DRAWING FROM
PHOTOS

In memory of

STEPHEN HICKMAN

(1949–2021)

Korero Press Ltd,
157 Mornington Road, London, E11 3DT, UK

www.koreropress.com

First published in 2022 © Korero Press Limited

ISBN-13: 9781912740178

A CIP catalogue record for this book is available from the British Library

DRAWING FROM PHOTOS

PROBLEM SOLVING & INTERPRETATION

PATRICK J. JONES

FOREWORD BY STEVE HUSTON

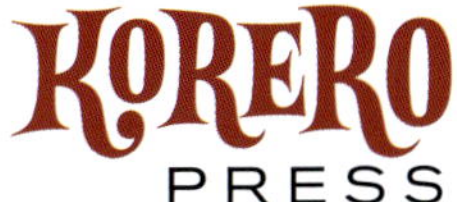

KORERO PRESS

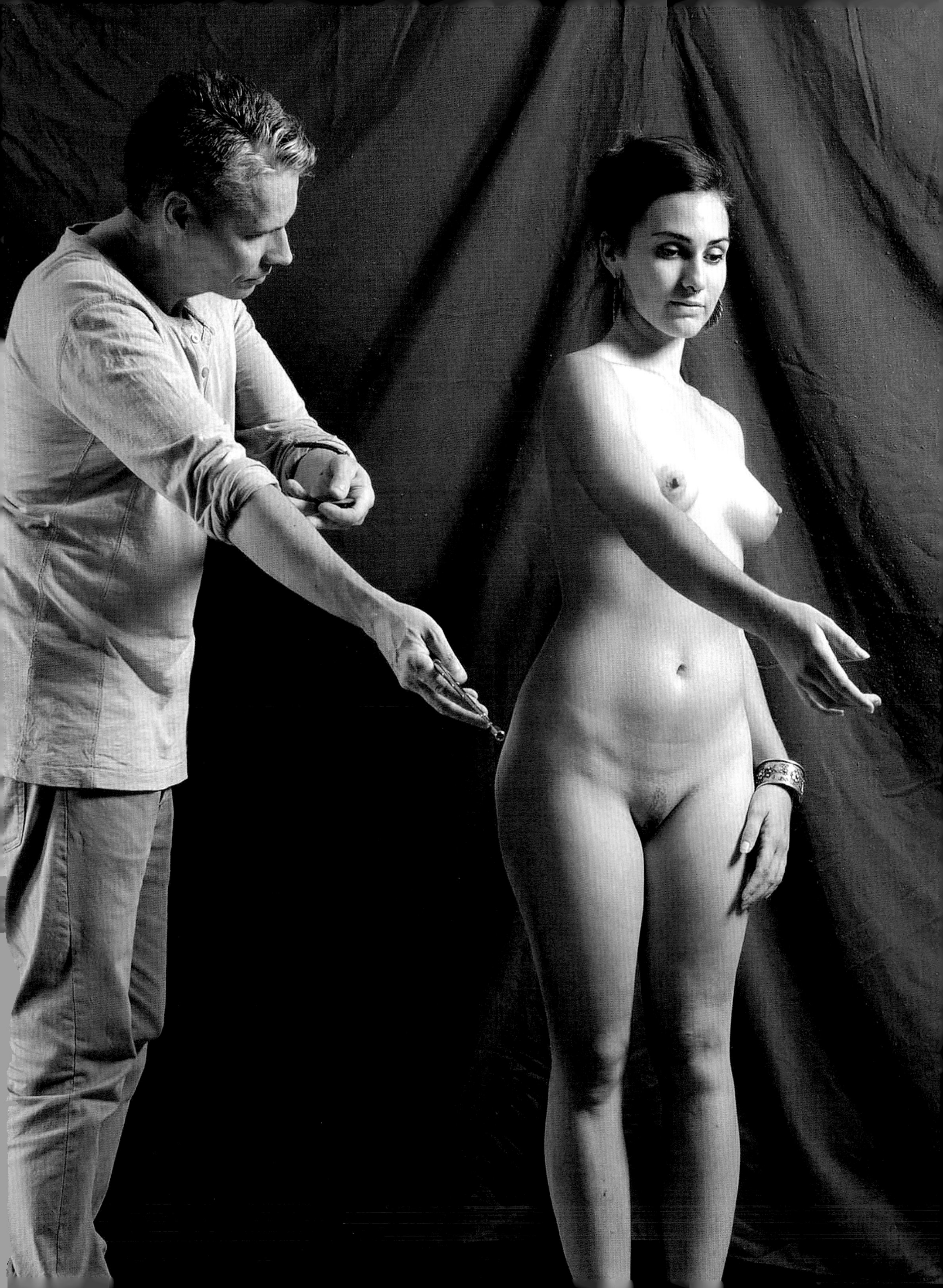

CONTENTS

*"Art is unquestionably one of the
purest and highest elements in human
happiness. It trains the mind through the
eye, and the eye through the mind."*

John Lubbock (1834–1913)

FOREWORD

STEVE HUSTON

I GREW UP IN ALASKA in the 1960s and '70s, and I know that Patrick fed from an equally art-bare cupboard in his part of the world. But there was the pulp fantasy and science fiction art to go on. Until I hit my twenties, that gave me more than enough: It became the escape pod I both craved and loved. Oh yes, I loved the stories, when they were at all lovable, but mostly, it was about the art. I loved the often very peculiar realism, along with the superhuman grace and strength that the best artists infused into their work. Even in the most uneven of stories, great artwork more than made up the difference.

Much of my childhood was spent poring over comic books and comic strips for their extraordinary figure drawings, created by such artists as John Buscema, Hal Foster, and Alex Raymond. For pulp novel paperbacks, it was the paintings, of course, and those included work by James Bama, Boris Vallejo, and Frank Frazetta. Looking back on my early heroes, I realize the common thread was their gift for bringing strength and grace seamlessly together. And I loved that they did it in a heightened way; in – what seemed to a teenager – a superhuman way.

Now, after forty years of looking at and doing art, I've seen very few figurative artists who've been able to cultivate "the chops" to pull off that superhumanness, let alone pull it off effortlessly. Patrick J. Jones happens to be one of those artists.

You won't be surprised to learn that I've been blown away by Patrick's work for years. However, it's only through a happy arrangement of events in the last few months that I've had the great pleasure of getting to know the human being. Normally when I'm asked to write an introduction, even to such an extraordinary work as we have here, I'll politely decline. Instead, I'm delighted to do so; and also flat-out excited. Because it means I get to pass on a little secret about Patrick...

I have the great pleasure of informing you and the rest of the world that the strength and grace we all see in Patrick's artwork is equally matched by the striking kindness and grace of the man himself. That makes him world-class on two fronts. And it's my great honor to call him a friend. It also makes him the ideal mentor to shepherd you through a subject which, in its way, is as critical to creating successful art as is learning how to construct a nose, or a thigh, or a full-figured pose, because the latter is entirely dependent on the former.

So, I leave you in the very privileged position of getting to feast your eyes on the fantastic art of my friend, while also being immersed in a masterclass on how to shoot and then use the photo reference from the gifted mind that's done it all so beautifully. Now, flip the blasted page and get to it!

Happy journeys and kind regards.
Steve Huston, Manhattan/Montana, USA

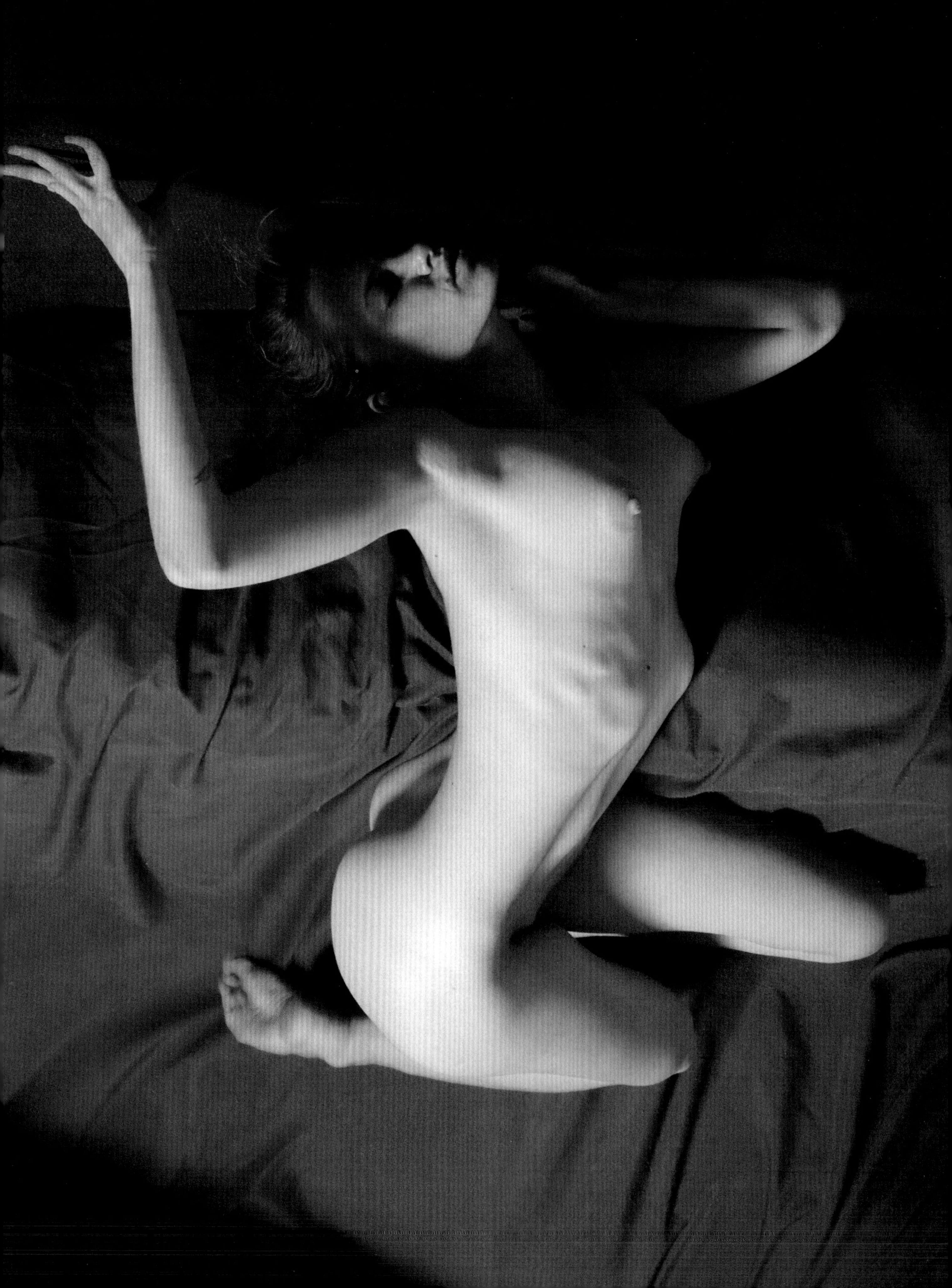

INTRODUCTION

PATRICK J. JONES

THIS BOOK IS BASED on the year's worth of workshops I created for *ImagineFX* magazine back in 2018. Fun and breezy as a magazine article is to write, there is only so much that can be said in a fixed word length over eight pages a week. So I decided it was time to rewrite and build further on the workshops, focusing more on the use of photography by artists. I'm writing these words in the midst of the 2020 coronavirus pandemic, which has created a world where gatherings are forbidden to prevent the spread of the virus. This has meant that, among many social events, life drawing classes are suspended, and the use of photos of models as reference, rather than live models, is a key topic for renewed investigation and discussion.

The use of photography as a reference for artists has been an incredible gift, but it has also created a shift away from observing life; in fact, there is no doubt that more artists the world over now work from photography than from life. So, what is the downside? Well, the problems, of which there are many, reside in the cold cyclopic eye of the camera lens and its relatively primitive idea of depth and focus. We have all grown up bombarded by images from this singular lens, to the point where most of us no longer notice their flaws, even though our binocular eyes see the world in a vastly different way. There are programs that fix photo-distortion to some degree, but they won't fix tangents or inform us what certain obscure shadows may represent. And more importantly, they don't train us to see the world as our human eyes do. There is a reason why the Old Masters' paintings, created in a camera-free world, still have so much depth and atmosphere.

Opposite is a photo with obvious camera distortion; now, this can be dramatic when created purposely, as I have done here, but most times, the distortion is more subtle and can creep into our drawings and betray us. In the following workshops, I will work with two of my most treasured artistic collaborators, Alana Brekelmans and Katy Woods. Together we will delve deep into the multitude of problems of distortion, proportion, edges, shadows, and tangents conjured by light during that brief moment in time when the camera blinks and whispers its lies.

Patrick J. Jones
Brisbane, Australia

Left: Model Alana Brekelmans

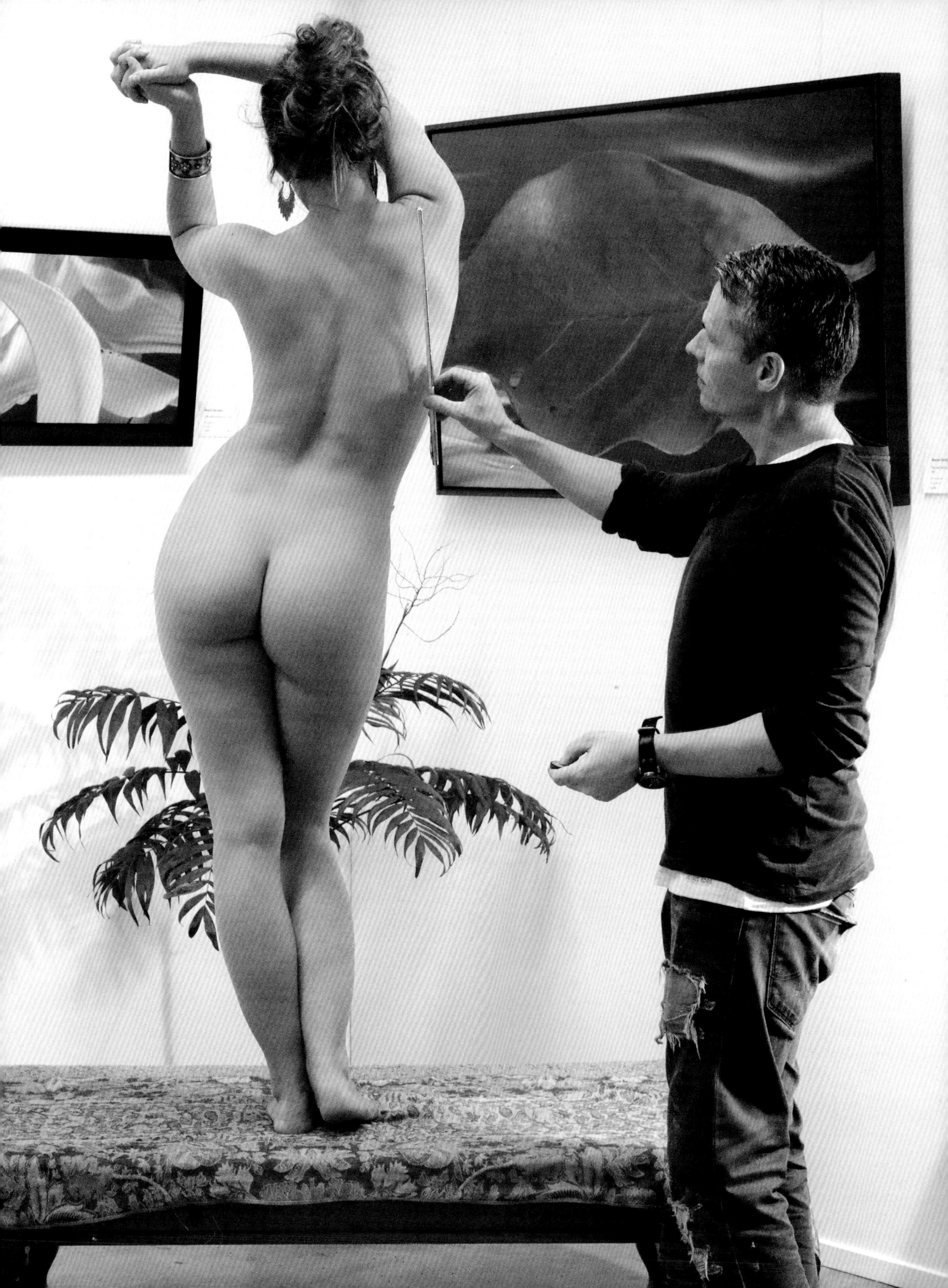

PART ONE

THE PHOTOGRAPHIC MODEL

ALTHOUGH I HAD taught drawing techniques in schools for many years, it wasn't until the publication of my first drawing book, *The Anatomy of Style*, that I was invited to teach live drawing workshops. Since the book was the spur for these private workshops, I decided to name the workshops after the book. The Anatomy of Style workshops then evolved to include more advanced teachings based on my follow-up book, *Figures from Life*.

In the workshops featured in this book, I will draw from photographs to recreate the atmosphere of my live workshops and will conduct each demonstration as if a life drawing class is in session with a live model posing. This will offer you a first-class opportunity to watch over my shoulder and draw along with me. I will explain my process and insights as we explore the beauty of line and form found in the anatomy of the human figure. A photographic model will take the place of a live model and will pose opposite the drawing stages.

Since we will be working from photo reference, I will also focus on guiding you through the minefield of problems typically associated with photography, and offer solutions. The camera's eye can be very deceptive, so we must be suspicious of every photo we work from. The prime suspect is distortion, which is often unseen by the untrained eye as we have come to accept the distortion in photos as "normal". Unfortunately, that level of acceptance doesn't extend to distorted drawings, so we trace photos at our peril. I believe that only professional artists up against deadlines should rely on tracing, and even then, only as a quick aid to getting the main elements down. To avoid leaning on the crutch of tracing, and the many evils inherent in that practice, I will demonstrate the sheer joy and freedom of drawing freehand.

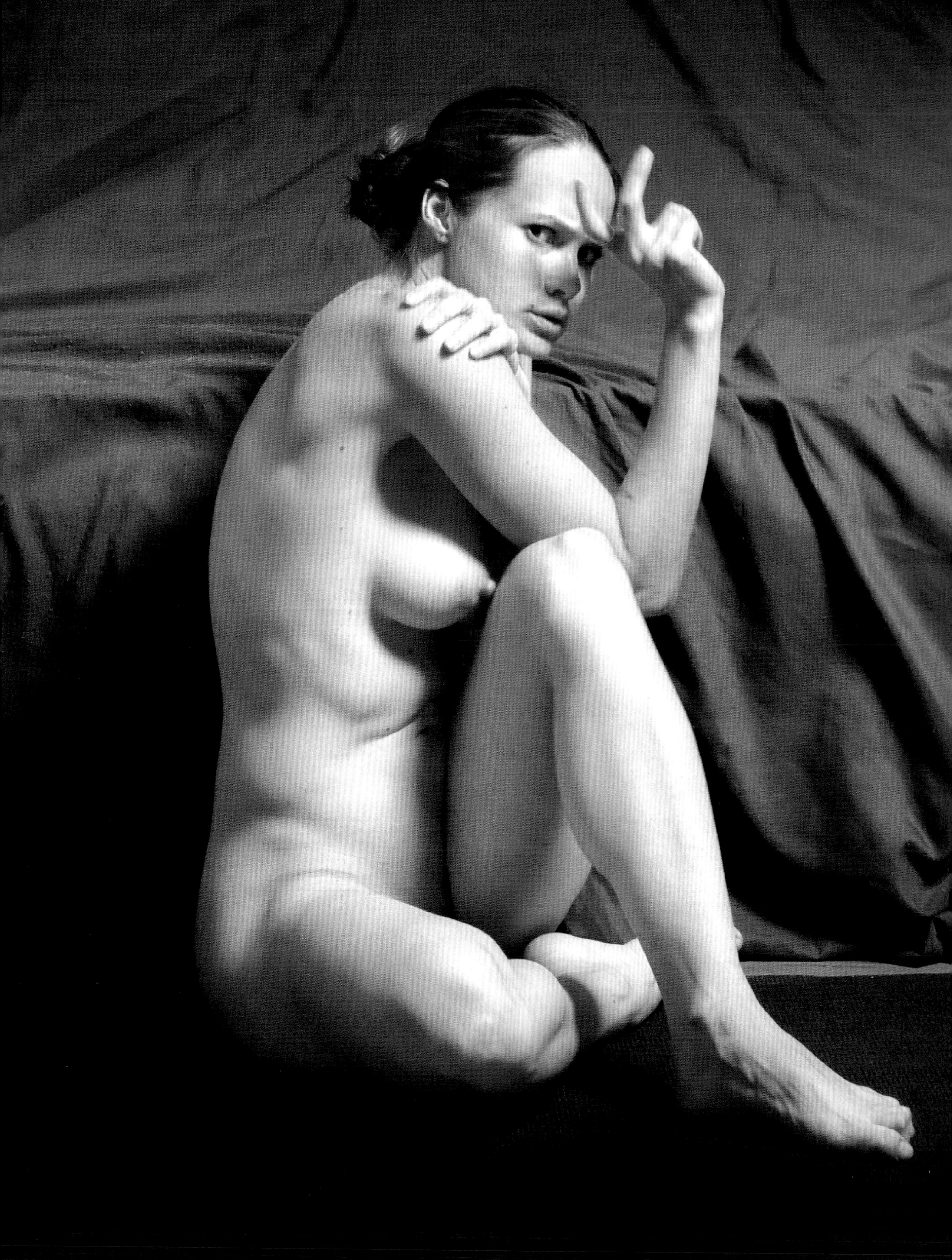

WORKSHOP ONE

THE LYING EYE

OUR CYCLOPIC NEMESIS, the camera lens: a duplicitous teller of falsehoods! Today, the camera sits in the pockets of billions of people on Earth, which is revolutionary if we consider that at the beginning of the 20th century a photographer needed an able assistant to help carry all their heavy photographic equipment.

Owning a camera is so commonplace now that literally trillions of photographs are produced each year, most of them taken through a warped 20–35mm lens. Most people have adjusted to accepting these distorted images as reality; show someone a photo and they won't see the distortion – *unless* they themselves are in the shot, especially near the outer edges, where most of the distortion lies. Thanks to the limitless choice of photo reference available online, artists can easily become lazy cobblers, grabbing what suits their purpose and frankensteining it all together. The unfortunate problem with doing so is that although we have learned "not to see" distortion and over-sharp edges in photos, we have not yet learned "not to see" those same anomalies in an artist's drawings.

The majority of the artist drawings I observe have a strangeness about them which reveals their photo reference source. When a drawing is close to reality in the sense of "camera lens reality", it becomes unsettling. We have all seen realistic drawings that are a bit awkward – not quite perfect, but still realistic in a warped way. Non-artists may not see the camera distortion in a drawing, but they still know something is wrong. When I see a beautiful figure drawing, it's usually drawn from life or from a photograph in the hands of an artist who knows how to see and correct photo distortion and lens anomalies to represent the human eye. In this first workshop, I will guide you on your way to becoming *that* kind of artist.

Let's get started...

Left: Model Alana Brekelmans

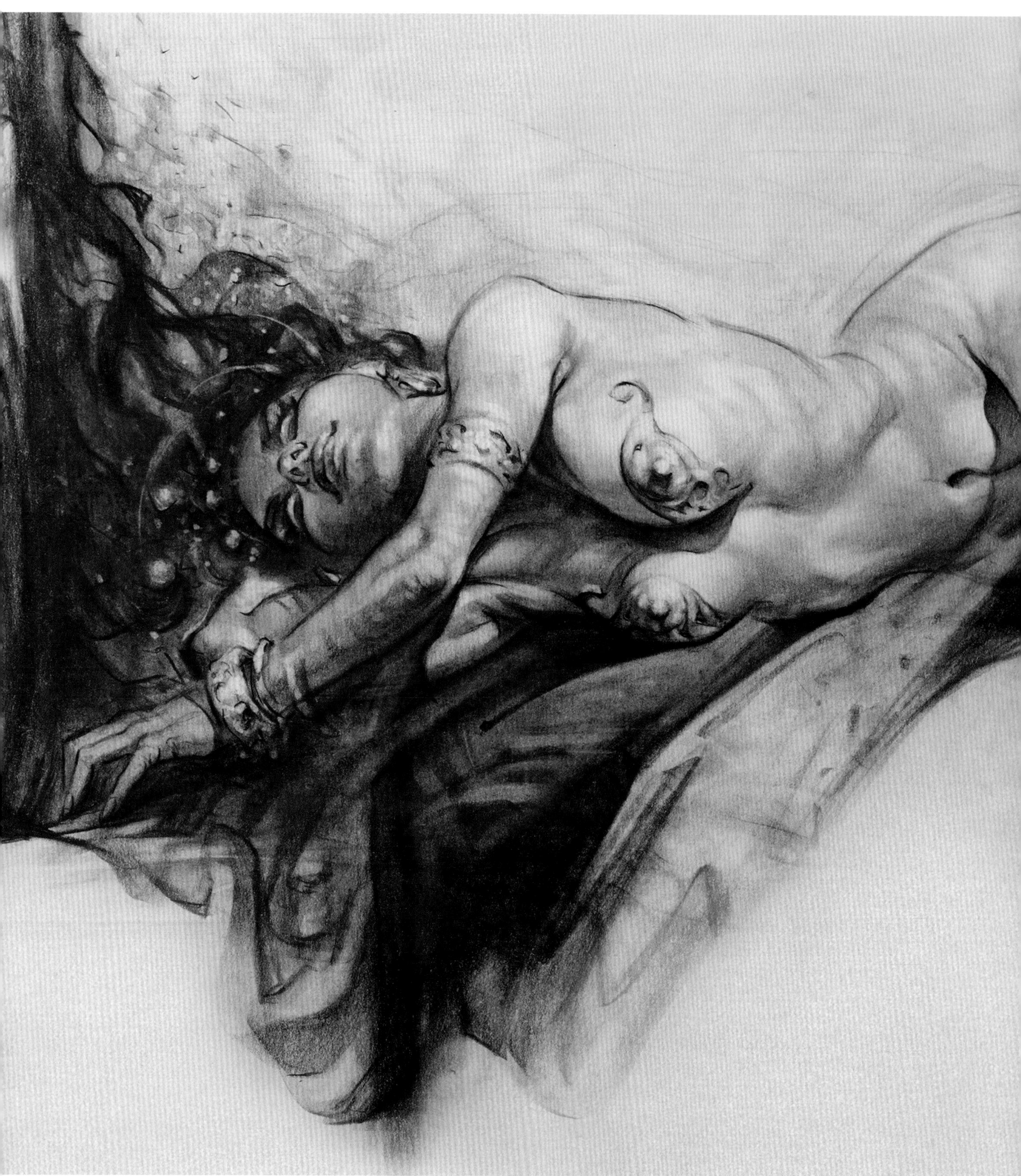

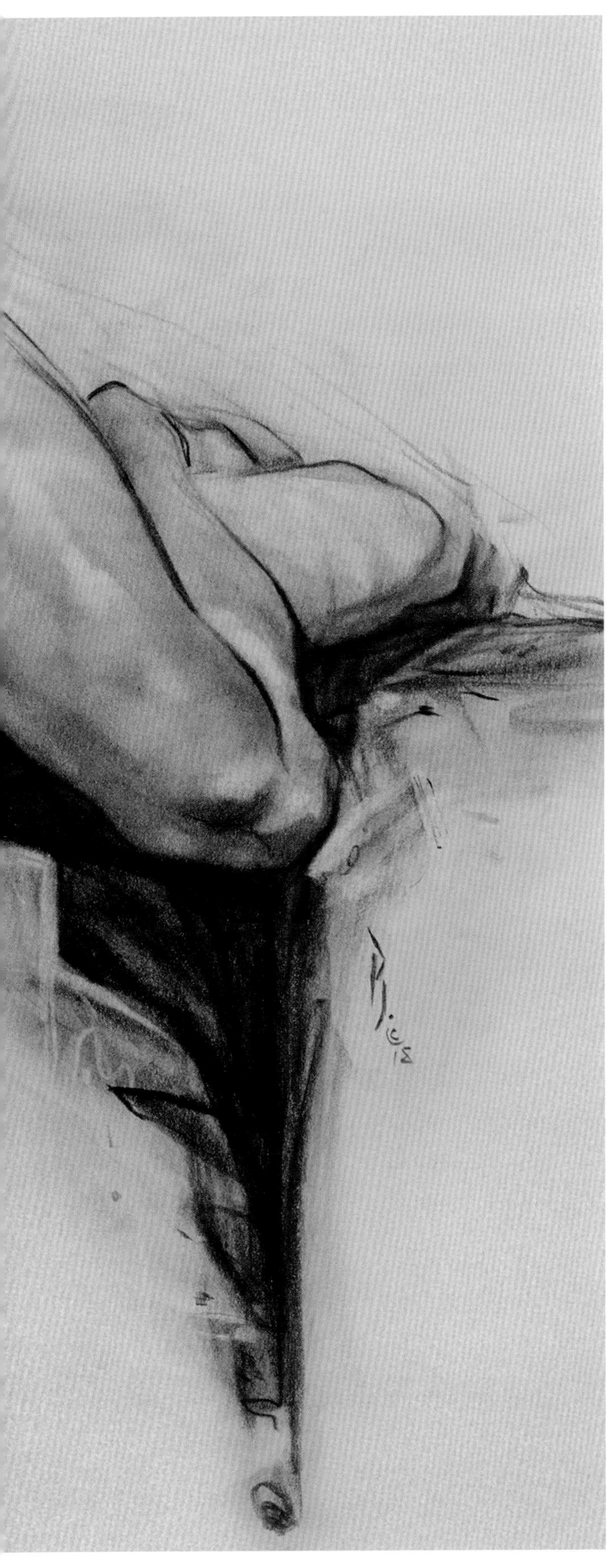

VAMPYRE'S TRANCE

Charcoal and pencil on A2 newsprint

Today we will be drawing Katy – a marvellous model who takes no prisoners when posing, which is precisely what I hope for when posing a model. An exciting pose like this will challenge us as figurative artists and help expand our imagination.

In my first figure drawing book, *The Anatomy of Style*, I explored average figure proportions, a practice we should return to often. Once we have thoroughly learned proportions we can store them in our subconscious and draw on them as and when we need to. We must keep in mind, though, that they are only a guide. Trying to shoehorn every figure to fit an eight-head-high ideal is a recipe for stiff, uninspired drawings.

When working with models, we can add fantasy elements through the use of costumes; or by studying the figure's contours and then adding elements using our imagination, which is the path I will demonstrate in this workshop.

To achieve style, we need to work with gesture, which is the spirit of the pose. If we take gesture too far, though, our drawing will look wobbly. To counter this problem, we also need to work with a solid structure; however, too much structure can make for a stiff drawing. And therein lies a key consideration of figurative art: the balancing of gesture and structure. We will explore this together throughout the workshops in this book.

1 · The Eye of the Cyclops

Here is Katy, perfectly lit and beautifully posed. We could wish for nothing more… until we take a closer look. I shot this photo with a 50mm Sigma prime lens, the closest lens to the human eye, yet even the best lens is still only a single eye – the eye of a cyclops. Compared to human binocular vision, a single eye is poor at judging depth. Look how small the foot (A) is compared to the head, for instance, and how long the torso has become. The distance from the shoulder to the navel should be similar to the distance from the navel to the curve of the upper thigh in a standing pose (the bottom of the gluteus in a rear view). With that in mind, we can appreciate how much distortion we accepted when first looking at this photo.

My awareness that the camera lies means I approach drawing from photo reference with extreme scrutiny before making a single mark. We must make it part of our artistic toolbox to learn to see photo distortion first and foremost, and then other problems as we go, such as focal depth – the difference between how we focus our vision to see depth compared to how the camera sees depth.

2 · The Slave Betrayed

Analyse the photo reference with me as I draw. Let's start with our attention level set to high. Using a two-finger wide piece of charcoal, I lay in the basic proportions. Aware of the lens distortion, I continue to examine and correct proportion as I go. I don't need to measure: it's mostly a matter of what "feels" right. Learning to see and constant life drawing with our binocular vision will attune us to seeing real-world shapes and proportions. I note that the far leg (B) is so foreshortened it looks amputated. This is a major fix.

I also bring the thigh forwards to create more rhythm within the figure and to show more of the far leg. I draw the thigh using natural foreshortening. Our eyes see objects shorten as they come towards us, but not to the degree of a camera lens.

Now this focus on proportion may make you think I'm overly concerned about achieving correct proportion, but that's not the case, as I will often push proportion for effect. What I'm changing is the mechanical mistakes of the camera lens, so they don't show in my drawing and betray me to the world as a slave to the camera.

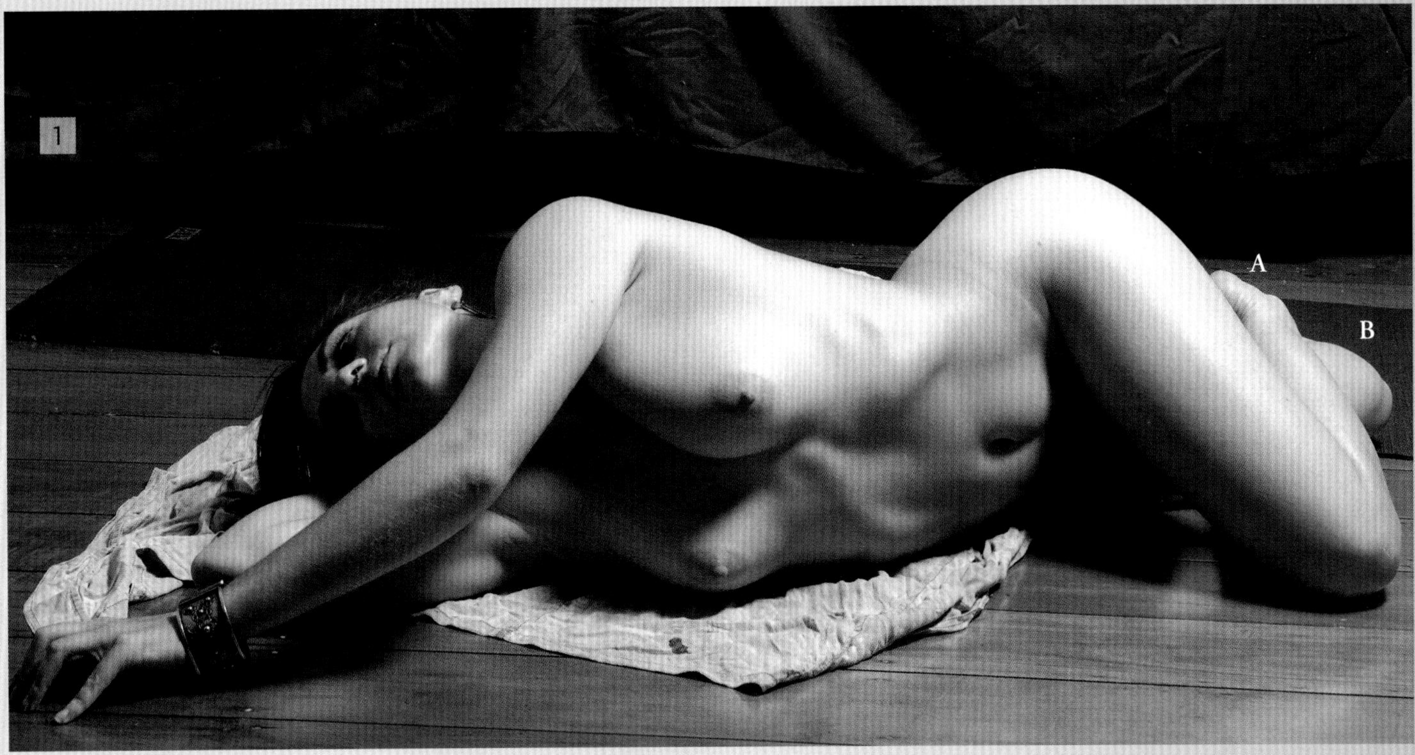

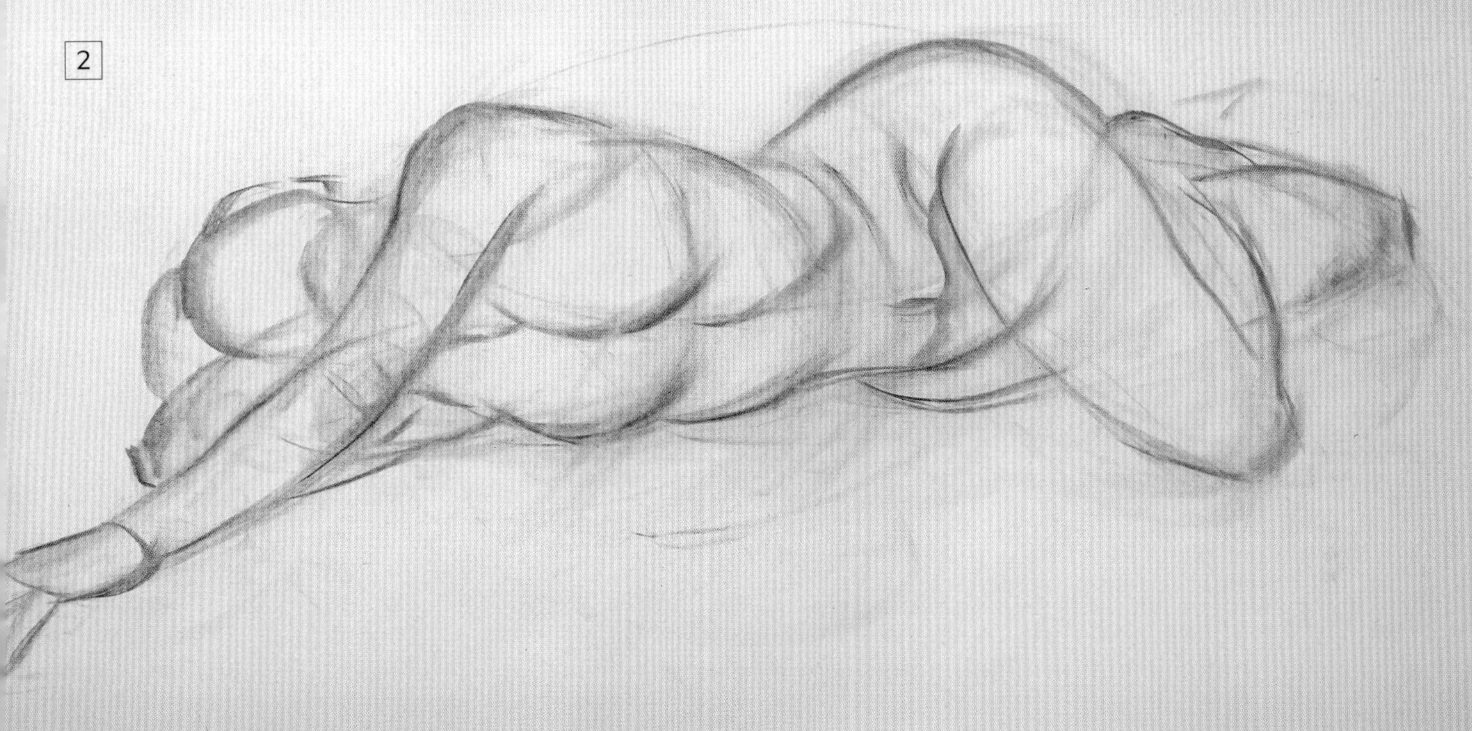

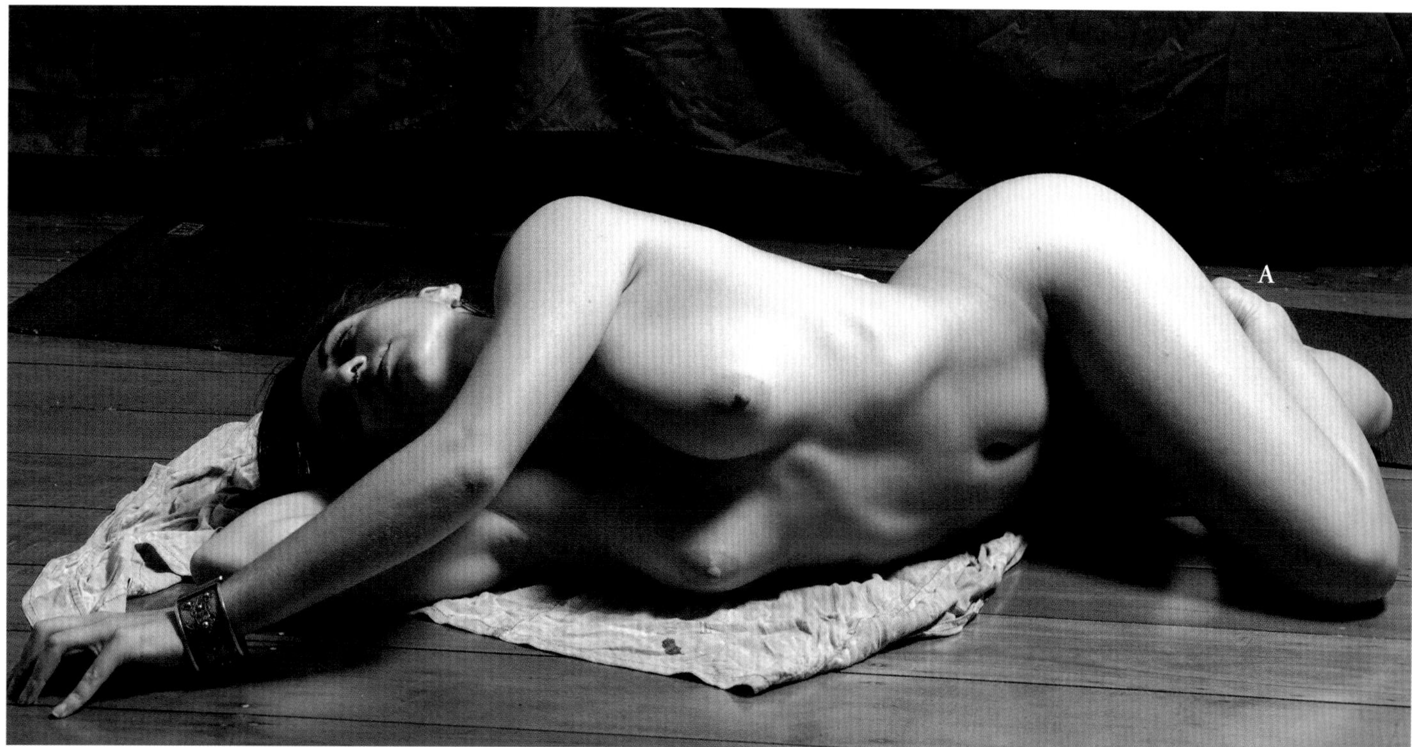

3 · Drawing with Rhythm

Once again, I look to real-world proportions for guidance. A standing figure is on average two heads long down to the nipples. Even allowing for natural foreshortening, I need to draw the head bigger and wider. In reality, Katy has a heart-shaped face, yet in the photo, it appears long. When professional portrait painters intend to work from photographs of their subject, they usually draw sketches from life first, to be aware of the distortion in the photos. Learning to see and learning to draw are essential skills for a painter.

By starting with basic shapes it's easier to draw more sophisticated lines on top. I draw the face using small shapes inside a big shape. This demonstrates two of my disciplines in action at once: big to small and simple to sophisticated. Note the gestural pencil grip in action. When drawing with our gestural hand, we use the rhythm of our entire arm rather than the stifled wrist movement of our writing grip.

4 · A Tilt of the Head

On closer inspection, what appears to be a foot (A) is actually a twisted ankle. In reality we would simply tilt our head to see and understand this in a 3D space. We need to inspect every anomaly within a 2D image, such as a photo. I decide to draw the classic shape of a foot to make the drawing clearer. I'm improving what I see in terms of artistic mark-making. Note also how many times I exaggerate the curves, using the gestural pencil grip, to make the drawing more lively. The gestural grip gives us the freedom to draw long, fluid lines from a multitude of angles.

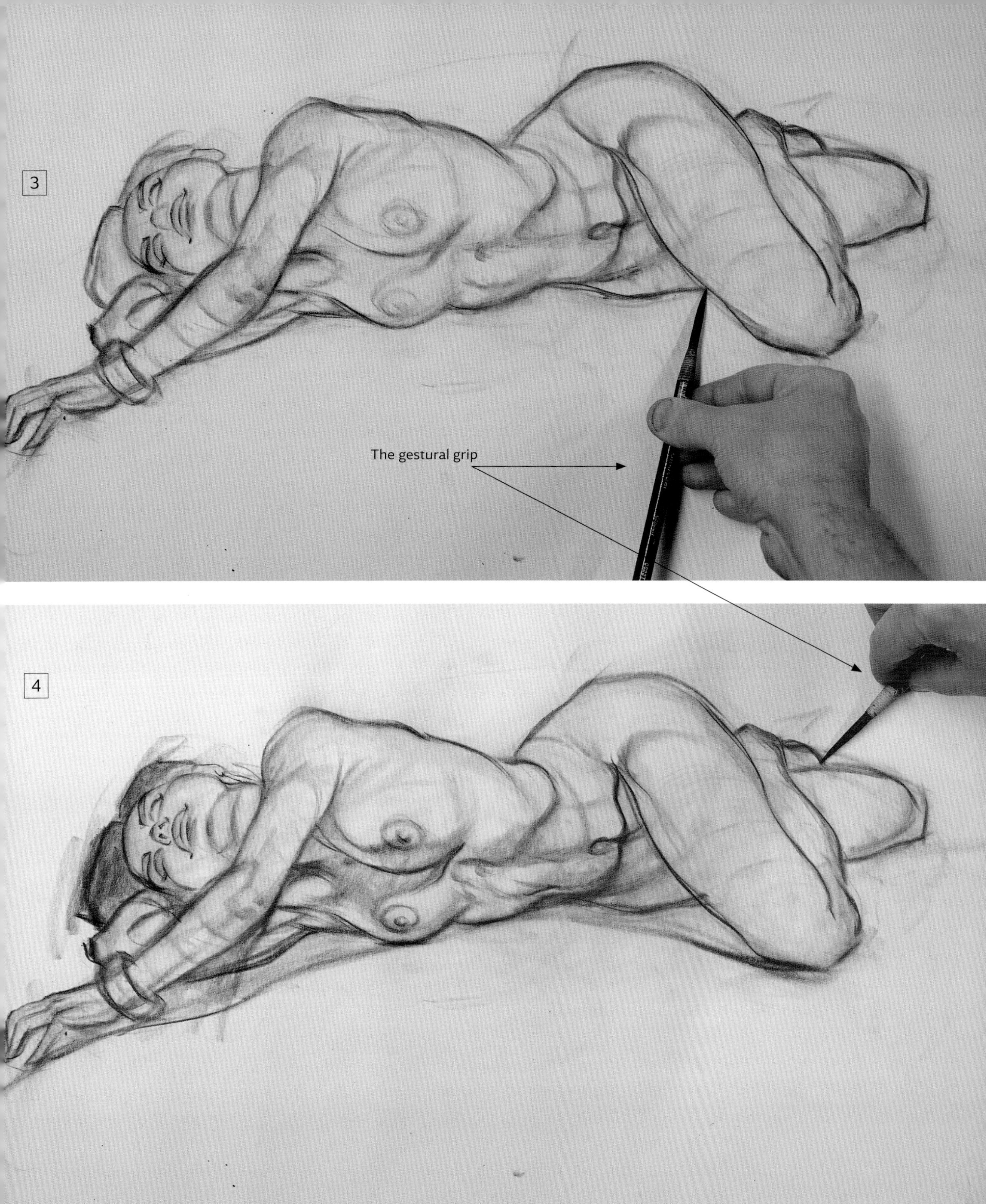
3
4
The gestural grip

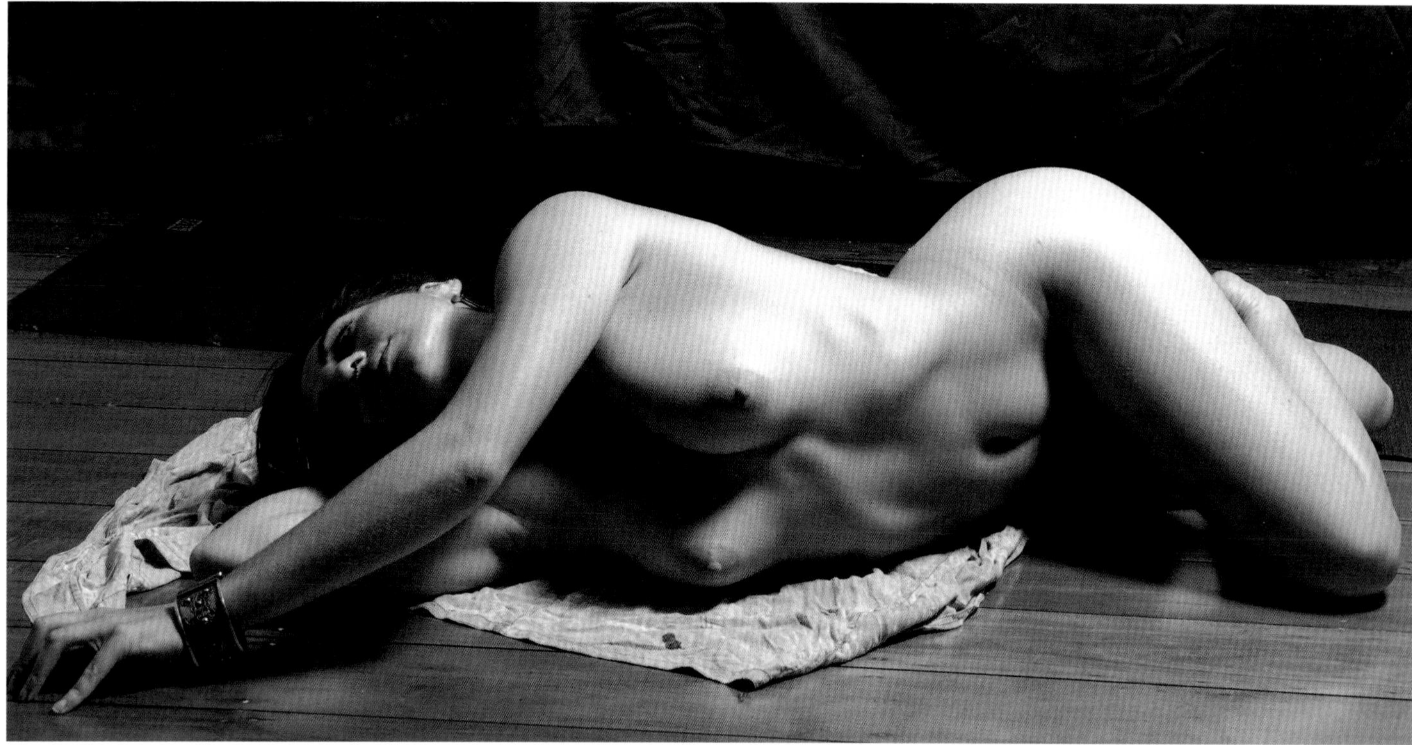

5 · An Odd Drawing

At this stage, I step back from the drawing to check that it has a solid structure. I lay in broad tones with my charcoal. Remember, our primary goal here is to interpret the reference. If we gauge our success by how closely we copy it, we will end up with a stiff drawing that looks like a distorted photo.

As I explained in the introduction, people will forgive a distorted photo but will see a distorted drawing as "wrong". As a learning experience, it's worth tracing this photo and comparing it to the adjusted drawing; you will see that the camera distortion becomes evident when its transformed into traced lines. The tracing will be an odd drawing.

6 · A More Interesting Drawing

Up to this point, I've juggled the fluid nature of gesture and the solid discipline of structure. The result is an OK drawing, but it's nothing stylish. This is the journeyman stage, onto which we can stamp our personal style. Using a tissue, I blend tone into form. This also fades the drawing, allowing me a second chance to draw better on top.

Here is an interesting point to consider. The camera, unlike the human eye, has a depth of focus that over-sharpens sharp edges and also over-blurs out-of-focus edges; whereas our eye has a depth of focus that sees sharp edges with a slight blur beyond each edge. For example, if I focused on Katy's face at this distance in real life, her hips would be less sharp but not blurred. In a drawing, I use softer lines and broken lines to give the impression of this idea.

Note how the difference in line darkness has already made the drawing more interesting and less heavy-handed. This is the first indication of a drawing approaching an artist's personal style rather than a drawing as documentation. Style need not be a wild abstraction, which it can be; for me, style is the recognisable hand of the artist who draws with thought rather than one who simply copies.

5

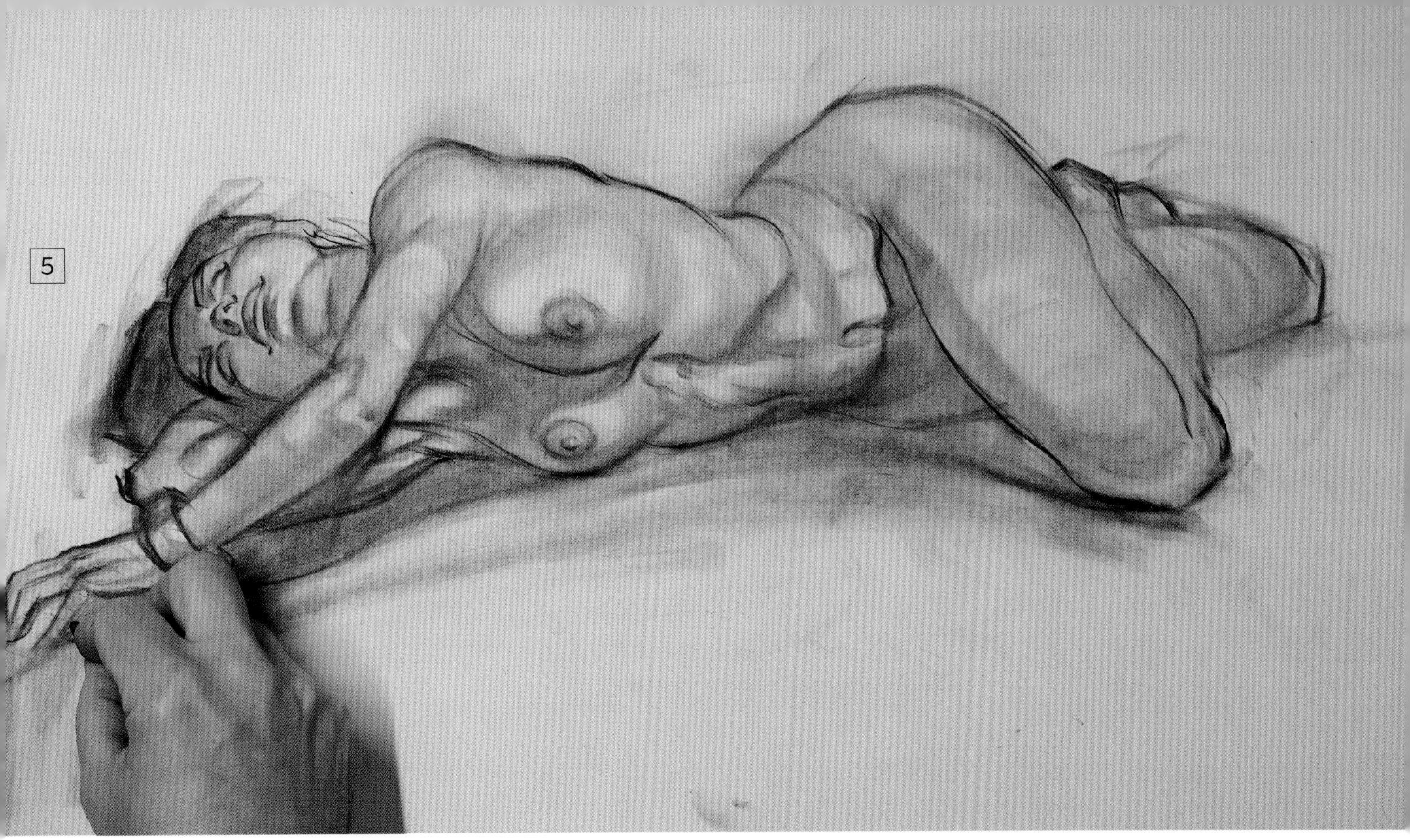

6

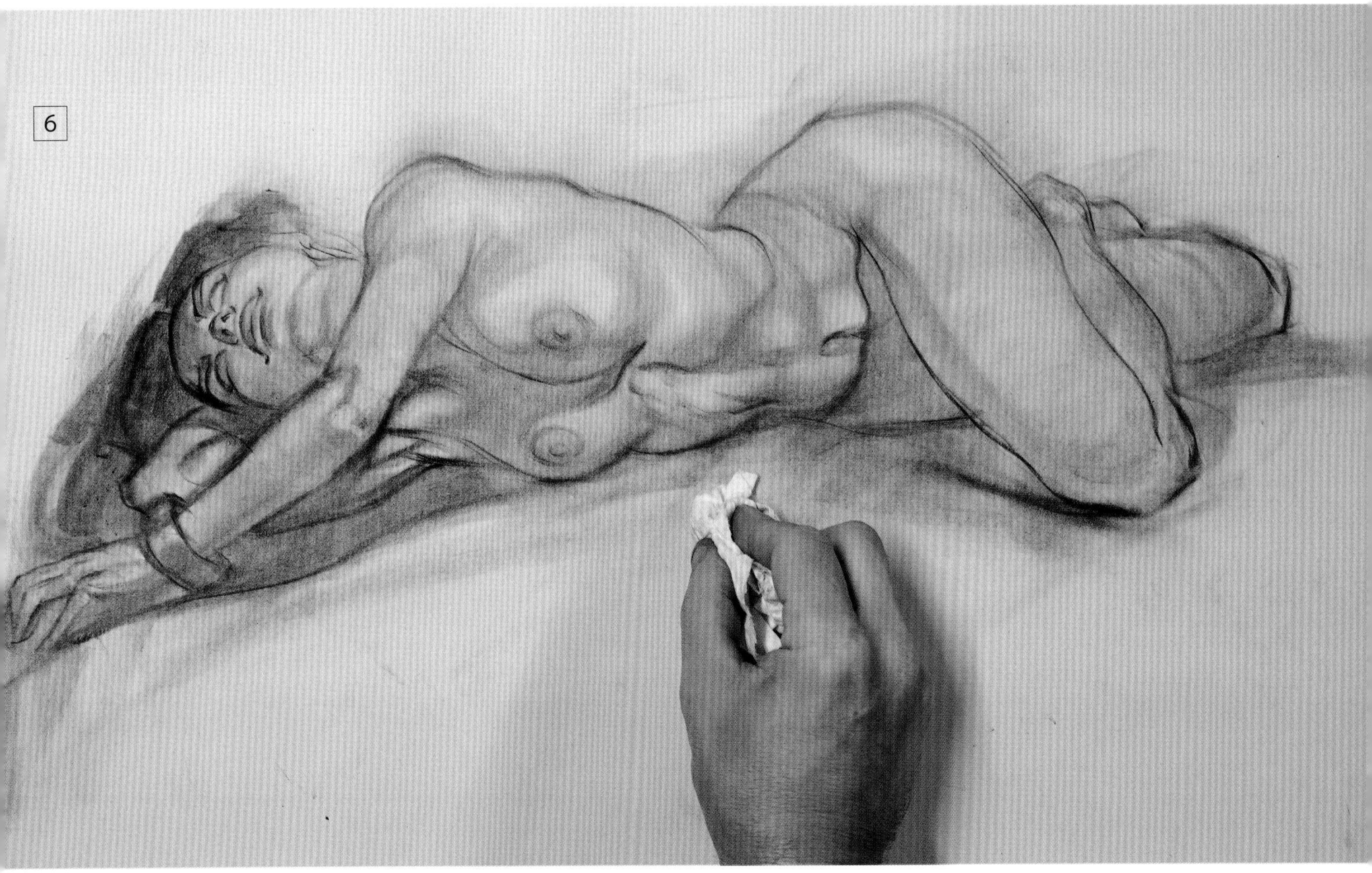

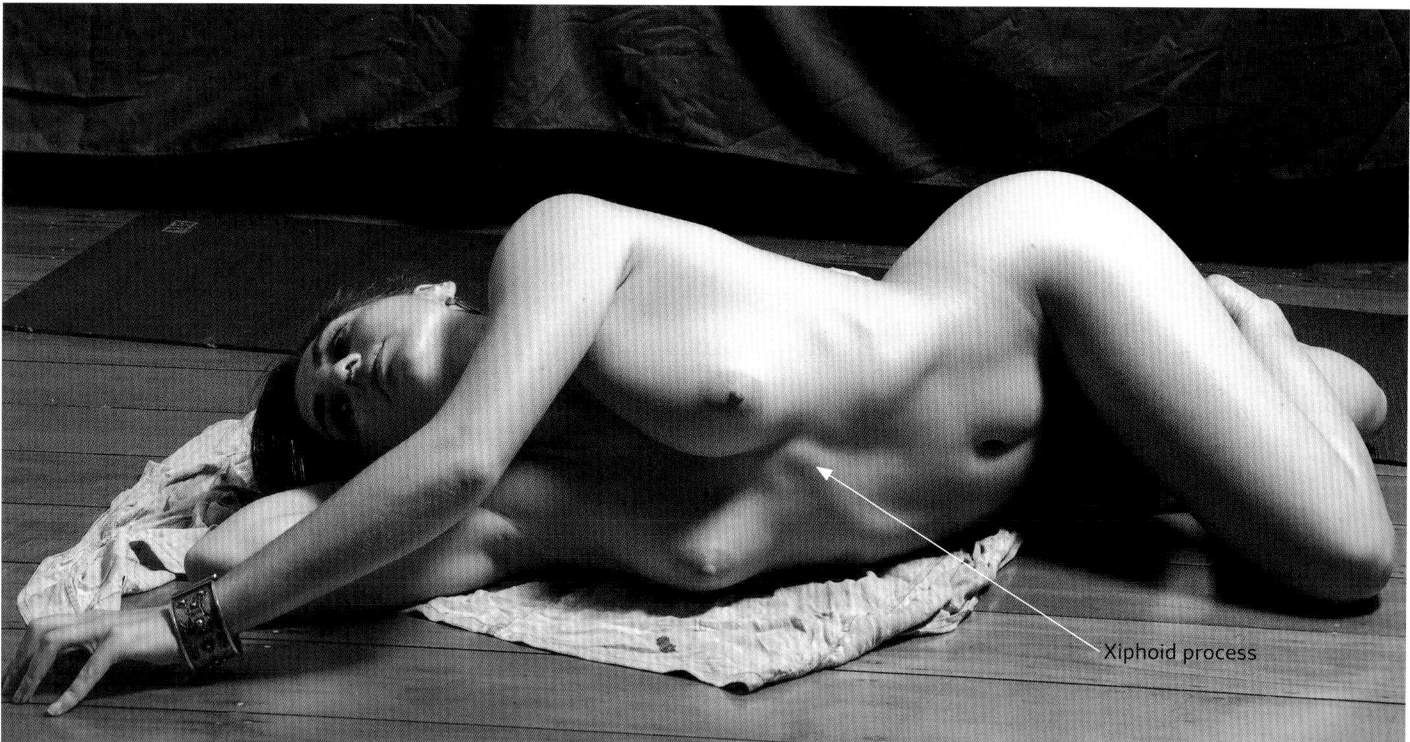

7 · A Small Investment

I'm now making minor structural adjustments and adding more tonal gesture with charcoal and finger smudging, considering the softer lines and edges as the forms turn. We tend to see more tone than the camera does, and so our forms should not "burn out" as quickly as they approach light. Note how sharp Katy's hips look in the photo against the dark background.

Adding broken lines and tone adds vigour to the drawing and freshens it up, giving it a more painterly quality. It also helps us feel the drawing as a holistic idea rather than a bits and pieces idea. This second time around goes quickly, just a matter of minutes, which is a small investment for an hour-long drawing. From this point onwards, my quest is to further explore style in the drawing and begin the process of breaking away from the photo source for reference.

8 · The Drawing is All That Matters

I use shadows to push the gesture, but in a considered decision, I omit the shadow of the xiphoid process (the small bone under the pointed arch of the ribcage). It looks odd here, and even though it's correct, it violates one of my art laws: "If it looks wrong, it is wrong, even if it's right!" The drawing is all that matters in the end – not what we see exactly or the correct proportions: only the drawing.

7

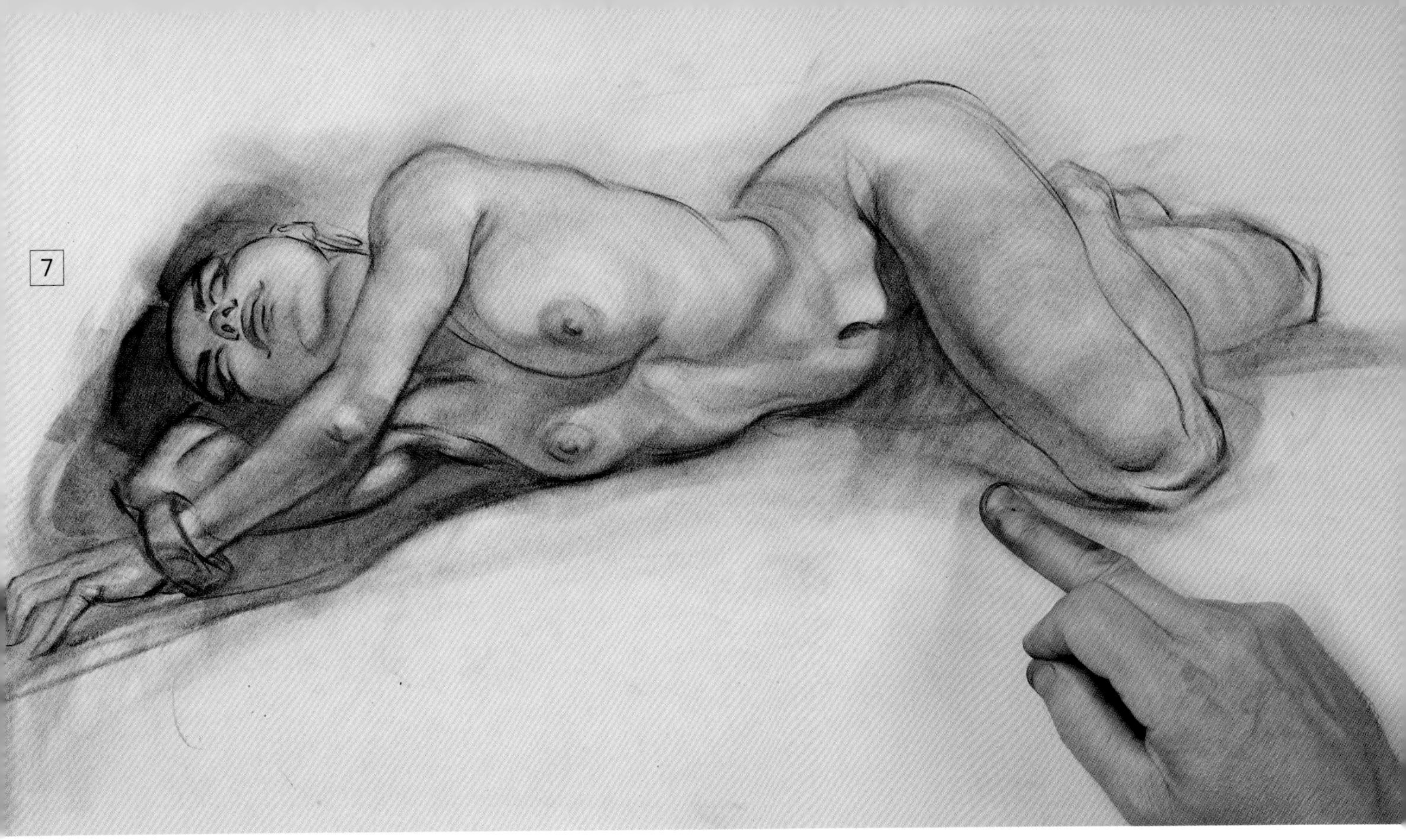

8

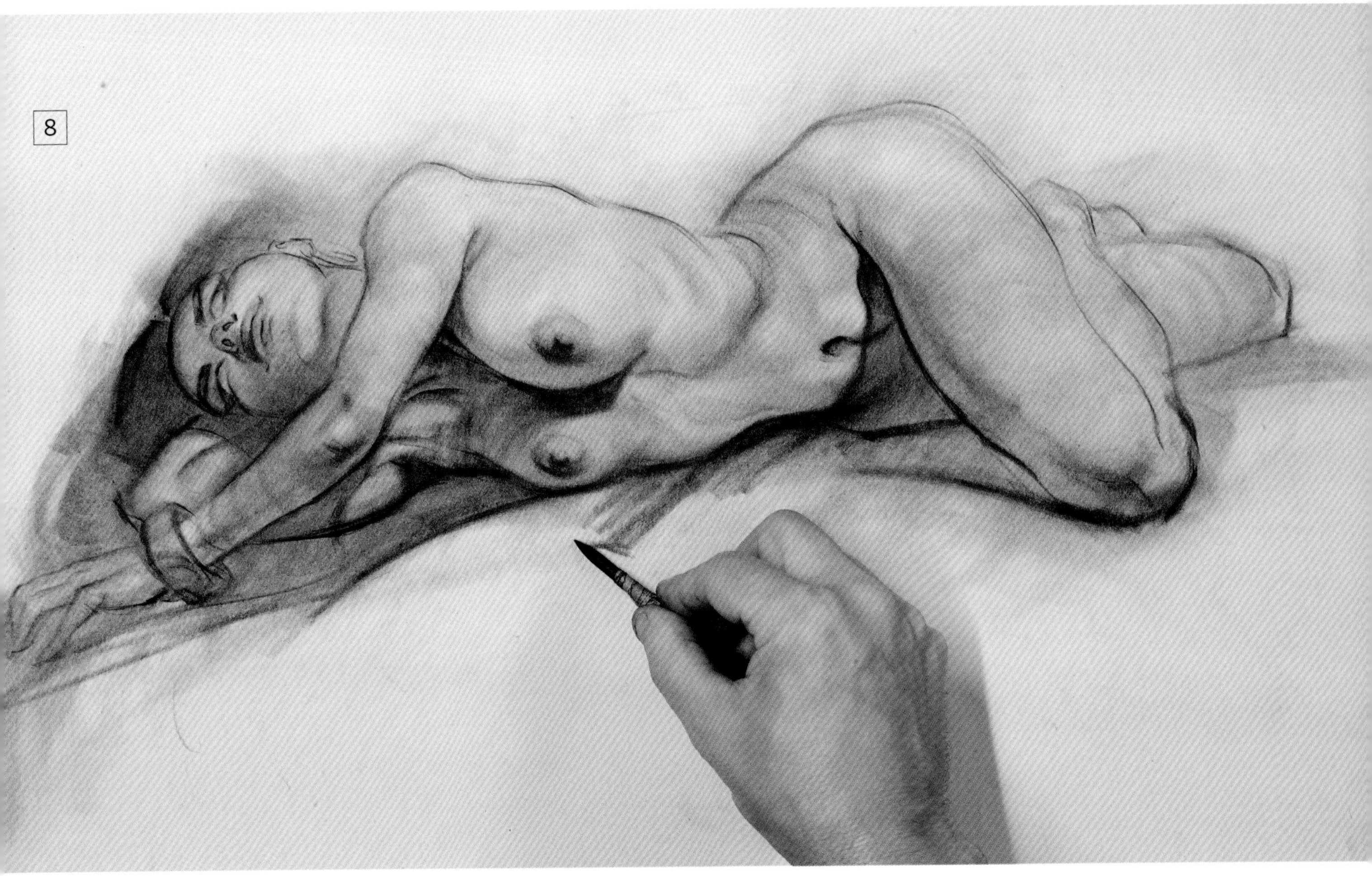

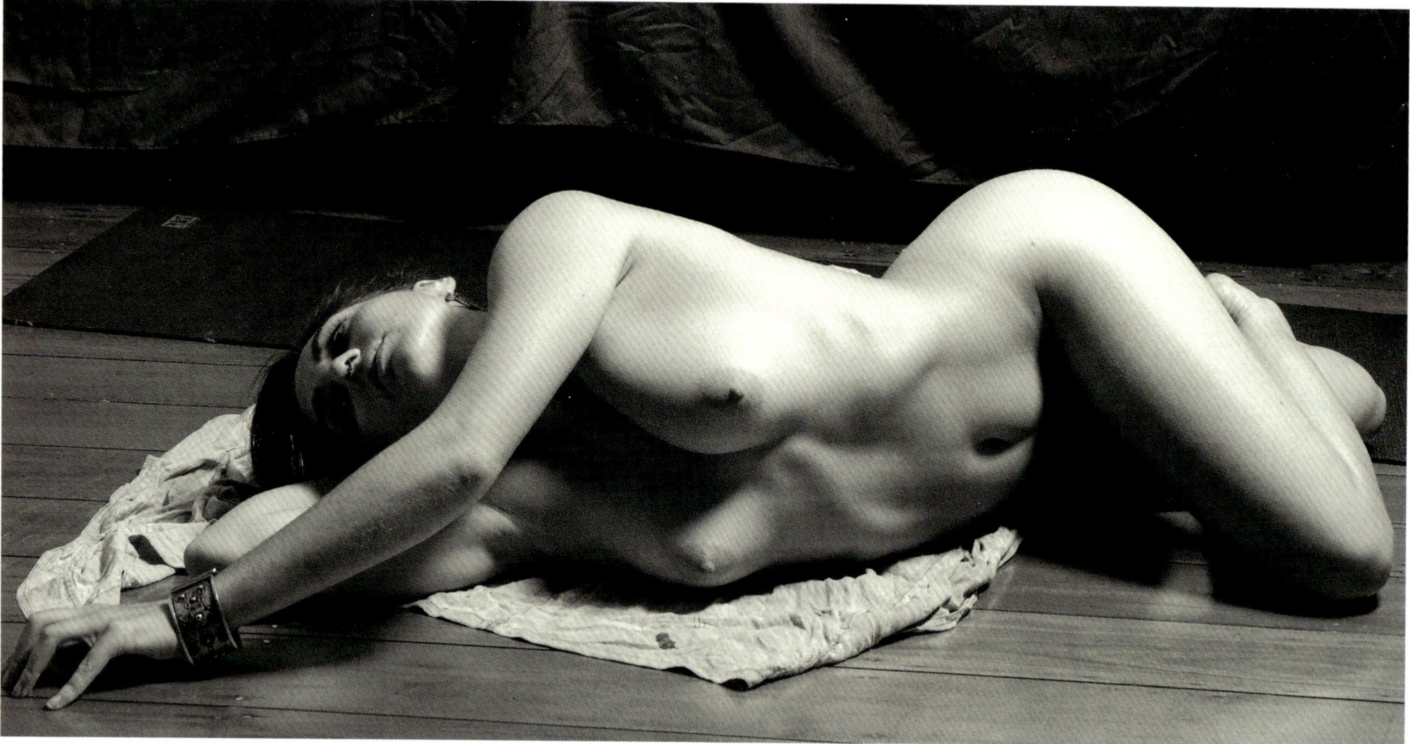

9 · Stumpy Fingers

Using a paper stump, I push around the charcoal that is already on the paper rather than lay down more. This keeps the drawing light and fresh. I'm also mindful to always be drawing, even when blending. To prevent smudging the drawing I rest my hand on a sheet of paper; this also prevents the oil from my skin leaving marks on the drawing.

I also keep my hands dirty with charcoal, as this also prevents oil transfer and allows me to draw and smudge with my fingers. You can use surgical gloves if you like, and also employ various-sized paper stumps to blend with, whatever works for you. For me, finger blending is the most natural way to work, followed by the more precise paper stump blending.

10 · Our Photo Friend

I "draw" highlights with a kneadable eraser. Photos can be our friend in finding highlights that are hard to detect. Photoshop and even apps on our tablets have features to enhance contrast. In the past, book cover artists had their reference images both over- and underexposed so they could see all the tones that might be tricky to spot in the original photo. The danger here is leaning too much on one reference source or the other, which could lead to over- or underexposed art. The "original" photo is still the main go-to for the final drawing.

Slowly does it, especially in the early stages. If we rush a drawing, we inevitably spend most of our time fixing mistakes. Every mark should be a thought.

9

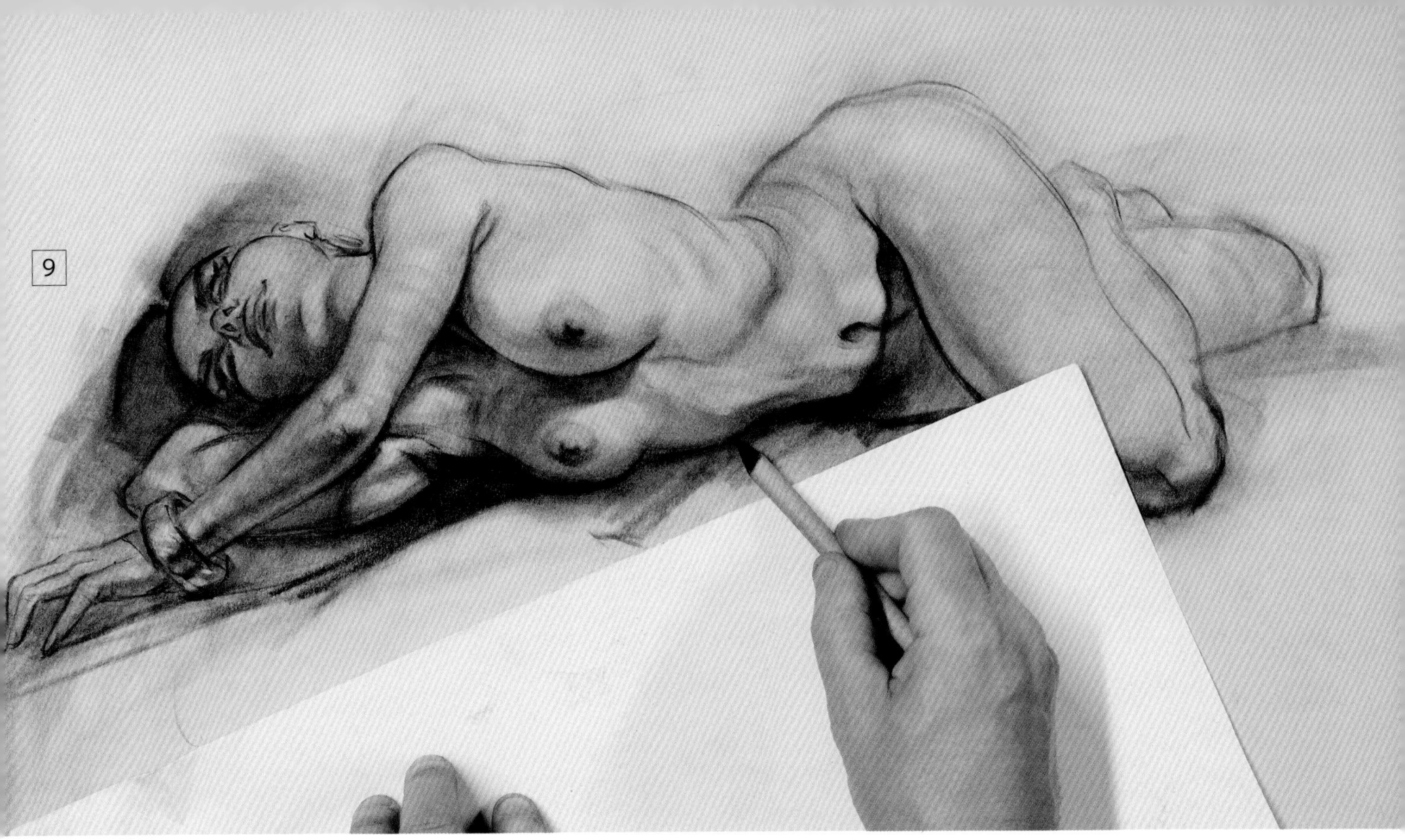

10

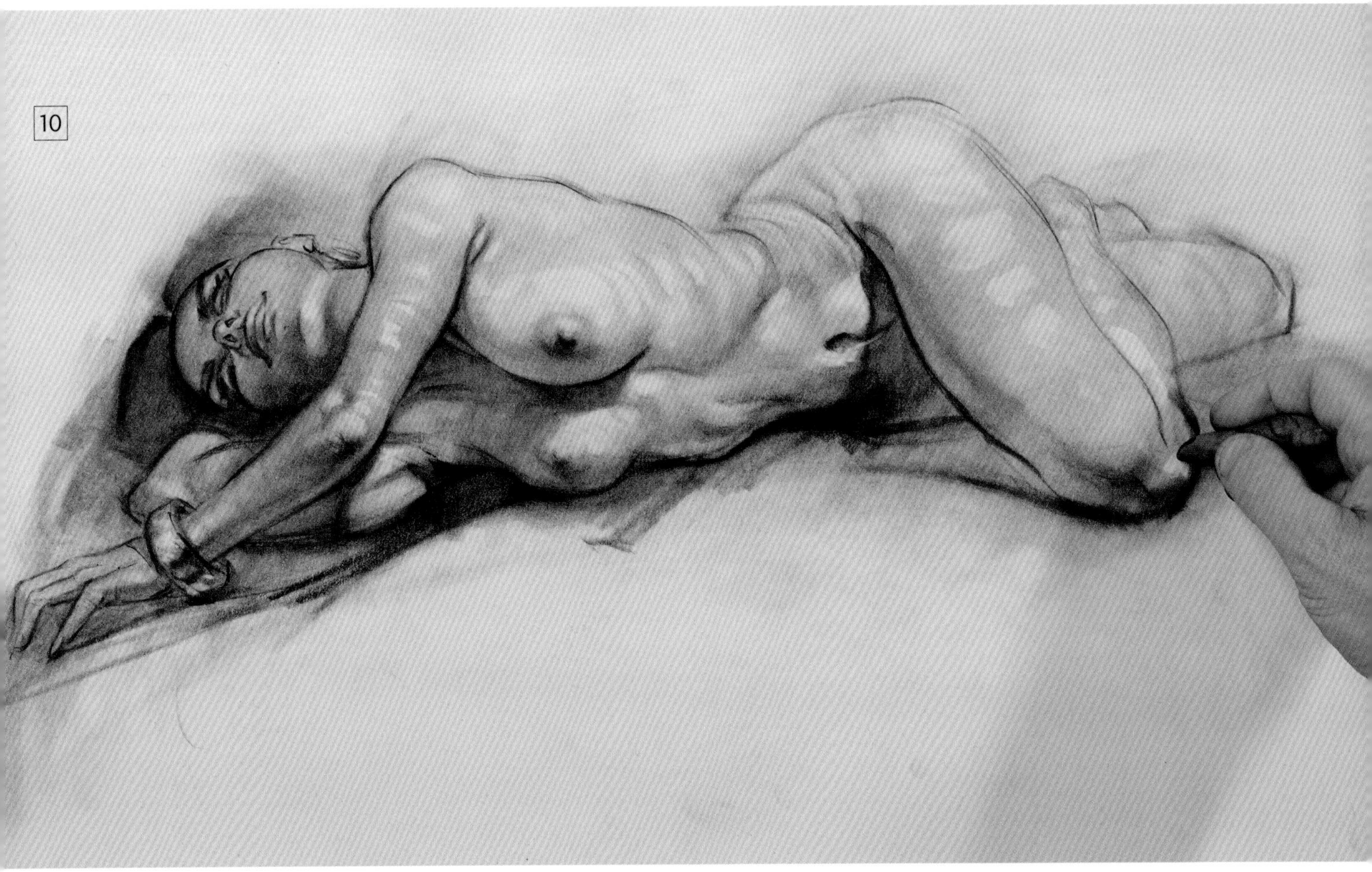

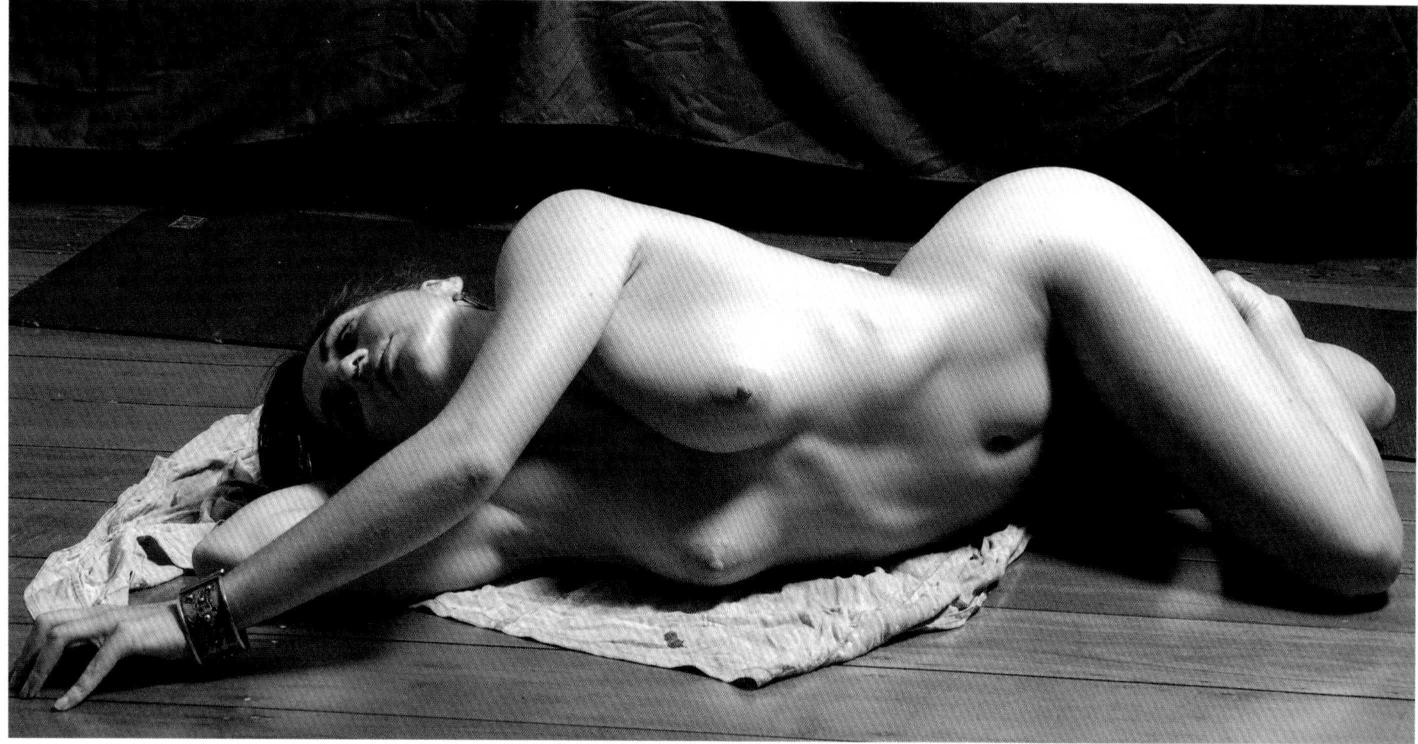

11 · The Bugbears

I take a short coffee break away from the drawing and come back with a fresh eye. A break helps me see the bugbears more clearly on my return. Bugbears is the term I use for elements in the picture that bug me. Sometimes I don't know exactly what the problem is; other times I do, and refer to the notes I make as I work detailing what needs to be fixed. A break will typically help me see problems that weren't clear when I was too close to the art – meaning I was so busy working on individual elements that the holistic nature of the drawing was suffering.

Another thing to be aware of with photographs is that we are looking at a frozen moment in time, when gravity may not yet have taken its full course of action during the model's movement into the pose. Here, I see that the breasts are too close in shape. This may be because they did not fully re-form into a more natural shape during the click of the shutter lens. Also, the lower ribcage looks too smooth, due to reflected light. I make minor changes to both bugbears and am now ready for the big finish.

12 · Two Birds with One Stone

I lay down a large swath of charcoal using a tissue. Jars of charcoal dust can be bought from art stores, but I simply dab the tissue on my sandpaper block, which is always thick with dust from my constant pencil-sharpening. This also cleans the sandpaper block, making it a satisfying way to kill two birds with one stone. I then smudge and tonk (dab) the applied charcoal with both the tissue and a chamois leather cloth, playing with textures as I go.

The tissue creates harder-edged marks than the softer chamois. A paper kitchen towel will give us even harder-edged marks. Between the three, we can achieve unique textures. I learned of the chamois technique from US artist Glenn Vilppu a few years back, and it has been part of my drawing arsenal ever since. Here I use it to make abstract marks that "ground" the figure and add style.

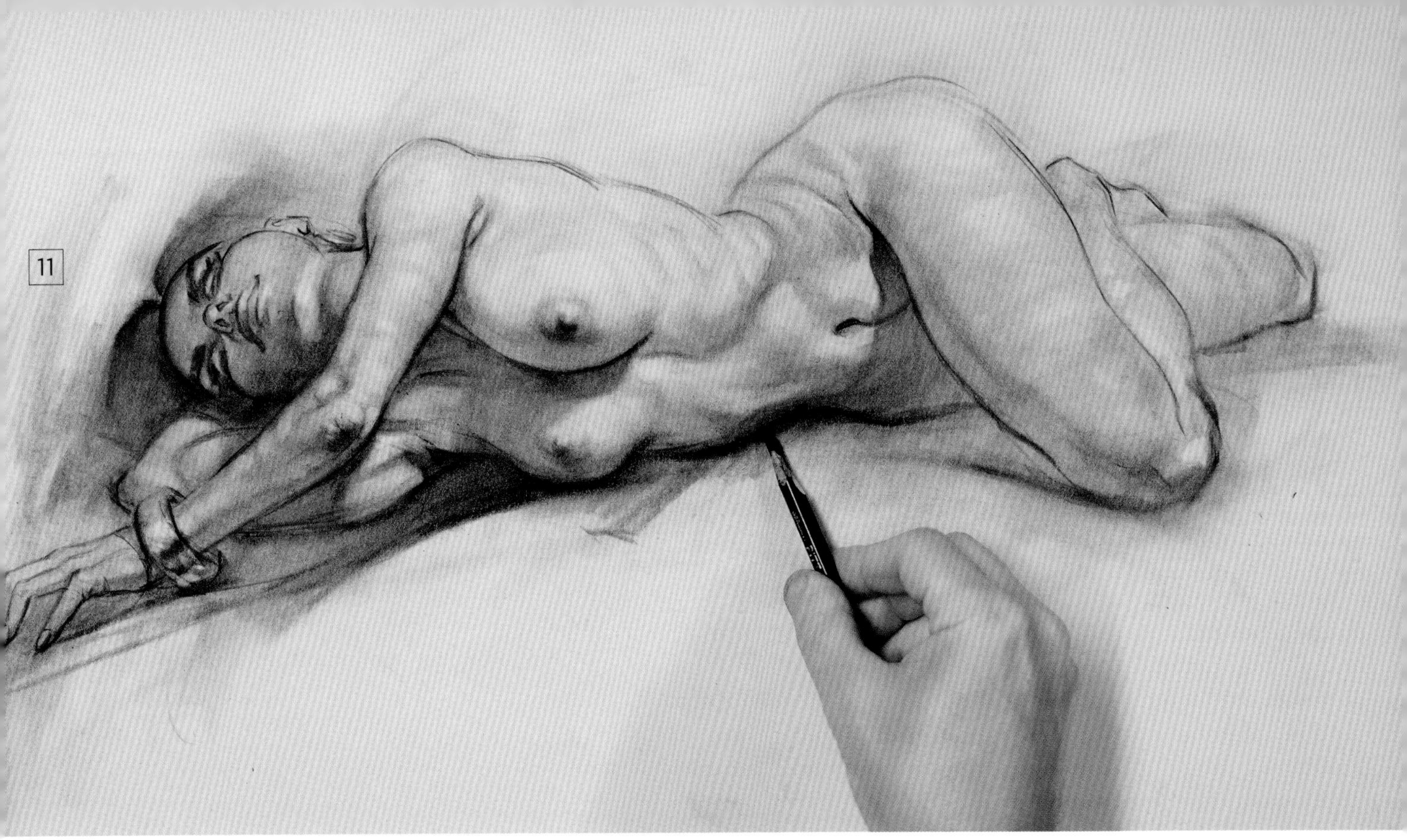

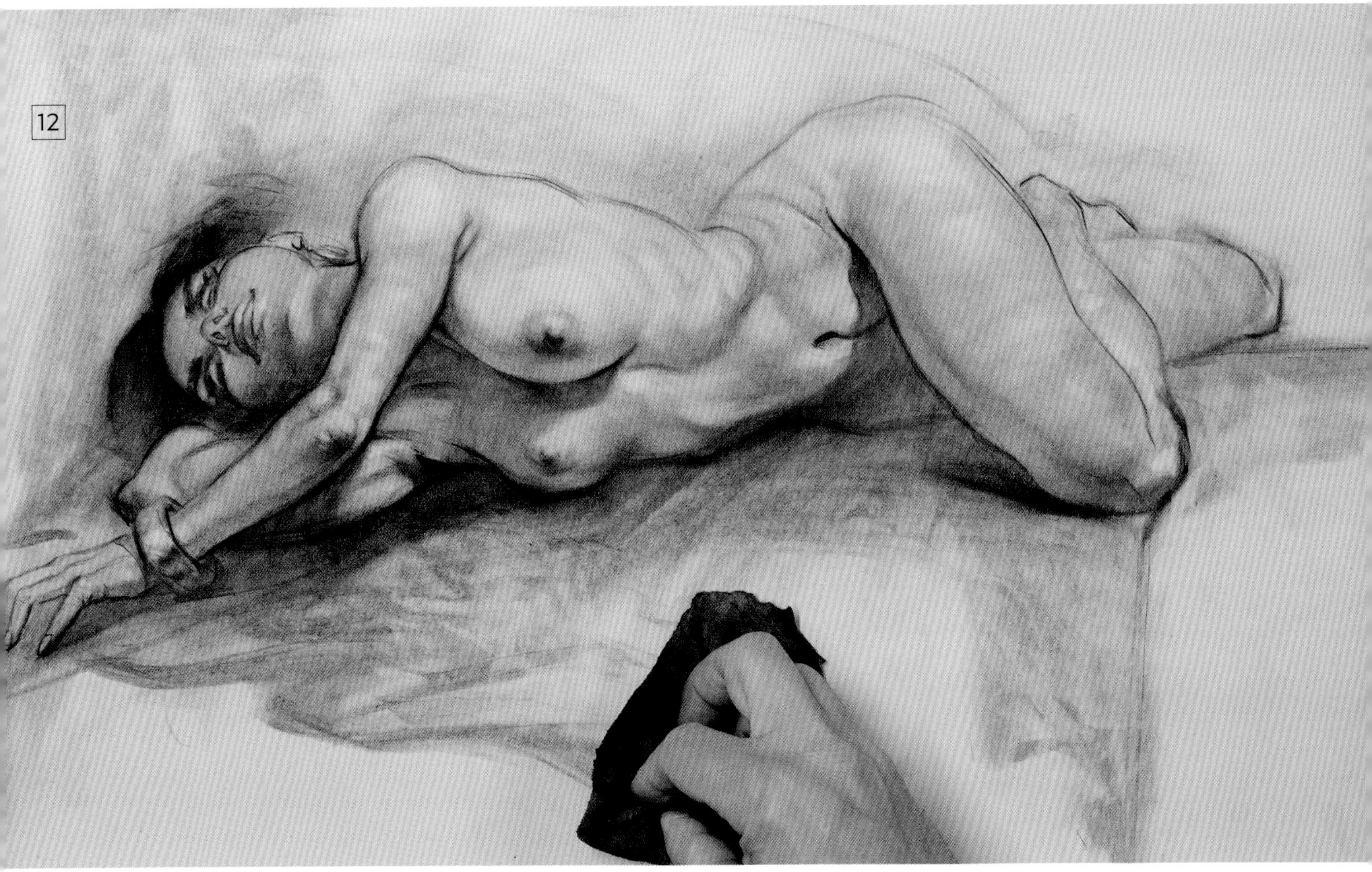

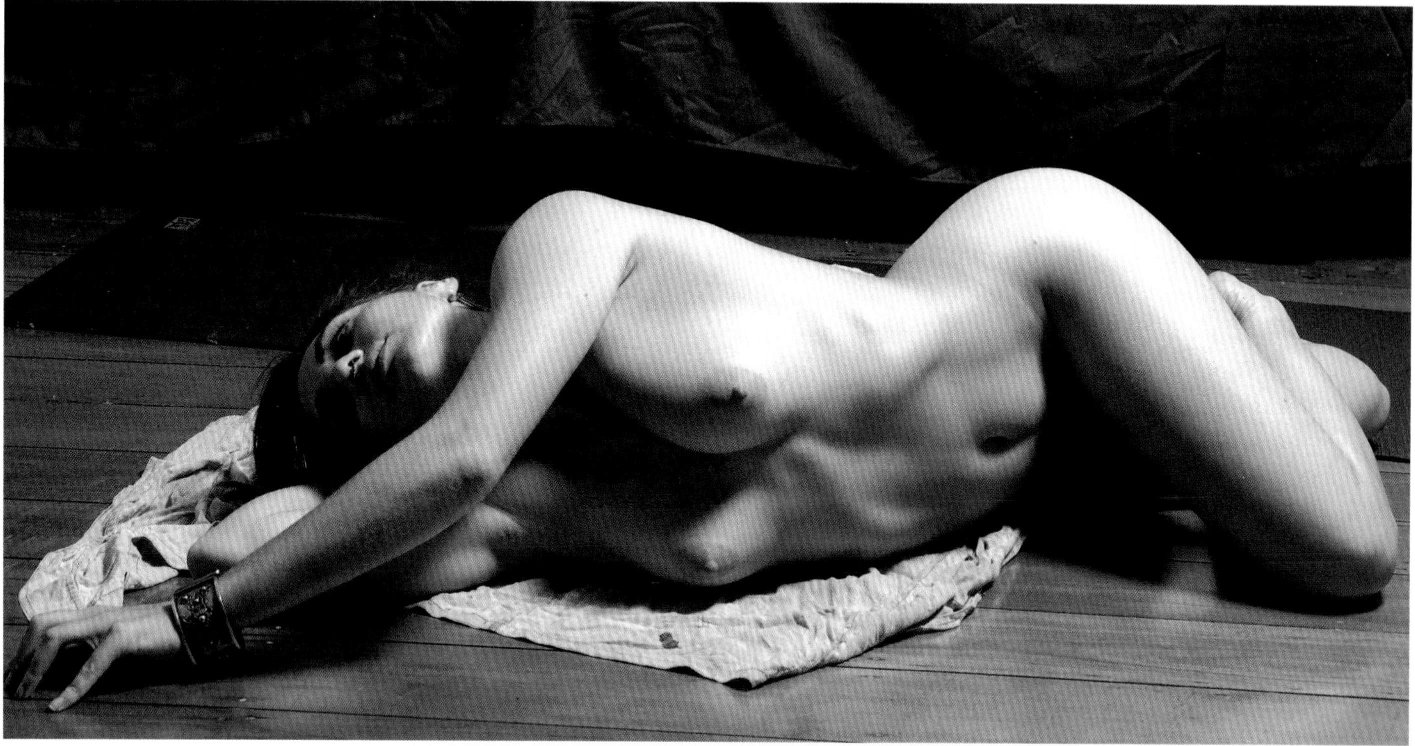

13 · The Elements of Fantasy

I usually give my model a story to work with, but for this shoot, I asked Katy to transition from one pose to another while engaging her emotions. Fear, horror, loss, anger, and loneliness were some of the emotional word "prompts" I used to bring out a stream of poses that transitioned into a spiritual ballet.

I now take the pose further and imagine a vampire in a blood-lust trance. With large charcoal sticks, I draw abstract shapes to create a magical dark mood. I push the hair up into the night air, as if it has a life of its own. I then pencil in the breastplates and jewellery using hard erasers for highlights. Throughout the figure, the variance in line width takes our eye on a liquid journey over the undulating forms, creating a sense of movement even within a still image.

14 · The Distrustful Friend

I now stop referencing the photo, beautiful though it is. If we continue referring to the photo as "correct", we might believe every change we make to the art is a mistake. I finish the drawing with gestural freedom. We must learn to separate the photo reference from the drawing, as the art must stand alone.

Look only at the drawing, and you will see the artist's style coming through due to choices of line, tone, proportion, light and dark – all of which are based on the decisions to change and move beyond the photo reference that was our initial source of inspiration. The photo reference, we must remember, is not our enemy – it's just a companion that once in a while, tells us lies.

13

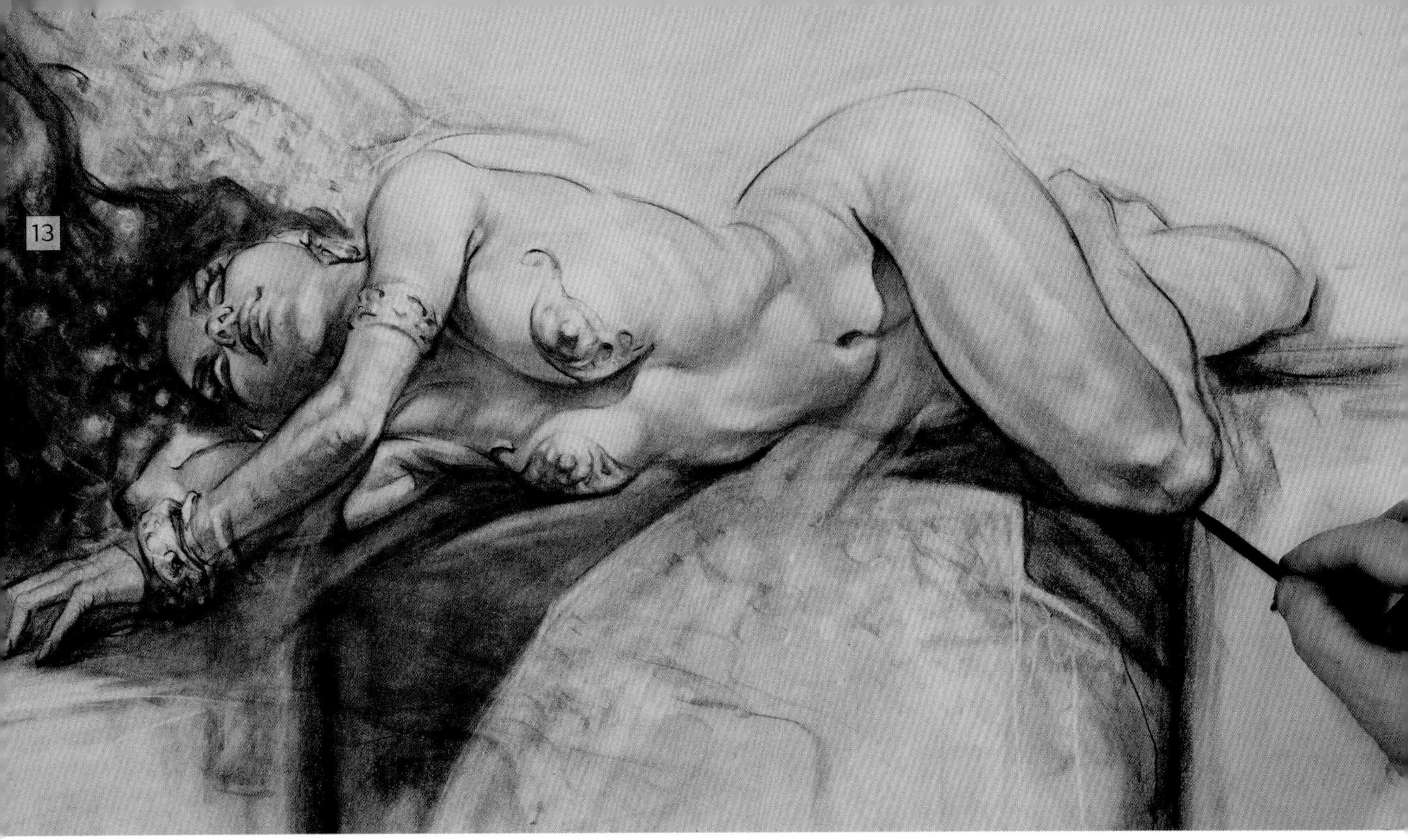

14

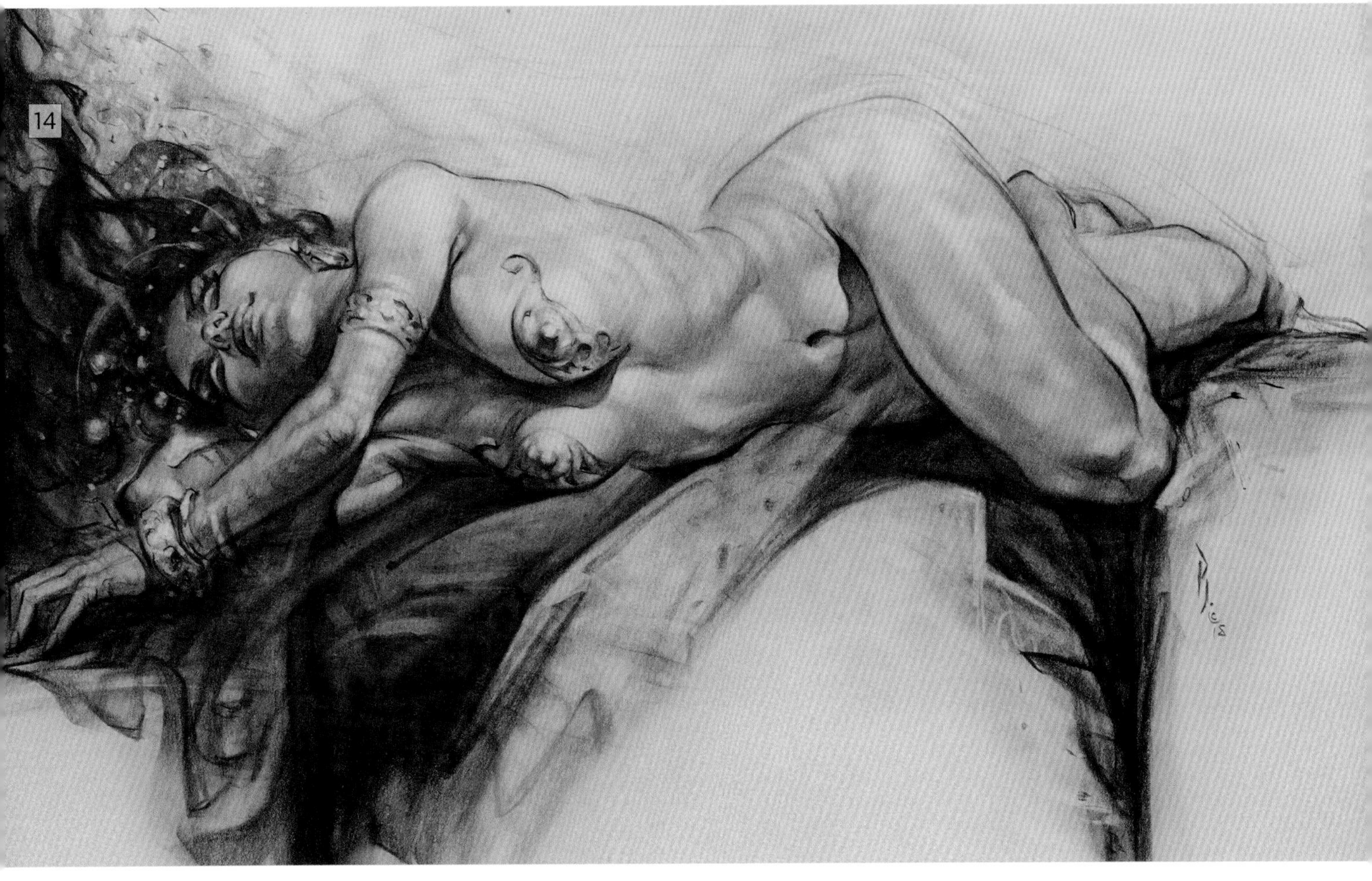

15 · Study Sheet

So, we end our first workshop with a drawing which resembles the photo reference in that it represents the same basic pose; however, it's now a world away from the photo in terms of its emotional reach. If I were to show only the photograph as the final result of my artist collaboration with Katy, the conversation would tend towards the lighting and what a marvellous model she is, and that would pretty much be it.

Conversely, if I were to show only the drawing, the conversation would explode in all manner of directions. "Who is the mysterious model who posed for this creature of the night? She must have been amazing to work with!"

"She was indeed!" I would reply, but there would be so much more to discuss. Things like "What does the title mean?" "Is she changing into a vampire via her trance?", "What happens next in the story?"

Study now the difference between the photo and the finished drawing. The annotated notes give a rudimentary idea of some stylistic choices I made during the process. These are a good go-to if you are starting out, but they are not hard-and-fast rules, just a beginning. I find that some techniques elevate the art out of the mundane, such as bringing reflected light into the shadows, but sometimes I darken a shadow that is too light to be more like the photo reference. It depends on what the rest of the drawing looks like in relation to the shadow. We began with a photo and we fought the lies it told us and rejoiced in what the frozen image conjured. It gave us the ability to study the figure for an extended period without the model shifting position – an impossible feat in real life. It is our friend and foe all wrapped up in a miraculous paradox.

The fact that the final process ends with a drawing rather than a traced image means the artist has invested thought and emotion into the art far beyond the photoshoot – so far that the photo is no longer involved in the process. The drawing now has a life of its own. The photo remains in a unique place as a documented memory of time, but the art has gained an eternal quality because the viewer can interpret their own stories based on it. The drawing may have stirred the imagination of the viewer, but now they have something more personal: ownership.

I've studied Frank Frazetta's *Egyptian Queen* so often over the years that I'm sure I've spent more time looking at it than the time it took Frank to paint it. I own it, and I own the stories I've imagined based on it. They are mine to treasure. Frank started a conversation that is eternal and belongs to us all.

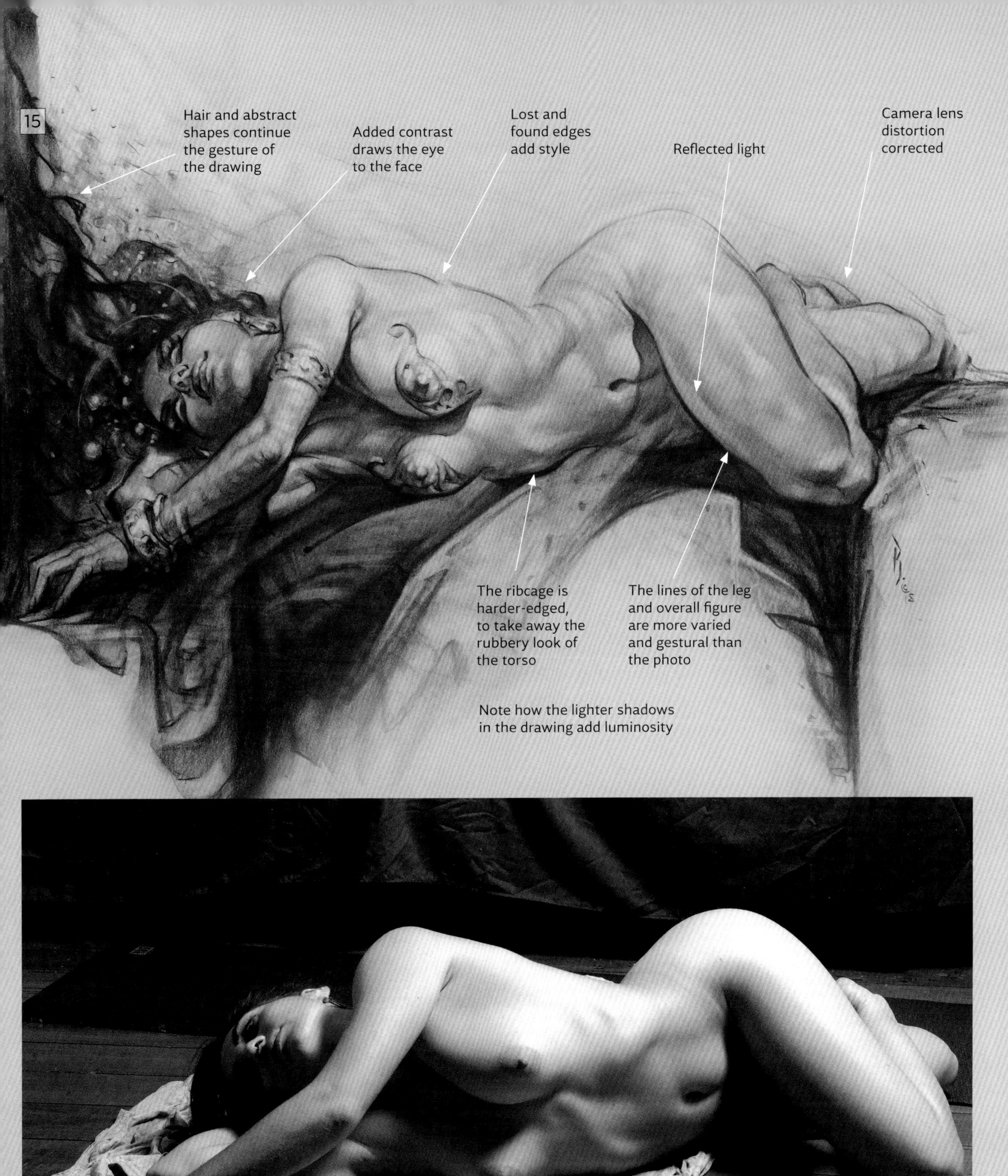

15
Hair and abstract shapes continue the gesture of the drawing
Added contrast draws the eye to the face
Lost and found edges add style
Reflected light
Camera lens distortion corrected
The ribcage is harder-edged, to take away the rubbery look of the torso
The lines of the leg and overall figure are more varied and gestural than the photo
Note how the lighter shadows in the drawing add luminosity

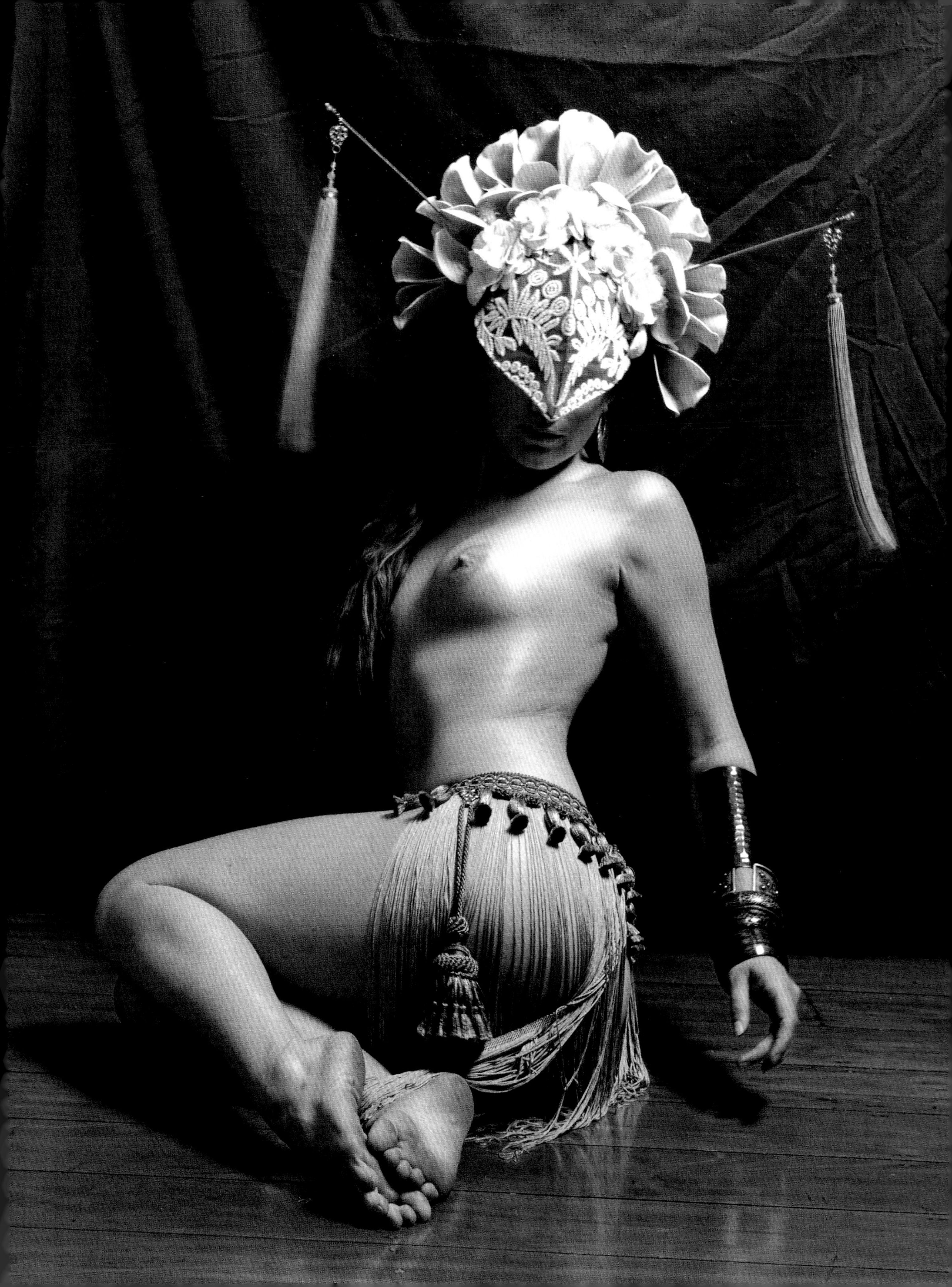

WORKSHOP TWO

THE POWER OF ILLUSION

ON OUR FLAT paper surface, we can draw only across two dimensions: we can draw up and down and left and right, but we obviously can't draw "inside" the flat paper, for therein lies the impossible third dimension of depth. Yet that doesn't mean we can't create the "illusion" of the third dimension.

It was the illusion of the third dimension that drew gasps of amazement when the Old Masters such as Rembrandt and Caravaggio first displayed their huge oil painted masterworks to the public. Imagine living in those times when photography and cinema didn't exist, and then imagine a giant canvas filled with heroic figures painted with the illusion of 3D space. Having stood in front of these monumental paintings myself, I can attest that it feels almost possible to step inside the canvas. Centuries ago, these works were not only the height of visual entertainment: to the average person, they were feats of magic!

Using charcoals and pencils to create the illusion of depth is a harder task to fulfil, though, as we don't have the benefit of colour and glazes, and in most cases scale, as pencil drawings are usually a small affair. But it can still be done.

In this workshop, we will explore the world of illusion, and endeavour through line and tone to trick the eye into believing we are looking beyond a flat surface.

Left: Model Katy Woods during a photo session based on emotion as physical movement.

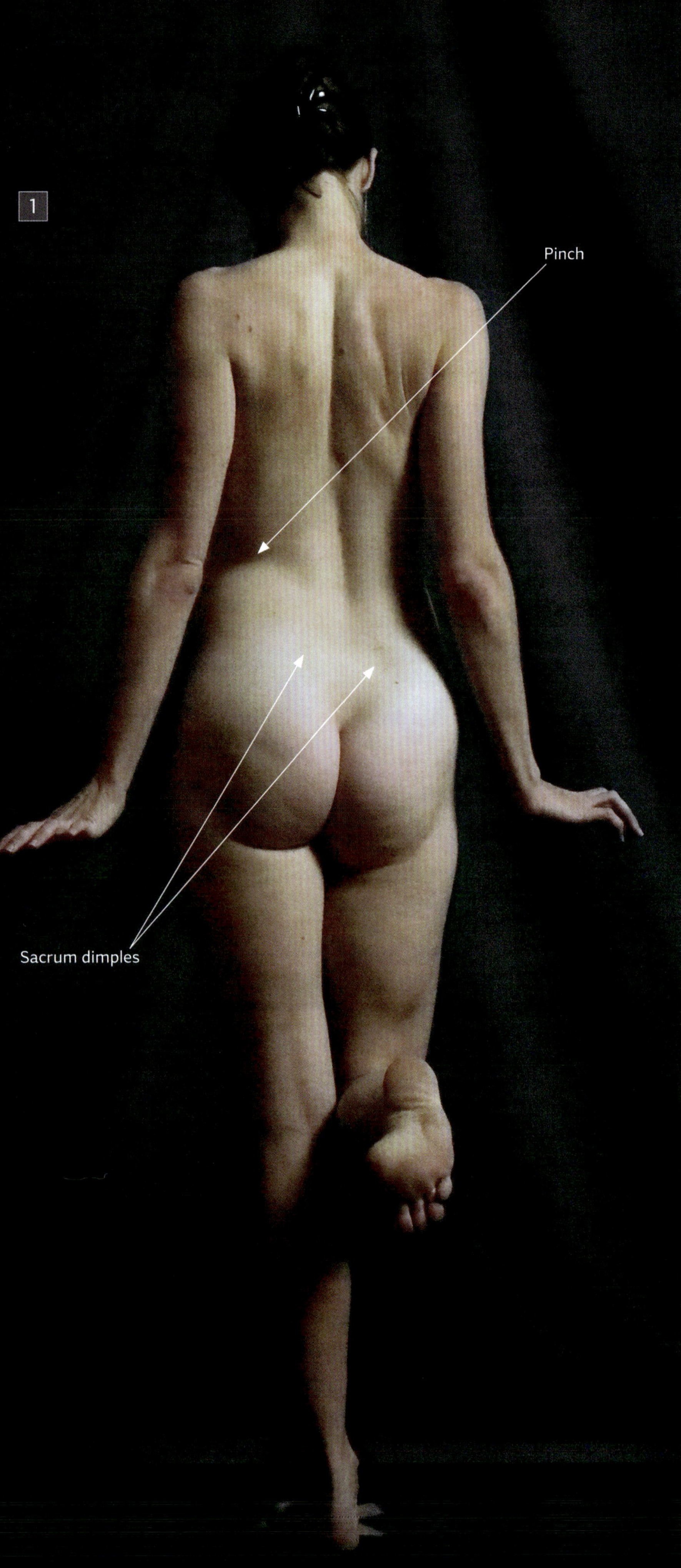

THE ENTITY
Charcoal and pencil
on A2 newsprint

Today we will draw Alana with a focus
on the gluteus, while creating depth
using tonal value. I've added to the task
by choosing a photo featuring very little
foreshortening. Apart from the foot
coming at us, the limbs, torso, and head
are roughly within the flatter 2D planes:
left to right and up and down.

To create the illusion of depth we
will work with a few ideas. Firstly, we
need to think like a sculptor and draw
the body as a dimensional landscape
of overlapping forms with a sense of
weight and volume. To achieve this,
we will work with tonal value – from
the darkest value, "black", towards the
lightest value, "white". In this case the
white value is the bare newsprint paper.

As usual, I begin with simple shapes,
big to small, taking time to assess how
I will construct the drawing before I
make a mark. Always be on high alert in
the early stages as there is no point in
rendering a badly constructed drawing.

1 · Feeling the Pinch

Although this looks like a symmetrical
stance, the hips are tilted downwards to
the right and the ribcage to the left. Look
to the left-side pinch of the waist for the
clue. The hips are a fused mass, so the
tilt affects each side. The pinch indicates
the oblique muscles bulging between the
ribcage and the hips.

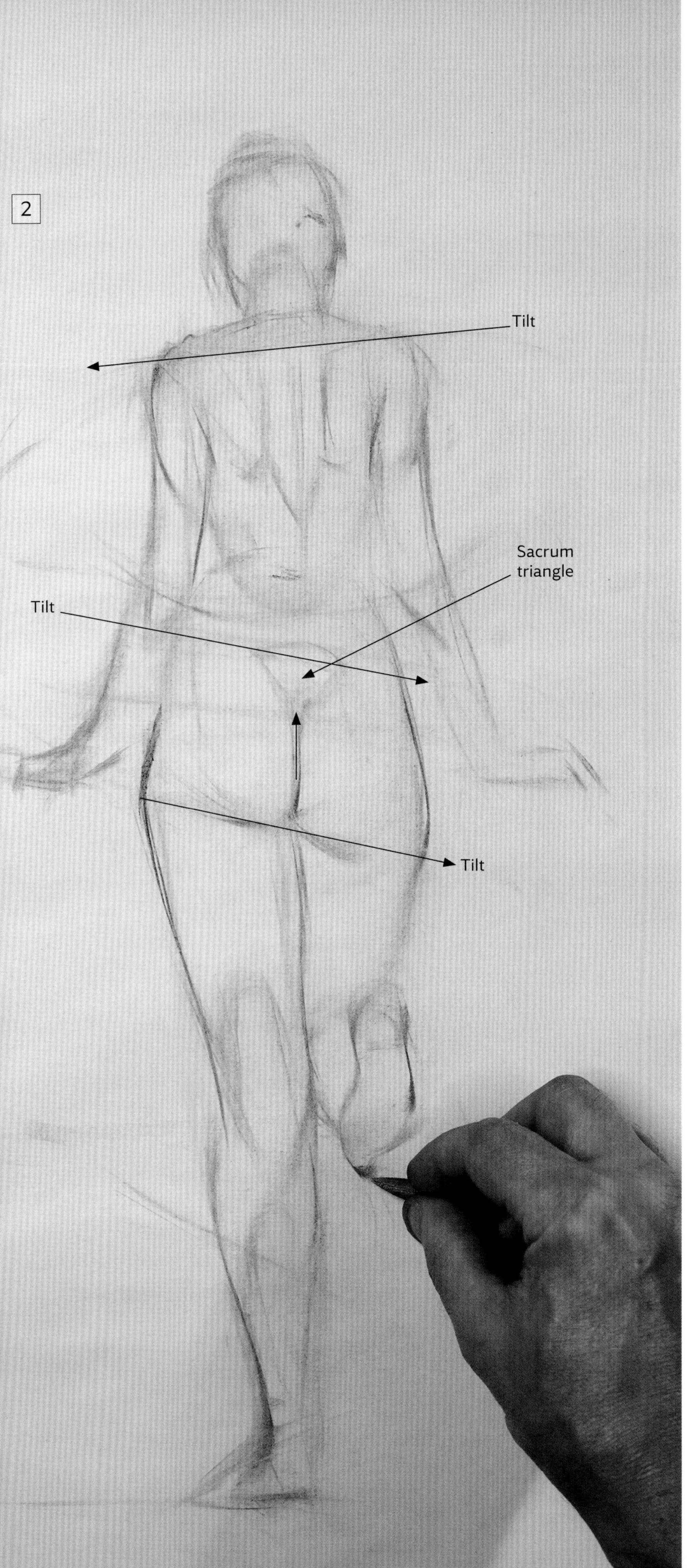

To give the pose more movement, I tilt the shoulders towards the higher hip. The shoulders will naturally tilt with the ribcage, but because the scapulae (the wing bones of the upper back) work independently, this can change. Using a small piece of willow charcoal, I also pull the right arm out a little to give the pose a more quirky feel.

Note the sacrum triangle above the gluteal divide; this is a central landmark to look for as it indicates the end of the spine and the beginning of the hips. As the hips are fused, they can only tilt and twist. The sacrum and its dimples are the cornerstone to look for as we begin our structure. In photographs shot straight on, the sacrum and its dimples can be hard to find. I recommend paying particular attention to this area in life drawing and shifting to a position where you can see the sacrum shape from the side. We can't do this with a photograph, of course, but constant study will help us see these vague shapes, as I've indicated in our photo here.

Placing the sacrum gives us a landmark to line up the hip bones and the bottom. The top corners of the sacrum will often show as dimples where we can run an imaginary line that informs the tilt of the hips. Once we have the hip tilt, we have an imaginary box form to work within, making the complex structure of the hips a simple idea to begin with.

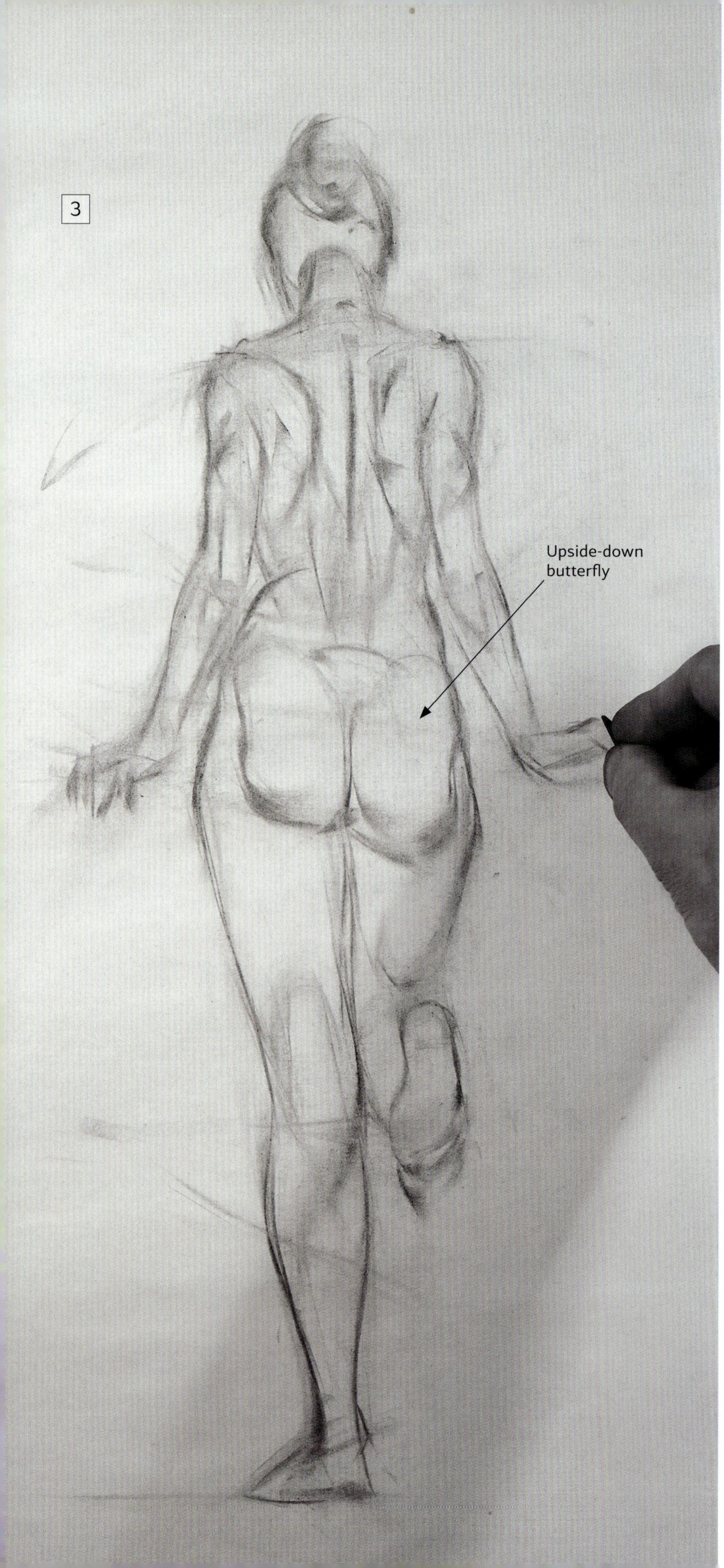

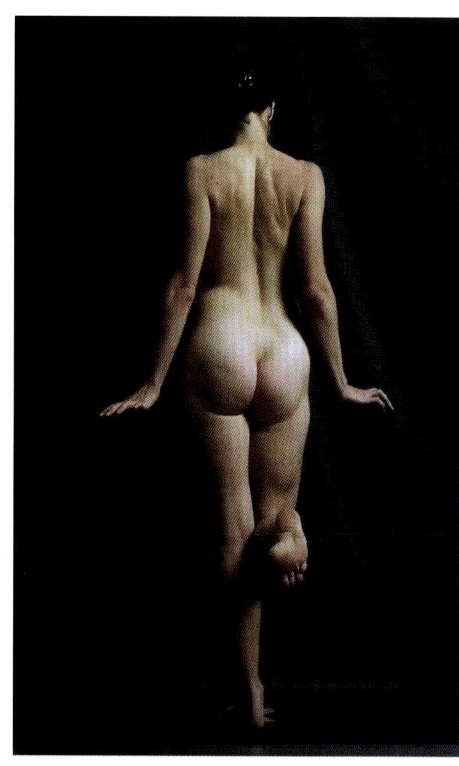

3 · The Butterfly Effect

I explore the body landscape, feeling the depth of the flesh as if drawing in the third dimension. Drawing the corners of the gluteus as I would a box, but with softer edges, helps clarify the idea. Note that the back side of the gluteal masses resembles an upside-down butterfly. This is a memory clue, known as a mnemonic, which helps me avoid the mistake of making the upper gluteus and lower gluteus equal-sized volumes. The lower gluteal masses are called the gluteus maximus for good reason.

4 · The Power of Illusion

With everything in place, I add some grayscale tone with the broad side of my charcoal. The tone immediately adds a sense of volume to our illusion of the third dimension. I'm keeping everything light to begin with, in order to have the freedom to change shapes and tones before going into detail.

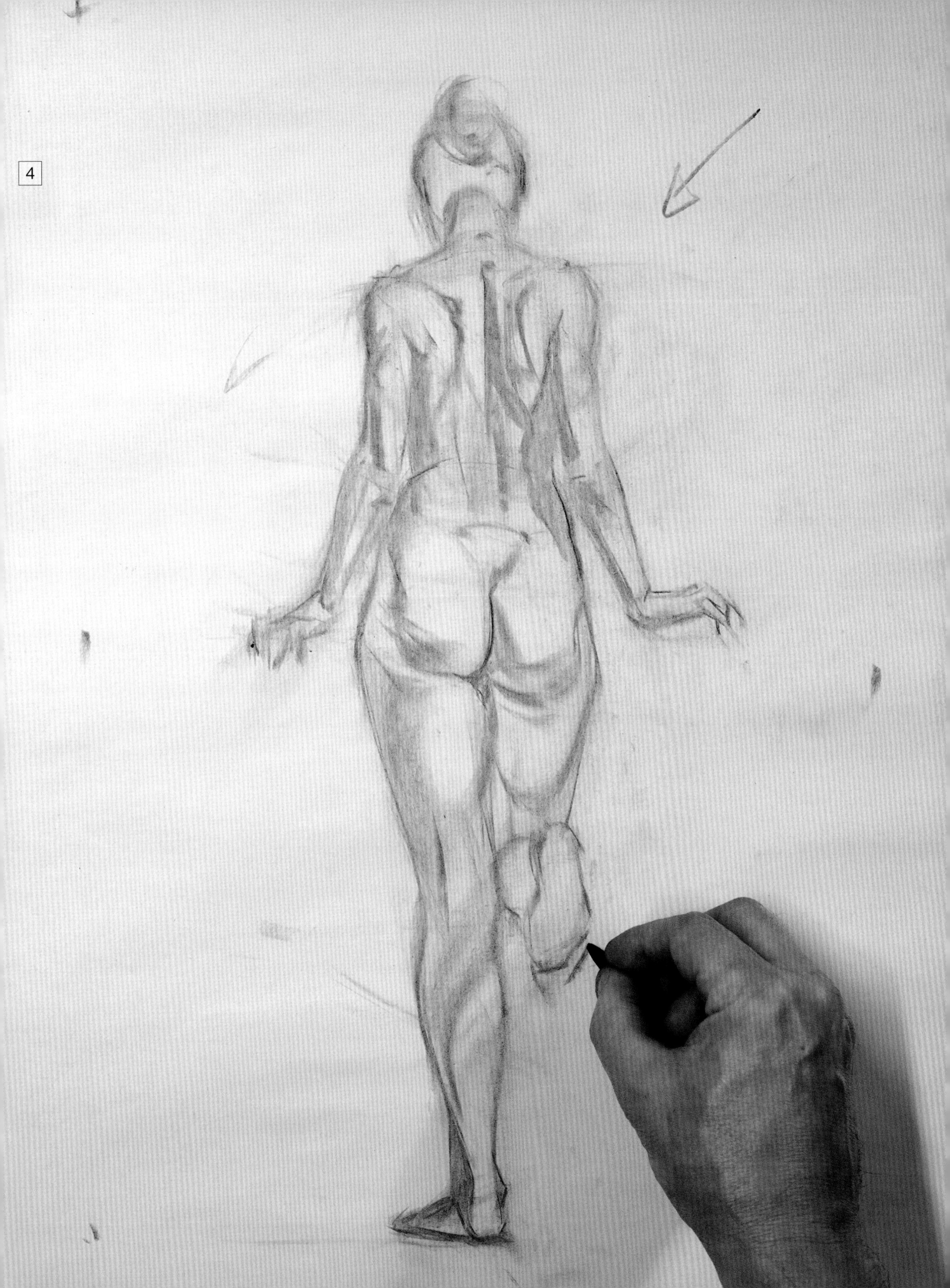

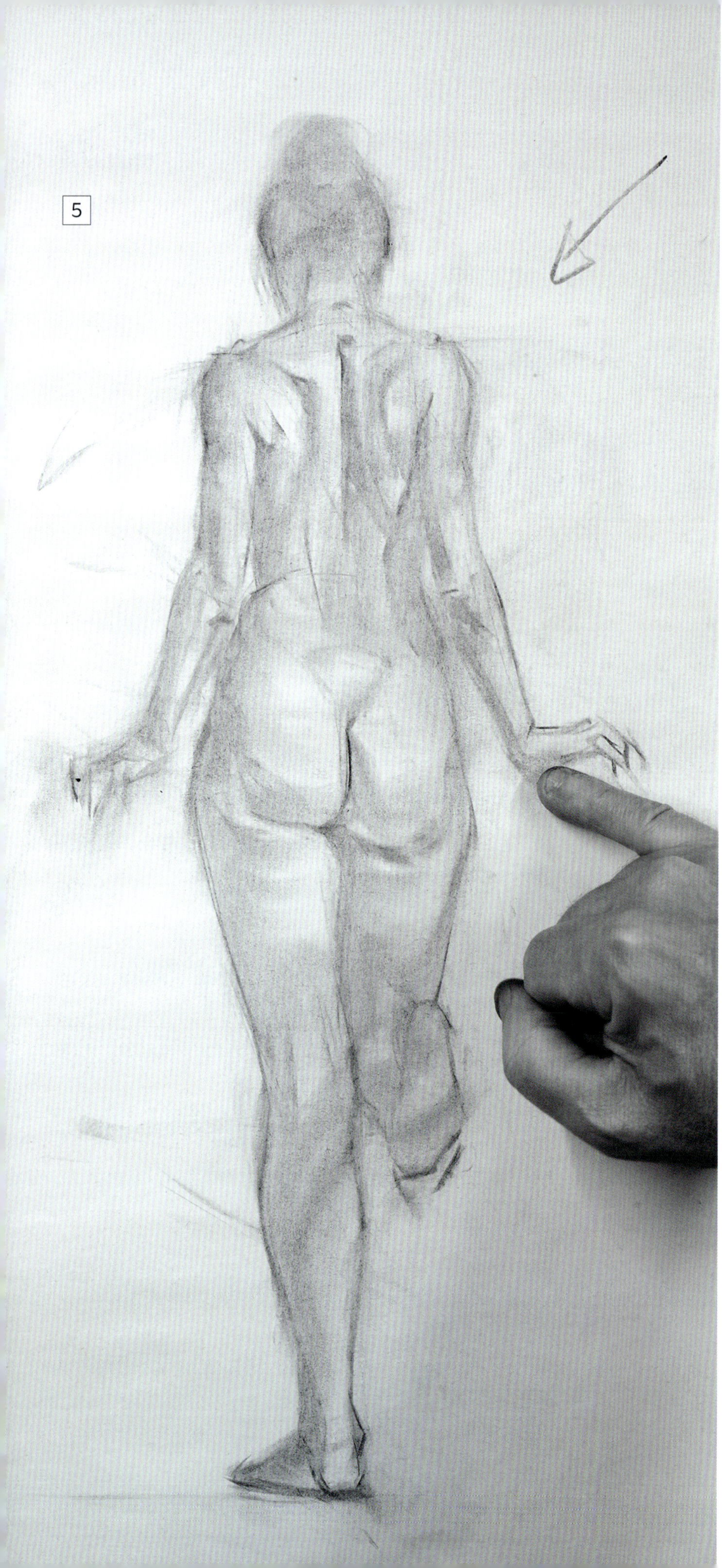

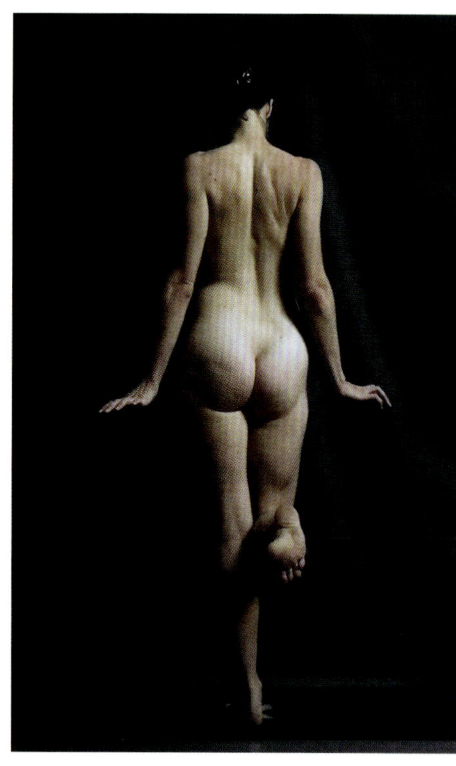

5 · Think Like a Sculptor

There's now enough charcoal on the newsprint surface for me to shape the flesh using my fingers alone. I'm thinking like a sculptor. This makes the illusion of flesh softer and fades the image. With the image faded, I have a less confusing drawing on top of which to put line.

6 · The Paper Solution

I use a scrap piece of newsprint to avoid smudging the charcoal as I draw. I could use a re-workable spray fixative at this stage, to hold the charcoal, but it can make erasing highlights difficult later. The paper solution leaves my erasing options open for as long as possible, as well as making it easier to smudge, fade, and redraw lines.

Here I'm drawing the bulge of the greater trochanter bone (ball of the femur) at the widest part of the hips.

The greater
trochanter bulge

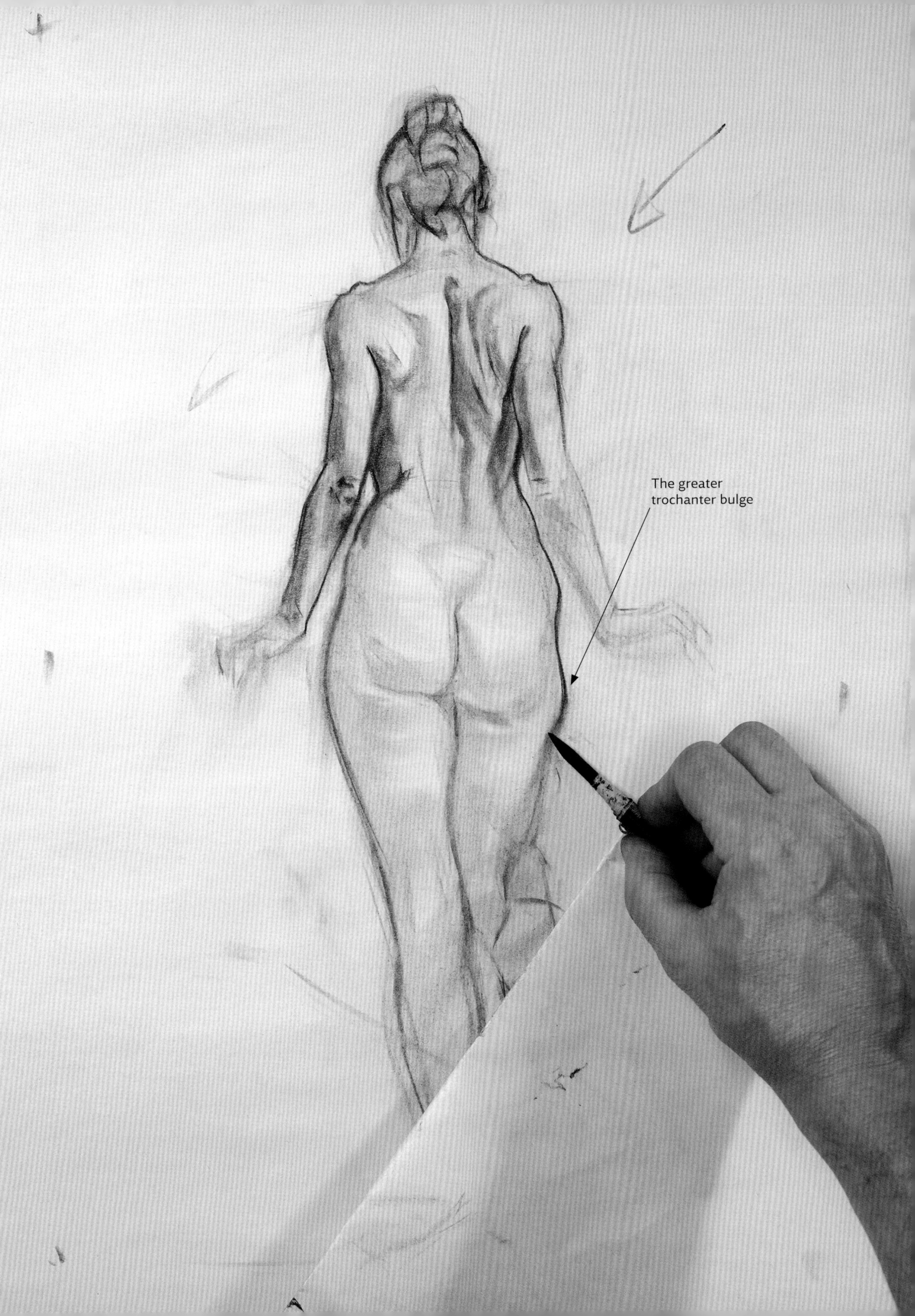

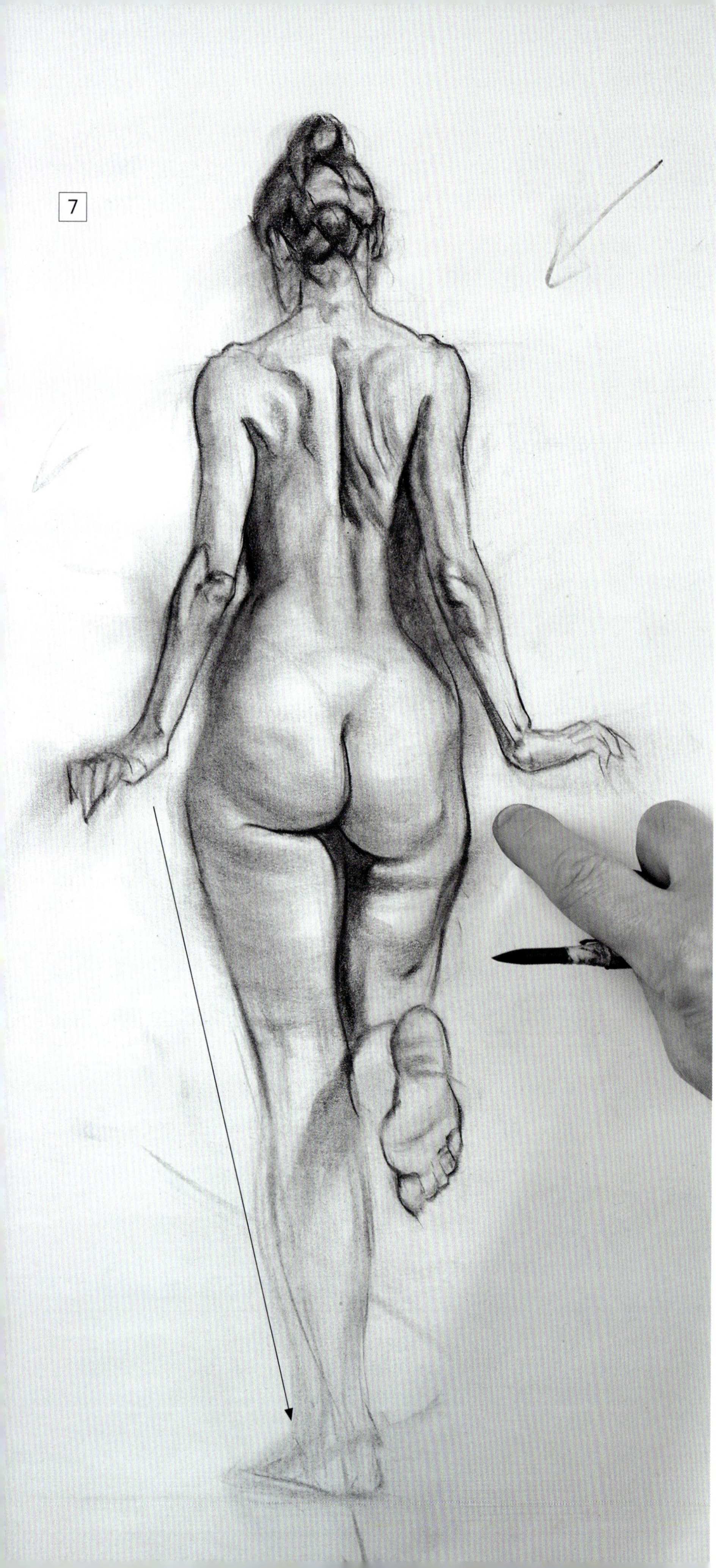

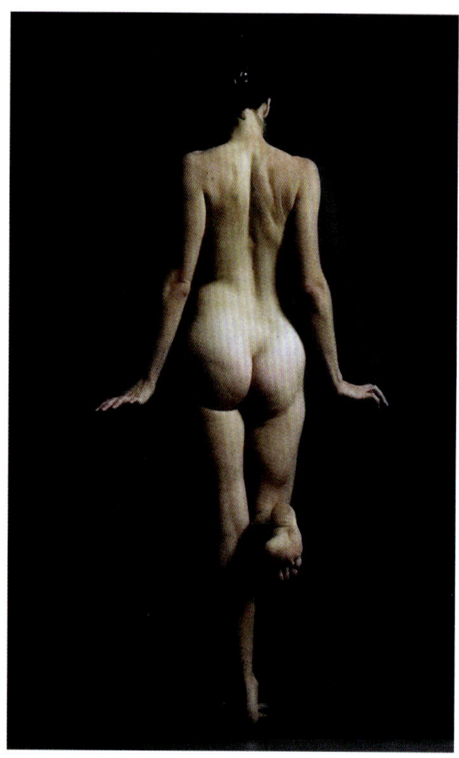

7 · Murky Areas

Alternating between finger smudging and pencilling, I work from dark to light tones to find further illusions of depth. Within photographic images we tend to find murky areas that we can't simply brighten with a light switch, so we need to know our anatomy should we decide to bring those unseen areas into the light. I decide to pull the standing leg inwards more before detailing. Remember: the early stages are the least painful time to make changes.

8 · Improving the Drawing

Adjusting the leg in the last step has made the figure more solidly balanced. I was lucky to spot the opportunity for change before I added heavier line work, which is more difficult to erase.

Every stage is a new opportunity to rethink and improve the drawing based on the photo (or live model) – interpreting what we see rather than simply copying without thought.

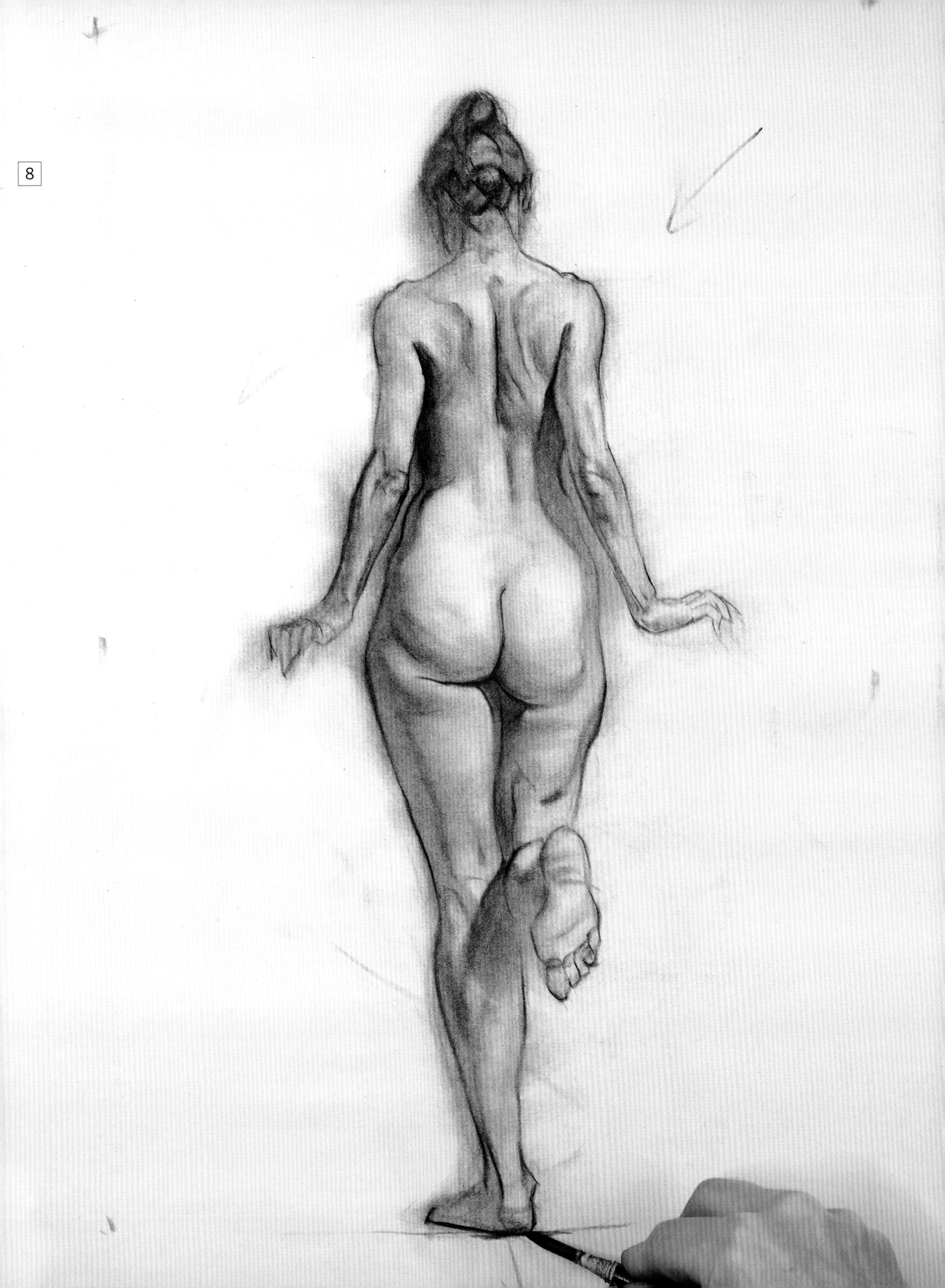

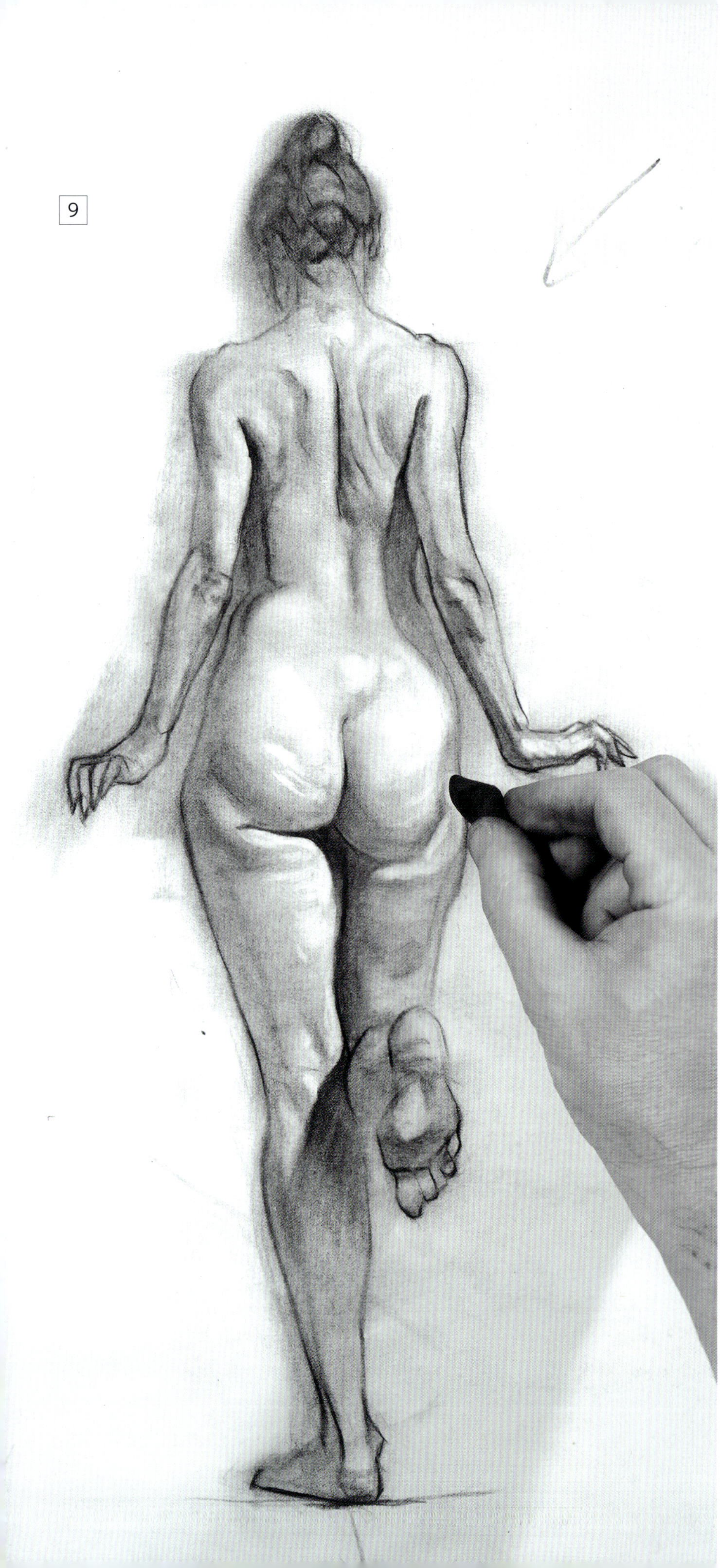

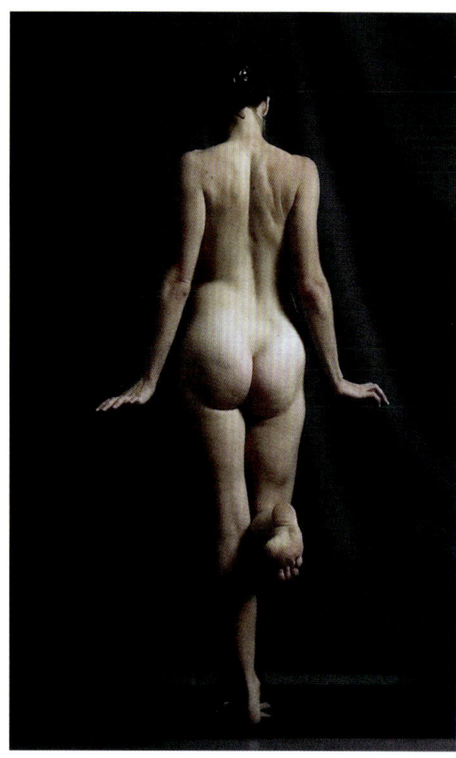

9 · The Shapeshifter

I continue to smudge into the flesh until I have a good mid-tone out of which to pull highlights with my kneadable eraser. By reshaping the pliable eraser as I go, I can vary the shape-making. As I mentioned earlier, I think of my erasers as drawing tools rather than mistake fixers. I don't fear the hard-edged marks the kneadable eraser makes because I'm thinking ahead to the next blending stage. Note how dark the eraser is. A dirty eraser is a more subtle eraser, and it leaves fewer gummy marks.

10 · A Light Touch

With a pencil eraser, I "draw" the brightest highlights. On flesh, extreme highlights are usually found on oily parts of the skin, such as the nose and the forehead, but also where the flesh gets pinched. The pencil eraser has a brush on the end for sweeping erased particles.

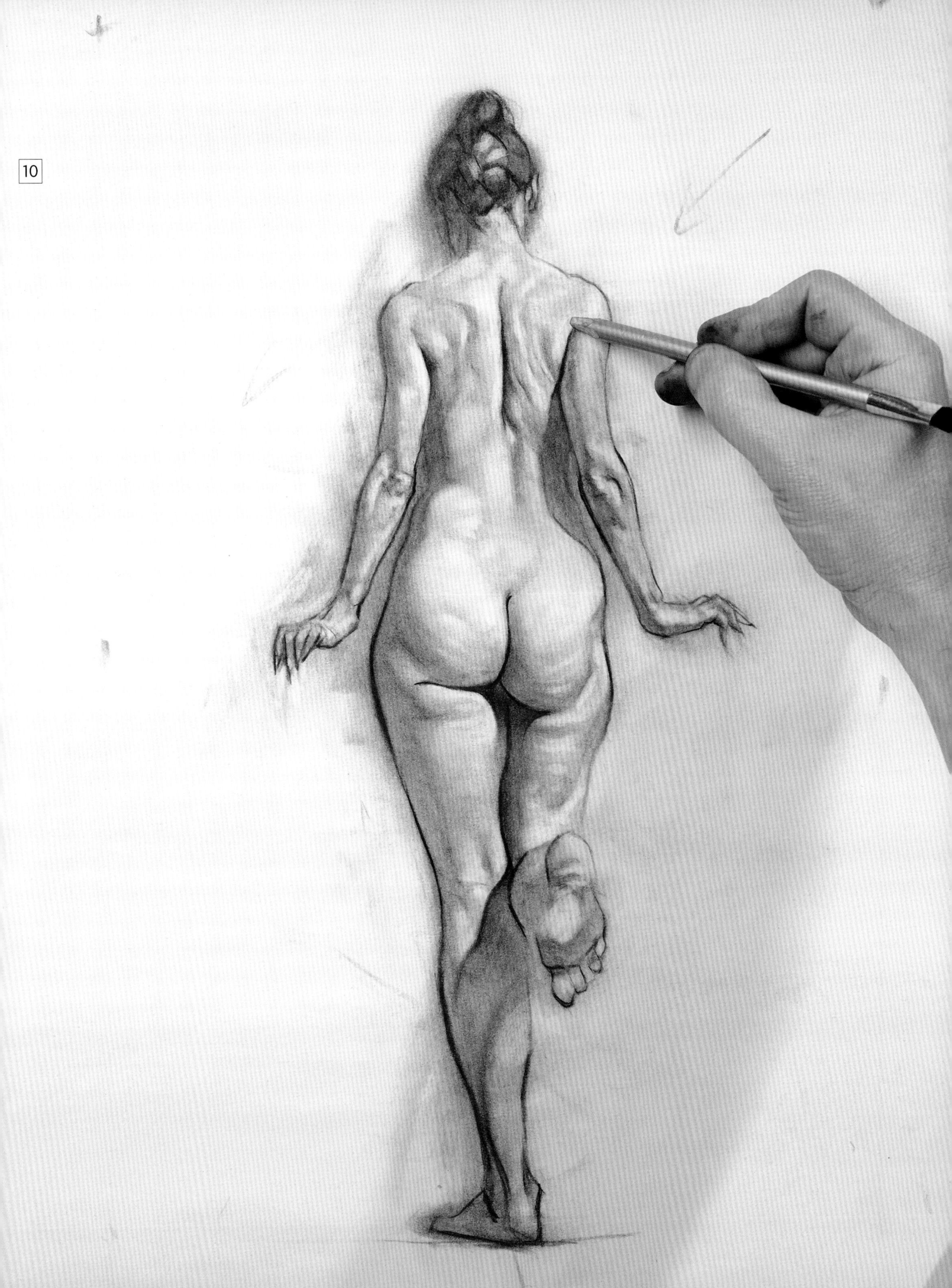

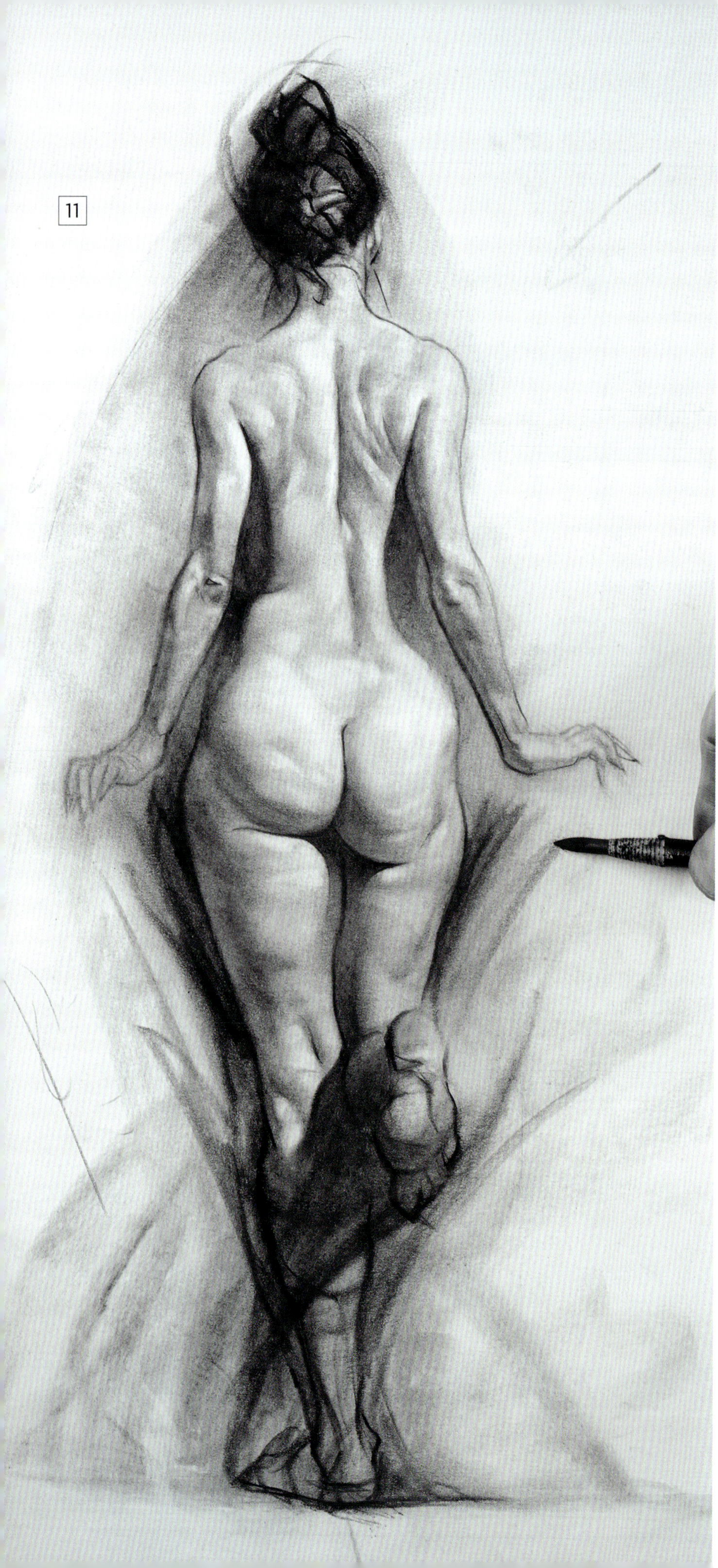

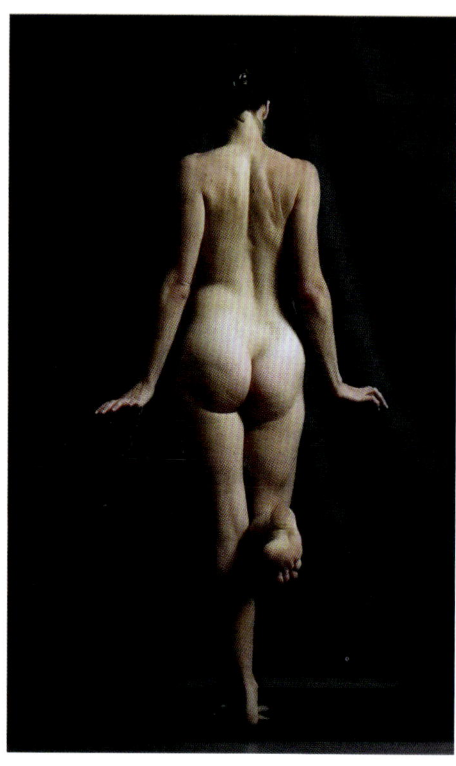

11 · Black Magic

Now I work into the absolute darks to get further dimension. The darkest darks will be in the occlusion shadows, where flesh meets flesh, such as in the creases of the gluteus and the arms. I also add some energetic strokes here to bring back my gestural hand, which can become stiff, in the "'drawing" sense of the word, after a lot of structural drawing. Abstract marks are one of the advantages an artist has over the camera, which, beyond capturing light, has no real thought process to speak of.

12 · The Mysterious

To finish, I tame down the strokes and shape them with my smudgy fingers, erasers, and tissue to create a mystical swirl. What is the mysterious "entity" in the drawing's title? Well, I'll leave that to your imagination as I like my drawings to be open to interpretation. Leaving some mystery creates a connection between the artist and the viewer.

12

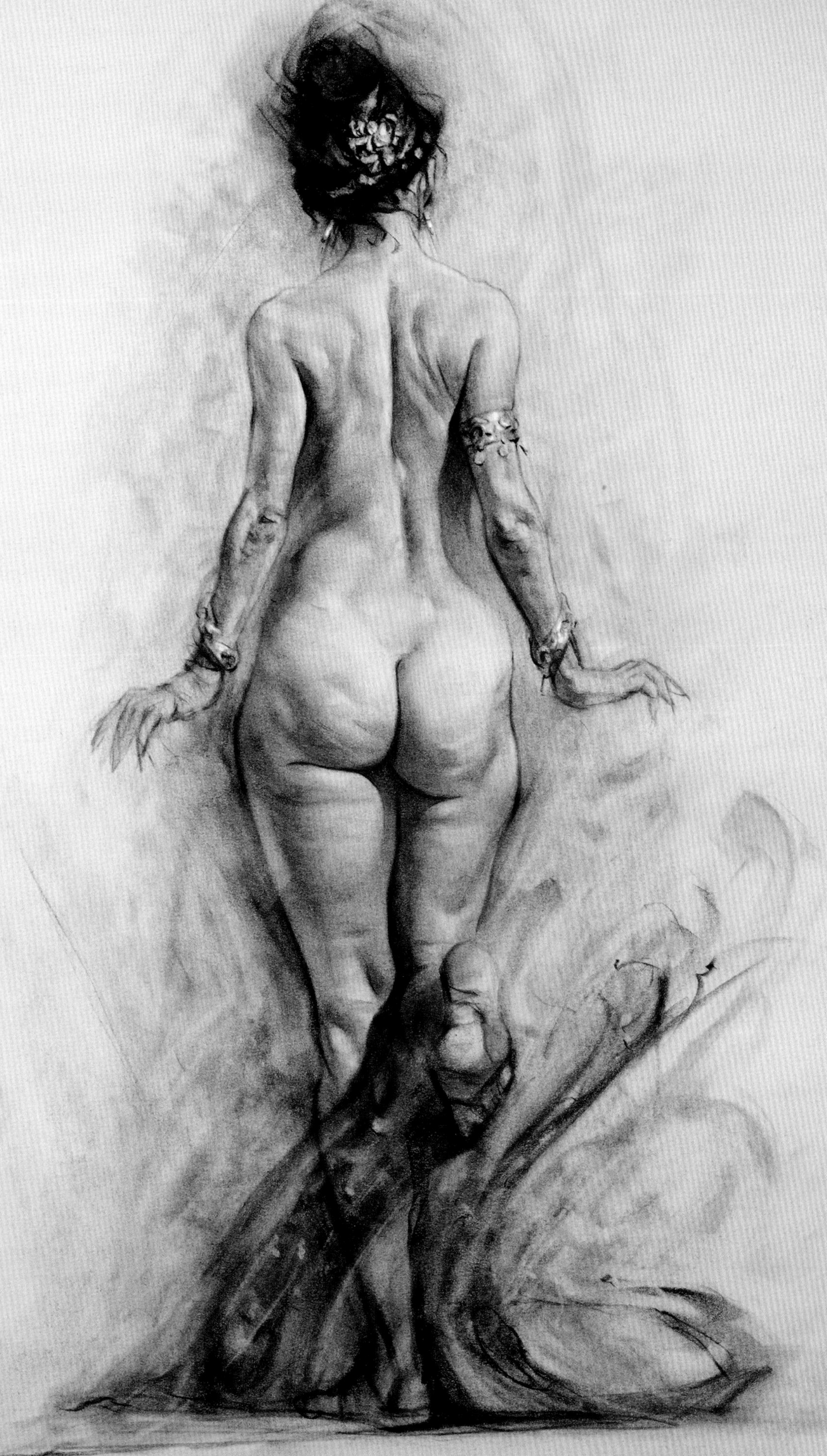

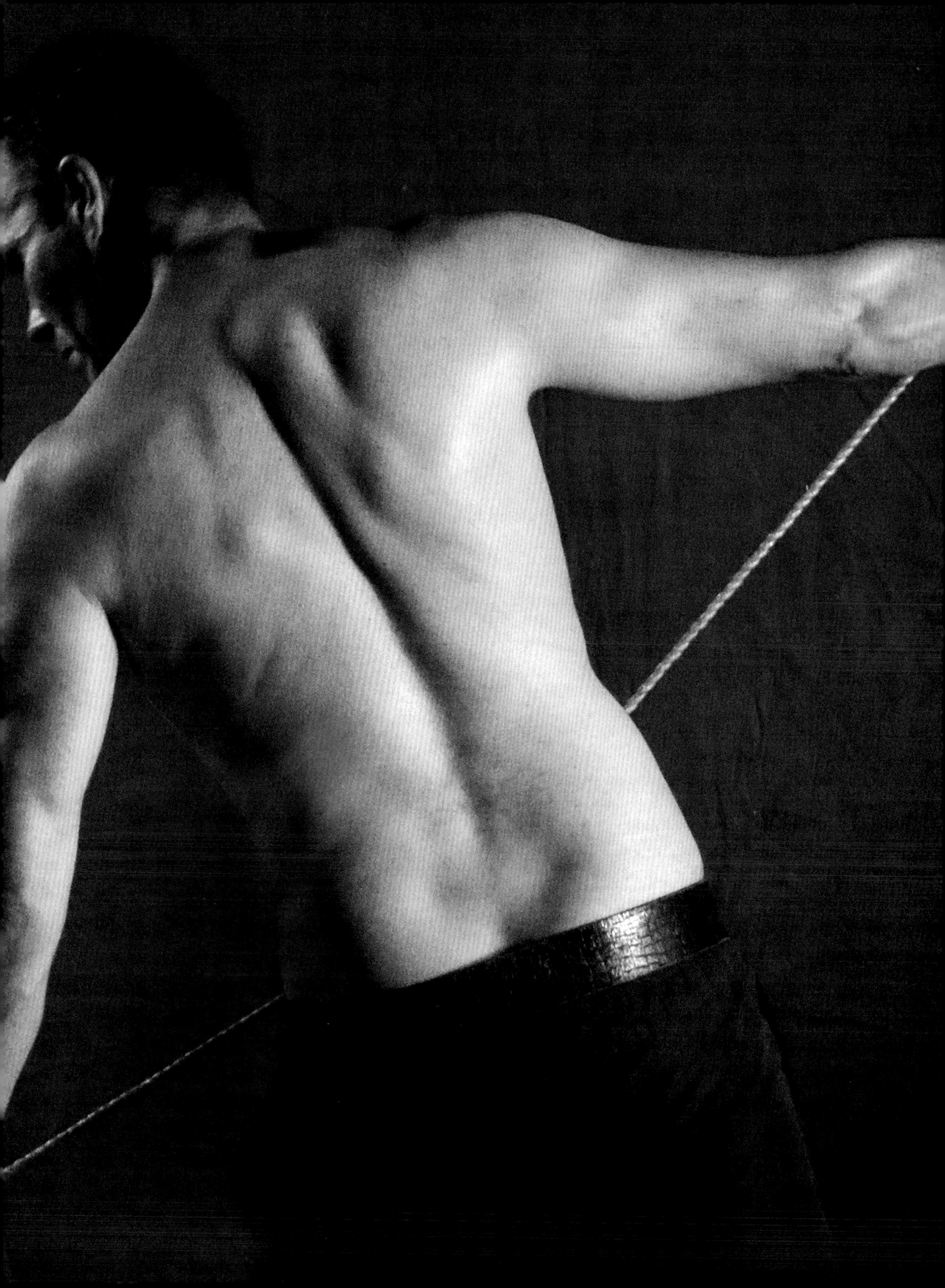

WORKSHOP THREE
NATURAL RHYTHM

CONTRAPPOSTO MEANS COUNTERPOISE or counterbalance, and in the visual arts it refers to a standing human figure carrying most of its weight on one straight leg, freeing the other leg, which is bent at the knee. The most famous contrapposto pose in an artwork is probably Michelangelo's statue of David, the biblical hero who slayed the giant Goliath, sculpted between 1501 and 1504. Incredibly, Michelangelo was just 26 years old when he started chipping into that 17-foot slab of marble!

The earliest known example of the contrapposto stance is the ancient Greek marble "Kritios Boy", which was sculpted around 480 BC. Before Kritios, figures were usually symmetrical or flat graphics, such as the figurative art found in ancient Egyptian temples. I guess it took a long time for a relaxed pose to be taken seriously.

What is it that makes counterbalanced figures in art so appealing? For me, it's their fluid asymmetry. When we are counterbalanced we are in a state of flux. I've stared into the eyes of counterbalanced Greek statues in silence and can understand how people in bygone eras believed they saw them move, or even speak.

Artists who are just starting out usually find photographic reference poses in magazines or on the internet, but with smartphones becoming cheaper and pixel resolution getting higher, we can now take our own photo reference shots. The most affordable models are our friends and ourselves. In this workshop, I will use myself as a model, as I have done since the start of my career. All we need when using the world's cheapest model is a friend to take the shot, or a self-timer, an understanding of rhythmic balance, and a sense of the dramatic.

Left: Patrick posing for a life drawing demo for *ImagineFX* magazine

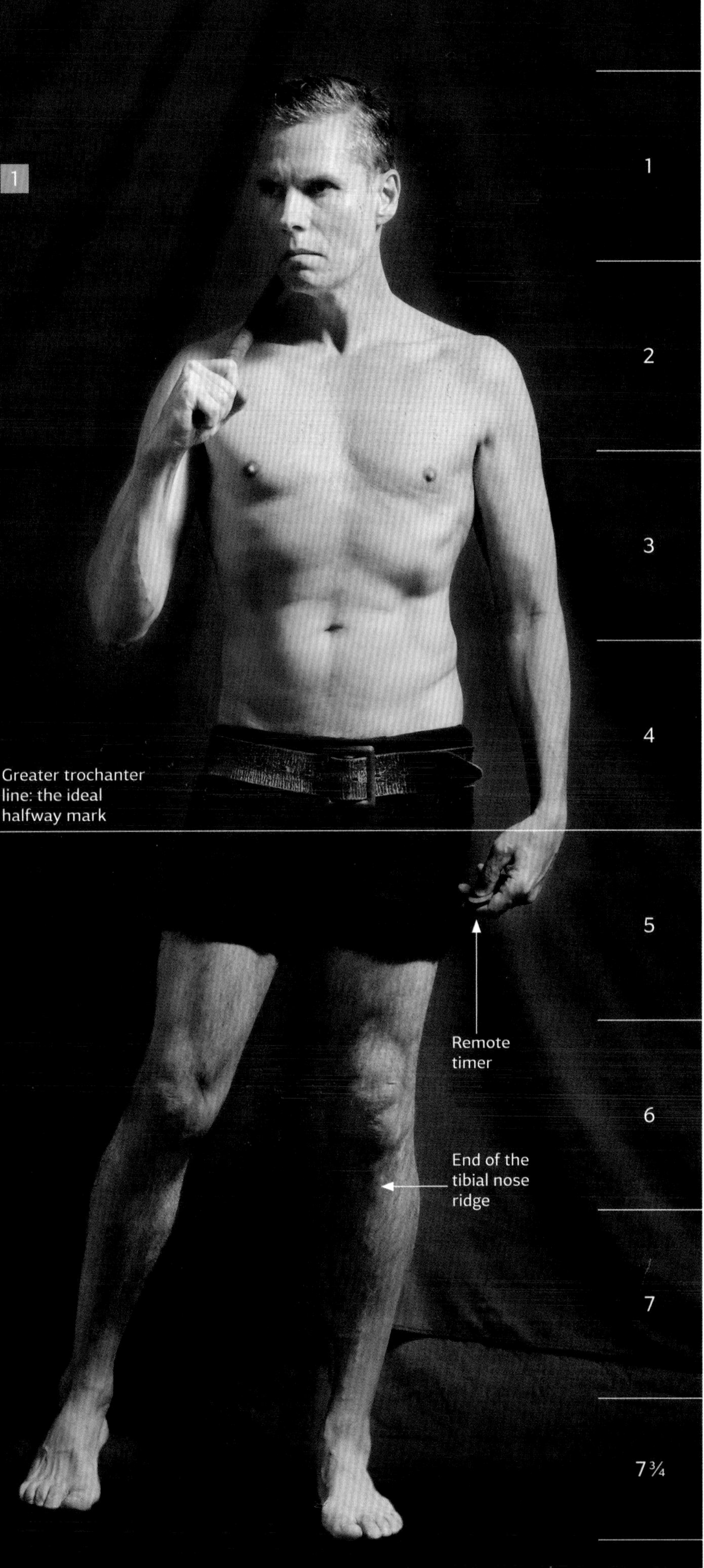

THE TRACKER

Sanguine pastel pencil on A3 toned paper

Today we will draw a male figure in contrapposto. To fill in for Michelangelo's *David*, I will employ my most reliable male model. He's always on time, and I pay him with simple foods such as cheese – a great deal for both of us.

I've measured myself in heads and I come in at around seven and three-quarter heads high (head included), which is close to the average proportion of seven and a half heads high. You can see the major landmarks: the bottom of head two lands just above the nipple and the bottom of head three just below the navel. The bottom of head four hits the ideal halfway mark of the greater trochanter (hip bone), and the bottom of head six lands just below the tibial nose.

An ideal division is eight heads, which would line up those major landmarks evenly – this is what the *David* statue appears to be. I expected less perhaps, as he has a large head, but he has a long femur. I have a small head, and at first glance, I expected I might be eight heads too, but I have a shorter femur. The point is, everyone is slightly different. Although we vary greatly in height, most of us are close in basic proportion.

1 · Always on Time

Look closely at my hand and you will see I'm holding a remote timer button to take the shot. Place a full-length mirror next to your camera, and you are ready to pose.

2 · Begin the Sanguine

For this drawing, I'm using a sanguine pastel pencil on toned paper. Sanguine means blood-red, and sanguine pencils can range in colour from dark brown to almost pink. I've chosen a dark sanguine and a warm, mid-tone paper. To find the right tone, just match the paper to the basic midtone of your pencil. The midtone doesn't need to be exact, just close. The paper will now represent the midtone of the figure.

As ever, I start with basic shapes, then identify the weight-bearing straight leg and tilt the shoulder towards it for more balance. I then tilt the head towards the higher shoulder. This is the ideal balance, but as in the *David* statue, I'm holding an object that tilts the shoulders a little towards the relaxed leg, throwing me off from the ideal contrapposto tilt. Tricky, but commonly seen.

I usually err on the side of a smaller head rather than a bigger one. A smaller head is more heroic as it makes the figure more majestic, whereas a big head can look comical – although a tiny head will also look comical. It's relatively easy to enlarge a head that's too small by adding to the jaw or the top of the skull, but to make a very big head smaller, we will most likely need to draw all the features, including the lips and eyes, smaller, and that's a bug fix. In that case, it would be a better and fresher choice to redraw from scratch.

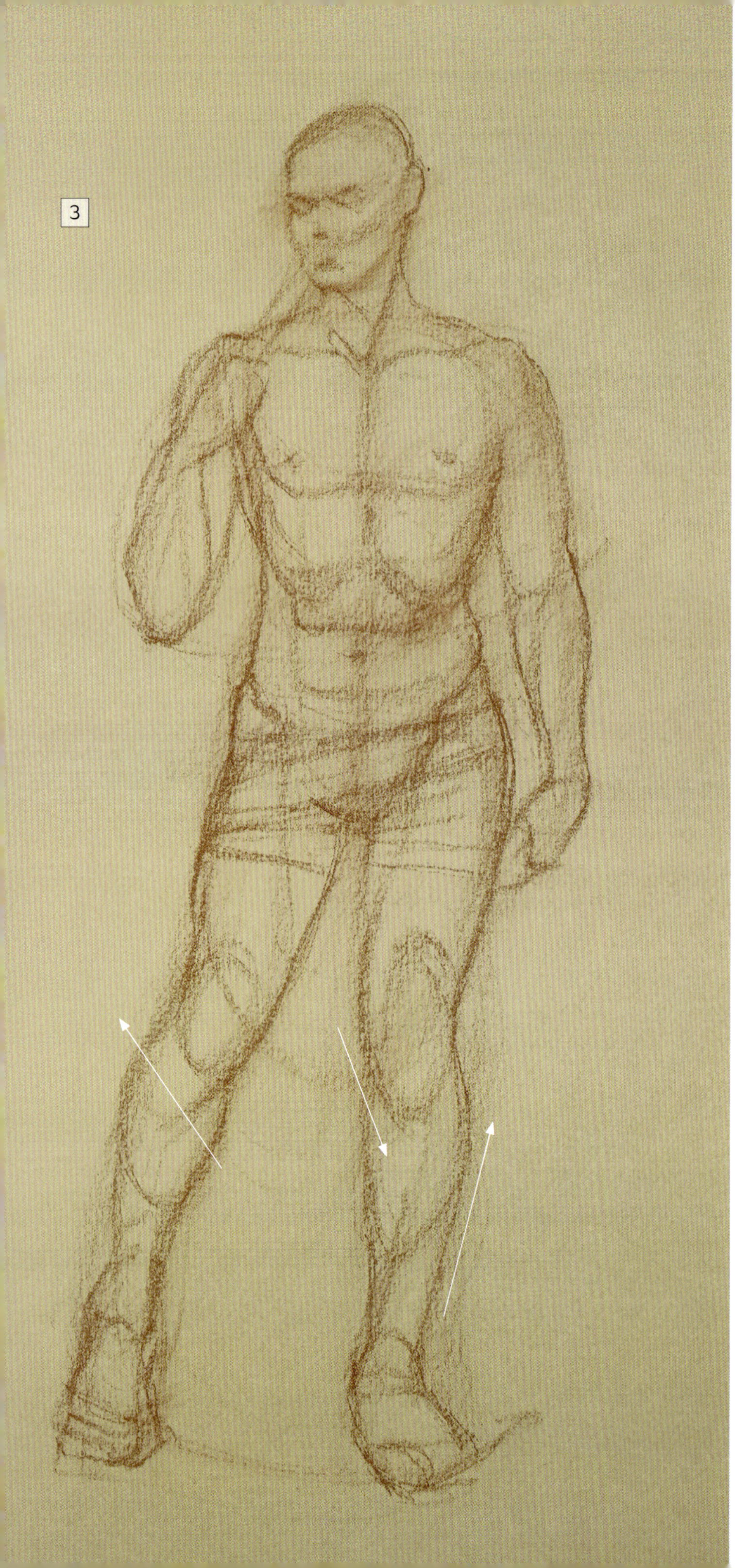

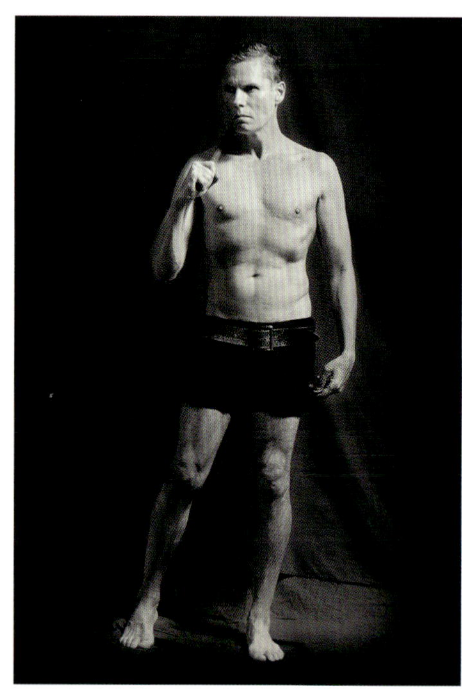

3 · An Individual Style

I draw smaller shapes inside the big, simple shapes. Note how I treat the rhythm of the legs, drawing from one side to the other. Study how the knees have a low, overlapping curve on the inside and how the calves are high on the outside. This is the natural rhythm of the body. Look back and forth at the photo and the drawing to see the micro changes I make as I go. They may not all be for the better, but each decision adds to my style; it also keeps me interested and constantly thinking, which by its very nature makes the drawing more vigorous rather than a stiff copy.

4 · Ghosting the Image

I'm using a high-grade pastel art paper. Pastel paper has a smooth and a rough side. I choose the smooth side, but it still has a "tooth" – micro pits that hold the pastel pigment. I blend with tissue to smooth the pastel pigment into the grain and also to ghost back the image.

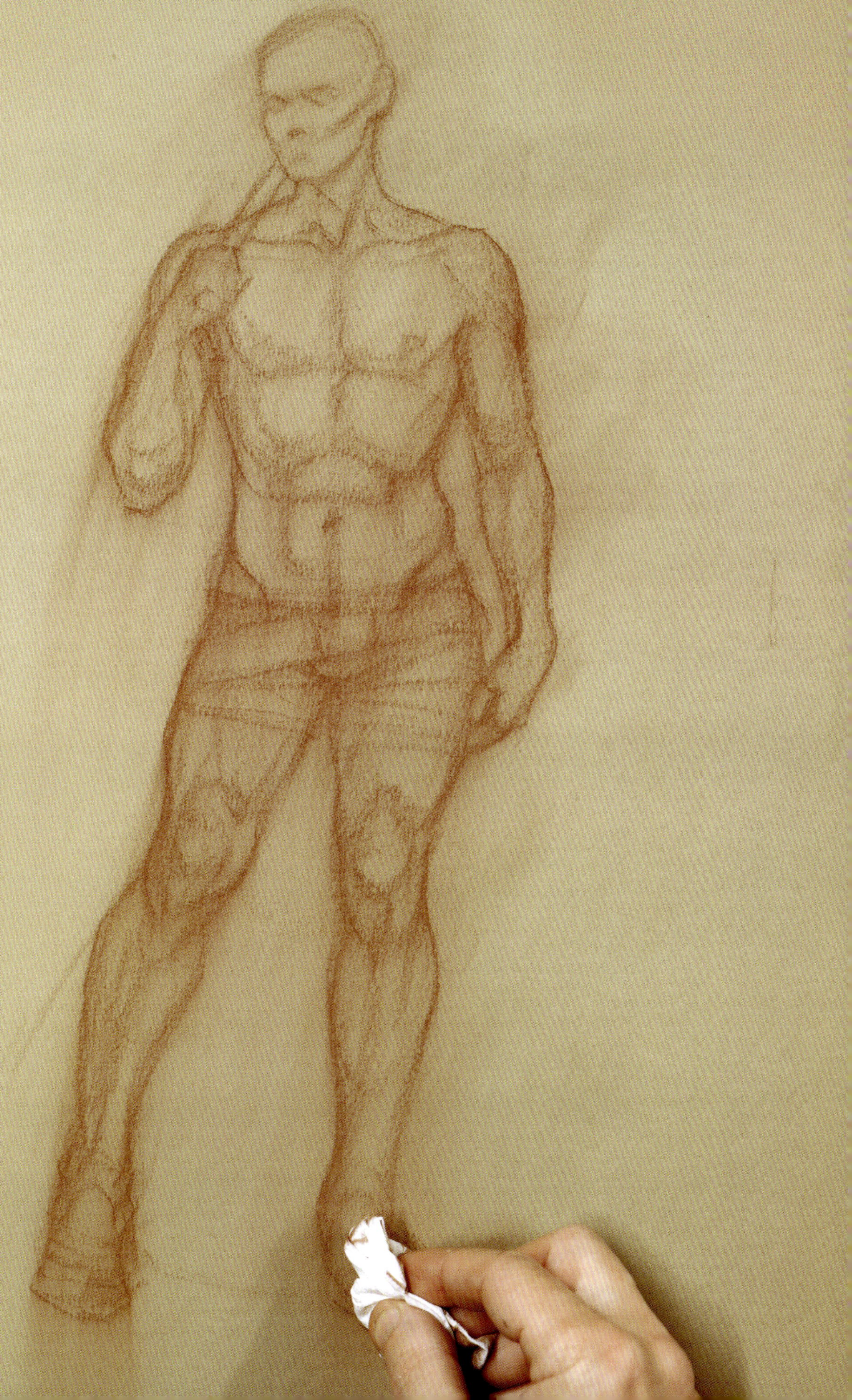

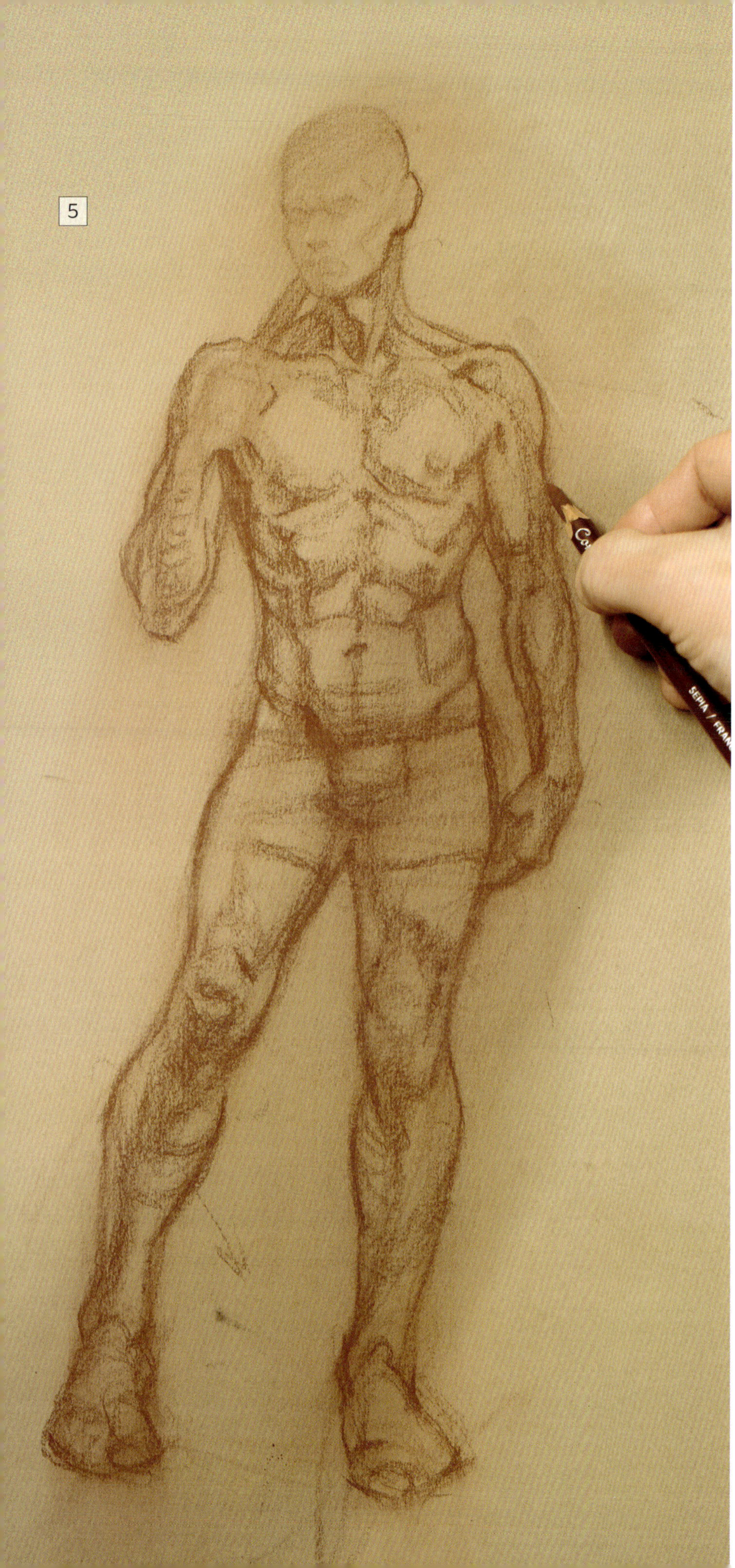

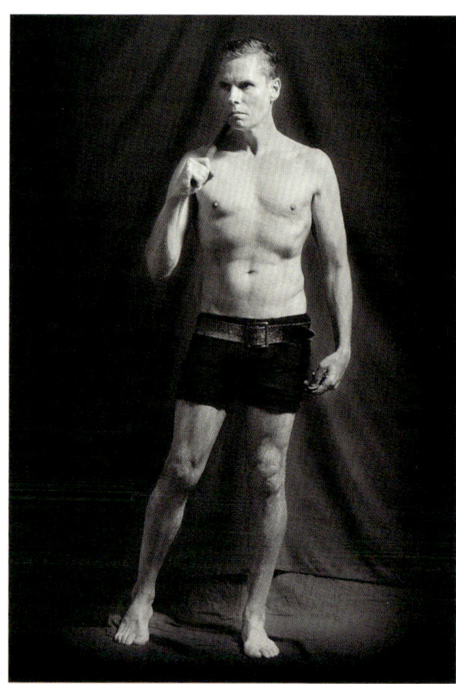

5 · Get out of Jail Free

I stand back from the art and see with a fresh eye that the head needs to be slightly bigger. I add to the skull, and this is all that's required. It's a simple tip to try that will save us from having to re-size all the features of the face. As long as we are not drawing a portrait likeness, this is a good "get out of jail free" card.

The great thing about using photos is that we can quickly reduce them in size to see the basic proportions better, rather than having to walk to the back of the life drawing class. Happy with the new head size and the basic proportions, I start detailing the anatomy.

6 · Don't Be Stumped

I blend the edges with a paper stump, improving as I go by reshaping and pushing the pigment around. I keep two sets of paper stumps and kneadable erasers – one set for sanguine and one set for charcoal, so as not to dirty my drawings. Always be thinking as you render and your drawing will reflect your inner feelings and energy in every mark.

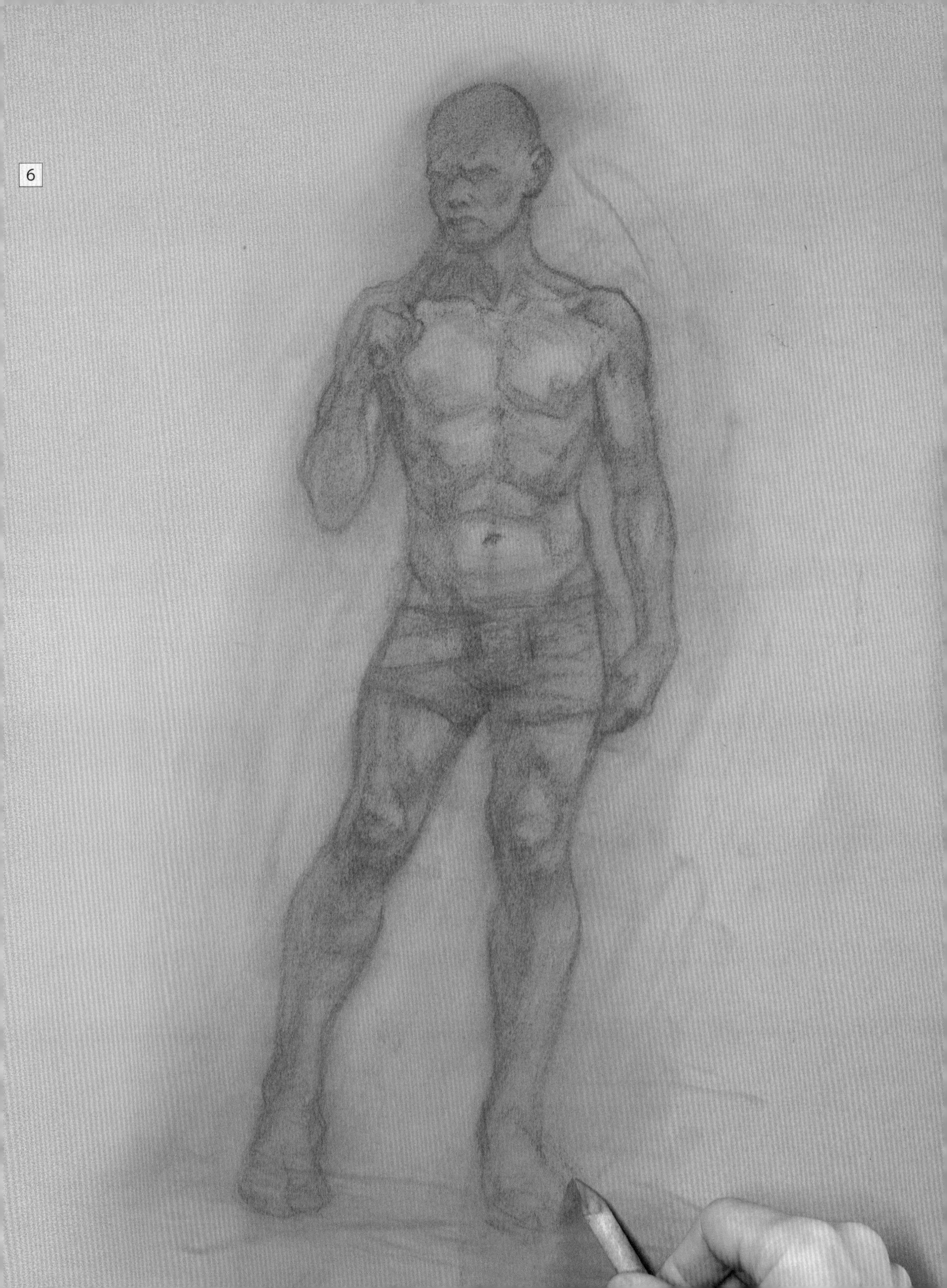

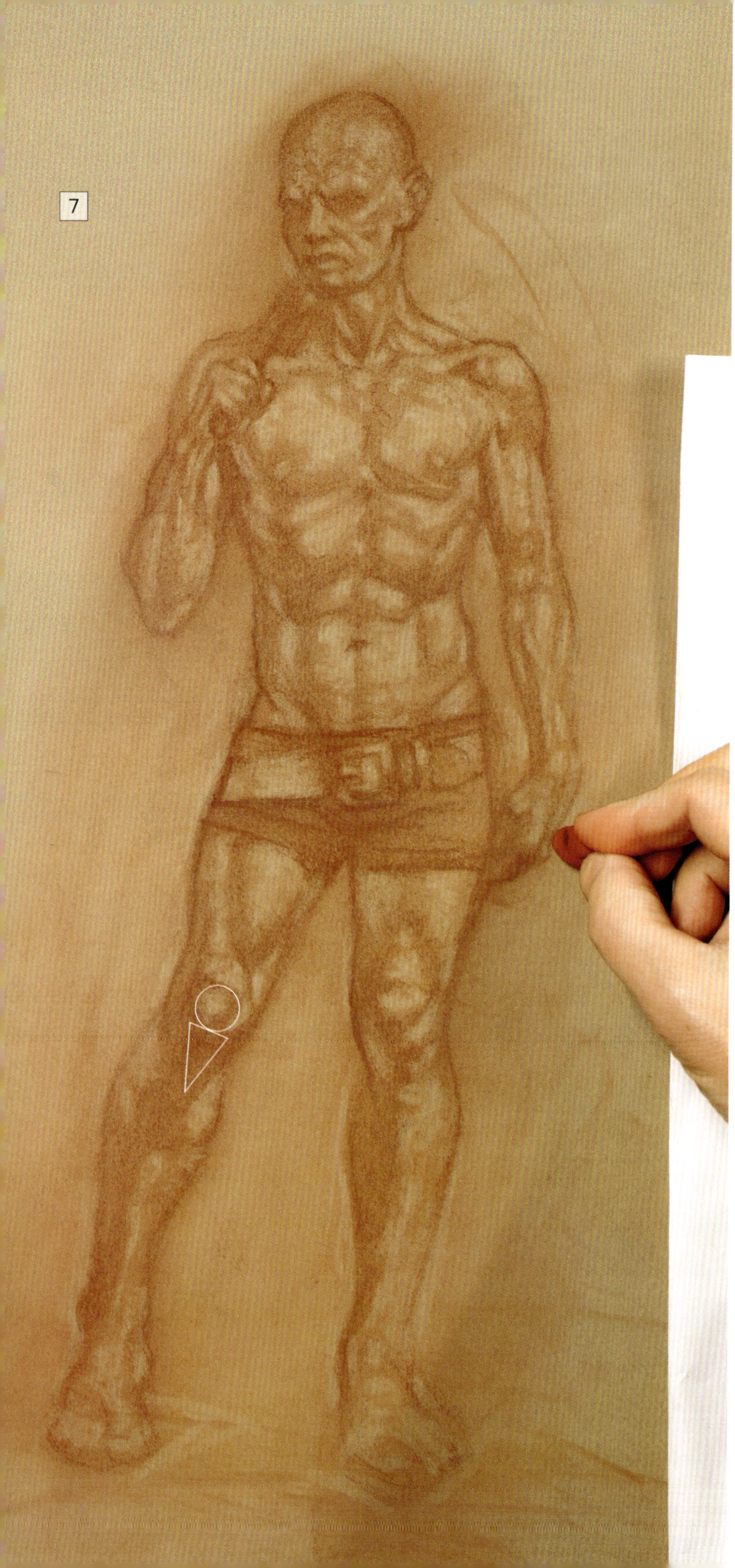

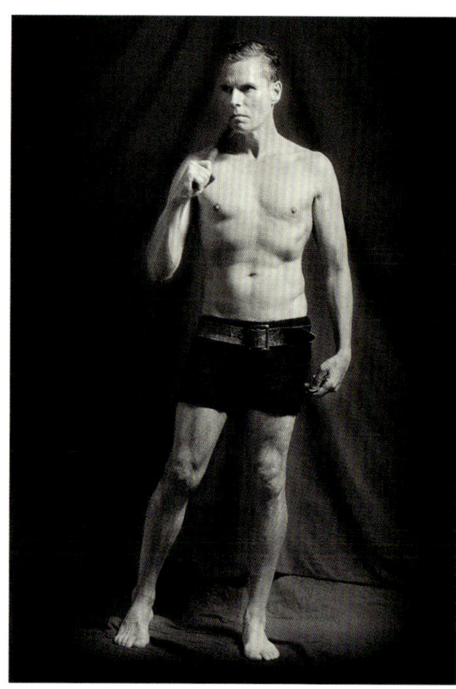

7 · A Simple Plan

I employ the same mindset for the eraser as for the blending stump, using it as a drawing tool. Kneadable erasers are pliable and can be moulded and shaped for use in pulling out highlights. Note how the knees are changing from simple shapes into something more sophisticated. Simple to complex is the best approach. A good tip for knees is to imagine an ice-cream cone – this will represent the patella and its ligament.

8 · The Same Squint

Keeping a piece of paper under my hand as I soften edges with tissue prevents oil transferring to the paper. Natural oil from our hands can be invisible at first and then appear as blots when we blend pigment later. It's no big deal on a textured background, but it could spoil the flawless skin tone you had hoped for.

To find the mass shapes of shadow and light, simply squint at the photo as you would at the model in a class.

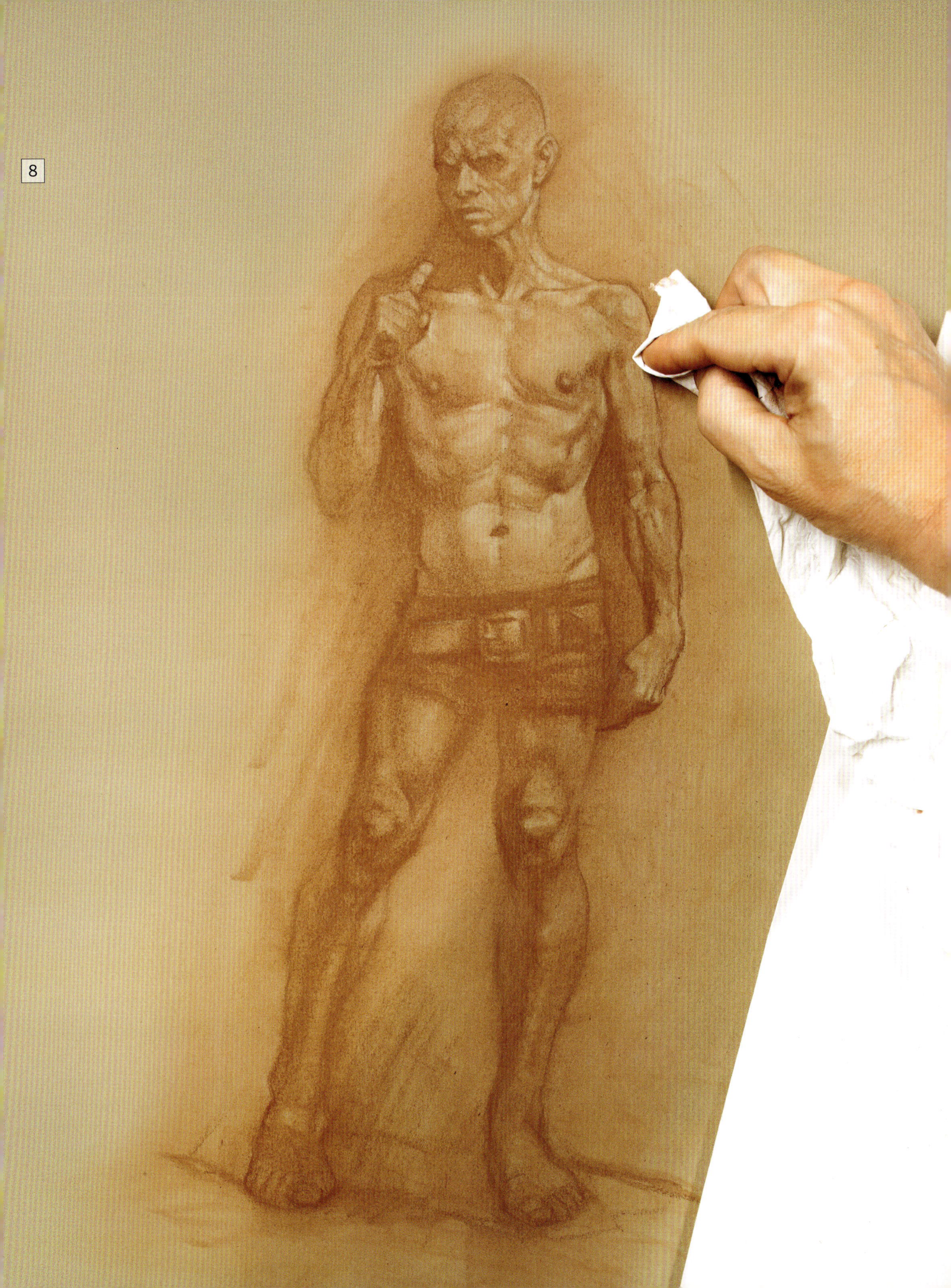

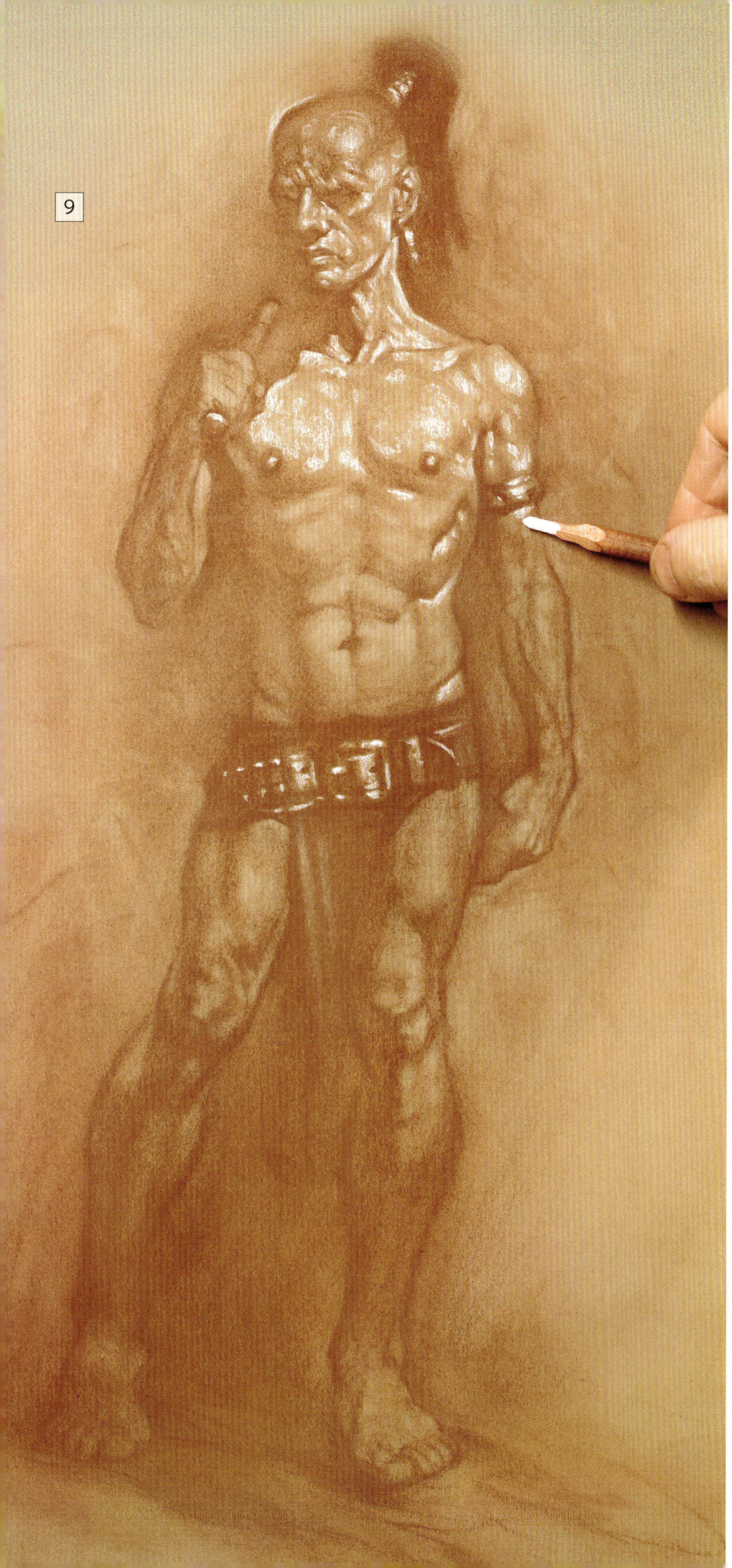

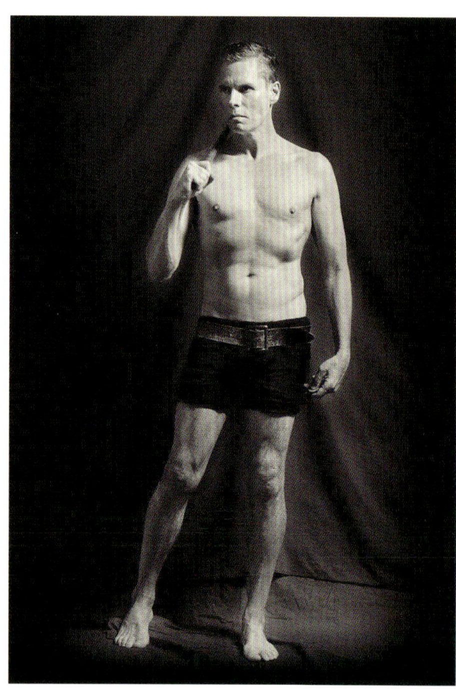

9 • The Big Crowd Pleaser

It's been a long time coming, but here it is: the white pastel pencil for the highlights. Ensure the drawing is strong structurally and gesturally, as the white effect should not be a crutch to prop up a poor drawing. It's also important not to mix the sanguine with the white. Since the mid-tone paper represents the mid-tone flesh, there is no logical reason for the highlights to reach the dark tones. This can be tricky as we sometimes have to butt the highlights up against the darkest areas where flesh compresses. Take care as white and sanguine mixed together create an unpleasant pink tone that screams "amateur!"

10 • Blend and Push

Using all my tools, I blend and push the white pigment into the surface. Note how fleshy everything has become, based on three simple values: the darks of the sanguine, the mid-tone of the paper, and the white highlights. I use the brush end of my pencil eraser to sweep away eraser crumbs.

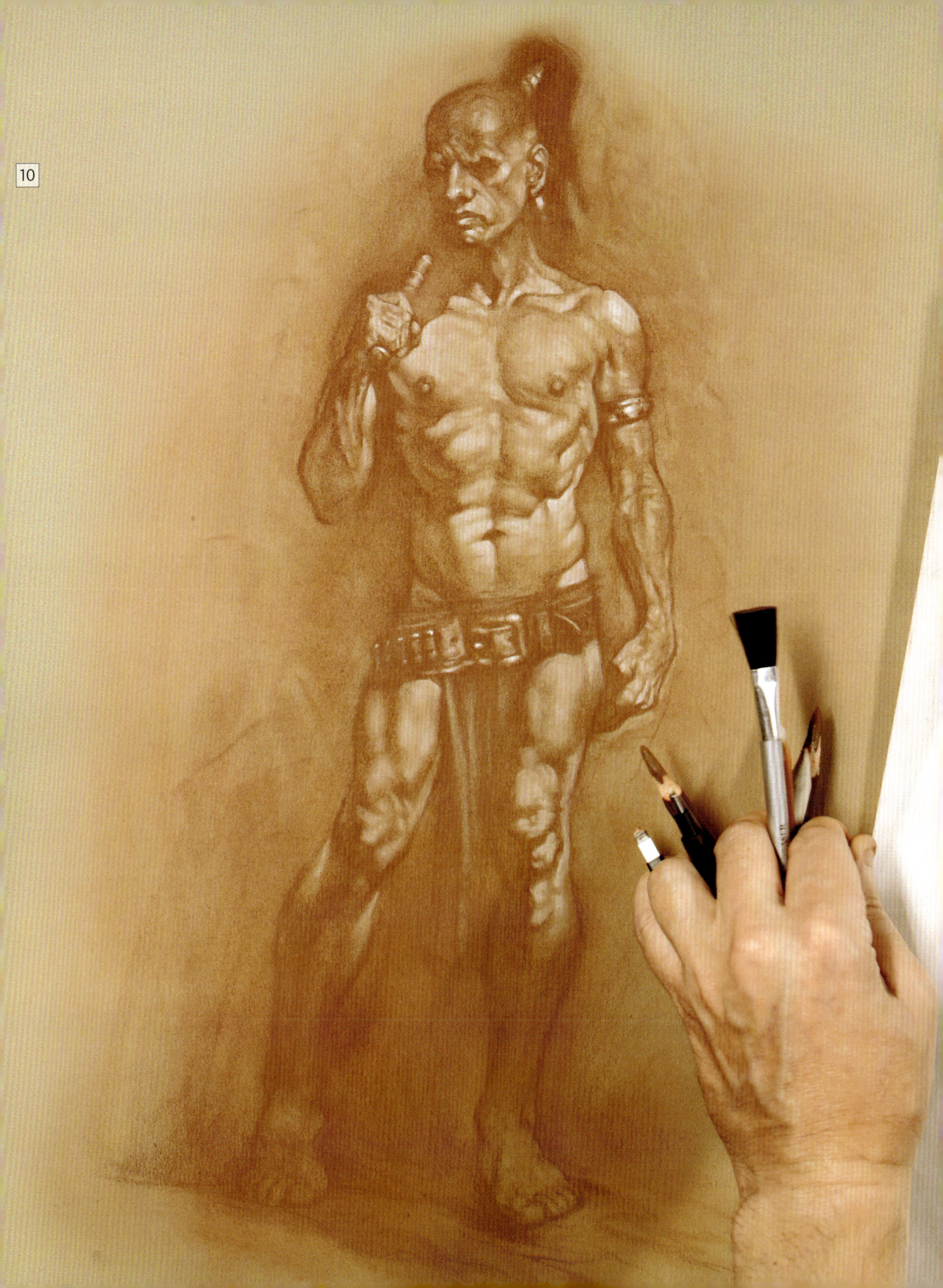

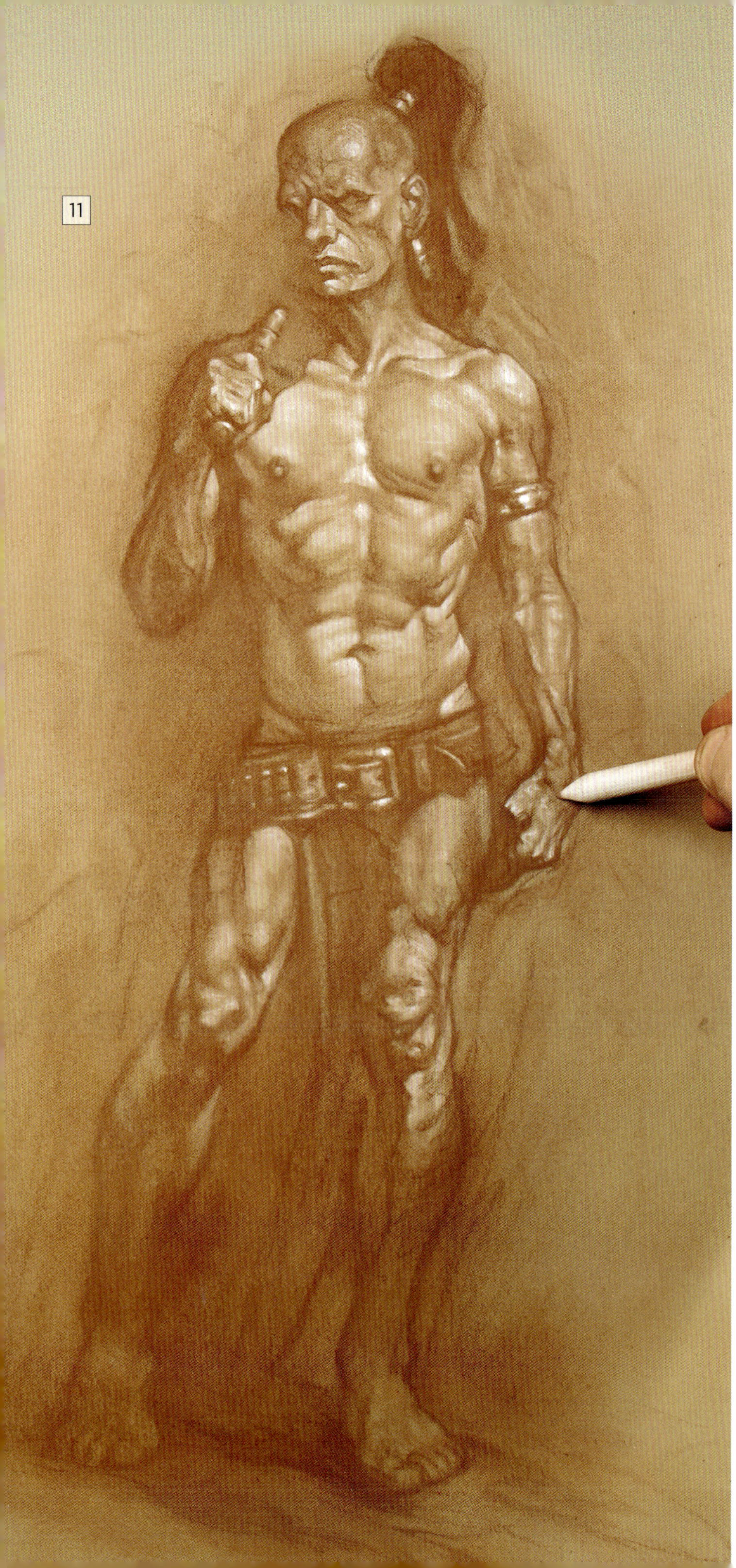

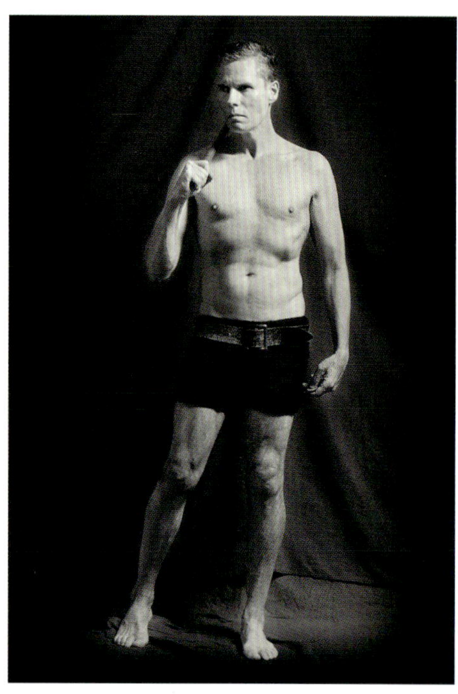

11 · The Dreaded Pink

Time to address the small stuff and explore the beauty of anatomy and form. Constant study of the knees is important as everyone's knees are different due to the variable shape of the bursa – the little fatty pads that protect the joints. Note that I'm using a clean paper stump to avoid the dreaded pink tone while blending whites.

12 · Spinning Rubber

Using a mono pencil eraser, I thin some of the line widths. I also use an electric eraser, as seen here, to add textures and erase stubborn areas. Test the electric eraser on a scrap piece of paper first, as it can run across your drawing if you are caught unawares by its spinning rubber. Pastel paper is wonderful to work with, but it's a fight to get thin lines when working on a relatively small scale, due to the grain. Ideally, this drawing would be easier to work with at twice its size, but there are always workarounds.

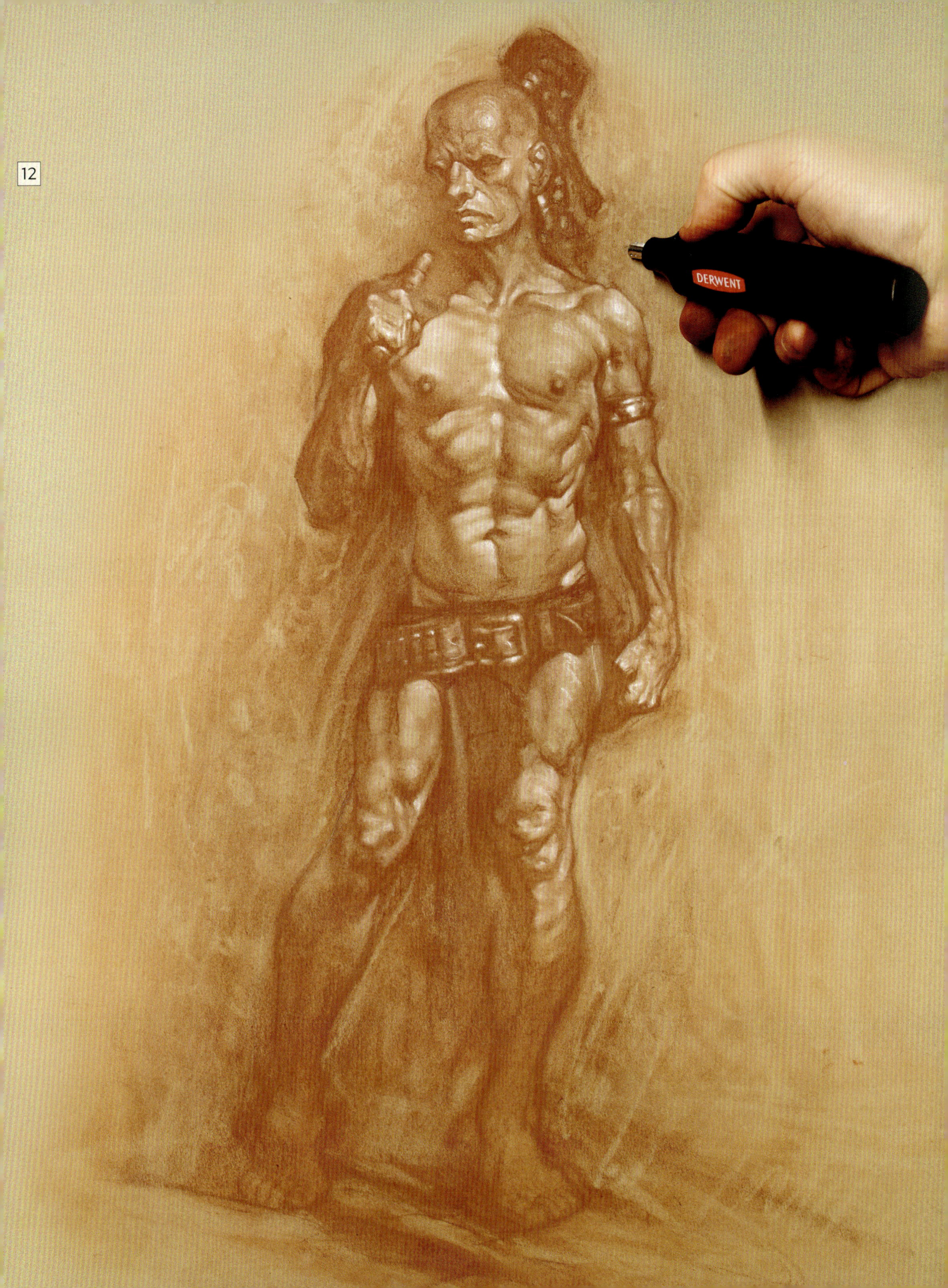

13 · The Back Story

I title the piece *The Tracker* after the indigenous warriors who in times past were employed by occupying forces to track down their own people; this happened the world over as colonial might took control. Having a back story, theme, emotion, or symbolism within our drawings adds depth. Betrayal is a strong theme in my art, due to the desperation and heartache it evokes; it connects strongly with every viewer as we have all felt betrayed at some point in our lives.

Making marks with erasers, tissue, and paper stumps for background texture draws the eye to the contrasting tones of the smooth skin. Sanguine on toned paper is slow but worth the effort. I probably spent three hours or more pushing and blending into the grainy surface. I tone down the whites with tissue and paper stumps, to take away the metallic look that can sneak up on the overzealous artist who has been seduced by the eye-popping effect of dimension. The less white we use, the more timeless the image will be. My advice is to take out as much as possible and keep it concentrated in the areas we want the viewer to see, which is the focus we consider most important. Note how there is less and less white the further we travel down the body. This keeps the focus on the torso and head. With hindsight, I would take away all the highlights on the face here, which would make the metal headdress read more like jewellery and add mystery to the shrouded face.

One of the reasons why some artists are just that bit better than most lies in the care they give to the final moments of their work. I almost always leave a drawing overnight before sending it off to a collector or a publisher, as we tend not to see the flaws during the battle. Some drawings viewed the next day can be littered with errors that just weren't visible the day before. This is known as seeing with a "fresh eye". Turning the drawing upside down or looking at it in a mirror helps us find even more adjustments we could make. Allowing some time away from the art and then spending a few minutes, or even hours, improving line, tone, and details can turn an OK work into an exceptional piece of art that will stand the test of time. So, take some extra time and thought over your drawings and you will be rewarded.

13

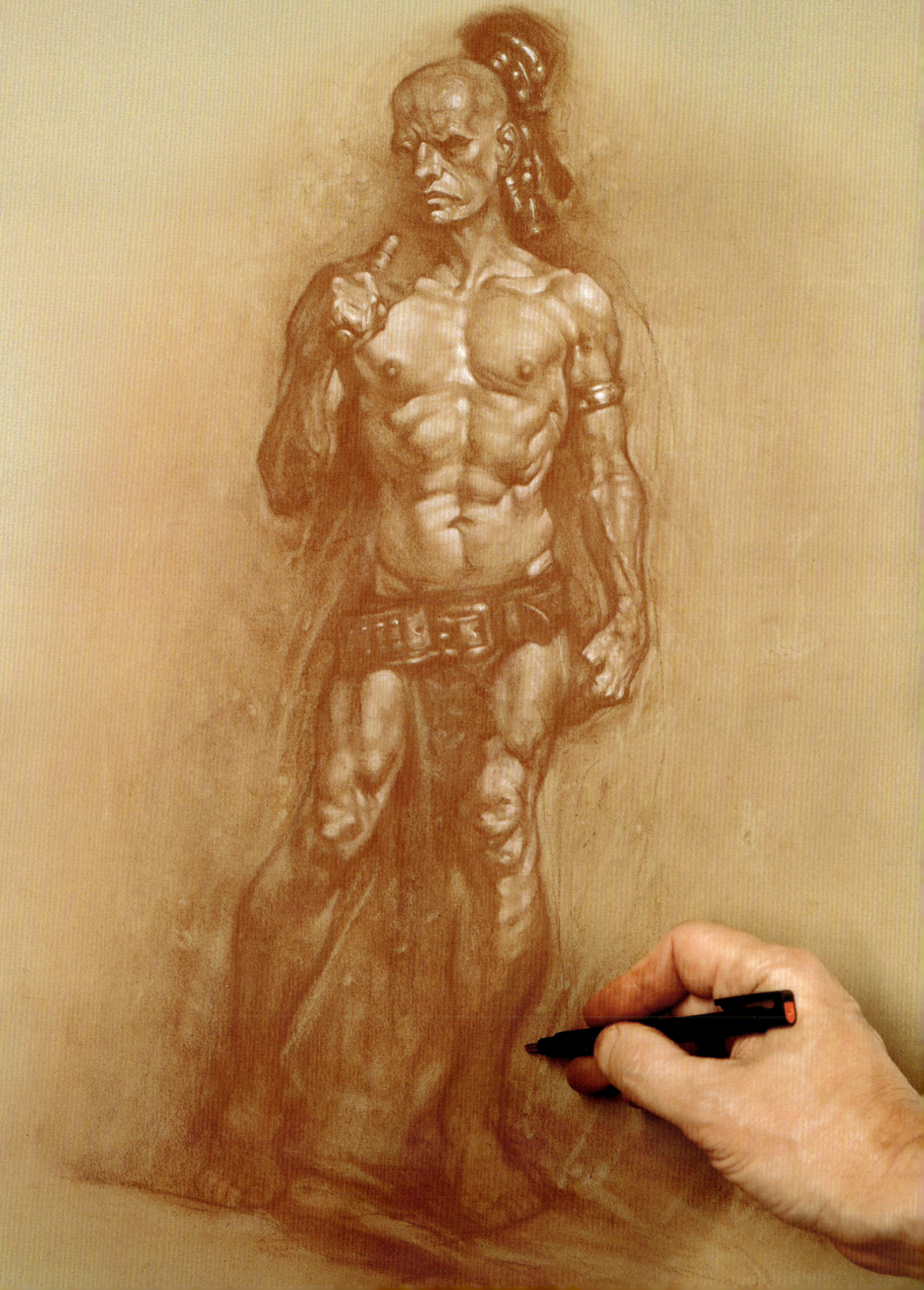

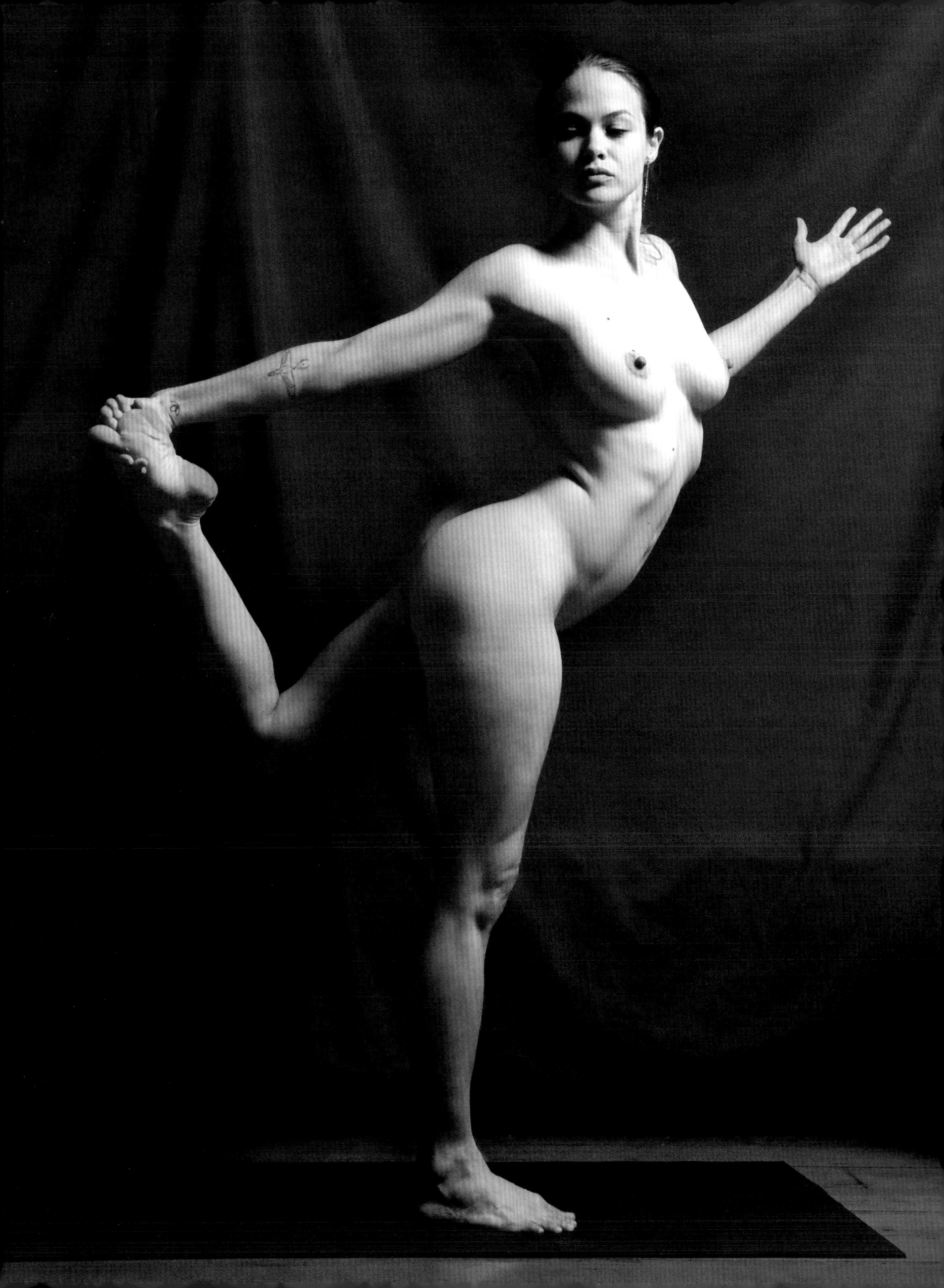

WORKSHOP FOUR

STILLNESS IN MOTION

DRAWINGS ARE USUALLY a series of lines on a flat surface that have no movement. So, with this premise, how can we possibly suggest motion in our drawings? We can add tonal values and overlapping forms to trick the eye into seeing the illusion of depth, but the illusion of movement is usually the domain of animators, who produce multiple drawings that flicker past in fast succession, convincing us that we are no longer looking at a series of static images but moving images.

Animators may have the ultimate answer to making drawings come alive in the mind's eye, but artists also have the tools to suggest movement in a static drawing. We may be working with a single, still image, but by using the power of gestural lines and rhythmic strokes, we can create the impression of life and movement.

Another method to suggest movement, and even chaos, is to throw the figure off balance. With contrapposto, we explore the beauty of balance using one side of the body as the support and leaving the other side relaxed, harnessing this asymmetry to create life and energy. We can push the idea of energy produced by asymmetry by forcing the figure off balance or having it fall or fly. Another tool in the quest for movement in drawing is the gestural rhythms found in foreshortened figures.

In this workshop, I will delve deep into these methods to project movement onto the static two-dimensional surface we have chosen as our artistic domain.

Left: Model Alana Brekelmans

THE WAKE OF THE BLACK WITCH

Charcoal and pencil on A2 newsprint

Today we will draw Alana with a focus on the torso and breasts, particularly on how the breasts change shape due to compression and gravity. At first glance, these simple forms look easy to draw, and for that reason, they are often drawn poorly. A common mistake is treating breasts as solid globes instead of shape-shifting mounds that move, fall, bob, and flatten out. Another common error is drawing breats as if both are facing frontwards like a pair of eyes, when in fact, each breast sits on the curve of the ribcage.

I've chosen this pose to demonstrate the changing shape of the breasts due to their shifting weight against a solid ribcage and the pull of gravity, which is evident even on a young woman in peak physical condition. Apart from drawing the illusion of soft flesh against a hard surface, we will also deal with relationships of form.

Although the ribcage expands when we breathe, the hips and ribcage are, to all intents and purposes, solid, with all the twisting done by the abdominals and the obliques (the waist side muscles). These hard shapes against soft shapes cause pinched flesh, most noticeably at the waist. I believe that learning proportions is essential for the figurative artist, but I do not see it as an inflexible rule, especially when drawing from photos. Note how long the arms appear by way of the camera's eye – the first obvious measurement to attend to. I always measure the forms by eye, analysing their shapes against each other, their boxed or tubular nature, and draw the biggest shapes first. With a twisting form, we will have a longer side being stretched and a shorter side being compressed. This is due to the incredible flexibility of the abdominals and the obliques. Measuring on the pinched side of the figure is easier where shapes are closer together and spaces are shorter. For instance, notice the difference in the stretch and pinch distances, from the top of the breasts to the top of the lateral portions of the hip crests, in the photo, as indicated by the lengths of the arrows.

If we keep all these ideas in mind as we draw, we will create a fluid figure that still feels as if it is made of flesh and bone. But more importantly, we will draw a figure that gives the impression of a living, breathing being – one that looks as if it's ready to move gracefully into another position. When I approach this moment of grace and fluidity in a drawing, I think of it as a state of "stillness in motion".

1
Stretch side 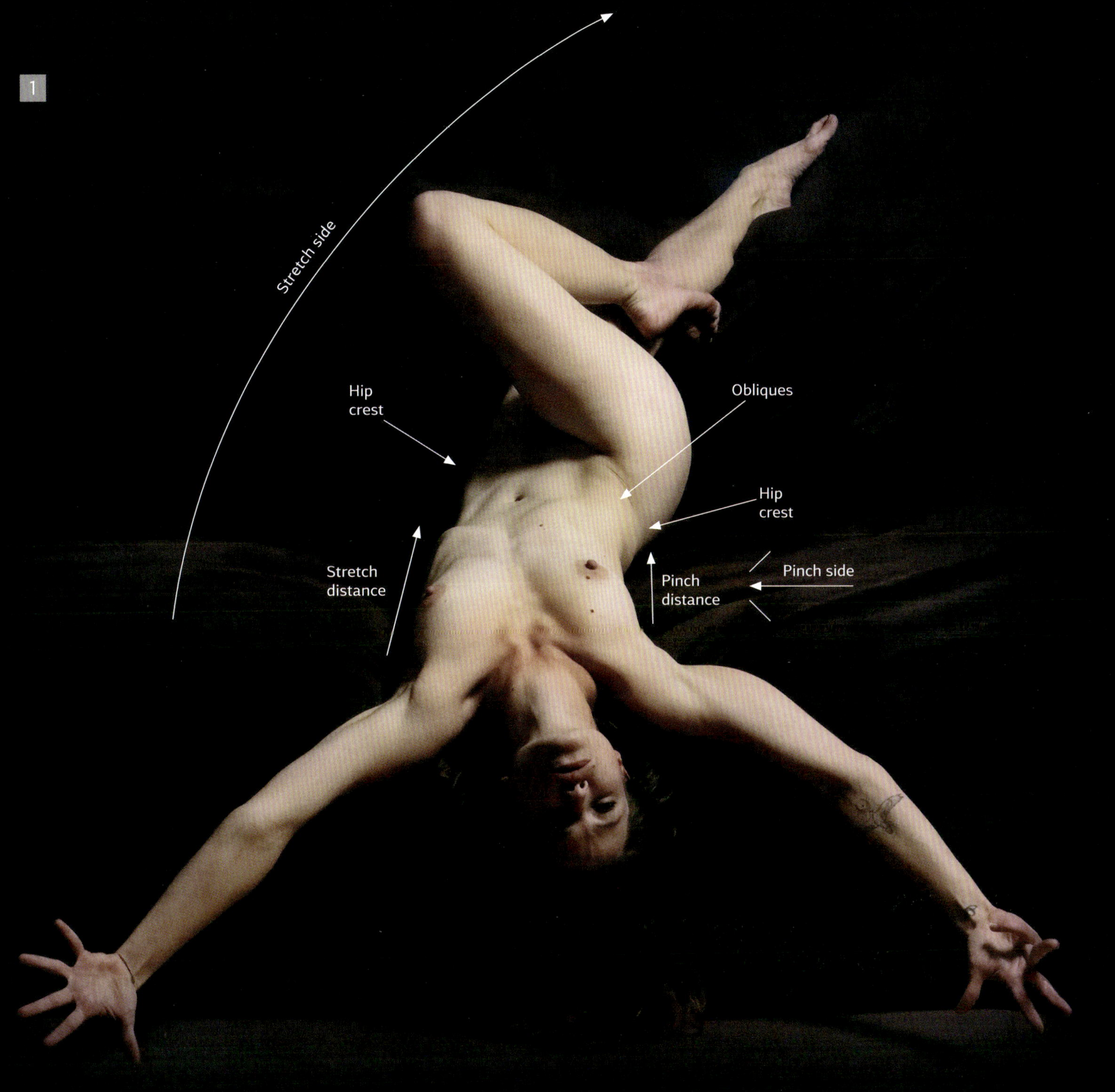
Hip
crest
Obliques
Hip
crest
Stretch
distance
Pinch side
Pinch
distance

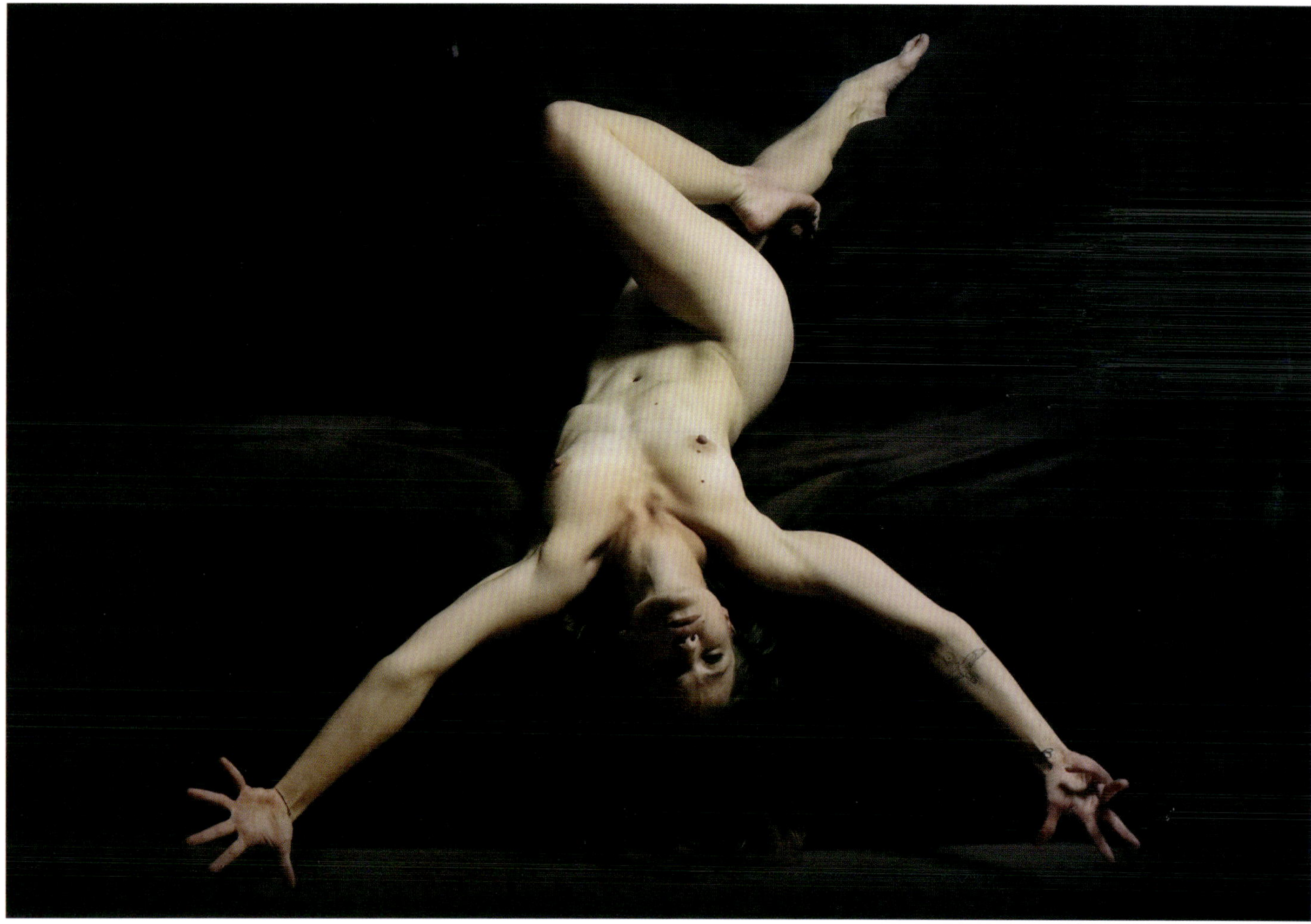

2 · A Symbol of Creation

When it comes to drawing the figure, I think about how the basic structures work together – making structural drawings such as this one helps me understand how everything locks together. Learning to see structure as a form of simplified anatomy is key to drawing with confidence.

Before the photoshoot, I sit down with Alana and discuss our plans for it. Having already communicated via email, we have a good idea of where to go artistically. I had sent Alana lots of ideas regarding mood, such as photos from surrealists and experimental artists and dancers, and she added her own collection of interesting ideas and emotional themes.

Although we are seeking inspiration, we are keen to extrapolate from themes that have gone before, rather than repeating ideas verbatim. Seeking out the past is an excellent way to ensure we don't do something that has been done previously. It's amazing how often we come up with what we think is an "original" concept, only to discover that it has already been explored and exhausted to artistic death. I decide on "creation" as the motivating theme for this drawing. To make sure we create a fresh adaptation on the idea, I call out the words cruelty, spite, anger, joy, and elation while Alana moves from one pose to another. As fun and "Austin Powers-like" as this may sound, it works. With this sorcery pose, Alana becomes a raging symbol of creation.

I draw lightly using a small piece of willow charcoal. As usual, I treat the photo with deep suspicion. I adjust the long arms, and find that the head feels a little small. I want the body to be flying rather than lying over a support. Therefore I lengthen the foreshortened midsection.

2

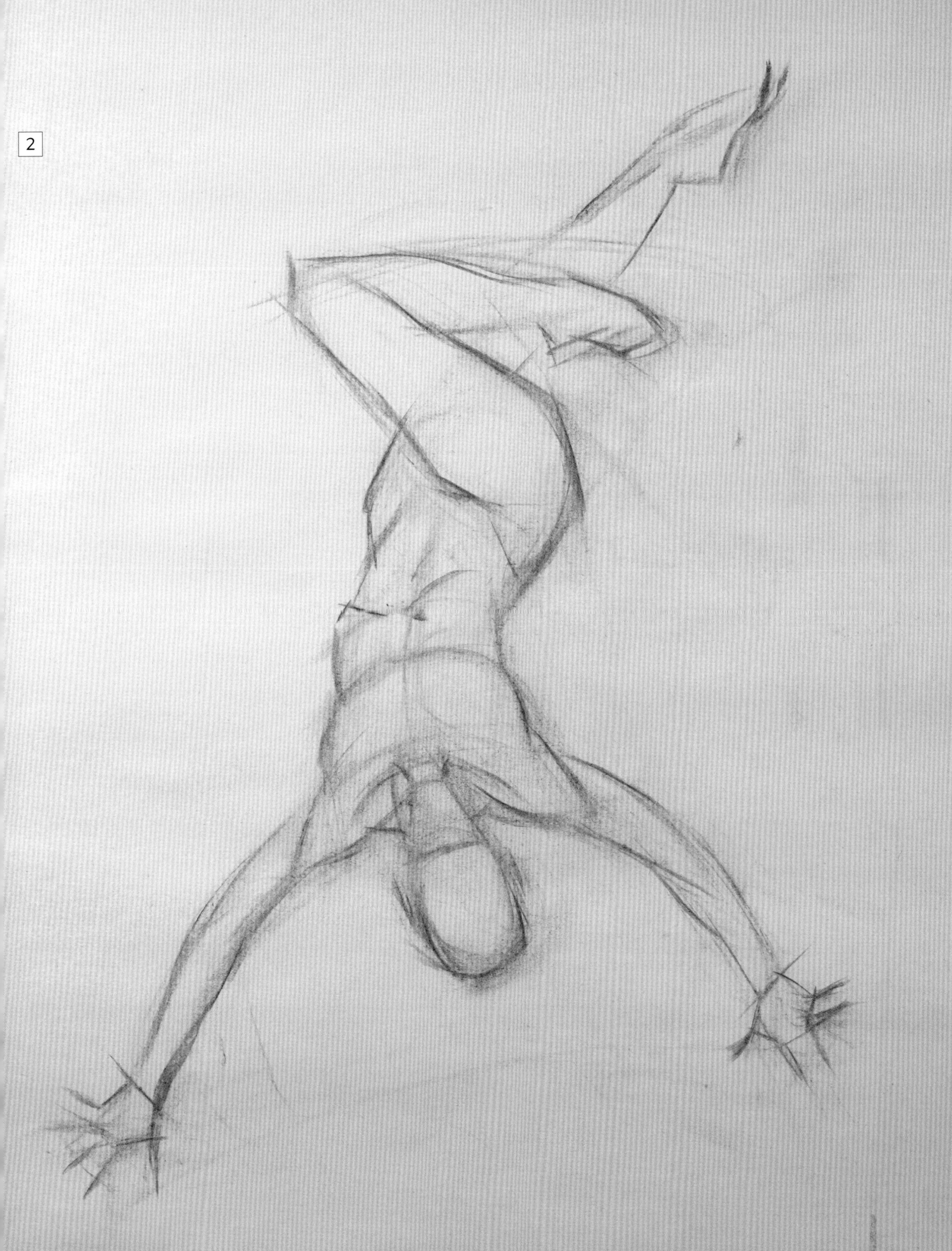

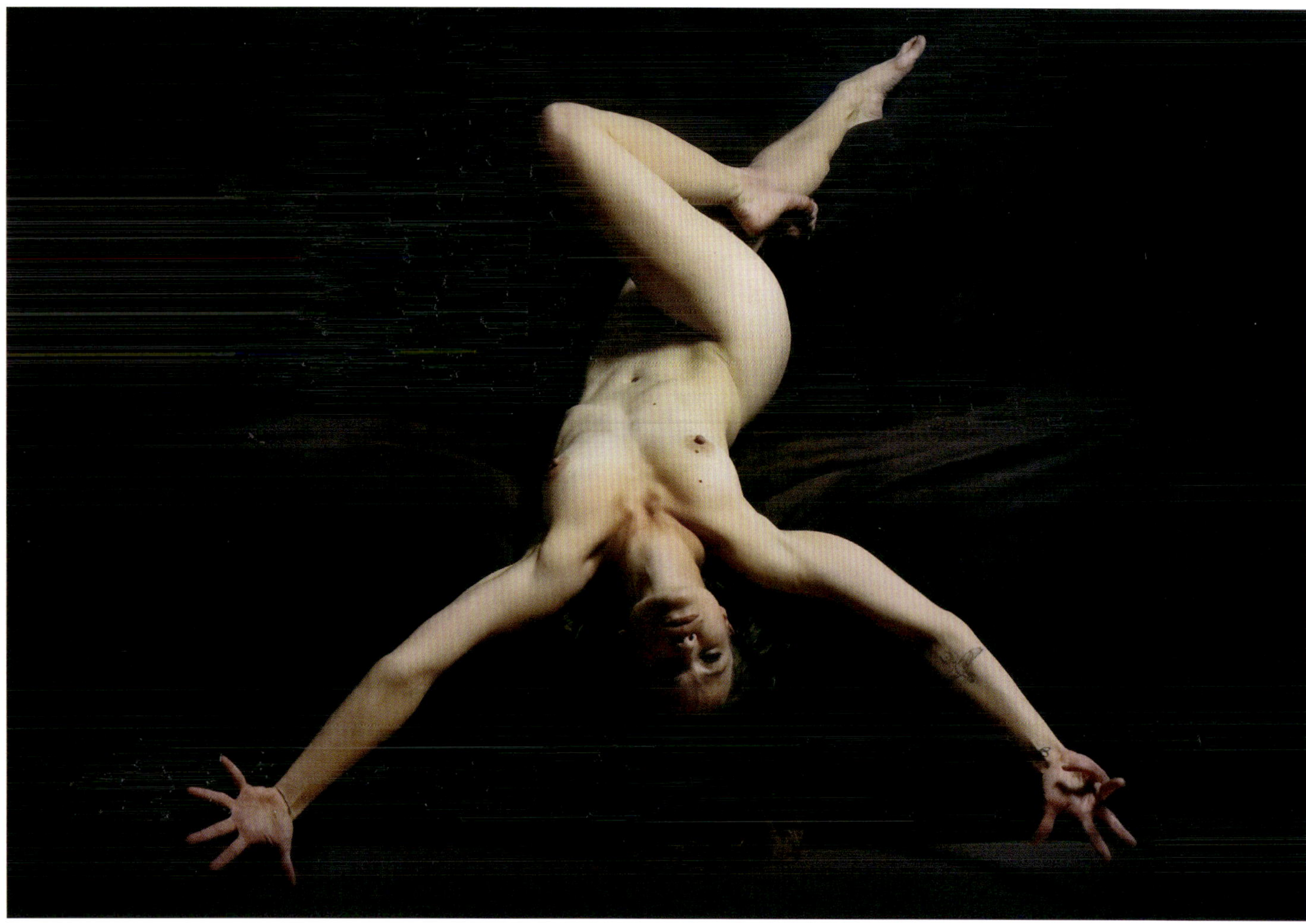

3 · Uncommon Fluidity

With our motivational theme of creation in place, I think about what kind of creature Alana is as I begin to draw. She can fly without wings and therefore must be a supernatural being rather than a winged fantasy figure from another world. I decide that she is a witch conjuring spells and name the drawing *The Wake of the Black Witch*. With a title and motivation, the drawing gains a driving force.

From here on in, I can build further on the theme and the title. A ship creates a wake in the sea as it churns through the waves, and I imagine what kind of wake a witch would make in space and time as she conjures her black magic, and how that would manifest itself as energy. A task to ponder on as I draw the form and feed off the energy of the pose for further inspiration in terms of gesture and life. Having an artistic collaborator rather than a posed model is what brings life to my drawings – a life they would not have if my model were merely a mannequin to be posed joint by joint. For this reason,

I no longer stick religiously to production sketches; instead, I make my sketches more abstract to allow further freedom of interpretation. With Alana free to express the overall theme without worrying about every limb meeting contact points, we have a fluidity uncommon in life drawing poses.

From this point onwards, it's up to me to add additional life, which I will do with the overlapping forms created by foreshortening. As a figure comes towards us, forms overlap, such as the breasts in front of the hill of the ribcage and the hill of the ribcage in front of the abdominals. Foreshortening, by its overlapping nature, creates a rhythm that is not found so easily in a standing figure.

Here, as I would for my live life drawing classes, I'm marking out angles – such as the high and low relationships of the forearms and the oblong width of the head. I've also bent Alana's right arm to add more curve to the straightness, implying a conjuring gesture as she flies through space.

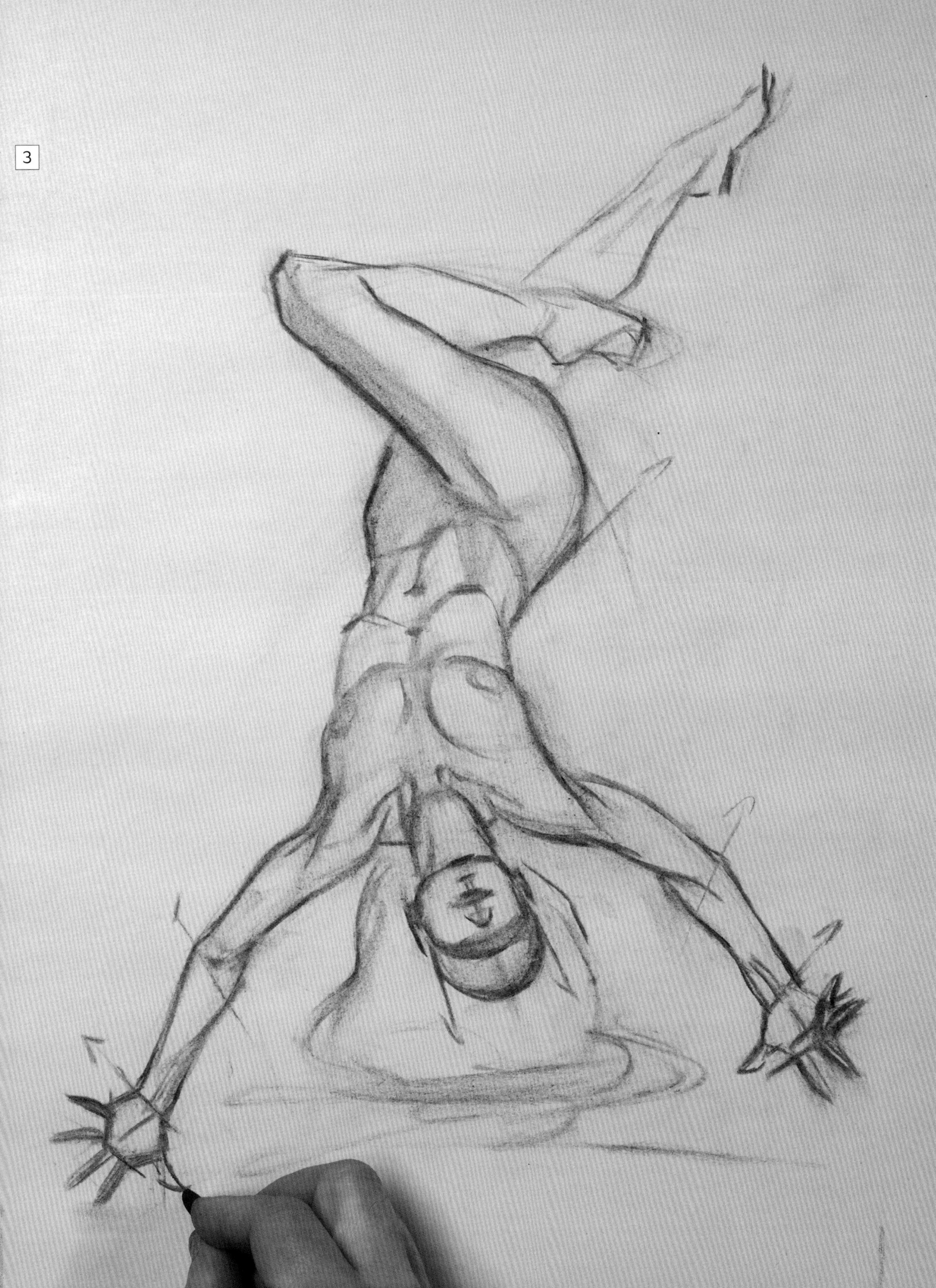

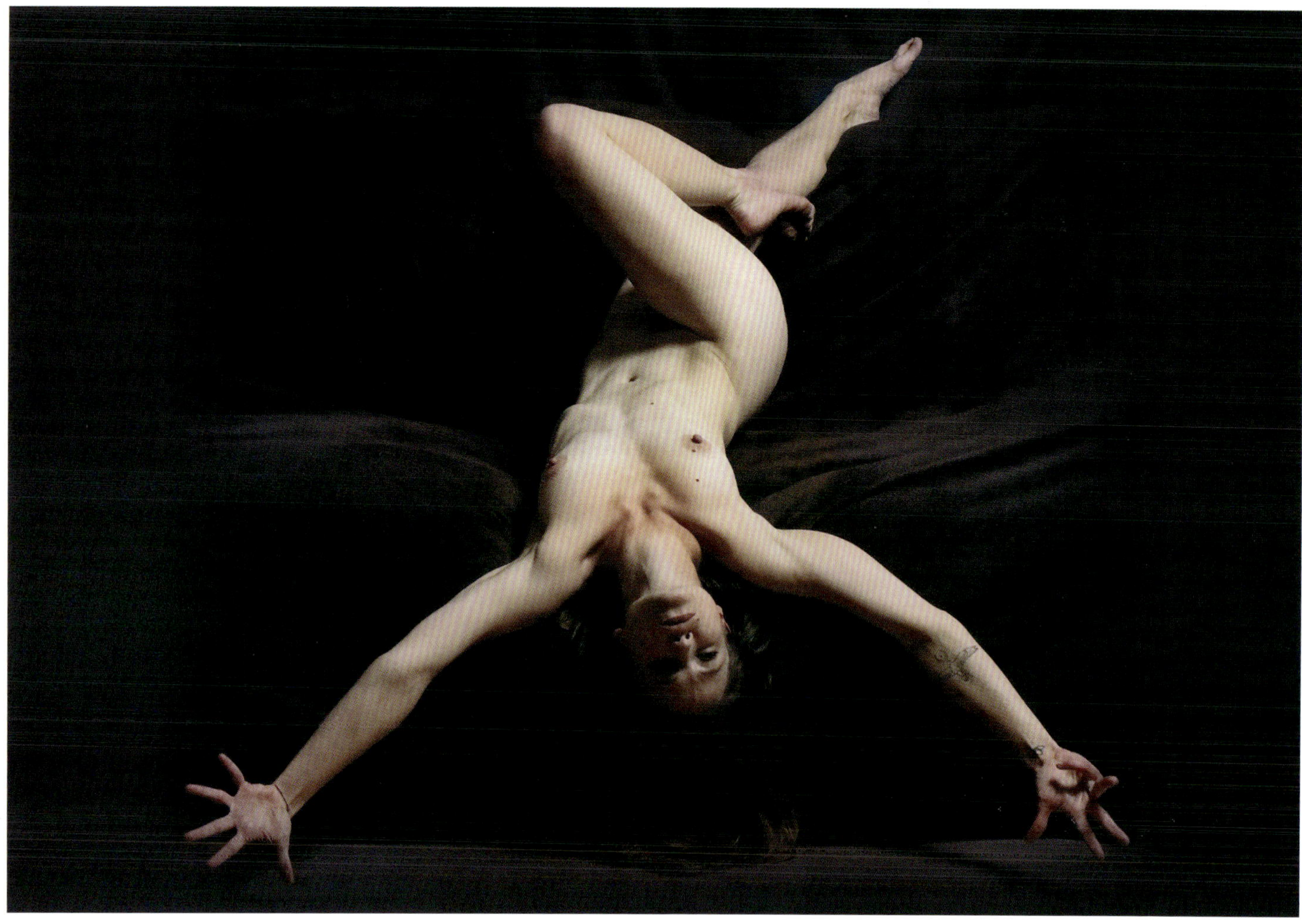

4 · The Subconsious Art Engine

With my fingers, I smudge tones around using the charcoal already laid down on the newsprint, then refine a little with a paper stump. Here we see the transition between the underdrawing and the next stage of refinement. It's important in the early stages to keep the drawing light as this allows for changes. I'm chasing the echoes of similar forms as I go, blending nature's rhythmic shapes down the body.

With the structural proportions pretty much nailed down, I move forwards with line quality and gesture in mind, which is the life of the thing. From here on, we are on a quest to avoid Structure Hell (an over-reliance on structure) and attain the nirvana of Gesture Heaven, as this flying figure needs to convey gestural elegance. I step back from the drawing and take time to evaluate it before committing to darker lines. I feel the overall drawing has solidity, and more importantly, a sense of movement. I lay in darker lines, placing a sheet of paper

under my hand to keep the surface clean. Using the broad side of the pencil dropped low gives me a thicker line. Rolling my cupped gestural hand up onto its fingers and down onto its knuckles allows me ultimate freedom of expression in line and tone. Another discipline is mastering the pressure required to blend light and dark tone. I recommend lots of mark-making on a blank piece of newsprint before starting a drawing. With practice, we build a subconscious "art engine" to fuel our work.

Once again, I'm aware of the hyper-crisp edges that photography creates compared to the less contrasting edges we see with our eyes. Take a photo of a glass of water on a table and then compare the photo to the same glass of water on a table seen with your own eyes; you will see harder edges in the photo, often with a crisp light edge after a dark edge. These are optical artefacts within the camera's lens. With that in mind, I thin the line along the hip to soften the edge.

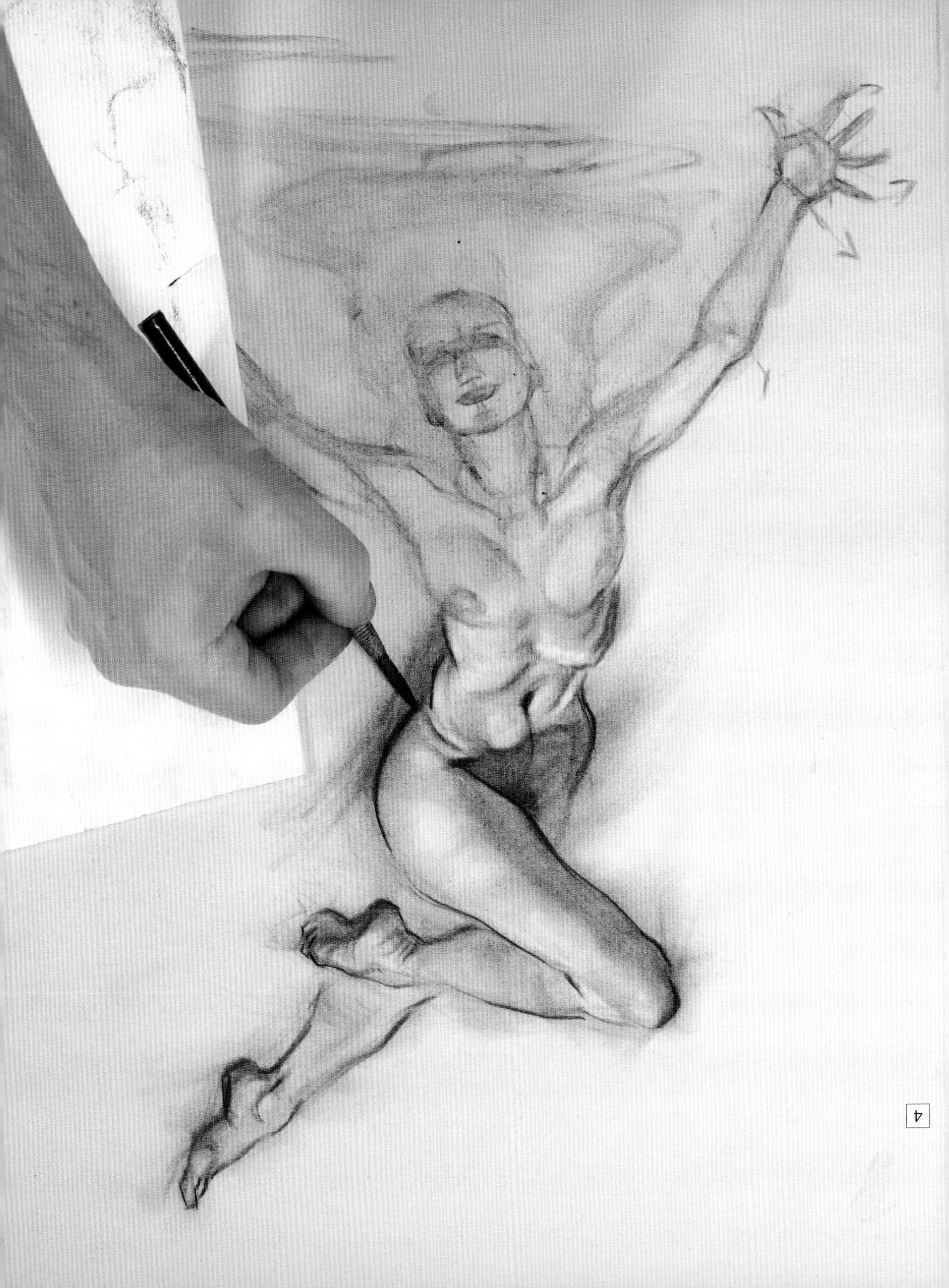

4

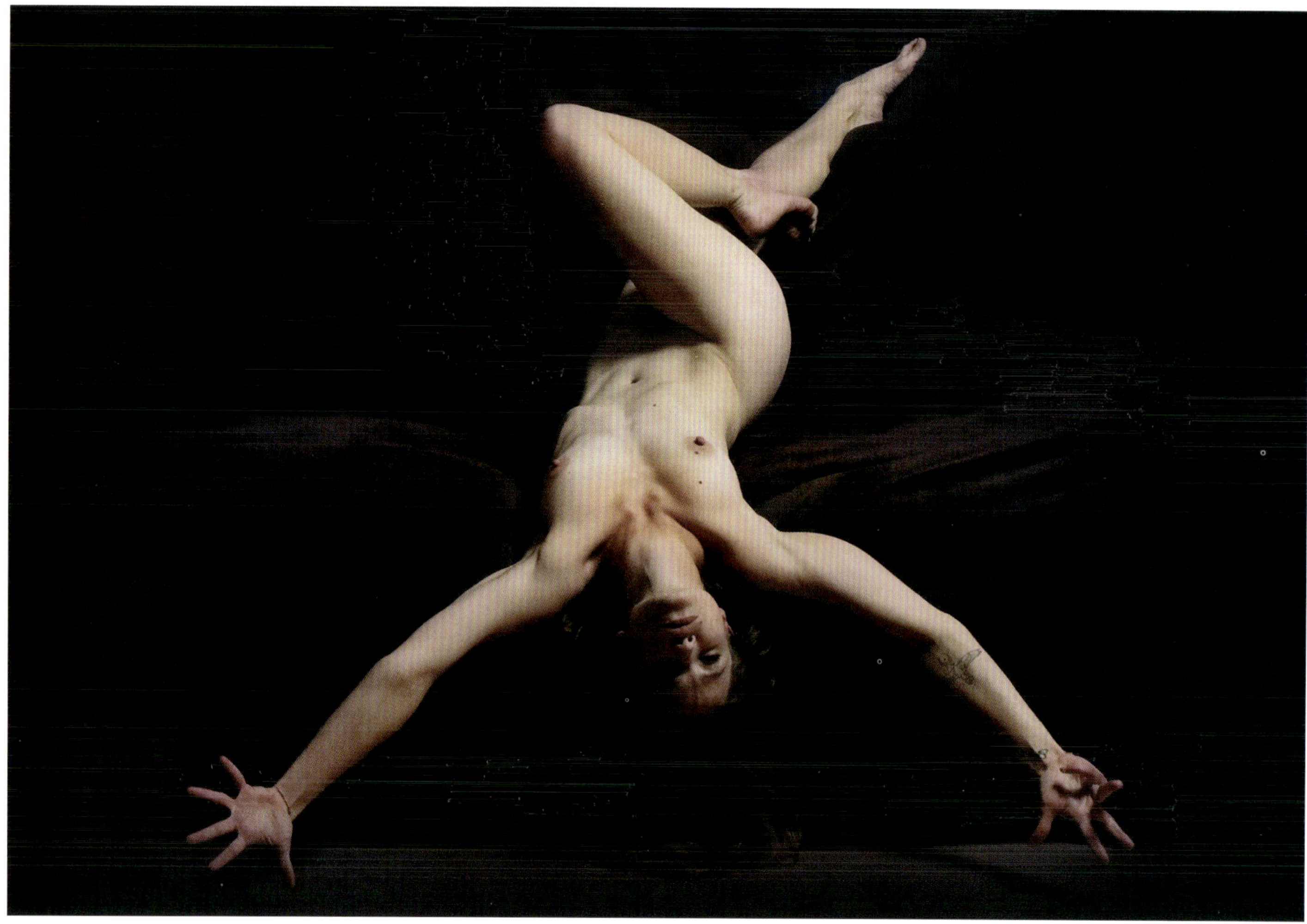

5 · The Gravity of the Situation

I continue to add line and tone down the body, moving from side to side as I go, aware of what one arm is doing as I draw the other. I don't myopically zoom into one area of the body, which is one of the biggest traps when working with photographs. I always resist zooming in until I'm drawing the final details, at which point photo reference becomes our friend as we can't zoom in on a live model.

It's important not to draw in "parts" as this will lead us into Structure Hell. I'm constantly aware of the figure as a living thing, with every imbalance counteracted in the natural flow of motion across anatomy. If one side is pinched at the waist, the other side will be more stretched. Our awareness of the figure in its entirety, from toes to fingertips, will make us the boss of our art. By being aware we take charge of the situation rather than flying by the seat of our pants and hoping for the best.

Add gravity to the situation and the breasts change shape. See how each breast is slightly different – because they always are. Note also how the nipples change shape as the breasts stretch or flatten out. We are not only studying anatomy as we draw, but also the skin suit we wear, which stretches and folds like seamless silk. As the nipples are on top of our skin suit they change shape when stretched. Take the time to study these ever-changing forms.

A big tip is to draw the breasts *after* the shape of the ribcage has been put in place rather than draw them first, because the ribcage will define the shapes based on factors such as gravity pressing them against the hard bone surface. In this upside-down view the breasts are more square shaped as they compress over the upper ribs, which have a flatter surface than the lower ribs, where the breasts would typically fall.

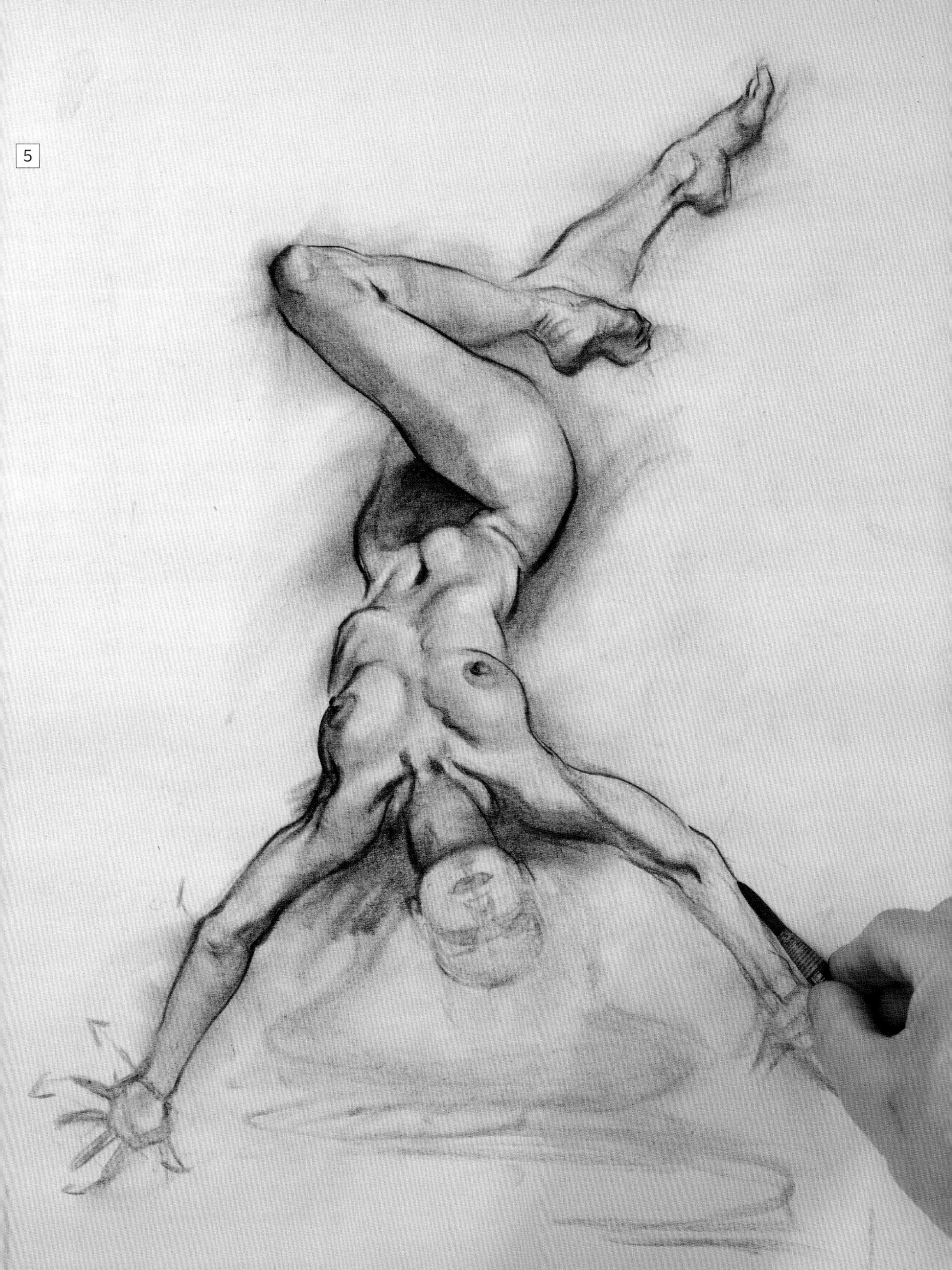

5

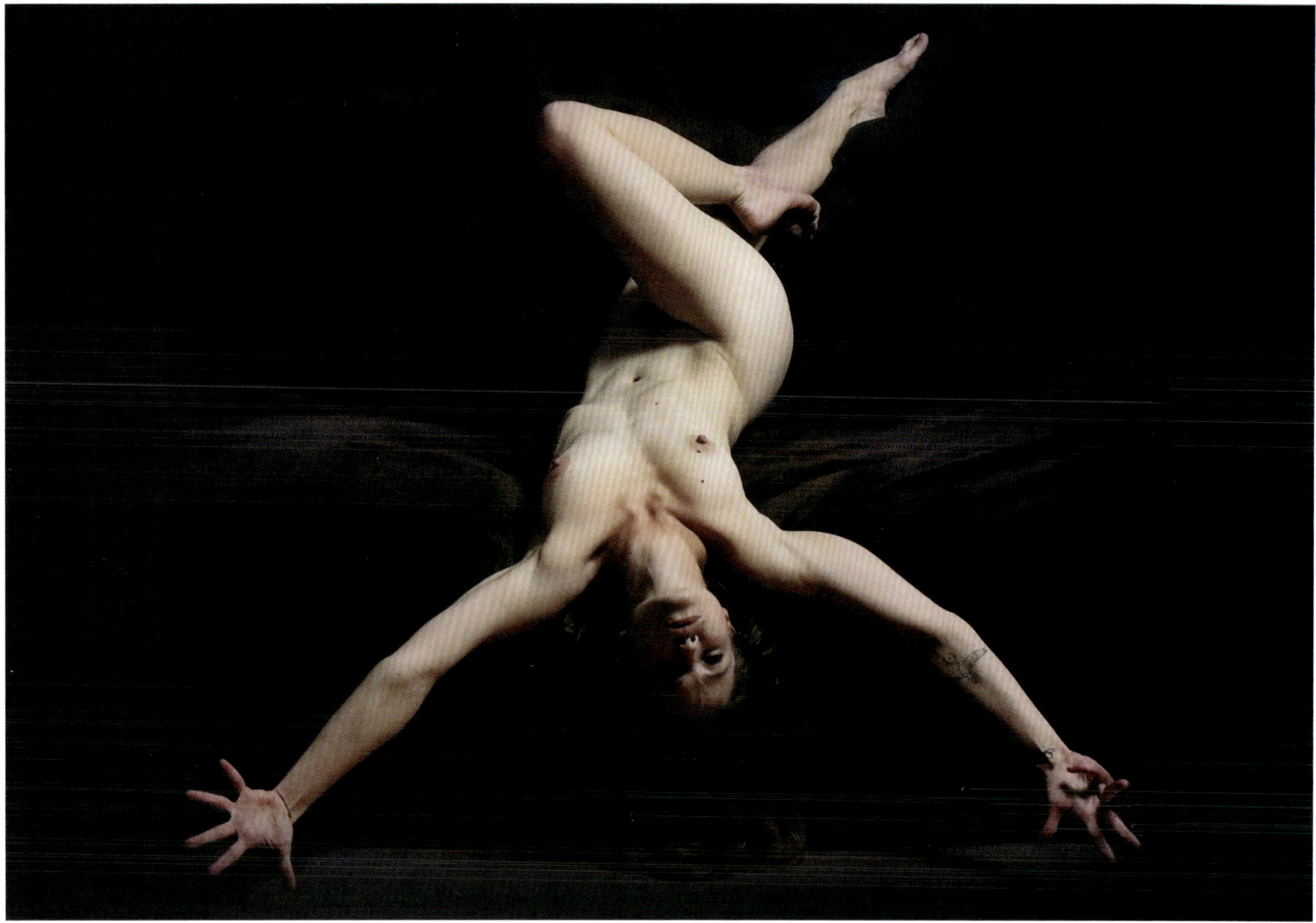

6 · Us Mere Mortals

When drawing hands there are points to keep in mind – for instance, the forefinger and middle finger take up more than half the hand's width, and the little finger splays outwards at an angle because it shares a carpal at the wrist with the ring finger. Drawing the outer edges of the little finger and thumb first makes it easier to plot and place the other fingers.

A rookie error is to draw the fingers one at a time as we go, which usually results in a giant, misshapen hand. That said, I've watched incredible artists, among them Kim Jung Gi and Eliza Ivanova, draw great hands one digit at a time. Try it and see: maybe you are a rare case of genius. For us mere mortals, drawing the basic shape of the hand first is the best way to go.

I make the bent lower leg and foot longer, to adjust for the camera distortion and also to accommodate my choice to elongate the torso. A glance back and forth between the drawing and the photo will reveal how short the leg is in the latter. There is enough charcoal on the newsprint paper for me to blend with a paper stump, and I improve the forms as I push the charcoal around. I also dim the torso area by lifting off some tone with tissue. This suggests a central light source which draws our eye down the drawing towards the face. Our natural senses draw our eye towards light and contrast, and this gives artists a powerful tool to use in composition.

Composing with light is as important in my art as is the composition of shapes. Shapes can be beautiful and elegant, but light and tone are atmospheric and emotional triggers. A misty day has its own unique sense, as does a hazy summer day, yet they have different elemental light shifts. Let's embrace all of the elements of nature at our disposal.

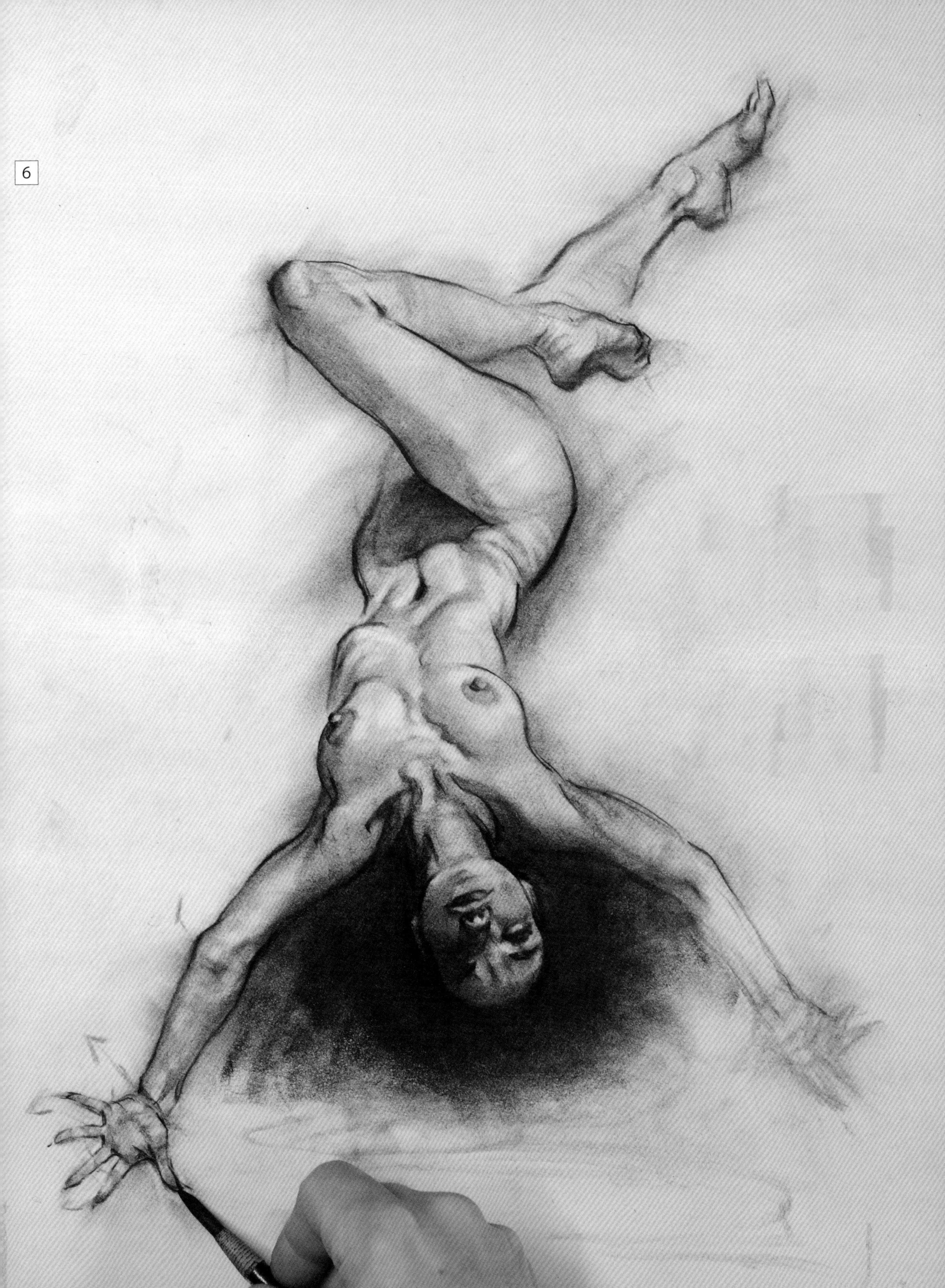

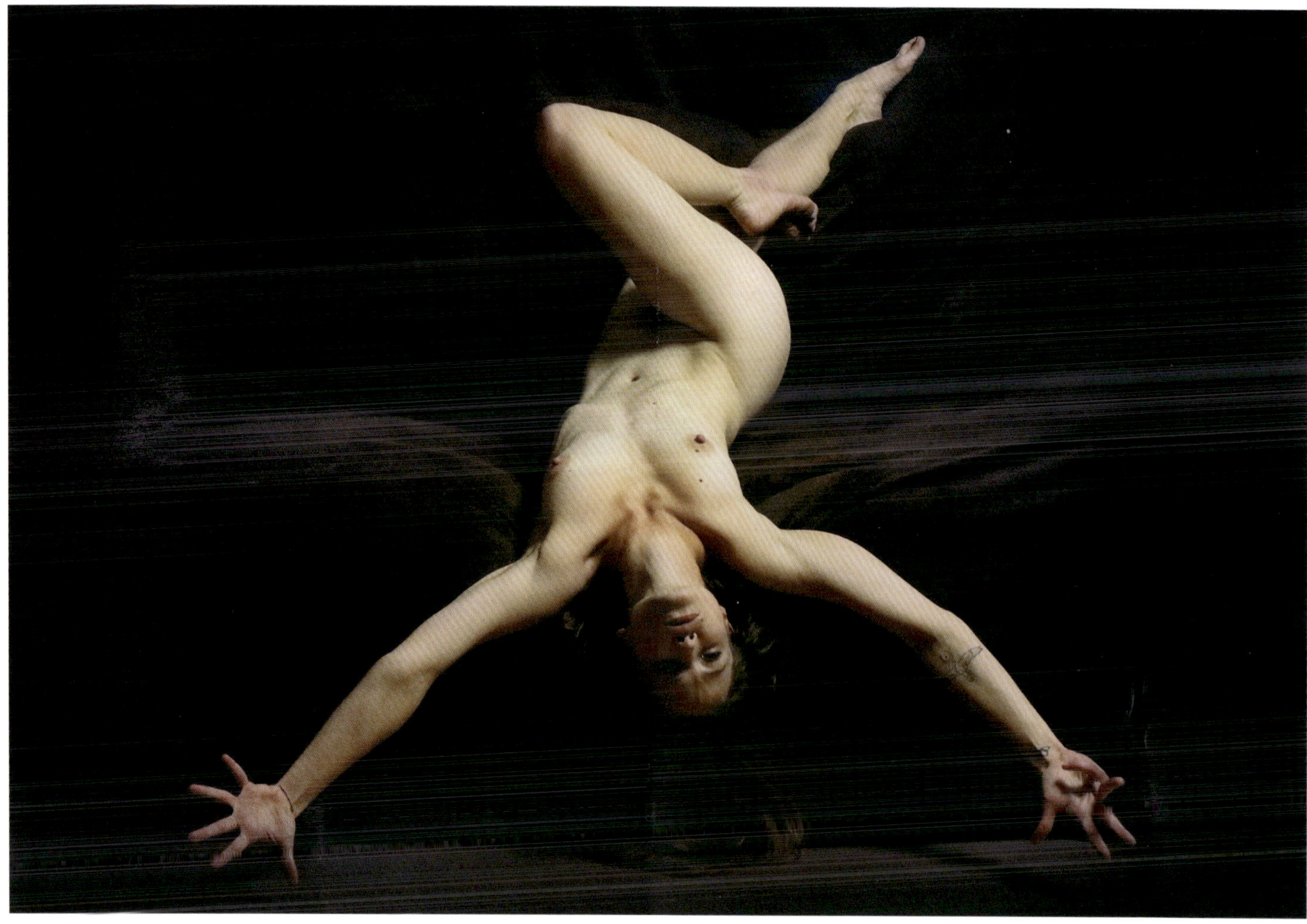

6

7 · Emerging Magic

When using photo reference we tend to draw what we see in the background without thinking of further possibilities, as it's difficult not to be influenced by what's in front of us. Here, I blot texture down with tissue dipped in charcoal powder, moving, twisting, and reshaping the tissue as I go, so as not to create duplicate patterns.

Within the textures I use a kneadable eraser to pull out highlights, reshaping it as I go, as I do with the tissue technique. I also lighten the flesh. A dirty eraser creates softer highlights whereas a clean eraser will give us a harder-edged highlight. Each has its own look. If you work in a blocky style then hard highlights will work, but for this kind of soft, blended flesh a dirty eraser is better. It also gives us the chance to pull

out tone slowly with several ponces (dabs) at a time. If the erased marks are too hard-edged we can come back and soften the edges with fingers, tissue, or paper stumps.

Slowly does it, especially in the early stages of a drawing. Take all the time you need to get where you need to be. The confidence that we gain as the emerging image magically takes shape before our eyes never gets old. Drawing faster than our thoughts is a false economy – if we rush, we inevitably spend most of our time in the negative world of fixing mistakes, which in turn dulls our confidence and results in dull artwork. Ironically, to draw fast we often need to slow down.

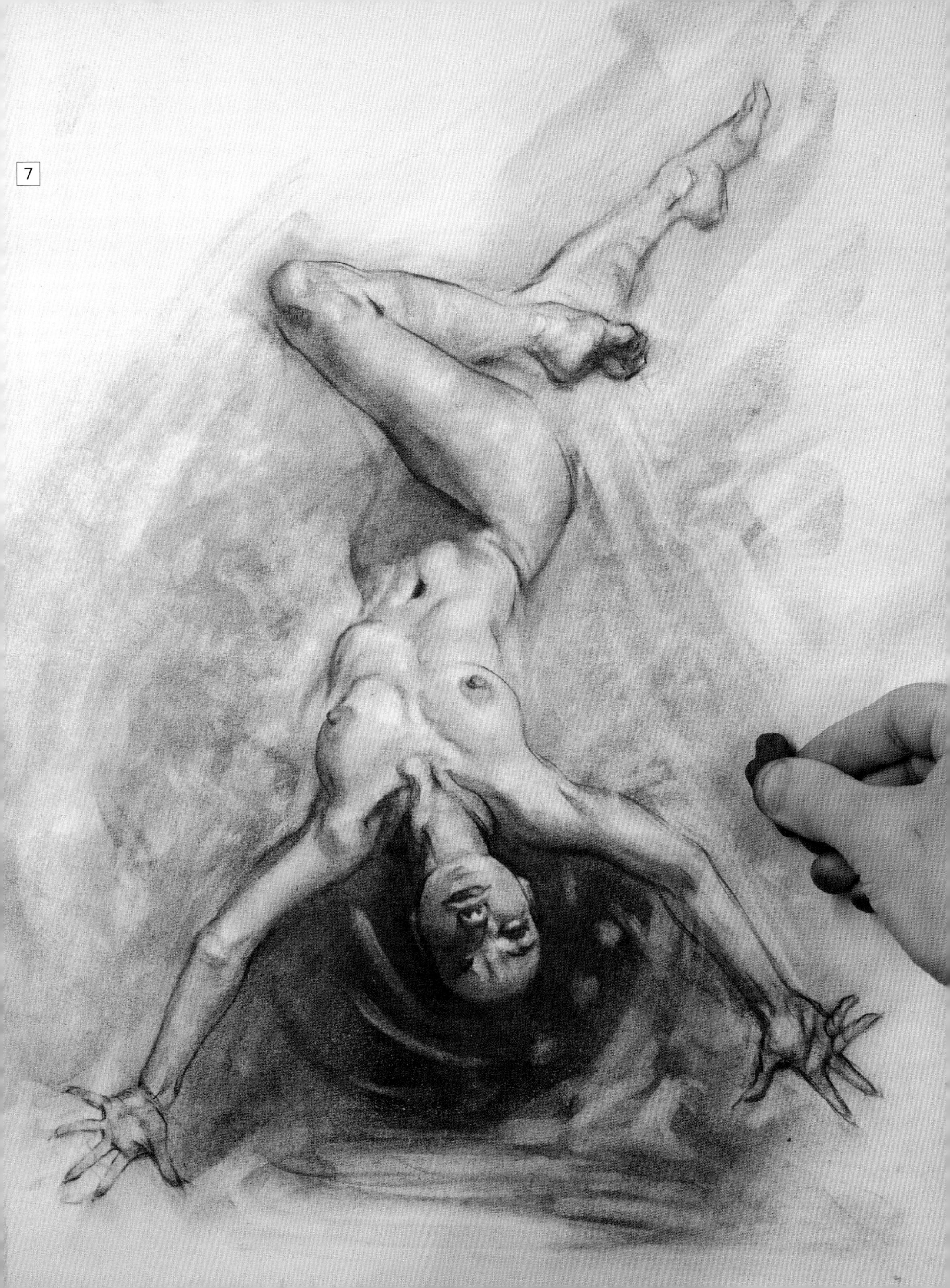

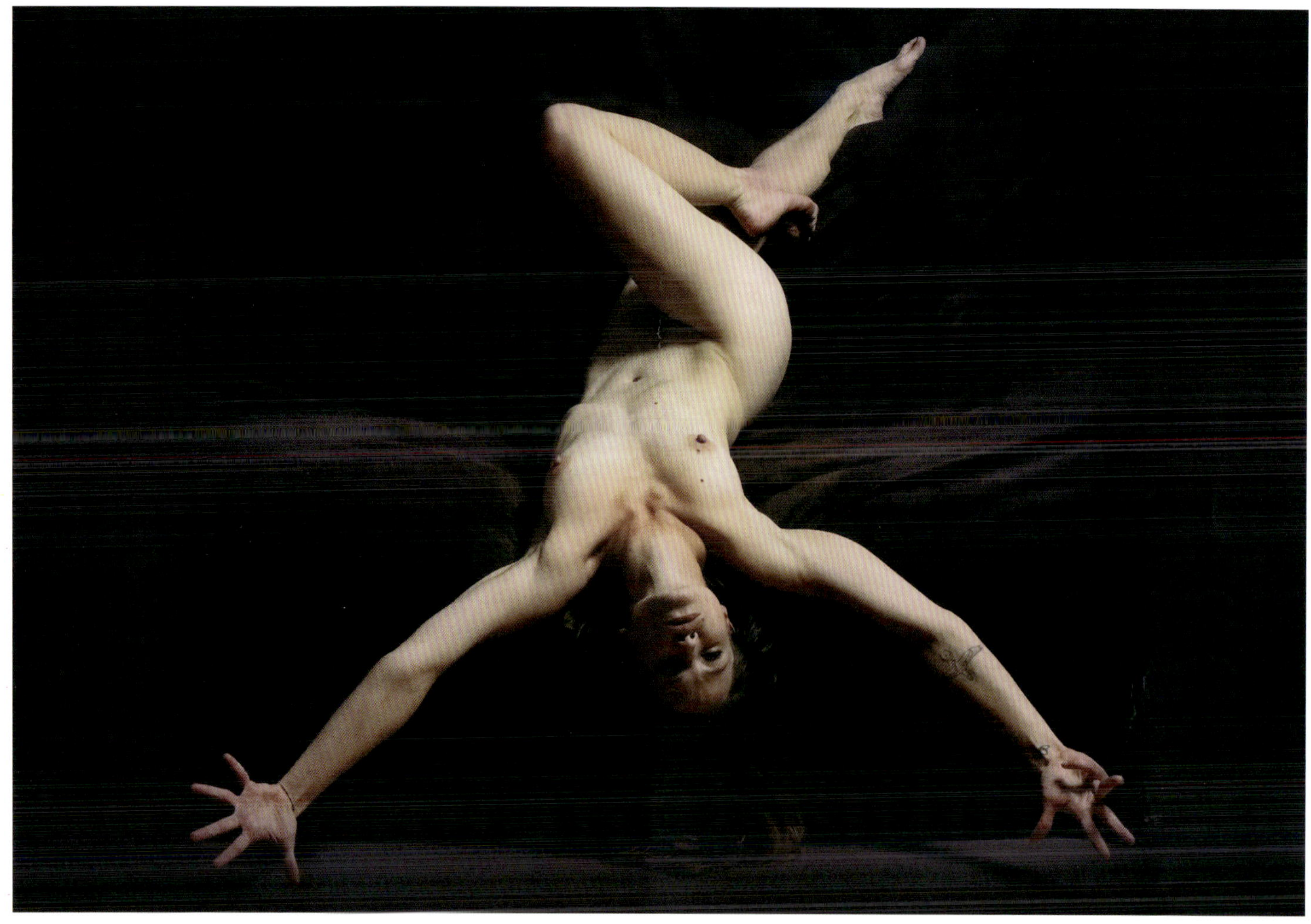

8 · From a Dark Room

The moody chiaroscuro lighting in the photo has inspired me to darken the background of the drawing. One of the advantages of photography is that I can pose the model in a dark room and then draw them in the light of my studio.

Using a large compressed charcoal stick I draw big swirls, twisting the stick as I go for thick and thin marks that suggest sorcery afoot. The compressed charcoal is more dense than the willow charcoal, as the name suggests, and for this reason it needs a light touch – the marks go down as black as night. This could be ruinous to the delicate work already achieved as the compressed charcoal is also more difficult to wipe back or erase. My advice is to practice how light and dark you can control the stick by using one continuous stroke on a separate sheet of paper. This is not only fun, it will also make your hand more confident. When I apply the charcoal strokes I do so with the ultimate confidence, as any doubt will show through with nervous mark-making. Time to be brave and sure.

I use my electric eraser to suggest crackling energy and then a Faber Castell grip eraser to change the swirls into more interesting shapes. I do this directly after the charcoal mark-making as I still have the gestural nature in my hand. In other words, we shouldn't take a break between the charcoal swirls and the erasing alterations – it should be done in one sitting.

Note how the figure appears visibly brighter now. This is mainly due to the darkened background rather than the small amount of highlight erasing on the figure since the previous step. This chiaroscuro light brings the black witch back into focus (we will look at chiaroscuro in depth in the next section).

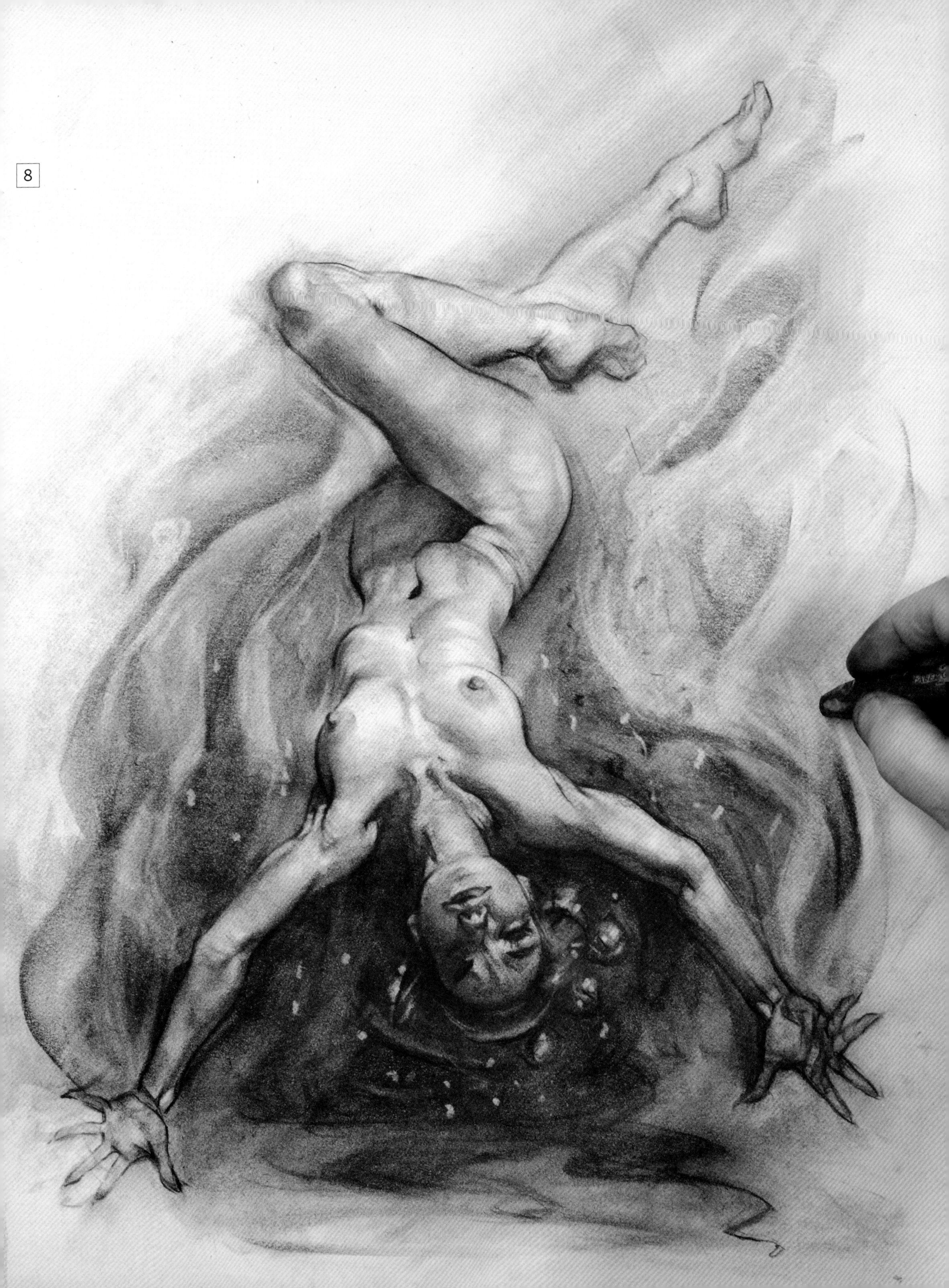

8

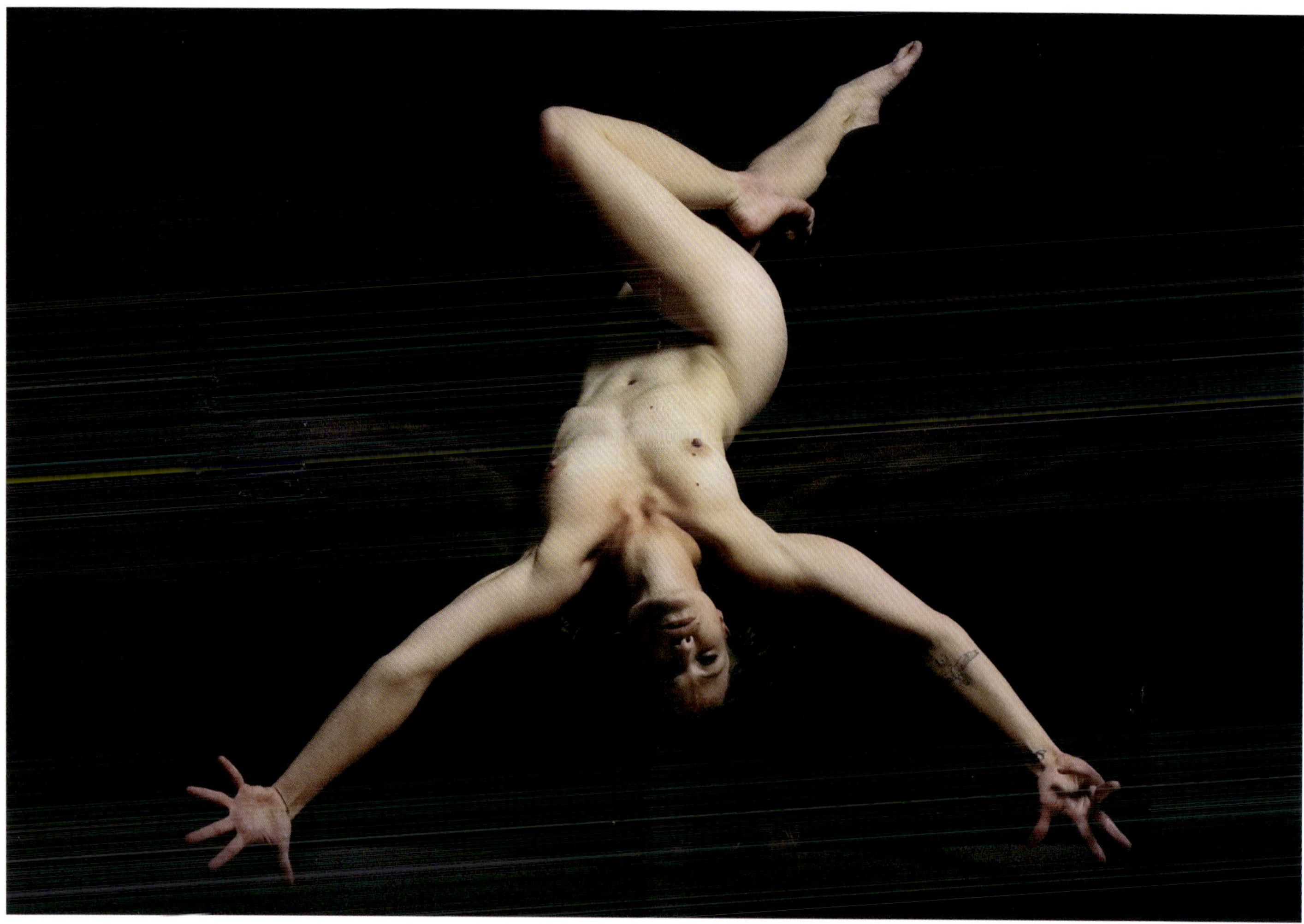

9.• Chasing a Dream

With smudgy fingers, thumbs, and tissue I make the swirls more gestural. Then, using a kneadable eraser and grip eraser, I further reshape them. Finally I carry the swirls upwards with compressed charcoal. I've darkened the bent lower leg along the way to further highlight the upper torso. We are working with light as composition here, as our eye will naturally track from the dimly lit foot down towards the more contrasting torso. The photo's lighting has helped immensely by guiding the atmosphere, so it's not all bad news on the camera front.

Putting in the small stuff of detail is always a danger as we tend to tinker and lose sight of the big overall picture. I'm feeling it's time to stop before the drawing suffers. Was this drawing better in the step before? Perhaps, but no one will ever see that stage, unless you write a book like this one or post progress shots on the internet. Had I not pushed further I may not have discovered the atmosphere created by fading the hair into inky blackness. By constantly exploring we get to understand more and will learn to feel the moment of completion in future artworks. As always, mileage – the act of drawing a lot – will not only build our memory muscles, it will also inform our general awareness of when a drawing is finished, or close to finished.

When I look back at my own progress stages I would say most of my drawings tip past their best moment. However, those best moments may never have happened had I not always chased a dream of better line and tone, seeking out emotional depth with story, atmosphere, and light in the quest to create the ever elusive "masterpiece".

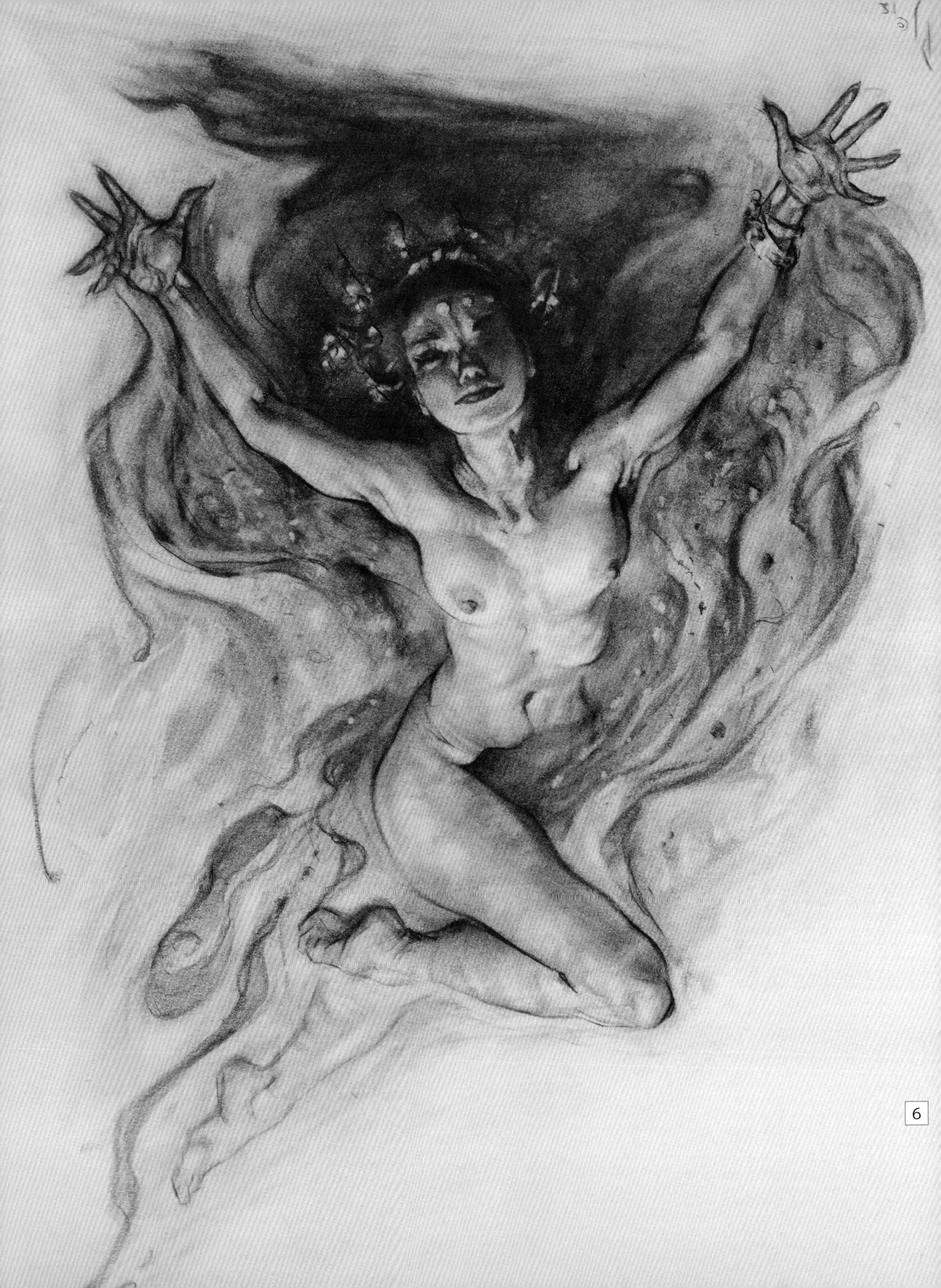

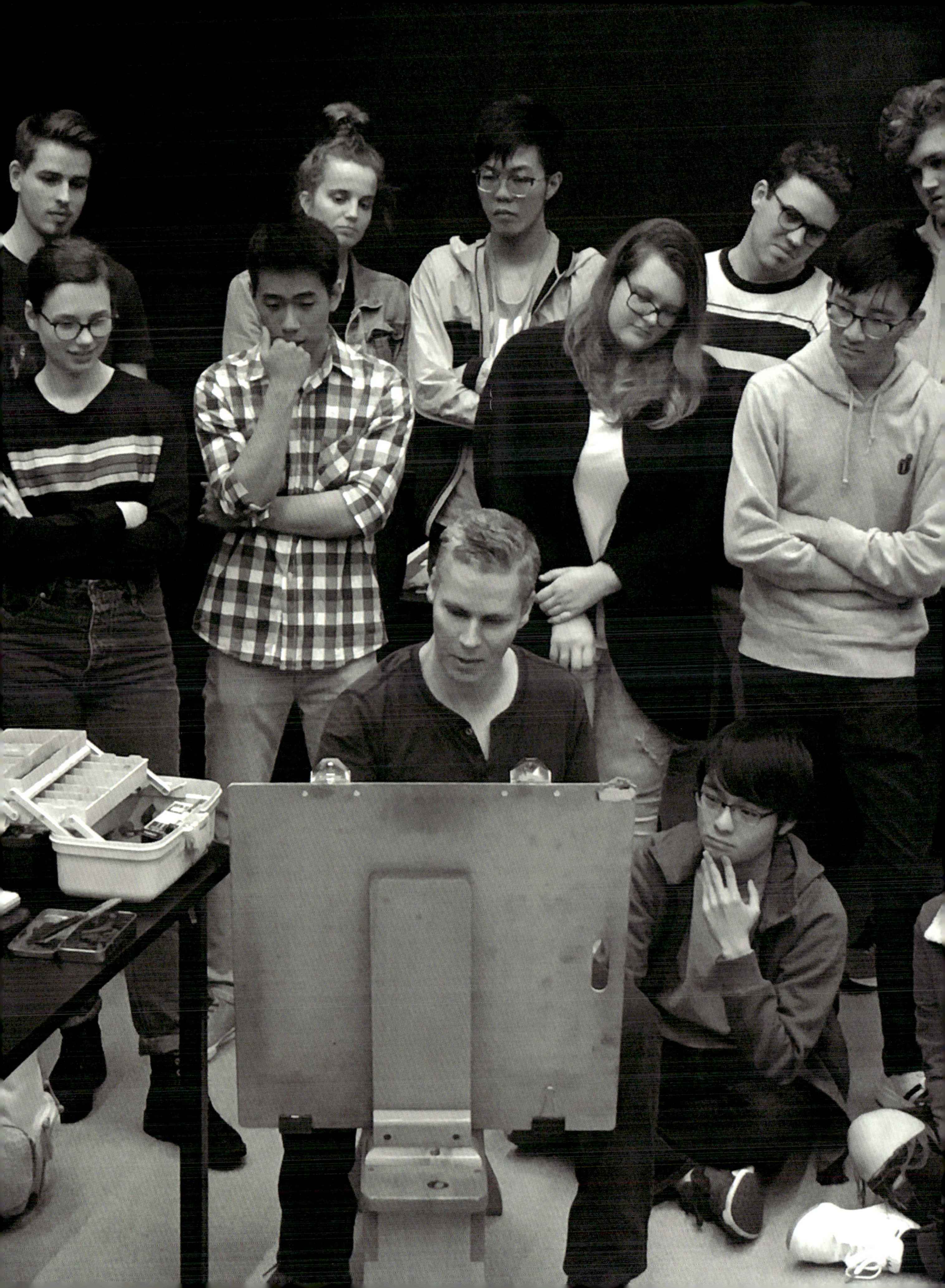

Remember, light and shadow never stand still.

Benjamin West (1738–1820)

WORKSHOP FIVE

MEMORIES SHAPED BY LIGHT

SO FAR IN OUR WORKSHOPS we have explored the balance of contrapposto, the rhythm of asymmetry, and the illusion of depth, and all the time we were working with the biggest illusion of all: the illusion of light to create an image in the mind of the viewer. In reality, a drawing is simply dirty marks on a flat surface arranged to fool the eye into believing it sees an image. In a similar manner, light enters the camera's aperture and burns into shadows to create tonal forms. The aperture, that winking eye we see in the camera lens, represents our pupil and iris. When a room is dark the iris widens our pupils to let in more light, just as a camera's aperture widens for the same reason; and when there is too much light, our pupils shrink. The brighter the environment, the less we need to open the lens of our eyes.

The photo opposite is a microsecond in time, a click of a button, and the opening of an aperture – enough time for the camera's eye to capture the light and dark of the classroom in various tones and make us believe we are looking into the past. What we are really looking at is a memory shaped by shadow and light. There is no depth; it's just an illusion. The moment we realise this, we can see it's a flat image. The people at the back of the photo are as close as the people in the front; this is due mainly to the broad lighting of the room. For us to create a drawing with depth and atmosphere, we need to simplify the lighting and create a more focused display of light and shadow. This brings us to chiaroscuro. Let's explore further...

Left: Patrick teaching The Anatomy of Style in Brisbane, Australia. Photo by Lorena Cappellone

THE ENCOUNTER

Charcoal and pencil on A2 newsprint

Today we will draw Alana with a focus on chiaroscuro. Chiaroscuro, pronounced kee-ahr-uh-skyoor-oh, is the composition of light and shadow to create depth, and more importantly, mood. Chiaroscuro creates an emotional atmosphere in both art and cinema. Movies that engage us with their skillful play of light and dark are sometimes referred to as film noir, meaning "dark film". This moody lighting can also be seen in centuries-old oil paintings, such as the startling *An Experiment on a Bird in the Air Pump* by Joseph Wright of Derby, painted in 1768, which is housed in the National Gallery in London. This work has to be seen in person to truly appreciate the skill of the artist, who was working in an era before the invention of photography.

Movies with artistic lighting are often the collaborative work of a director and a cinematographer. When I first watched *Apocalypse Now* I was entranced by the cinematography and the way it created a constant mood that flowed from one scene to the next. As an artist it felt to me like the emotional and gestural flow through great figurative art.

To create a chiaroscuro photoshoot, it's not necessary to buy an expensive lighting set up: all that's needed is a sunny day and a dark background. An old abandoned building with a hole in the roof will give you the right light, or alternatively, any indoor space with an open roof. Add a smartphone on a makeshift tripod and you can create a professional photoshoot.

And so we begin our own chiaroscuro adventure of shifting shadows and light, using our humble charcoals and pencils.

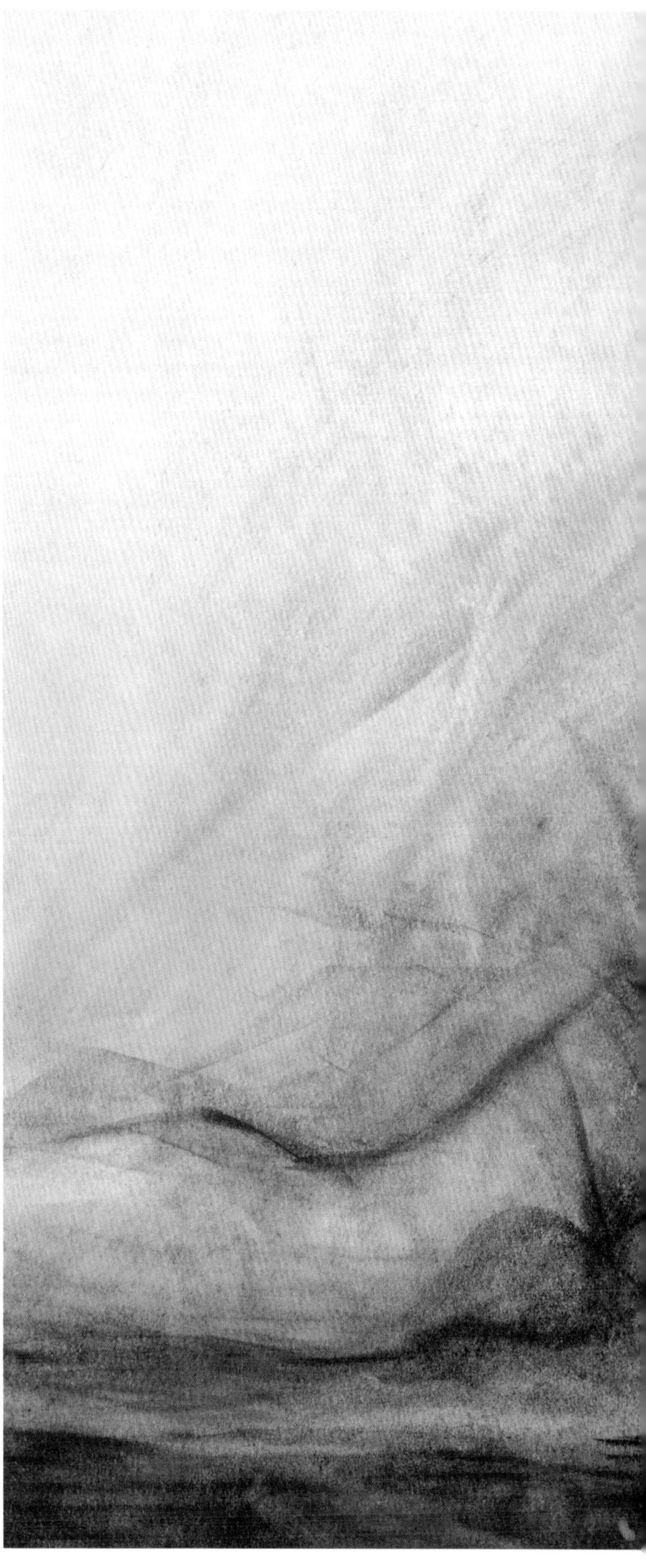

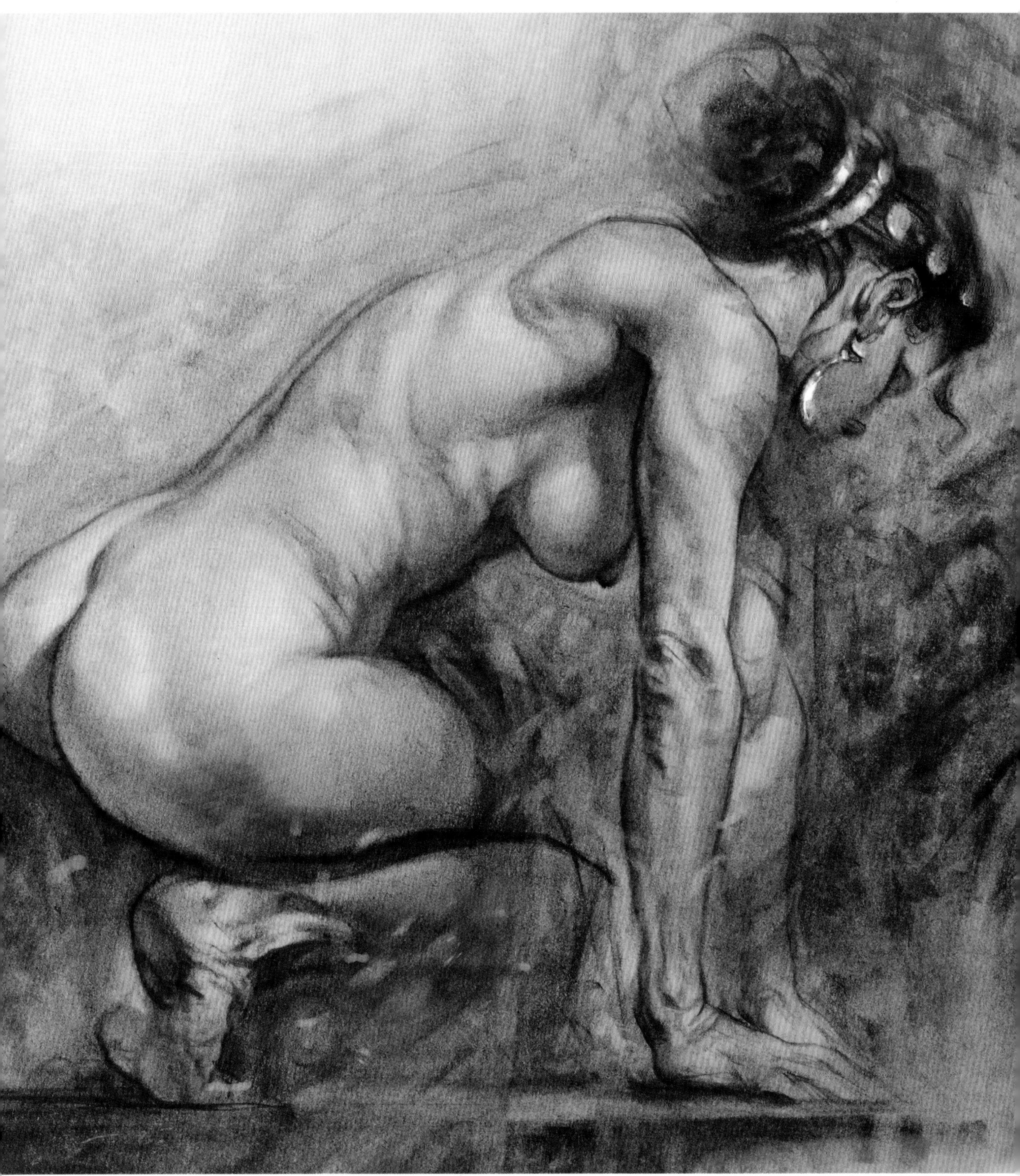

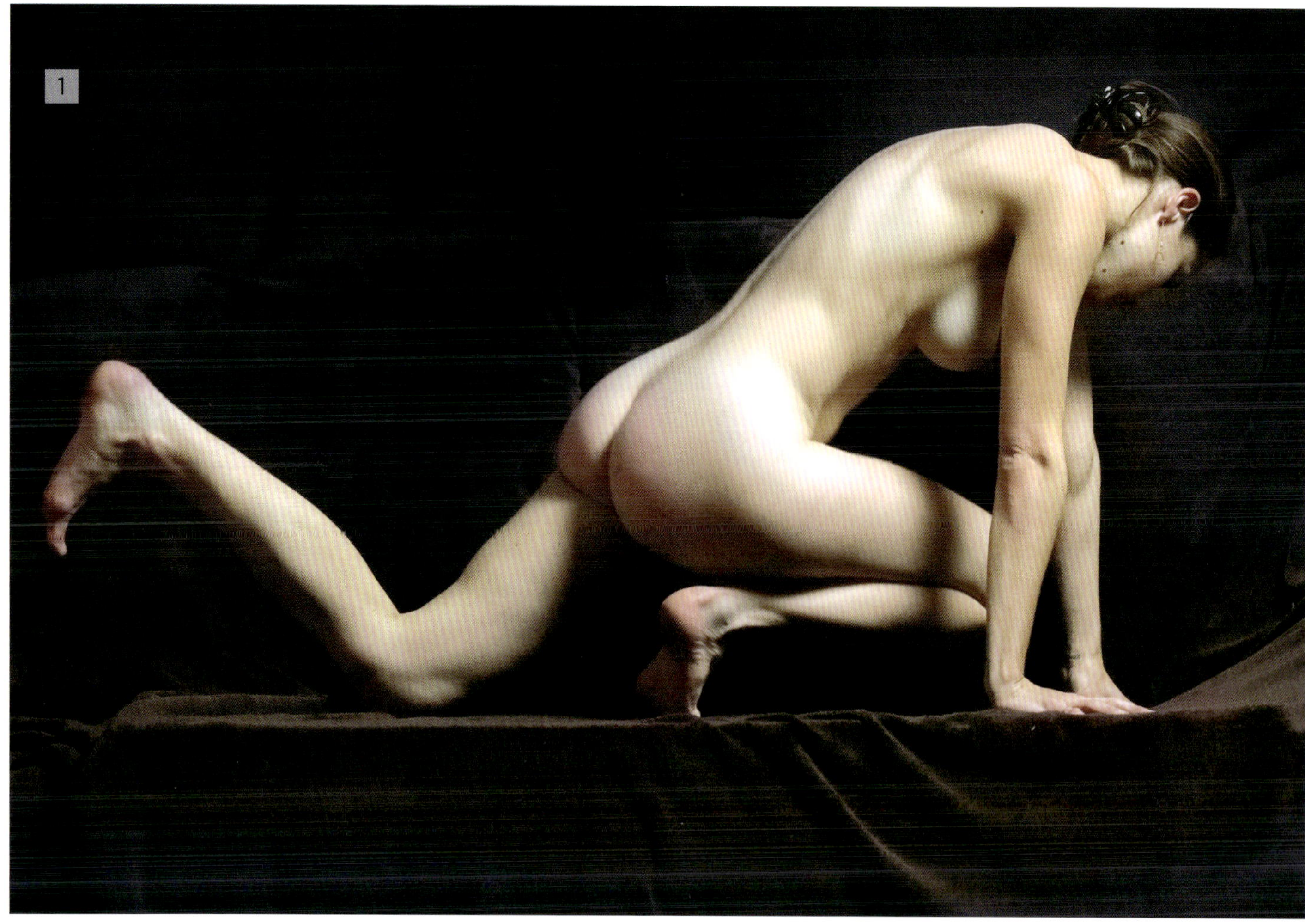

1 · Separate Lives

Above, we have a wonderful photo and pose to draw from. We can see how clearly the figure stands out from the background – so defined, dimensional, and atmospheric in tone – and for that reason, it holds our attention. This is due to the single directional light source and a dark, uncluttered background. My lights are positioned high in order to recreate an artificial afternoon sun in a dark studio background.

One benefit of artificial light is that it's unchanging and remains constant, with no dimming due to passing clouds. But how can a drawing compete with such a great photograph? Well, it doesn't have to, as photographs and drawings live separate lives in the world of art.

2 · Major Structures

With my willow charcoal, I plot out the figure with two major structures: a long tube for the upper torso and a ball for the hips. Working big shapes to small, I add the scapula (wing bone), and below the scapula, I indicate the serratus and latissimus bulges as a converging "V" shape.

3 · Versions of Anatomy

I continue adding smaller structural shapes to define areas such as the hip bone. Structural shapes are simple versions of anatomy. If I were to draw the intricacies of each anatomical shape as I go, the drawing would get so complicated that I might lose the sense of the whole figure.

2
Scapula
Serratus bulge
Latissimus bulge

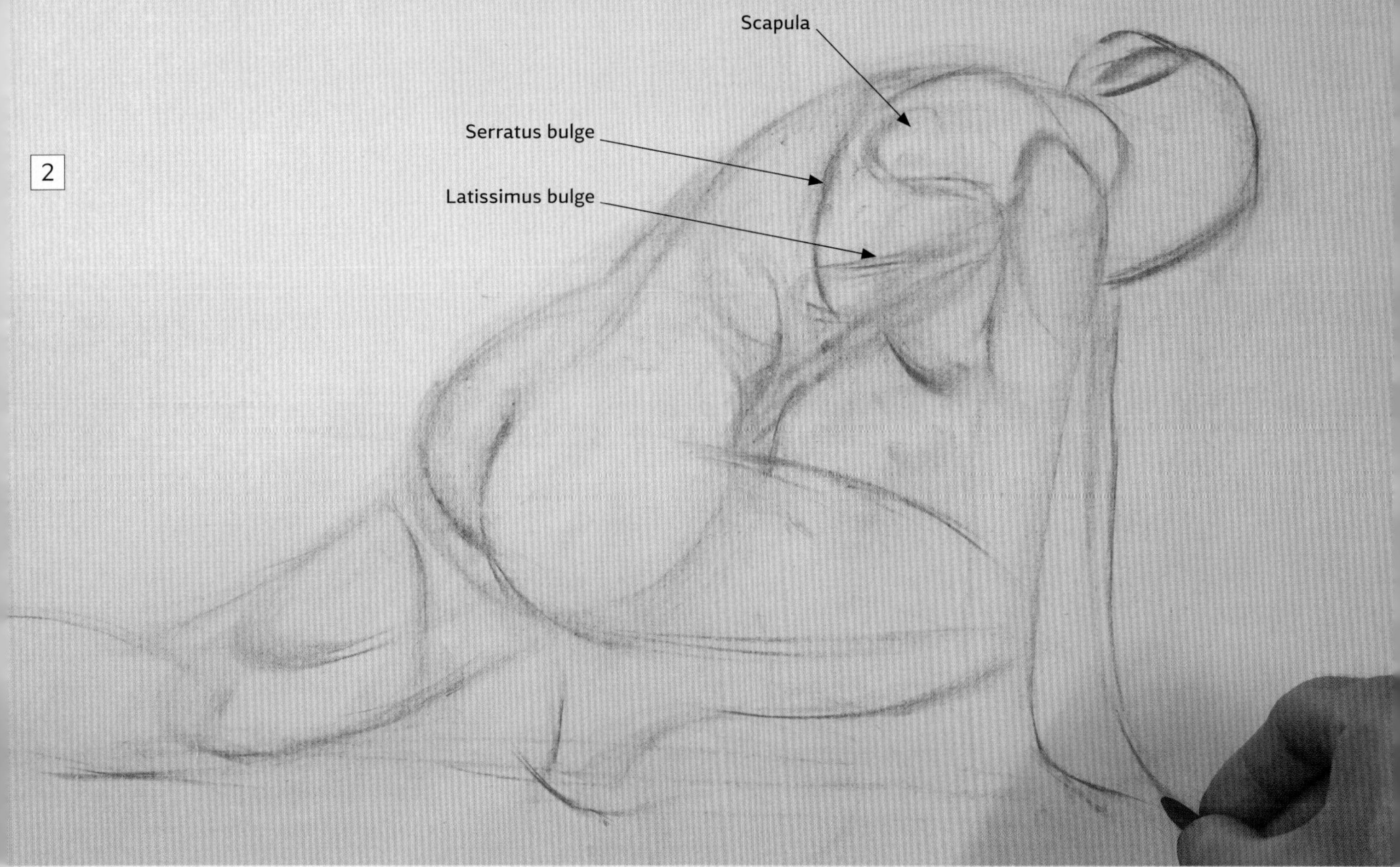

3

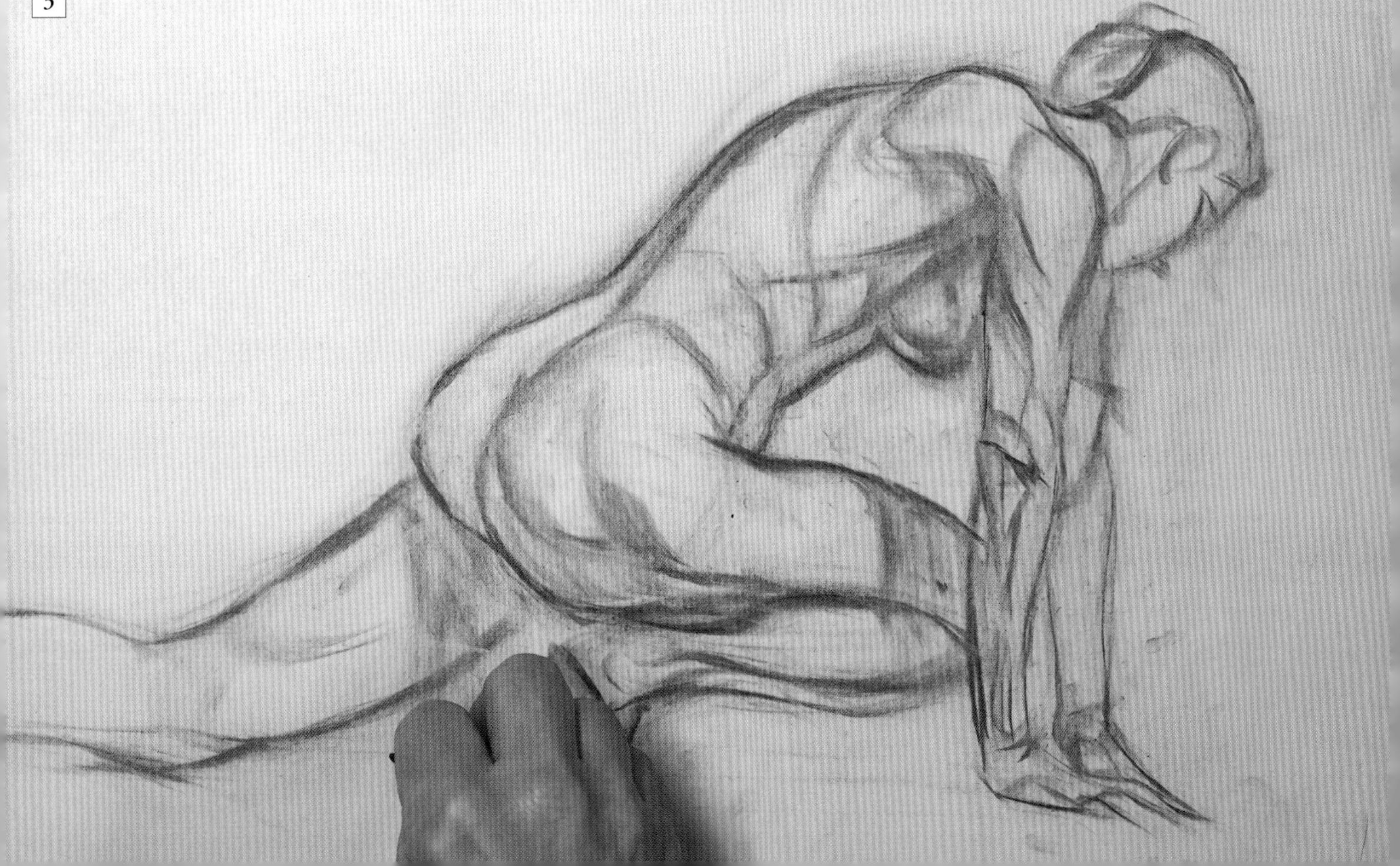

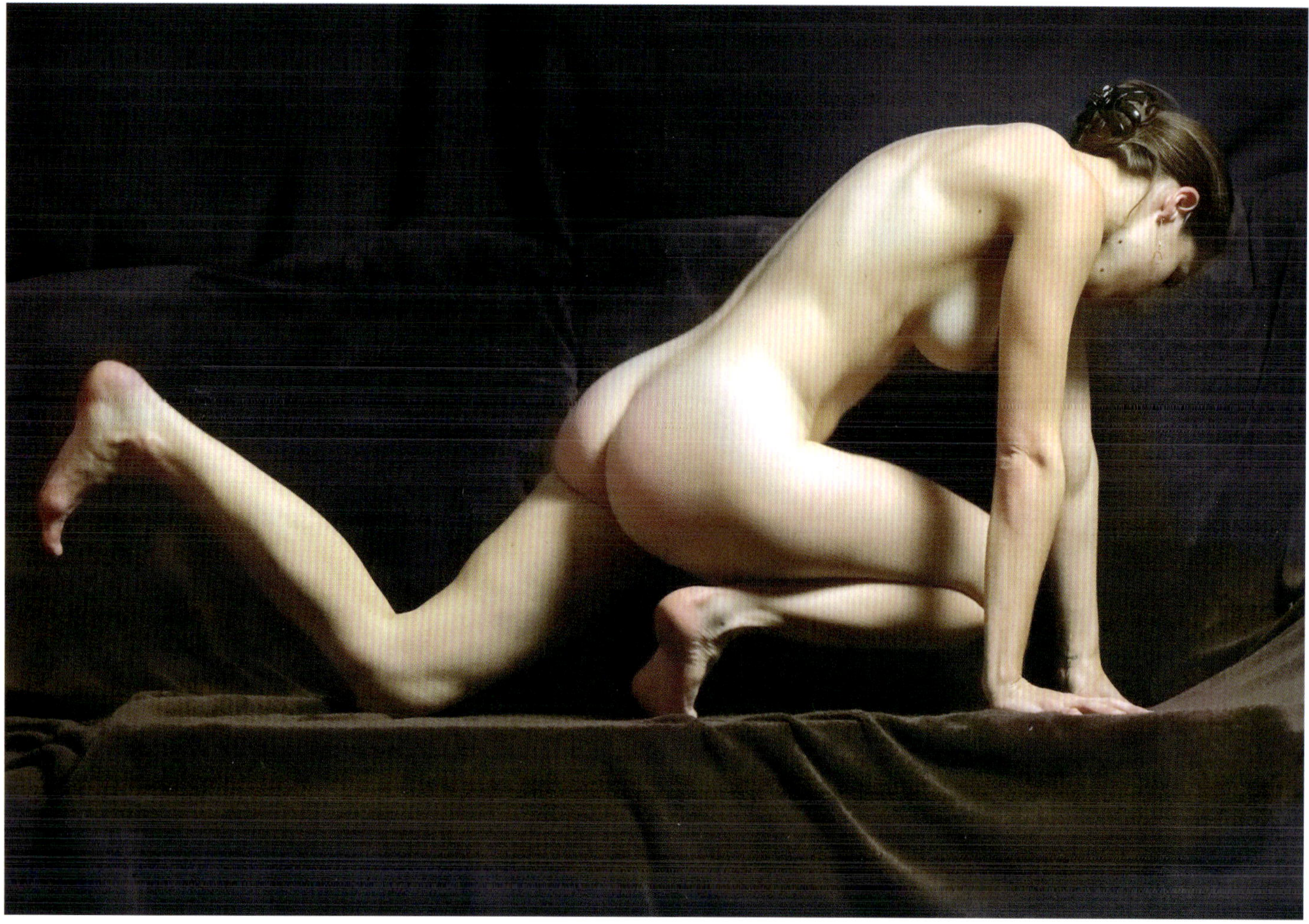

4 · Burning Candles

Note the way the reference photo carves out the form, almost like a statue. Chiaroscuro is the most dimensional lighting we have to create an illusion of depth, and it reveals natural muscle form like no other. Caravaggio would have given anything to have photography to help with his chiaroscuro paintings. Gone are the days when artists had to burn candles through the night in order to paint a figure lit like this, keeping the light constant after daylight ended.

From here, we begin to reap the benefits of a strong structure. As I go over the drawing's simple shapes again, it's easy to add smaller anatomical details, such as the ribs, the sacrum pad above the gluteus, and the two serratus notches visible to the left of the breast.

5 · Flickering Changes

I smudge the charcoal into softer forms to freshen the image and introduce tone. In life drawing classes, I have students step back at this stage and glance back and forth between the drawing and the model until they see every flickering change between their work and the pose before making adjustments. Time spent analysing forms early on, is time saved later.

Serratus notches

Ribs

Sacrum pad

4

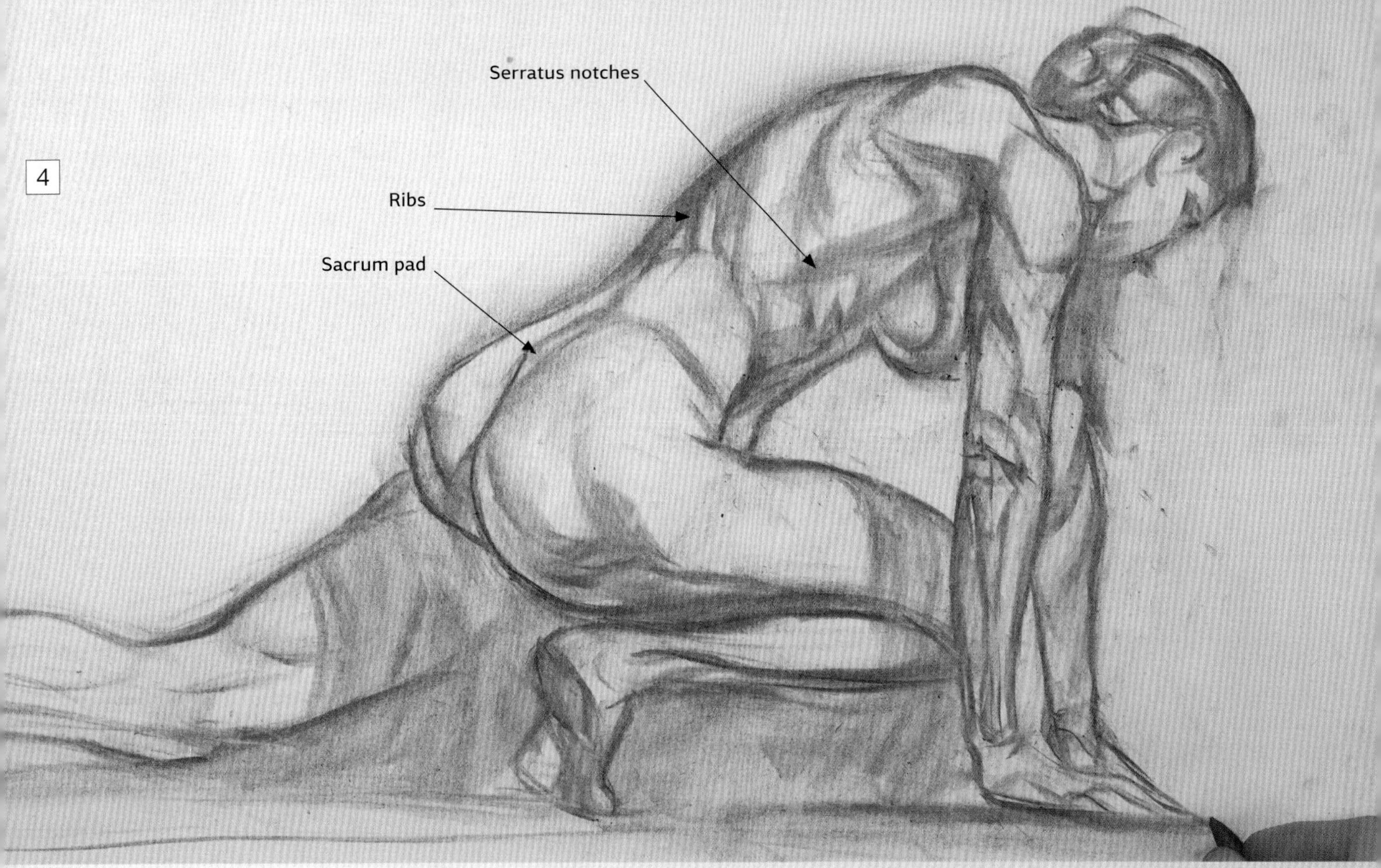

5

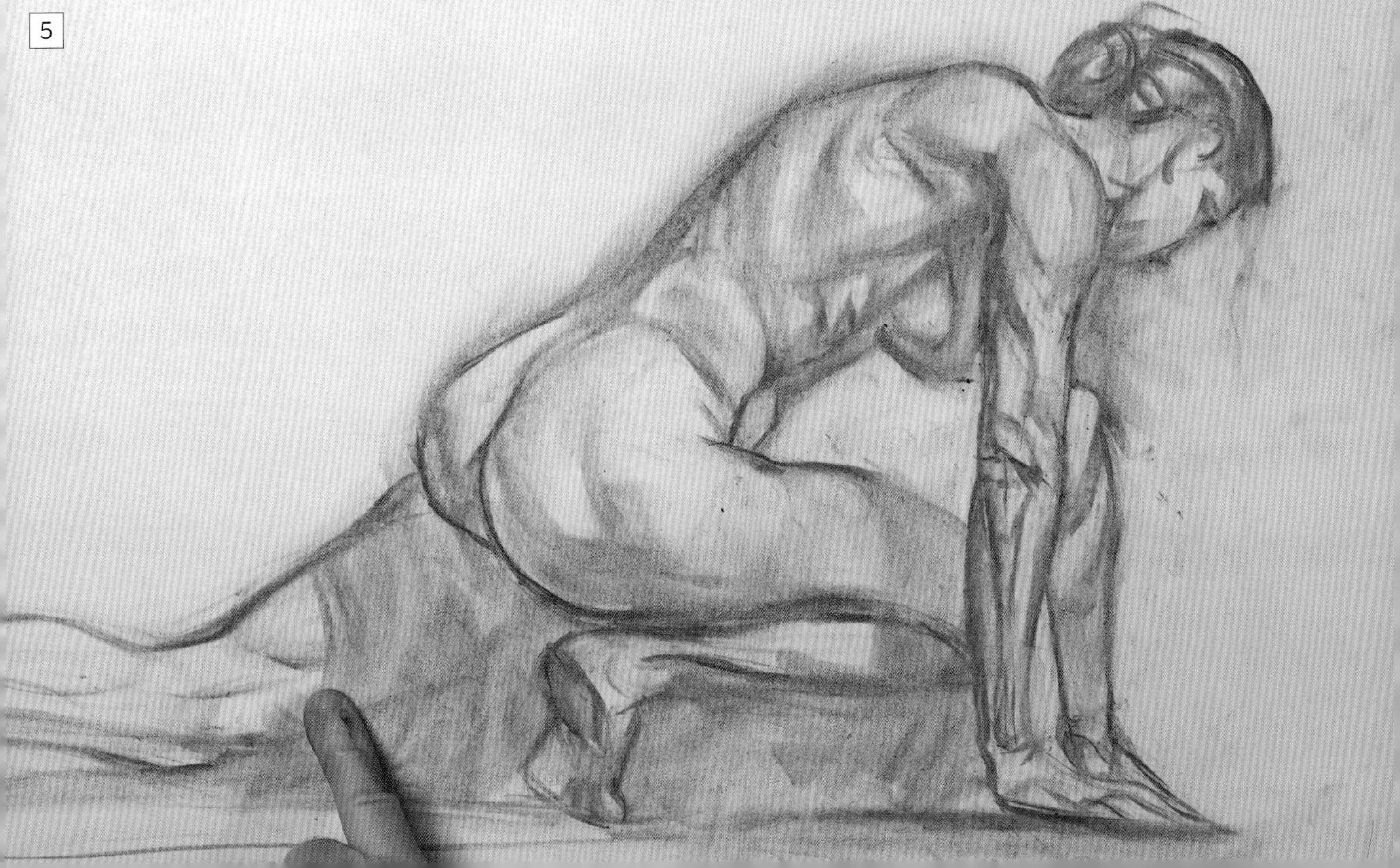

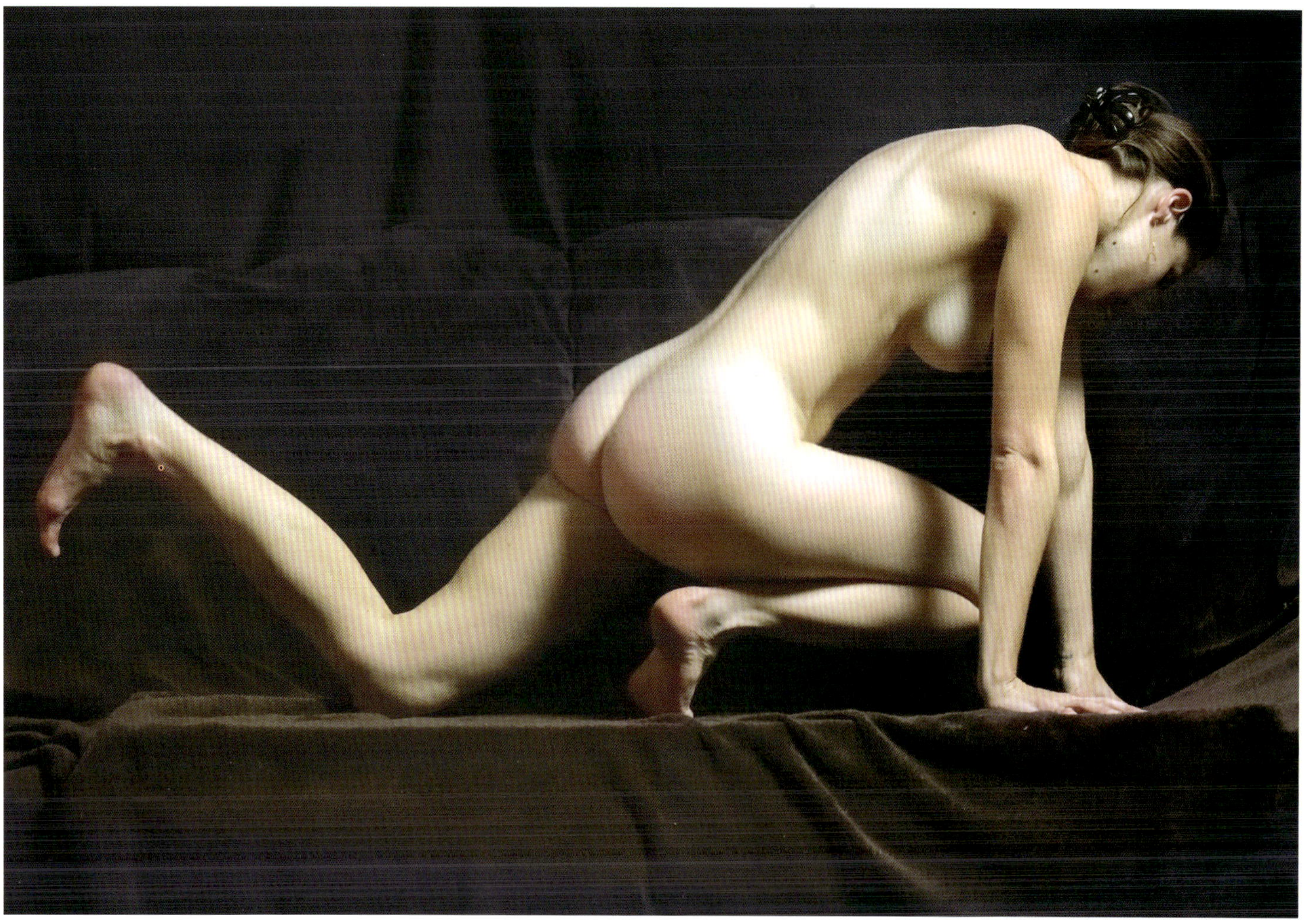

6 · Interlocking Forms

With due diligence done, I step back from the art for a final assessment. This doesn't mean I want exact proportions. I'm simply making sure the anatomy and interlocking forms, such as the hip crest fitting into the obliques, work both structurally and gesturally. The chiaroscuro lighting makes the drawing go in fast, as I'm not searching so hard for the muscle definition, as is often the case in poorly lit life drawing classes. With everything working to plan, I pencil on top.

7 · The Magic Light

I'm strolling down Easy Street now as I pencil over my self-approved structure. Or so it seems… In my quest to make every line more gestural, I've made the suggested scapula too rounded. Keep in mind that structure and gesture are a delicate balance of back and forth that can fall apart at any time.

Now on to the subject at hand: the magical chiaroscuro. As I blend with my fingers I'm thinking of the single source of light and how it tumbles across the forms. To study the power of chiaroscuro, turn any object in front of your bedside light and observe the strong changes in light and shadow produced.

6

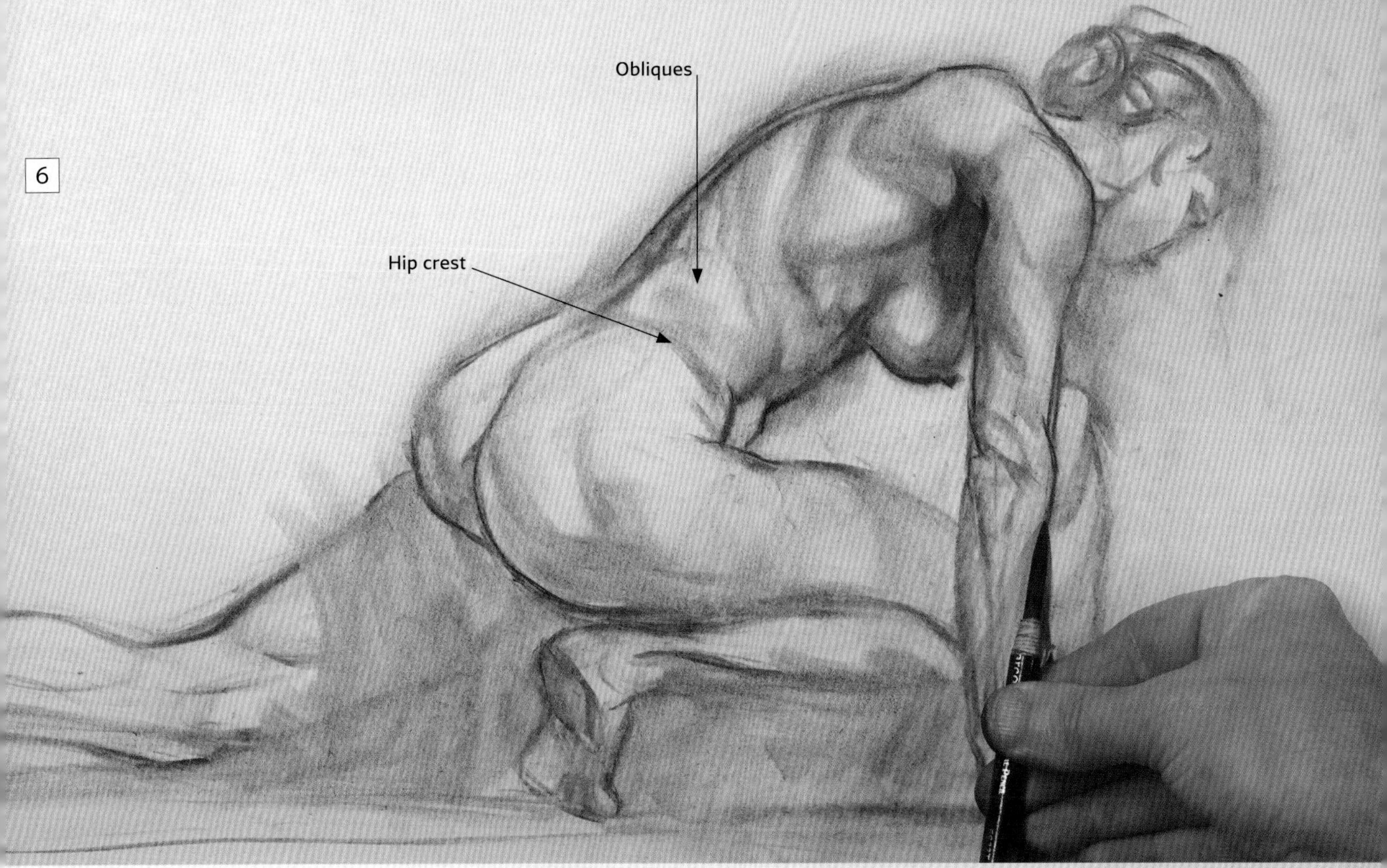

Obliques

Hip crest

7

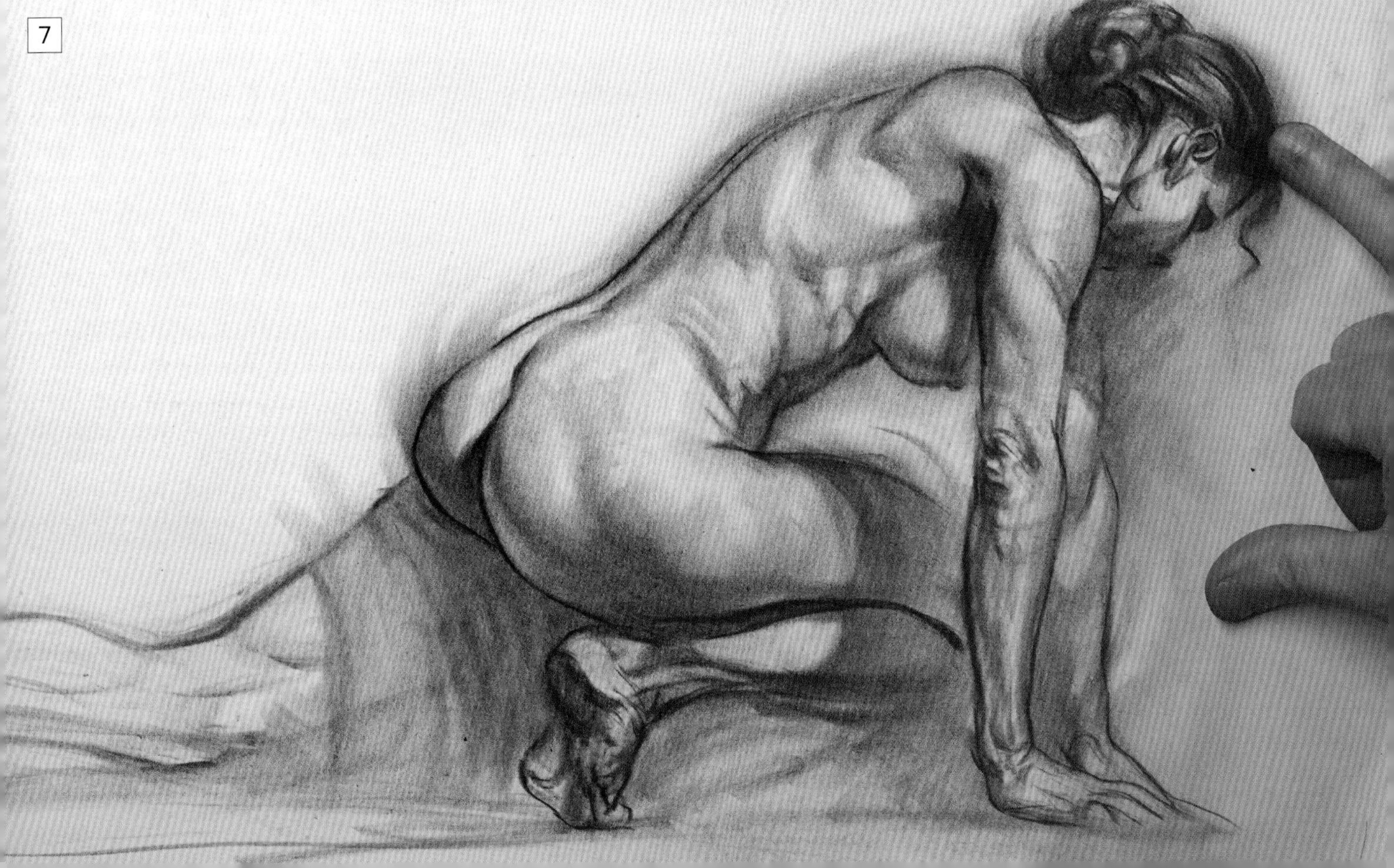

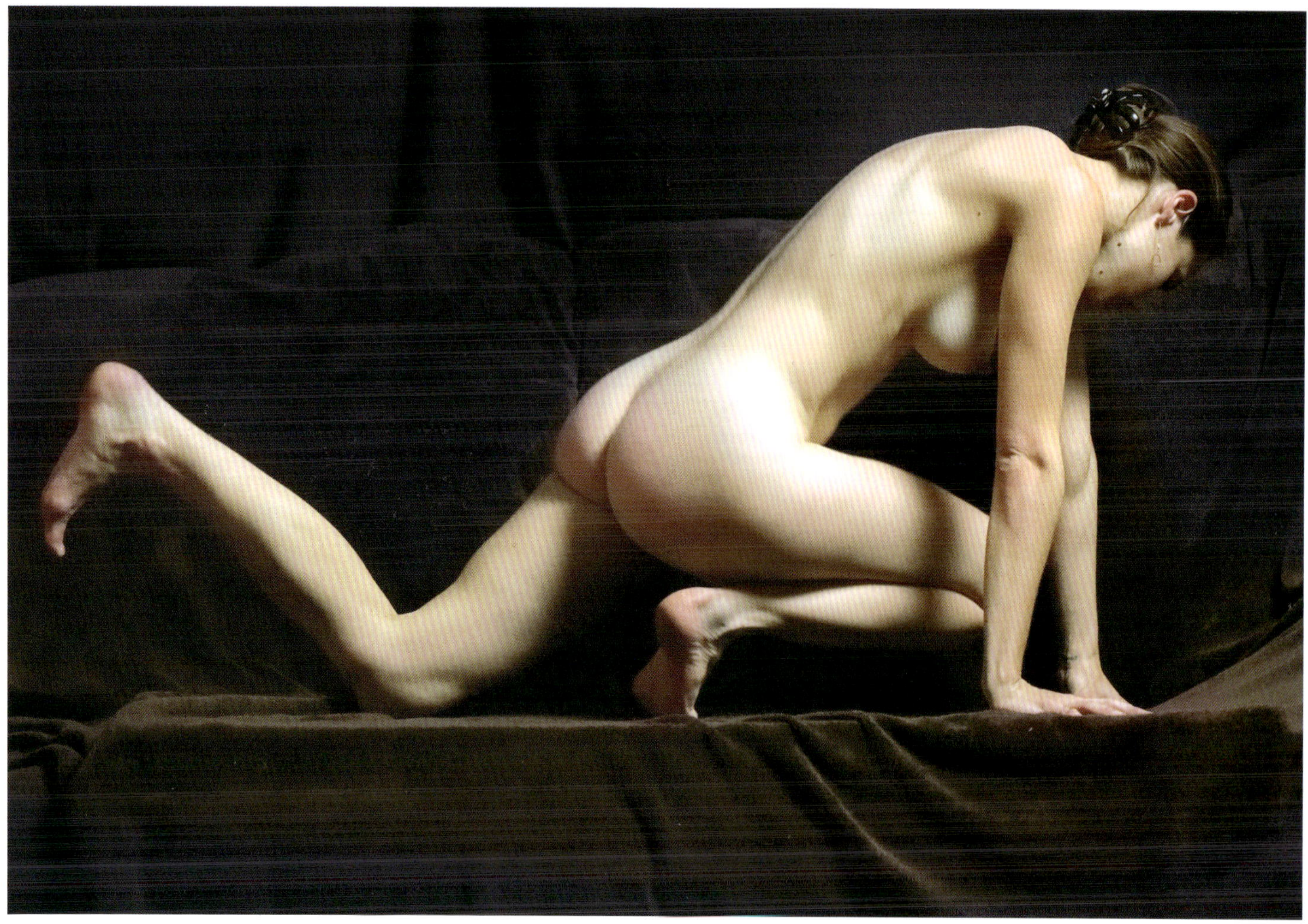

8 · Sfumato

I make the shadows darker than necessary, so I can better judge the light. Charcoal is "live", which means it never "sets" like paint, so I can choose to lighten these darks later with a dab of soft tissue. To seal the charcoal, I wait until the end before spraying a few coats of fixative. I could also choose to use a light spray of re-workable fixative between stages for a drawing that can still be smudged. If you fix the drawing though, it will need more push and harder erasing because the hold on the paper will be stronger. This will slow down the drawing, which is why I leave the fixative until the end.

Note the misty quality of the shadowed leg – this soft and subtle transition used to blur edges and forms is called sfumato (sfoo-mah-toh) and it gives us both atmosphere and a clearer focus towards the more contrasting upper figure.

Often, what we don't show is more interesting than what we do. One of the most dangerous aspects of working from photographs is that we tend to draw every detail and miss out on the beauty of sfumato.

9 · A Lighter Affair

I've finally addressed that pesky scapula by drawing a straight line across the upper curve. Placing straight lines on top of curves can add authority to a line; it's something I do more often on the male figure, to add a more rugged look, but it can work on the female figure too.

After a round of tissue blending, the drawing becomes a lighter affair. I add a head ornament with an eraser and then pencil in some detail. I could call the drawing finished at this stage, but it's a little too bright and breezy. I will explore further in search of more depth, mood, and atmosphere.

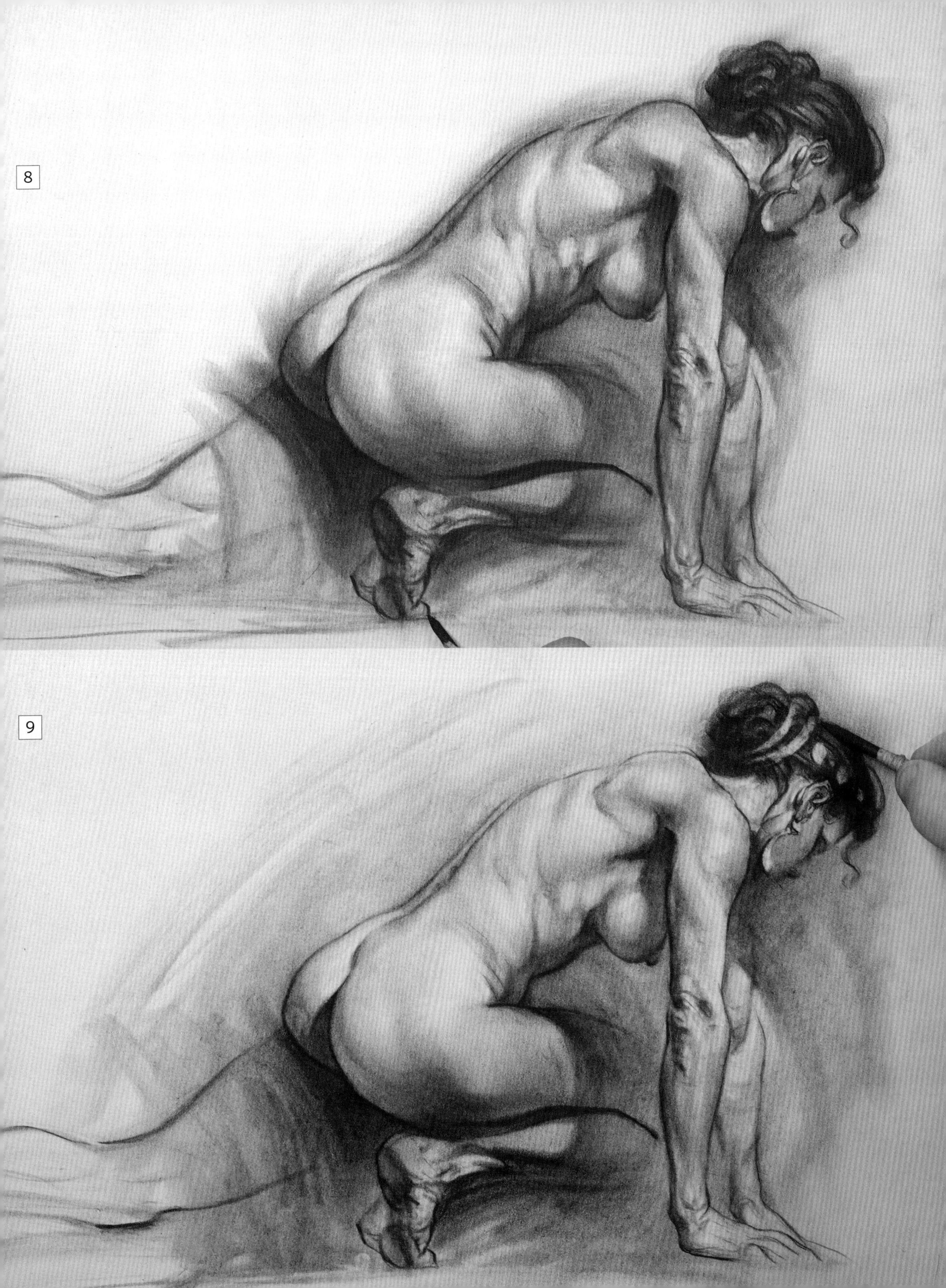

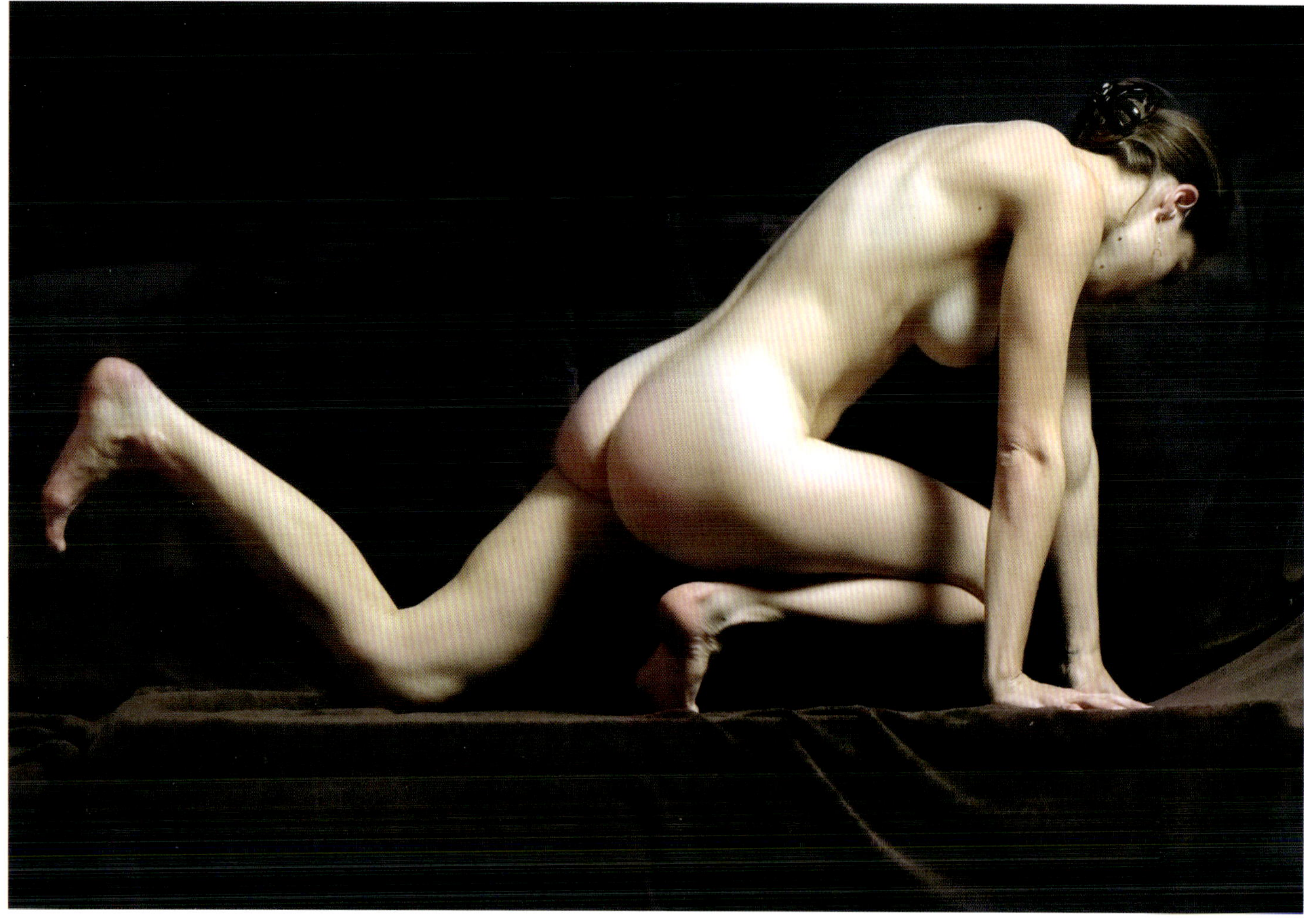

10 · Echoing Textures

With a block of square compressed charcoal, I lay in a gestural abstract background. Artists of the past, most notably Rembrandt, often kept their backgrounds dark, sometimes black, to bring the figures forwards for the ultimate chiaroscuro effect. The echoing texture here also adds suggested movement to the figure.

11 · The Artist's Hand

I continue texturing the background with tissue, chamois, and a kneadable eraser, turning my hand as I make shapes, to avoid repetition. Texture not only adds interest, it can also make flesh seem softer by contrast. At this point, I use a paper stump to soften some edges.

As long as the light comes mostly from a powerful single source, the figure will appear to be carved from light and shadow, regardless of time or place. I now call the drawing finished. As incredible an asset as it was, the photograph is already a distant memory, a component that has been put aside to live its own life elsewhere. Look now only at the drawing. It stands alone – a newborn creation of organic line, tone, and gestural energy: an energy that can only come from an artist's hand.

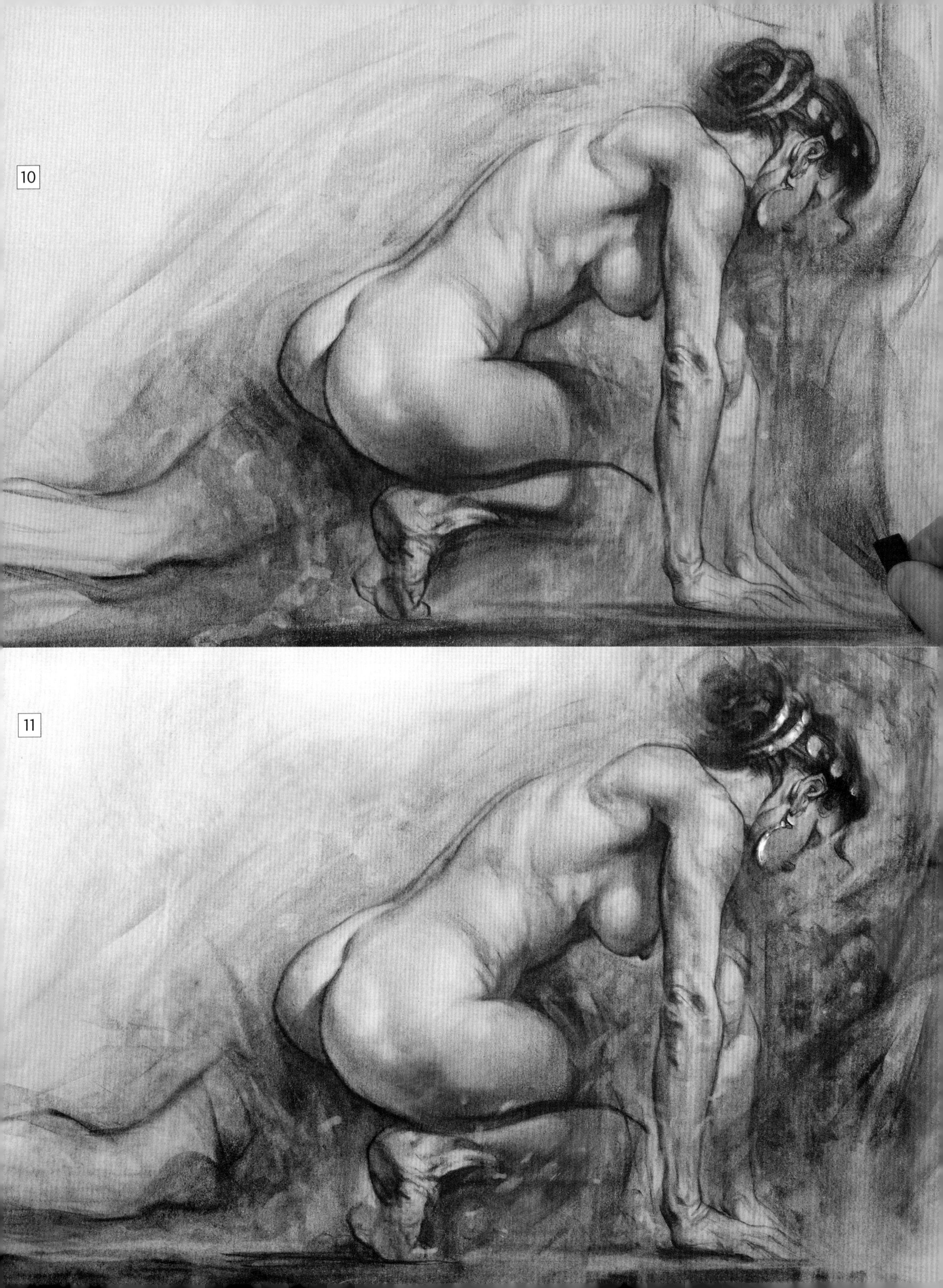

10

11

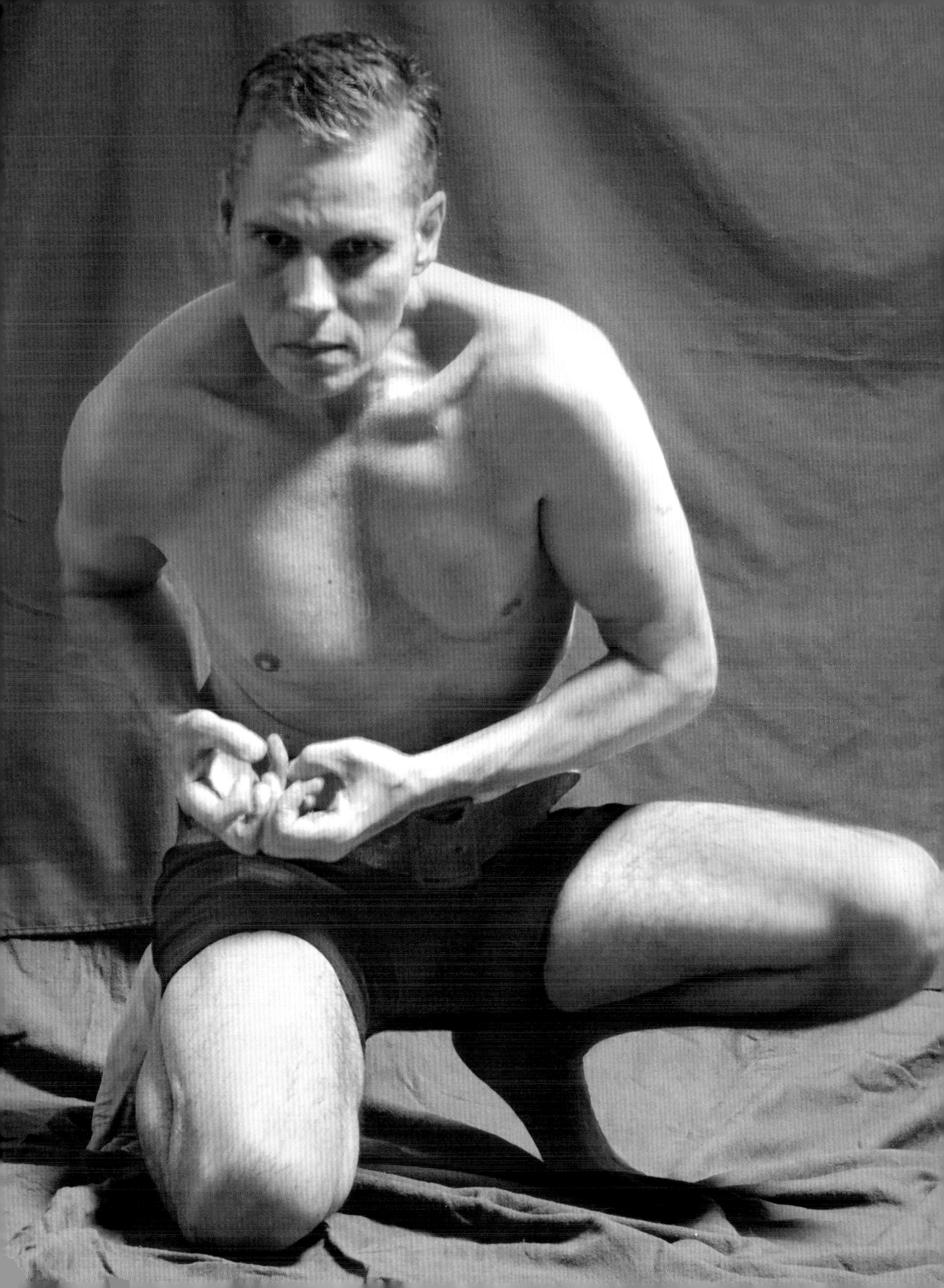

Robert Henri (1865–1929)

WORKSHOP SIX

EMBRACING FAILURE

IN THIS SECTION, we will study the male back and arms, exploring the natural rhythm of muscles and the expressive nature they display as they counterbalance and work in unison to move the body with style and grace. For someone who loves anatomy, this is simply a beautiful thing to observe, but being an artist also opens a world of possibilities, flowing shapes, lines, and rhythmic tones.

But why do live anatomical studies when we can study anatomy books instead? The answer is simple: in a non-action pose, anatomy looks basically the same for everyone, but the moment we move, the muscles change shape and affect each other as they jostle and push for position. In other words, muscles are shapeshifters. This is a marvellous thing – we are all different shapes and sizes, with different personalities and degrees of bearing, and we therefore end up with unlimited chances for expression within the human figure. Look at the way a boxer moves or even stands compared to a ballerina, and you will see a world of difference in aspects of line and tone within what is basically the same human anatomy.

With that said, studies are by their nature a notoriously slow affair, with a studied drawing usually ending up on the stiff side. Photos are also frozen in time, adding to stiff art if we stick too closely to copying them. This is when life drawing trumps working from photos, and it's why I recommend studying the life model as they move in and out of the pose to truly understand how the muscles shift in position.

Unfortunately, I hadn't drawn for a month before creating the workshop in this section because I'd been in the US for the wonderful IX show on imaginative realism, where I'd given a lecture based on my most recent book, *Figures from Life*, which, ironically, is about creating gesture through an understanding of anatomy. Although I was out of practice, there was no time to faff about, as the workshop was due at the magazine within days of my return. That experience leads us to our next adventure in the pearls of an artist – working with rusty arms, and the value of failure.

Left: Patrick posing for a life drawing

THE PEARLFISHER

Charcoal and pencil on A2 newsprint

In this photo, the rhythm of life in muscle movement is evident – *when* we learn to see it. Note the waves created when the ribcage bites into the side obliques and the rolling muscular hills. Here, the body suggests motion even in stillness. I've struck a fluid pose by acting the part of a fisherman, and then stopping, but most posed models can be a lot stiffer if they are directed with limbs positioned to match a rigid sketch. If you can do a photoshoot, I recommend giving the model the freedom to interpret the sketch rather than mimic it.

Opposite is my final drawing based on the photo reference. I consider this a failed drawing, for within it, I entered several drawing "hells"; firstly, Structure Hell, where I was overly concerned with getting proportion correct, which ironically can result in getting proportion wrong. The reason for this is that we tend to measure parts rather than relating broader shapes. Measuring structure to the detriment of rhythm and gesture will result in a stiff drawing. Now I know this, and I was aware of the balance required, but still I struggled. Why? Well, sometimes we just have an off day. It's worth remembering that should we ever doubt ourselves, we are still better artists on our worst day than we were previously, when we did our best drawing – provided we have constantly been drawing.

And therein lay my main problem with this art – a dip in mileage. A month away from drawing had left its rust on my muscle memory. My hand had lost its fluidity. The mind was willing but the rhythm was stifled. I even resorted to Render Hell – over-rendering in a bid to bamboozle the unwary. Let's explore something not often discussed art books: the flawed drawing, and how difficult drawing can be when we enter drawing hells. But most importantly, how to embrace failure.

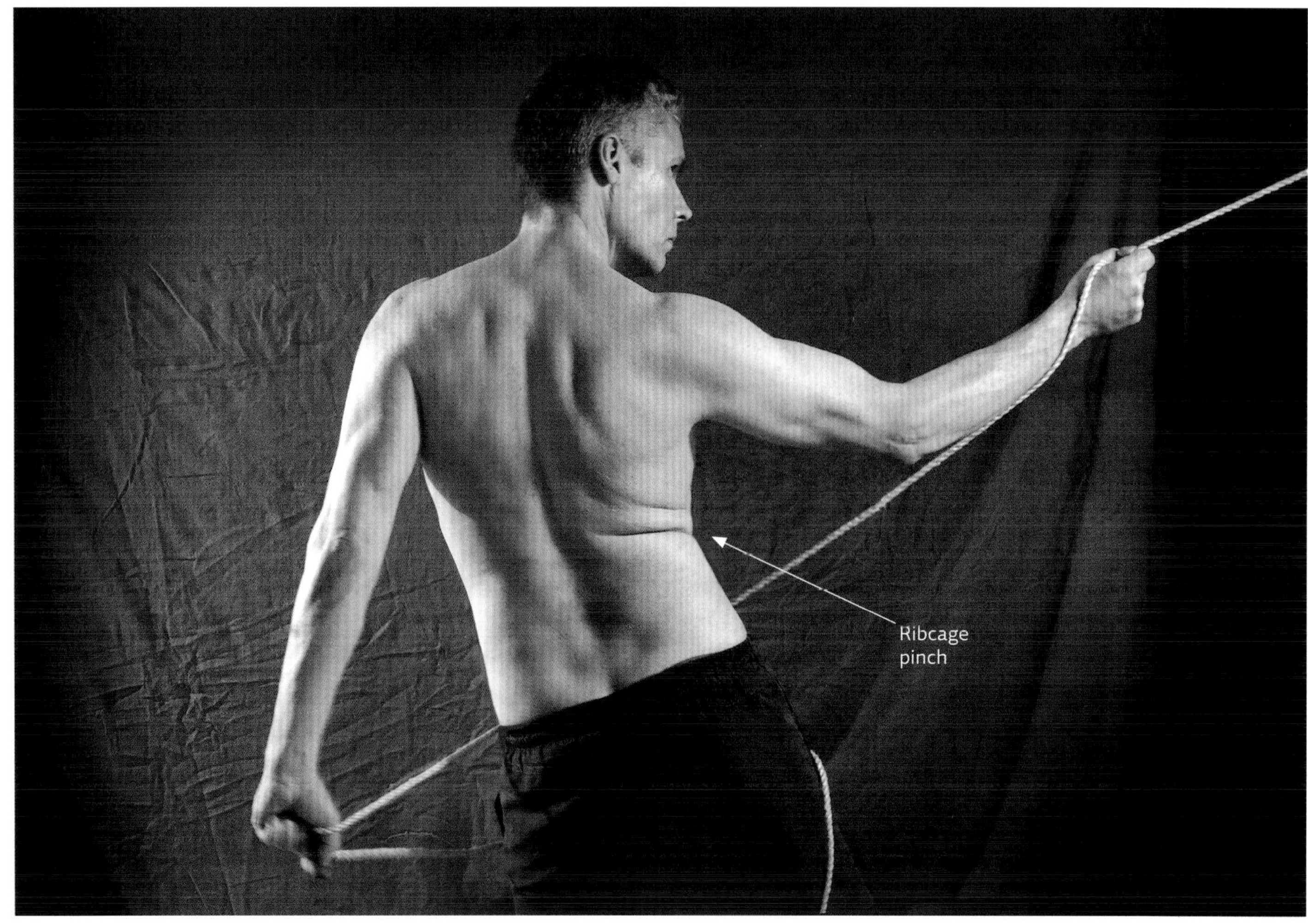

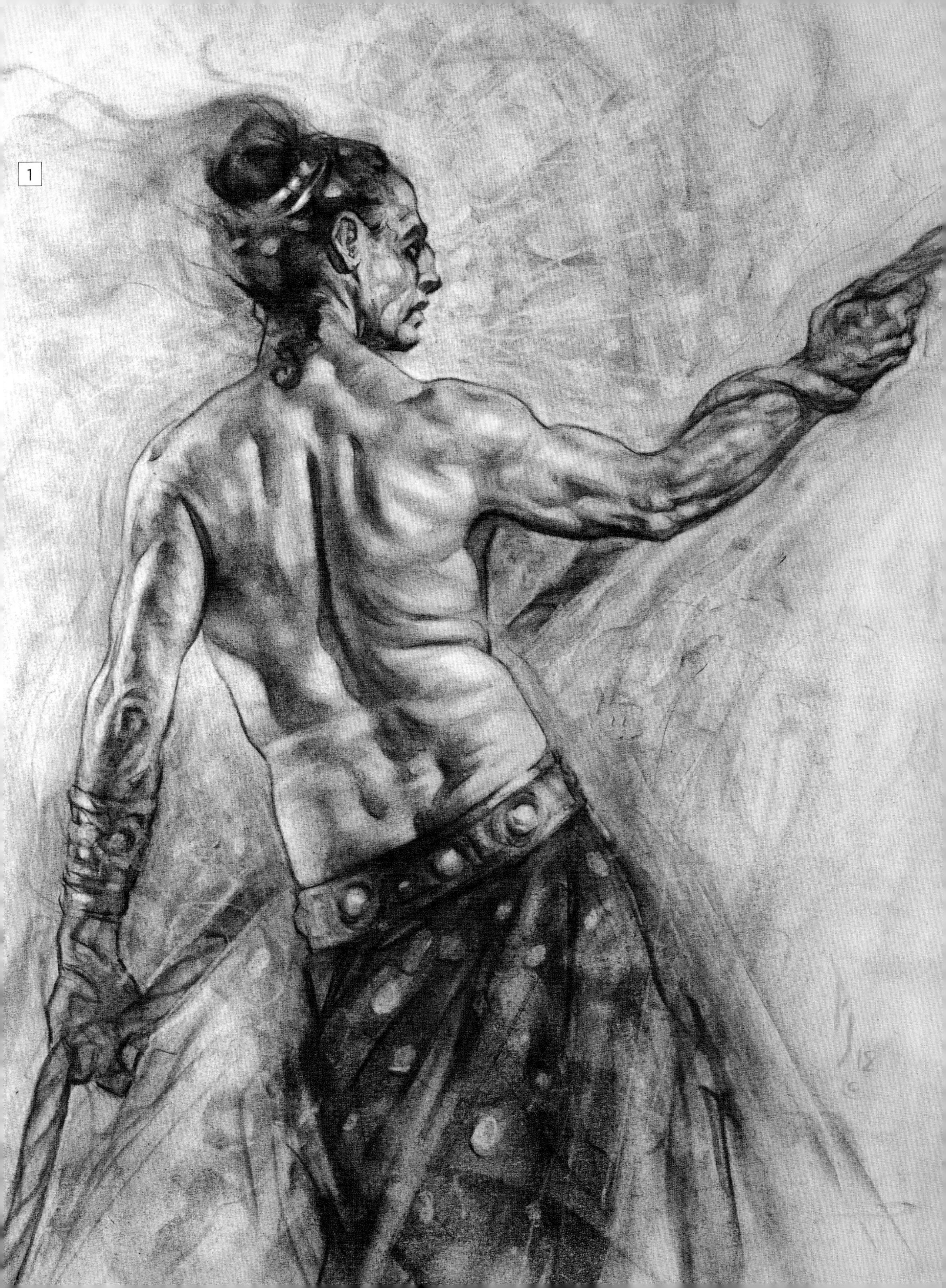

1

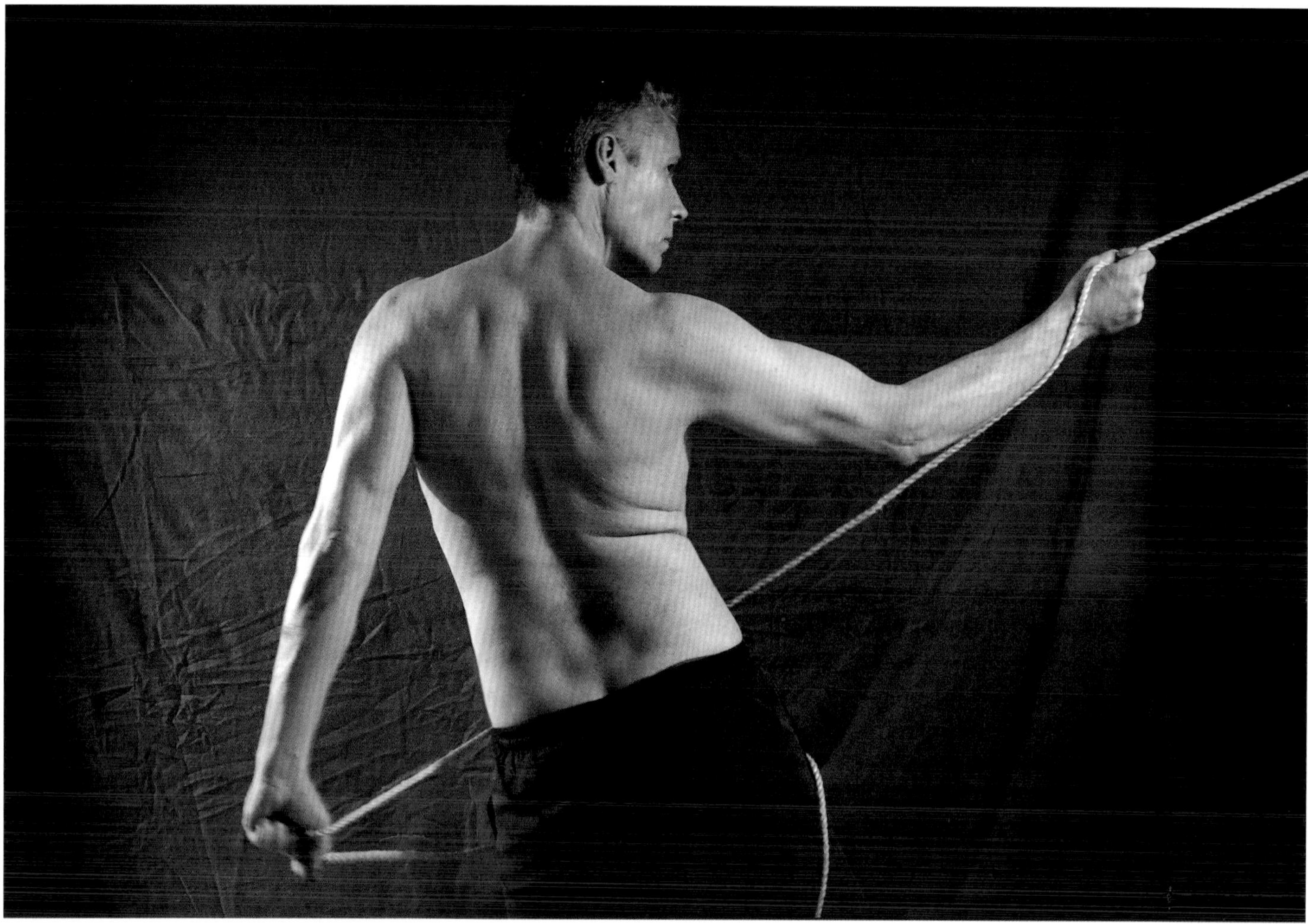

1 · The Spectre of Doubt   **2 · An Old Adage**

· An Old Adage

Using my two-finger wide sharpened charcoal piece, I draw in the simple shapes. The male figure is notoriously "blocky", and therefore I need to find as much gesture as I can. By finding simplicity, we can uncover gesture, even in blocks. All is going well here as I did a few warm-up gesture drawings beforehand, which loosened some of the rust. But in the back of my mind lurks the spectre of doubt. The art is due for submission by the end of the day, so I only have one go at this. I already feel I'm not on my game, and so the seeds of ego are also sown.

I work on the "pinched" side of the body first as the distance between forms is shorter and easier to judge than on the wider and longer "stretch" side of the body. This is an invaluable tip I learned from master draughtsman Steve Huston. How could I have missed this simple technique after years of drawing and painting? It reminds me of the old adage "We should never graduate from drawing".

As usual, I'm working with simple shapes first, to deal more easily with the complexities ahead. I can feel the head is too small, but as this is a heroic pose, I lean towards the smaller head and know the addition of hair will visually enlarge the cranium. So, I'm not too concerned.

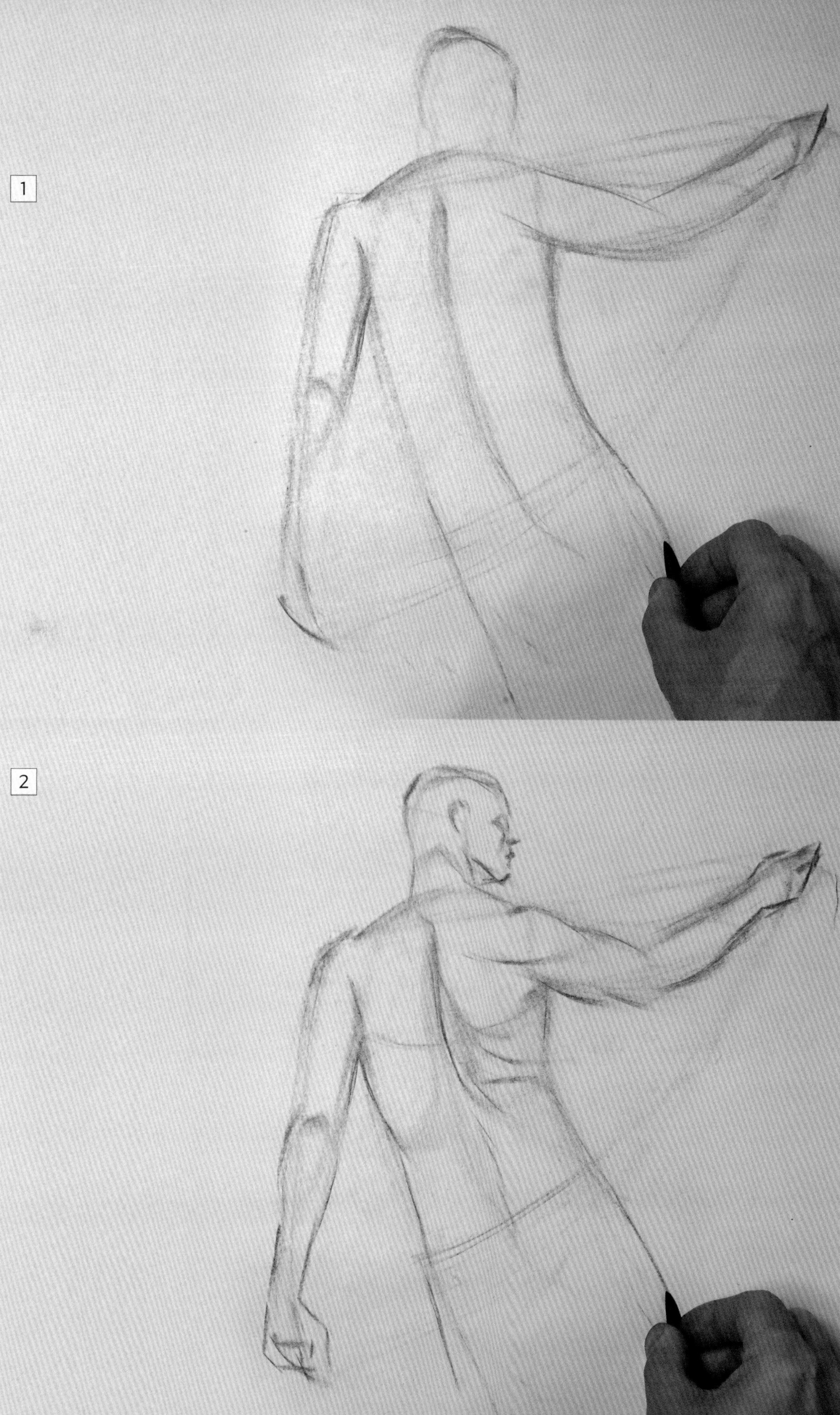

1
2

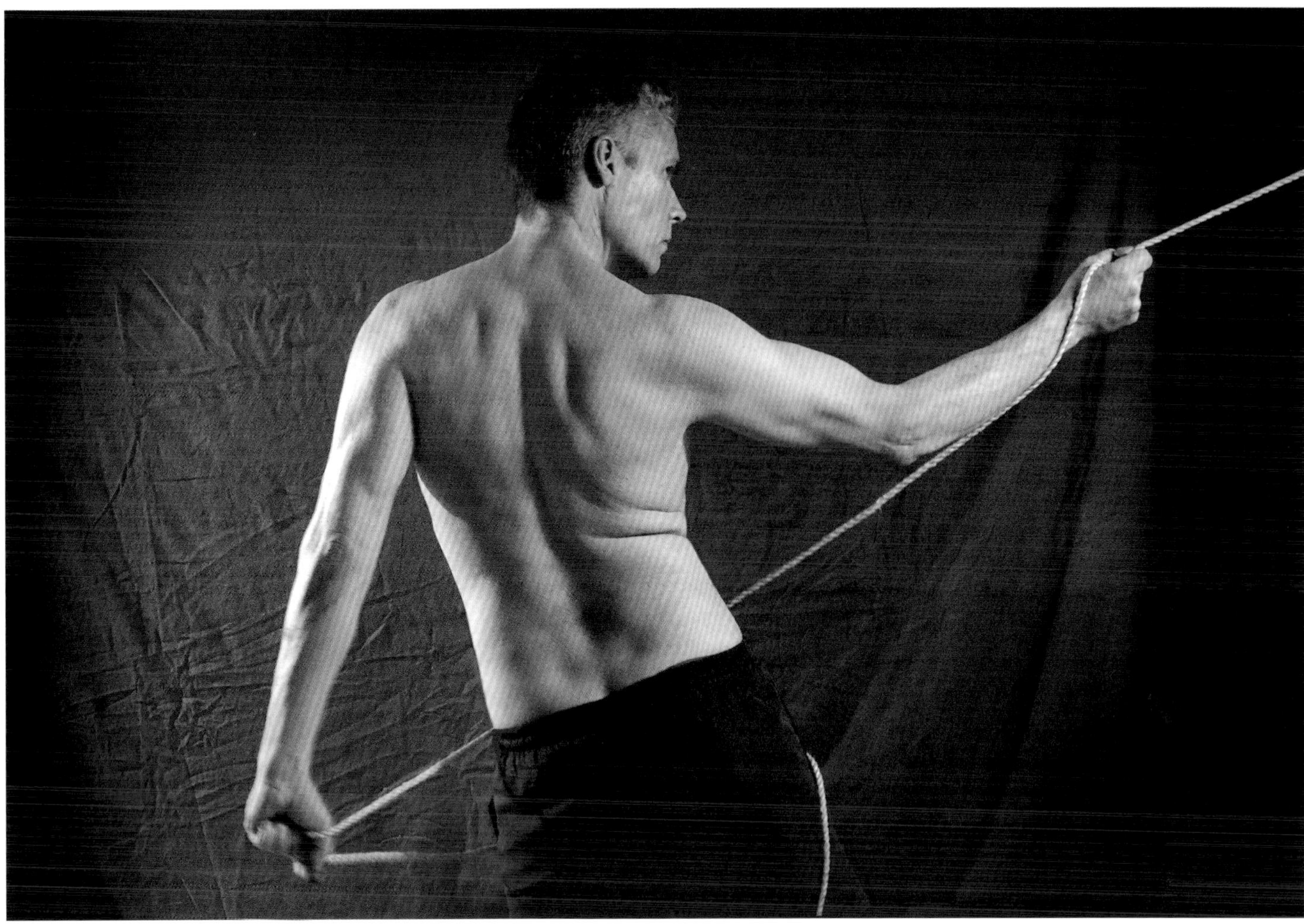

3 · Time to Dance

Gesture is king. If we work only with structure in mind, our drawings will be stiff. Keep lines long and loose whenever possible. With the block-in stage mostly complete, I once again employ the help of gesture to regain some fluidity. By working from one muscle to another, it becomes apparent they share similar shapes at their borders. It's time to dance, time to chase the rhythms of muscle and flesh.

Working with gesture has relieved some of the doubt, and for a while, I ride the crest of a wave. However, I've sailed by without properly examining the reference, which in this case is not badly distorted, and have drawn the upper right arm too short, which makes the left arm seem overly long by contrast.

The reason? I've fallen for one of the most ridiculous rookie errors, which is to try to fit the image onto the page regardless, in the hope of fixing any shortcomings later. The raised arm is too short, but there is no page left to make it longer! I'm embarrassed even to admit it, but there it is.

With this major error identified I would normally stop the drawing, get a new sheet of paper and start again. However, I'm not in my right mind here, for in the background, a camera was also rolling, recording the drawing as a movie, which was part of the commission. There was too much going on, and I was running out of time. Pressure is not a friend of the artist.

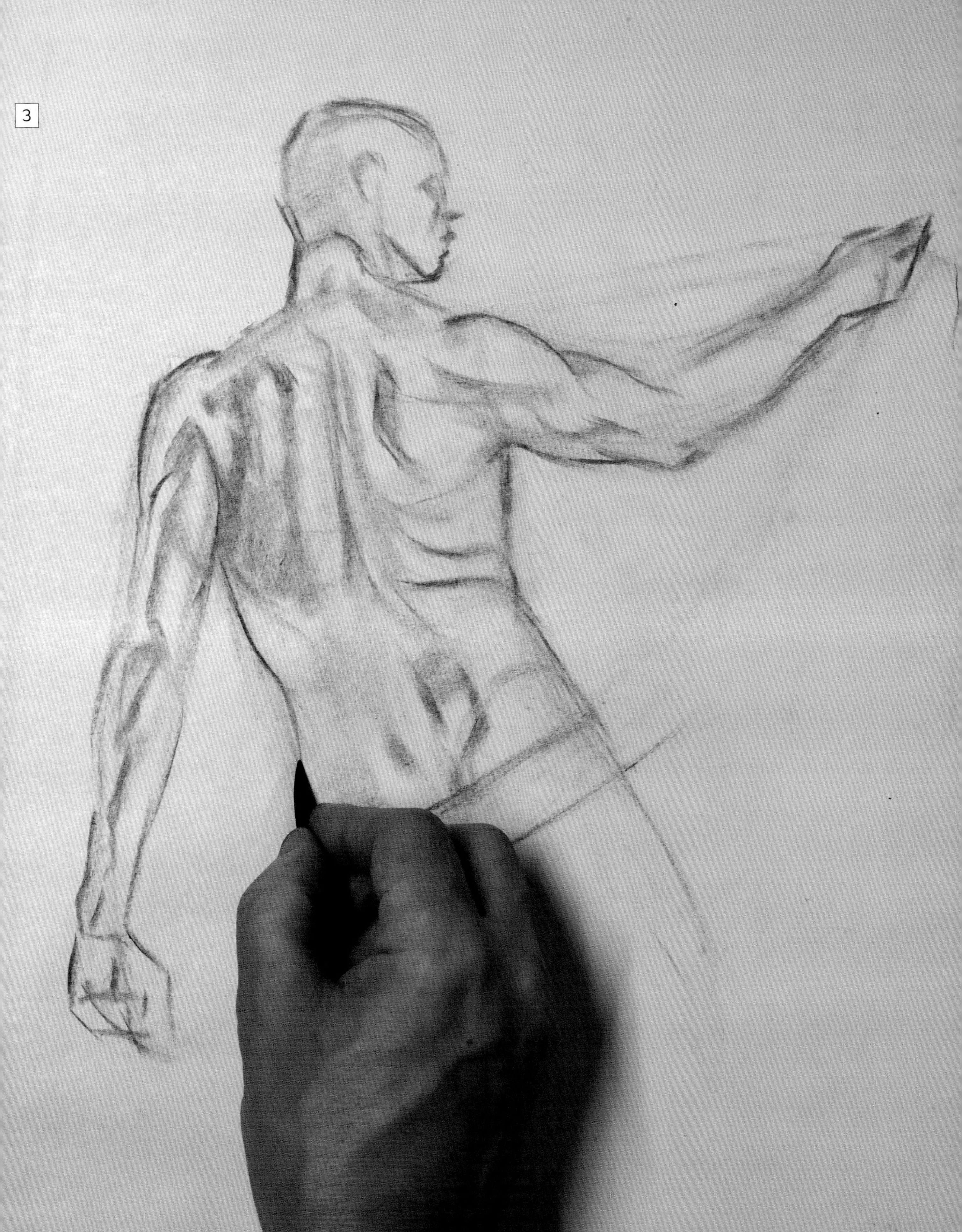
3

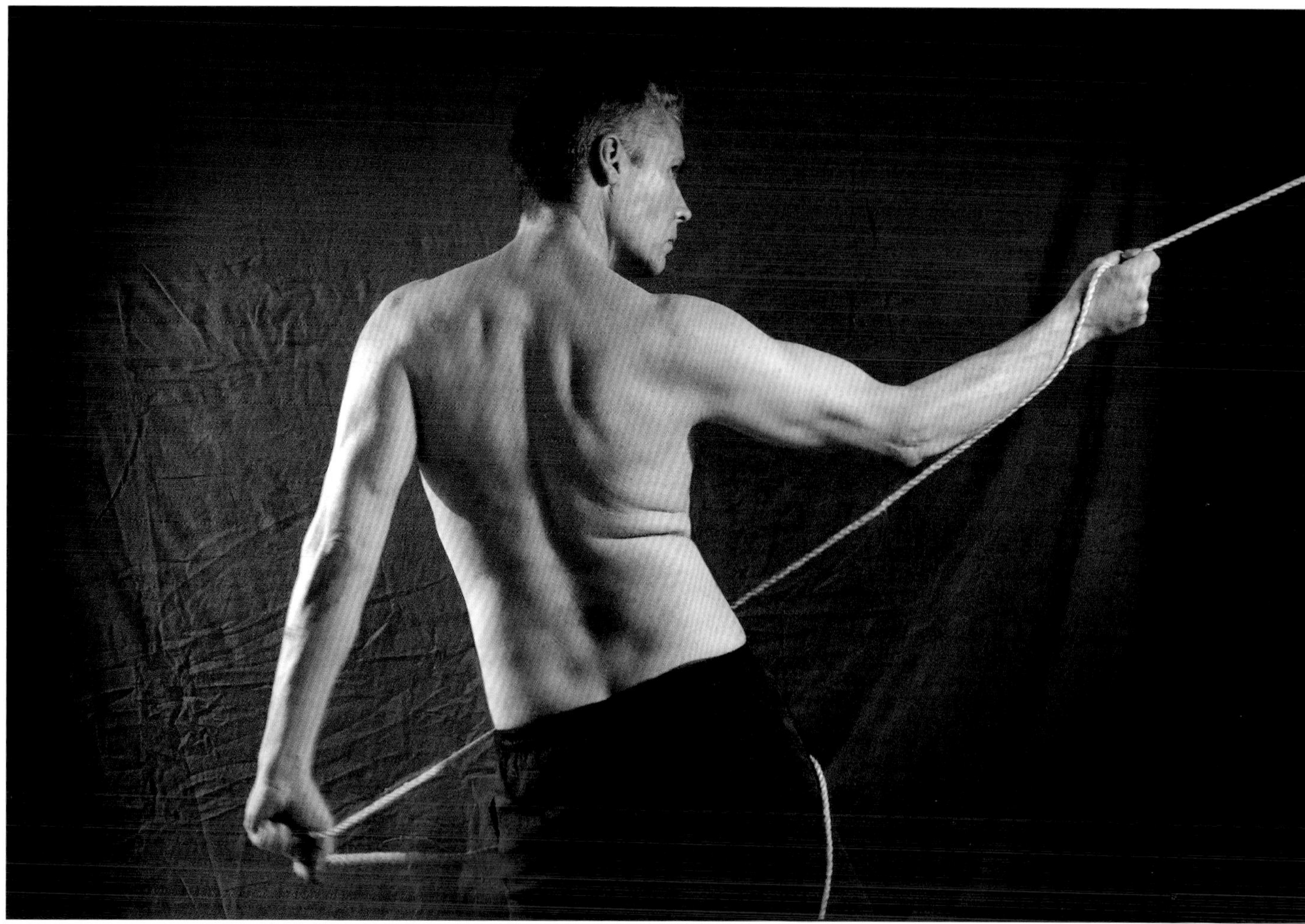

4 · To the Ends of the Earth

I put the short arm problem in my subconscious for now and work down the left arm, continuing my rhythmic dance by drawing from one side to the other. Note the natural flow of things – how the forearm bulges are higher on the outside, much like the calves of the legs. I'm chasing rhythms again: left to right as usual, but also high to low. All great methods that would typically see me through, but that arm isn't going to fix itself and it's constantly on my mind.

This is a rare occasion where the photo is more successful than the drawing. Having been a merchant seaman as a young man, it was easy for me to harness the adventure of those incredible years. Brief as they were in the scale of my life, they contained a lifetime of experience and exposed me to the tropics, the Arctic, and cultures far and wide – literally to the ends of the Earth.

The reason I've back-lit this photo, which is unusual for me, is to recreate the glow of moonlight on the horizon – at sea, night time is one of the most atmospheric and beautiful periods. The ability to light a night scene during the day makes a camera a remarkable asset for artists.

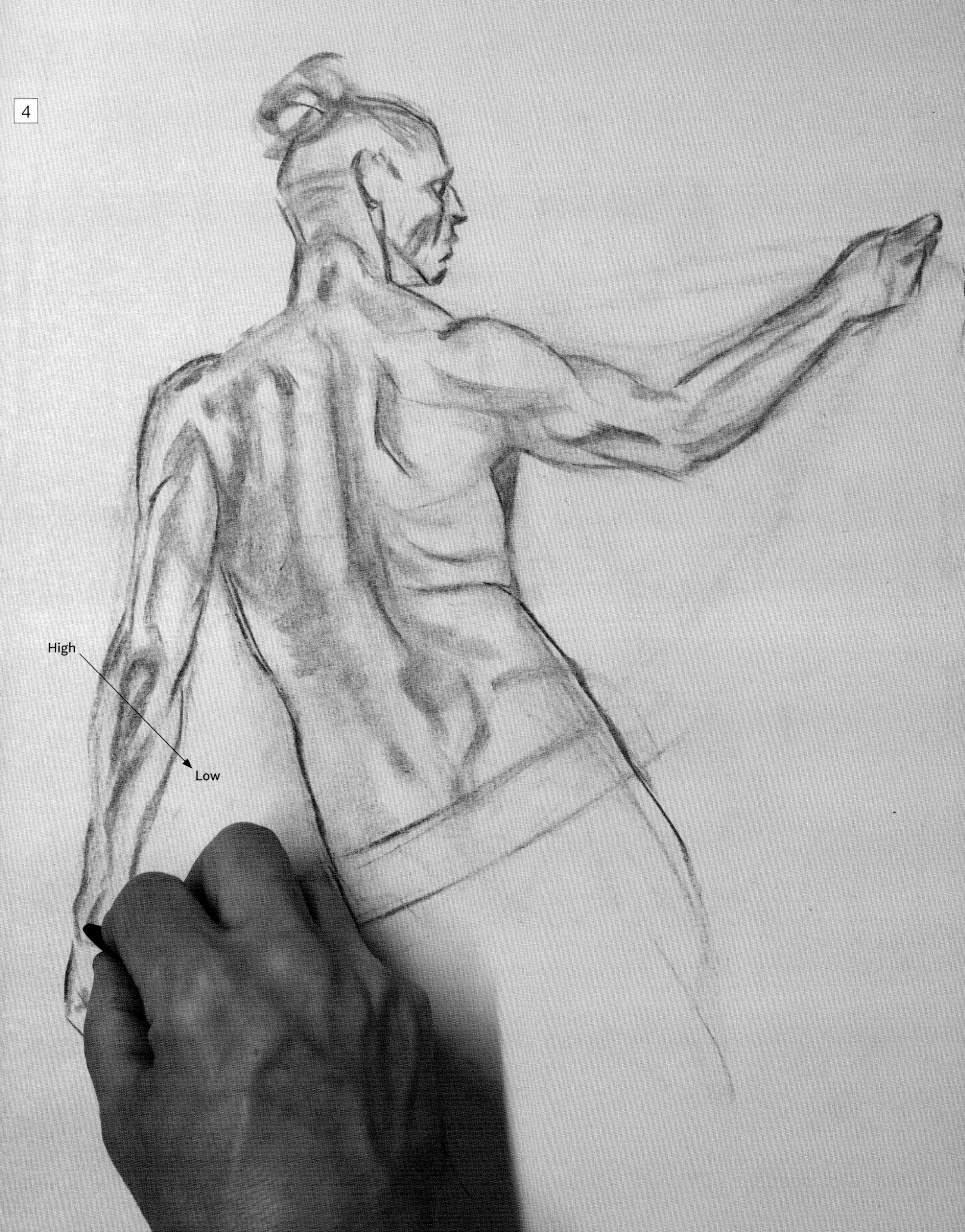

4
High
Low

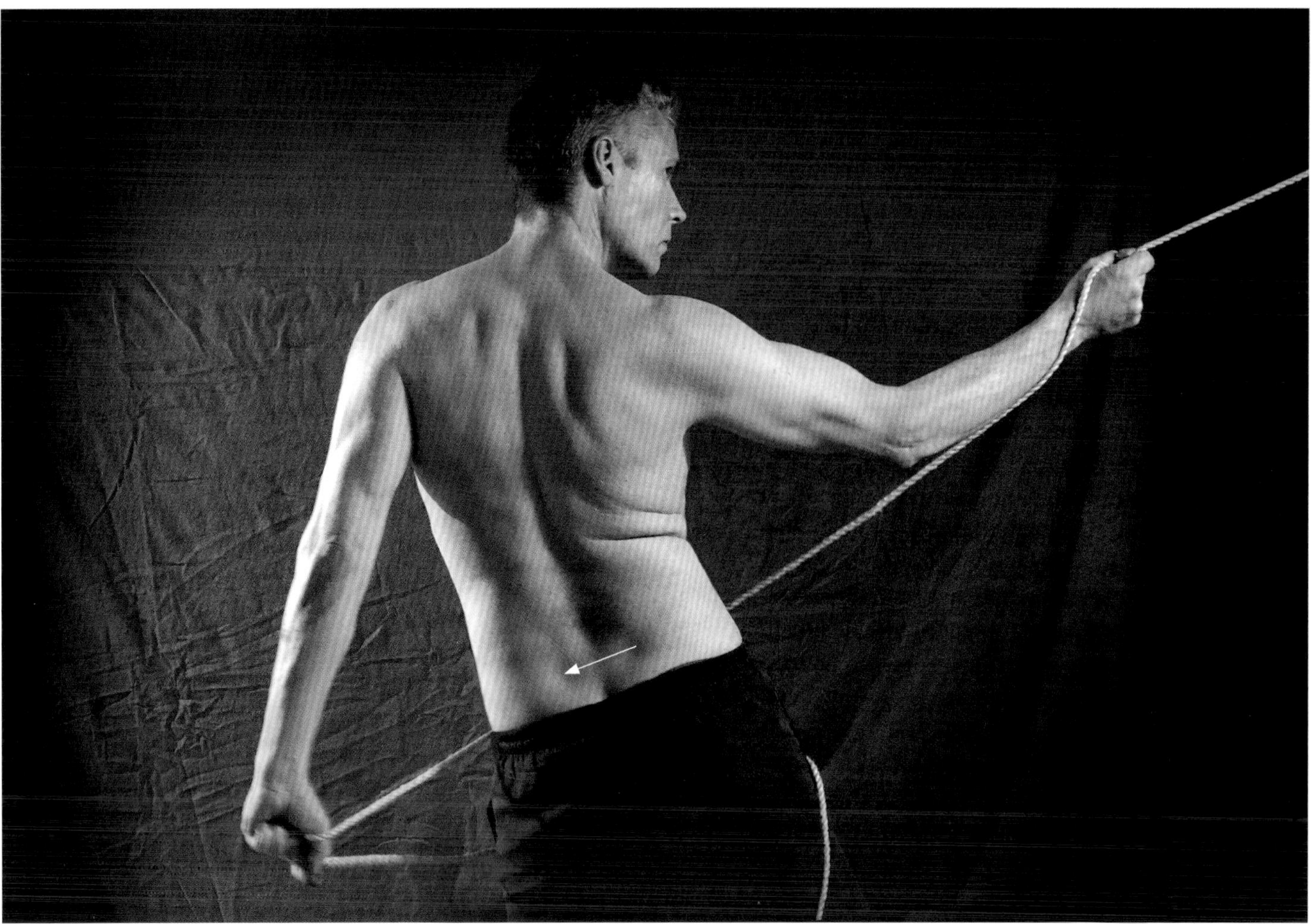

5 · Echoes of Rhythm

I title the art after a haunting duet from Bizet's opera *The Pearl Fishers* remembered from my childhood. To get into the mood, I play the music as I work and find it a great motivator, with its similar echoes of rhythm and gesture.

I add a broad belt to echo the tilt of the hips. Note how the sacrum dimples above the shorts dictate the tilt. On a nude model, we can use the dimples as an indicator for tilting belts or imaginary clothing by tracing a line through them. As the hips are fused, these dimples will always line up.

6 · The Shame

With the rhythms taken care of, I dust the drawing back with tissue in order to get a softer undercoat out of which to work the darks and lights. I begin rendering the forearm and work up into the upper arm, rendering with the same rhythm as before. To my deepest shame, I'm relying on render here to trick the eye into believing the arm is correct in its proportions.

Therein lies the problem with rendering from photographic sources. When we see lots of detail, we lose sight of proportion within photo distortion. We simply accept that all is well because it looks "realisic". I know this, and here I reverse my usual method of fixing distortion, using my powers for evil rather than good.

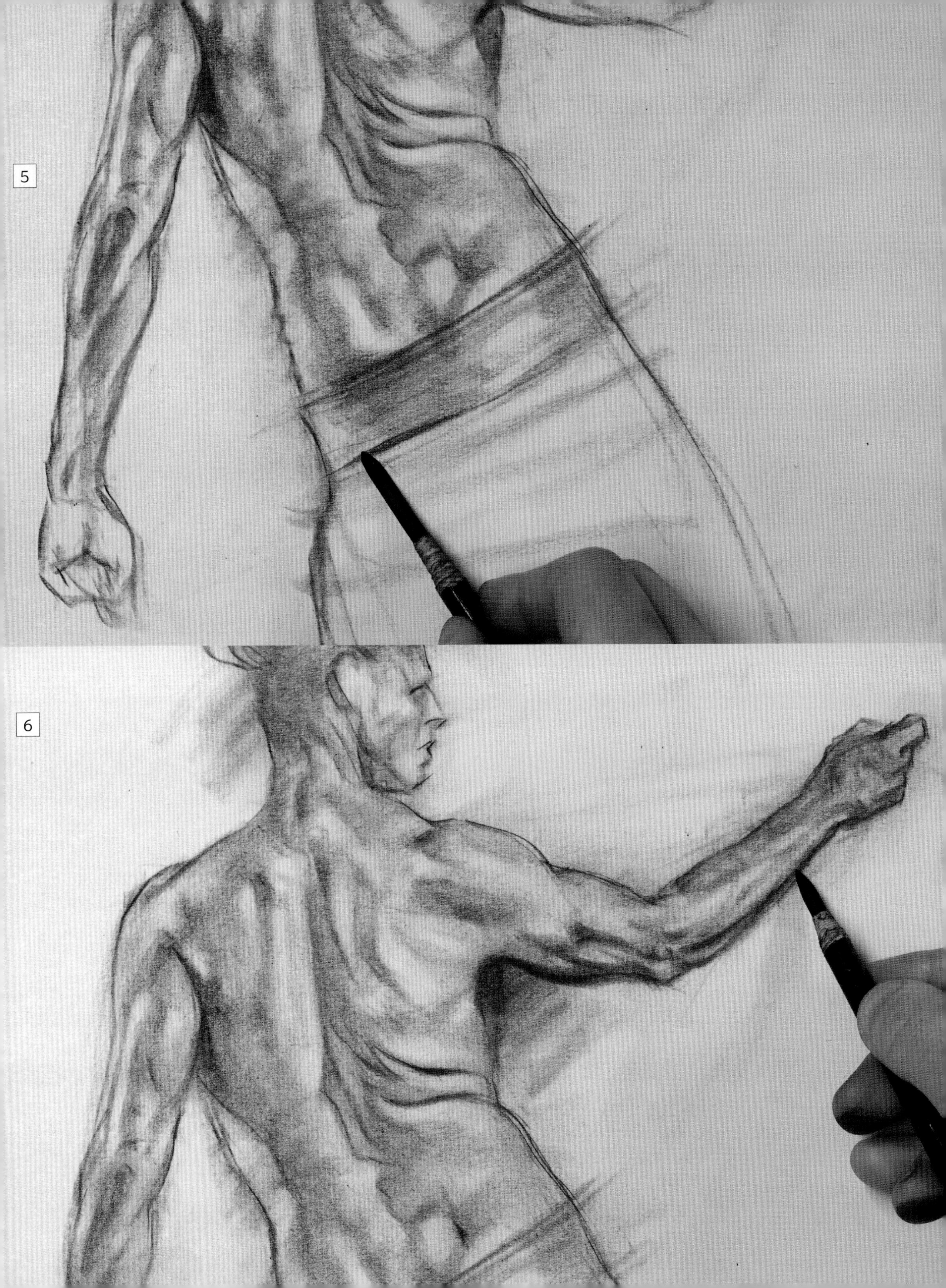

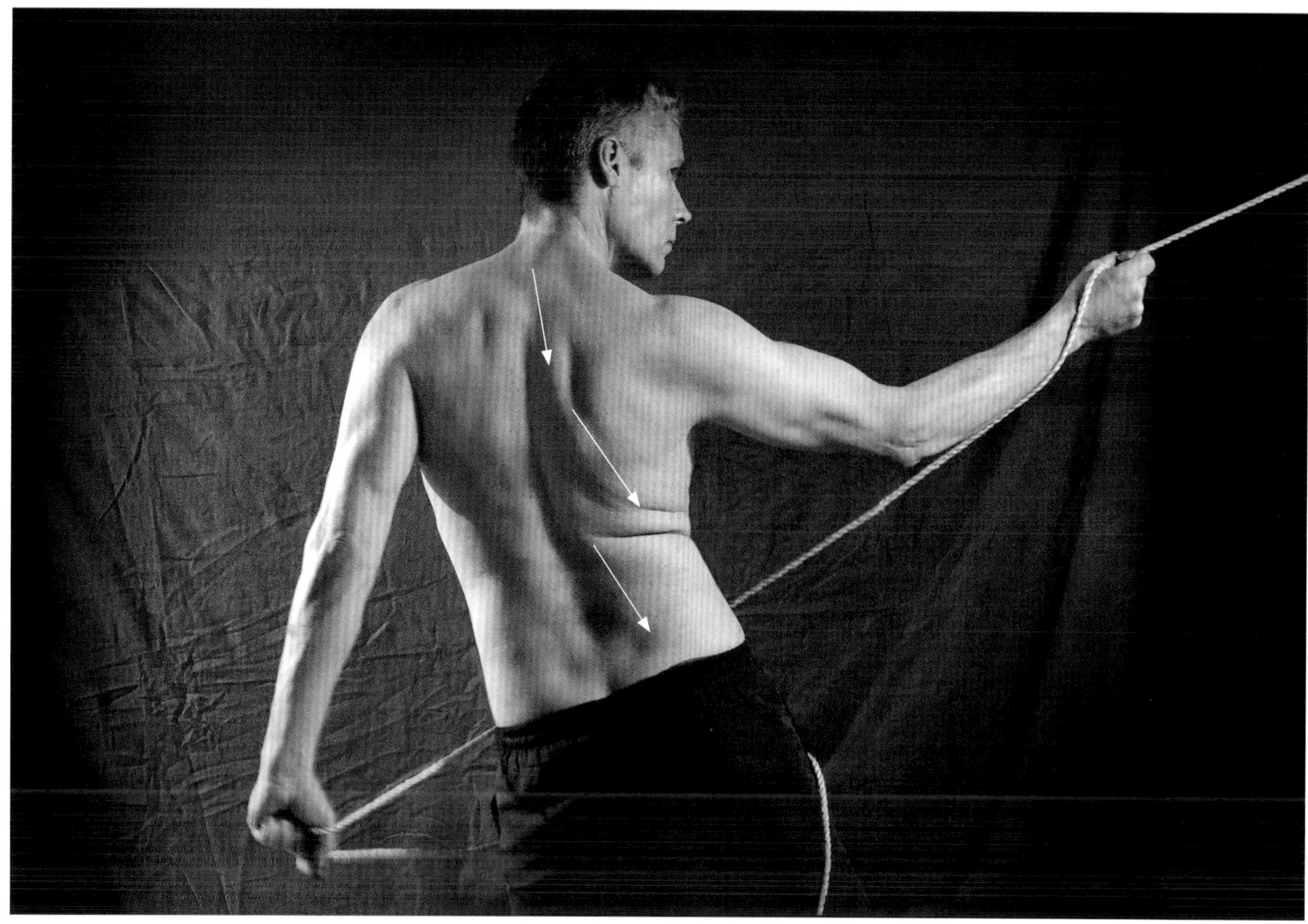

7 · The Language of Rhythm

Laying in the darks reveals the nature of muscles pushing into flesh to create ripples. See how the scapula pushes into the rhomboid muscles, creating wave-like echoes all the way down the spine to the sacrum dimples of the hips. All this poetry leads me to draw a sensitive face; such is the power and language of rhythm. The figure is at its best at this stage, but because my ego is dented, I decide to continue, playing the hero who can still win this fight. This reminds me of one of my mantras: leave your ego at the art studio door (you can always pick it back up on the way out).

8 · Render Hell

With the game afoot, I continue further into the depths of Render Hell. Having pulled back some confidence and a little dignity, I draw a thicker rope than the anaemic one I posed with in the reference. Thanks to my Merchant Navy days, I'm well aware of the kind of ropes used on a ship and how thick they can be. The drawing gains a mass of authenticity from that one thought.

My past life helps me rekindle the atmosphere of life on deck: the salty sea air and the way it adds moisture to the skin; the overly tanned forearms; the matted hair – it all comes back to me. All good, honest stuff, but I'm also using the thick rope to shorten the appearance of the forearm, which is less honest.

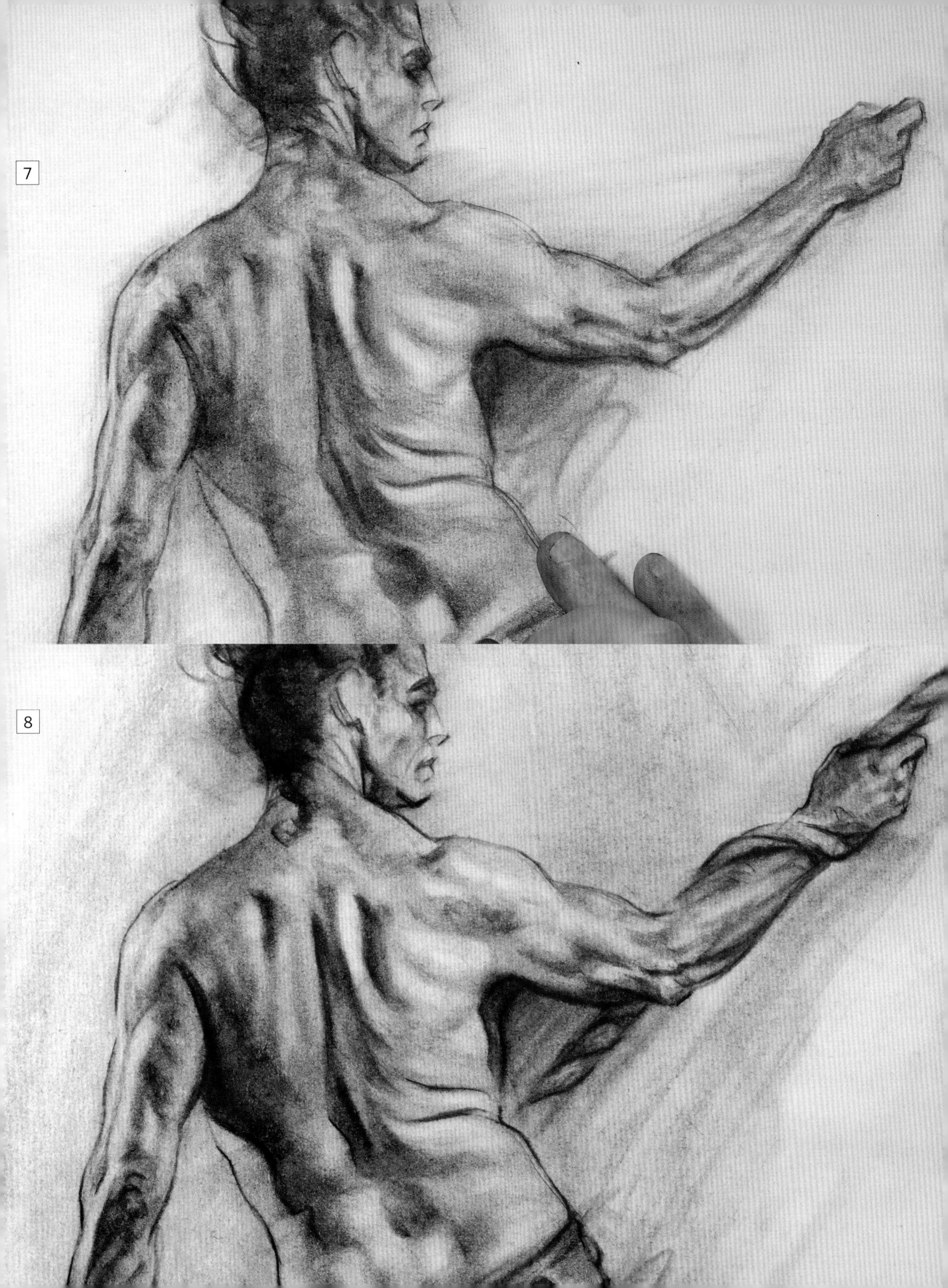

7
8

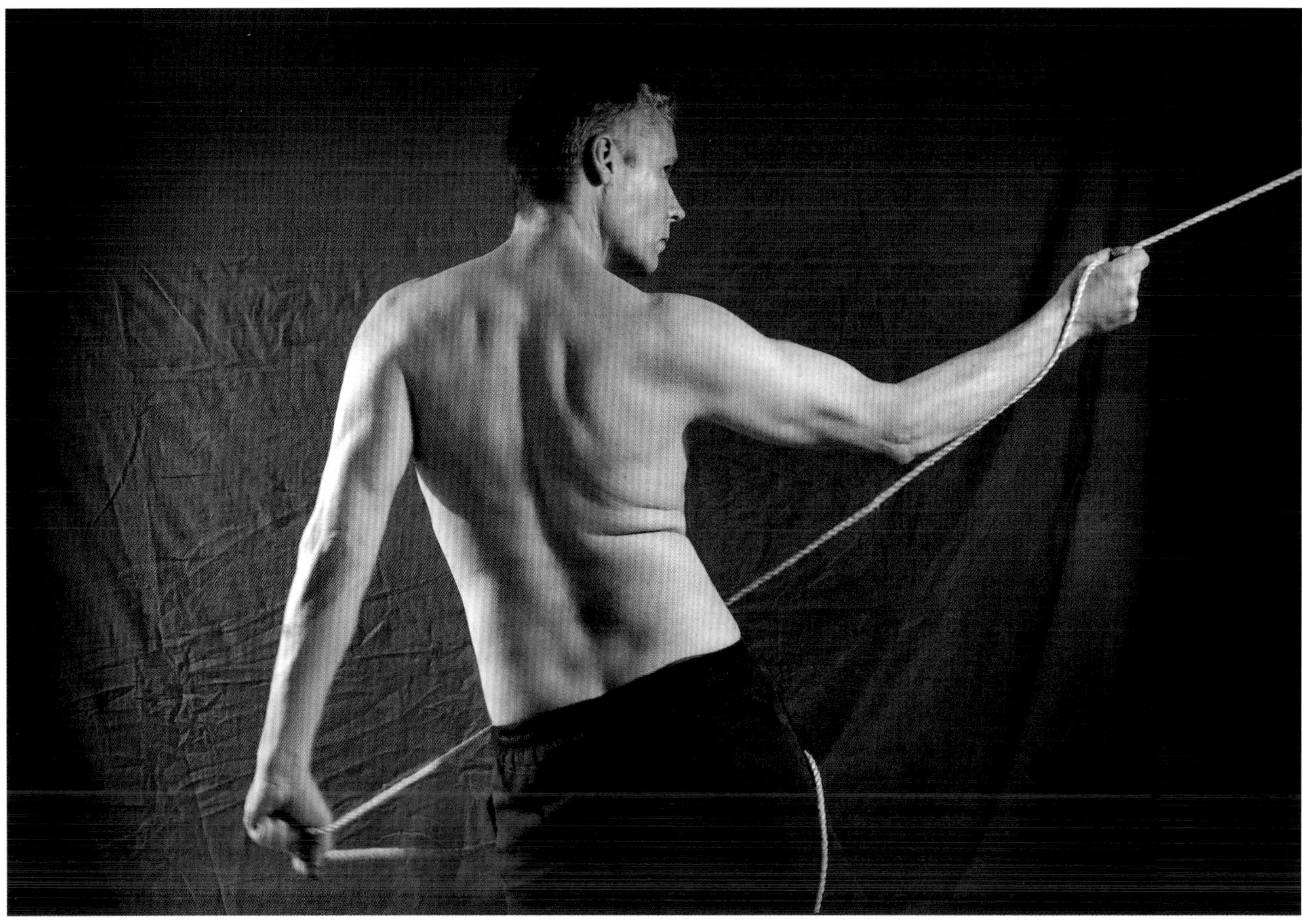

9 · The Depths of Hell

Drawing the arm bracelet leads me into a stiff corner, and the depths of Render Hell. I break out a piece of compressed charcoal and engage my gestural hand again. I also add some abstract shapes in the background with willow charcoal for added movement. Normally, a textured background will help bring a figure forwards and make the flesh look more fleshy by contrast, but here it simply highlights the too-short arm.

Looking back at the previous stage, we can see that the white background made the arm seem longer due to the amount of space behind it; this demonstrates the law of relationships and how it affects our perceptions – for example, dark clothes making us appear slimmer. The texture also makes the outreaching nature of the arm seem less distanced.

Adding a metal hair ring and a row of bolts to the belt creates additional exotic elements and more movement, but the chimes of doom cannot be quelled. At this point, I've pretty much conceded that the drawing is a magnificent failure. But nothing kills creativity more than doubt, and so I blaze ahead regardless. Working broad strokes into the Polynesian lavalava sarong brings some hope of redemption, and also stokes my optimism that the drawing can still be saved. This is a perfect time to take a break, reassess the situation, and plan a strategy to escape this hell of my own making.

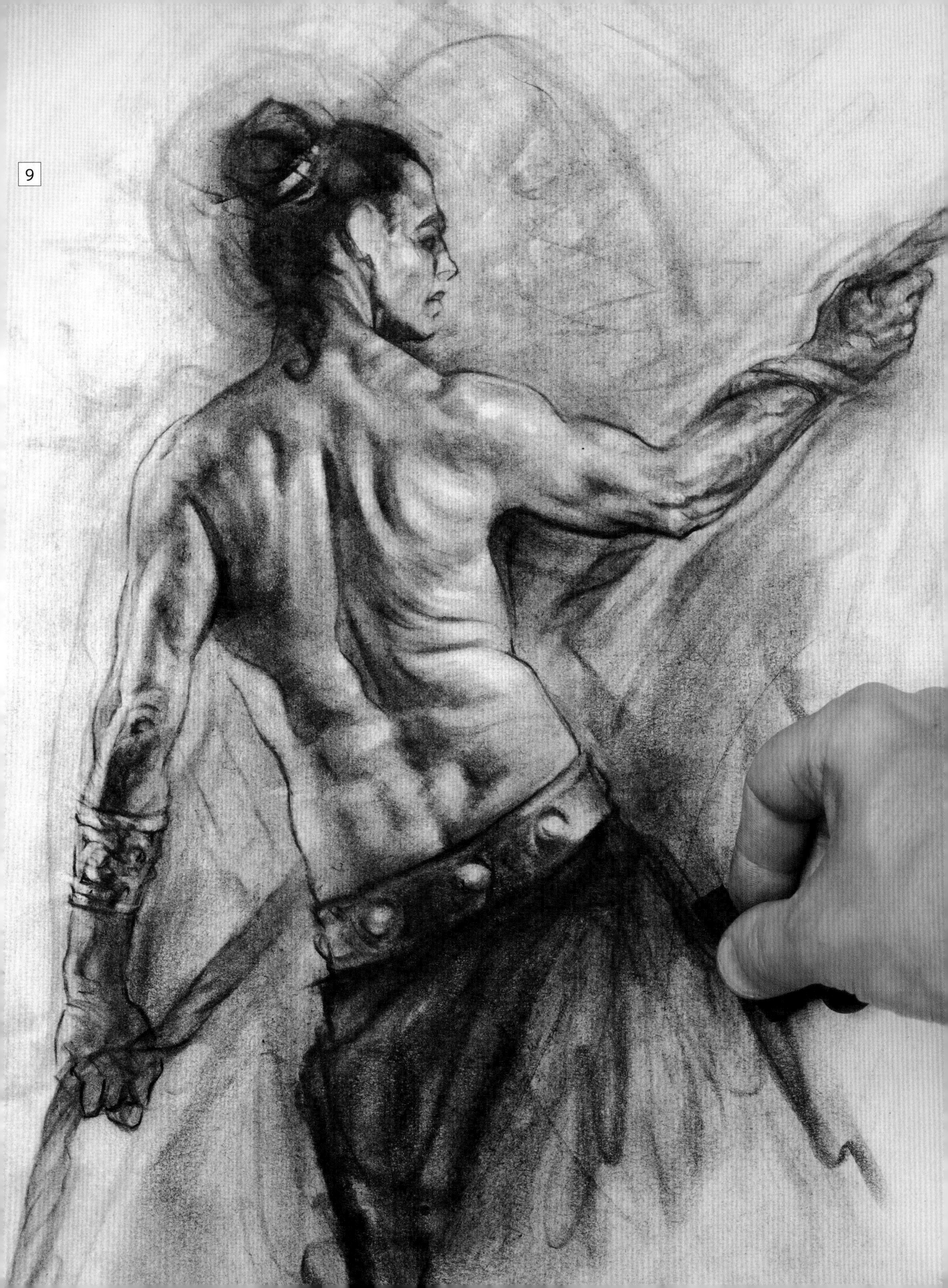
9

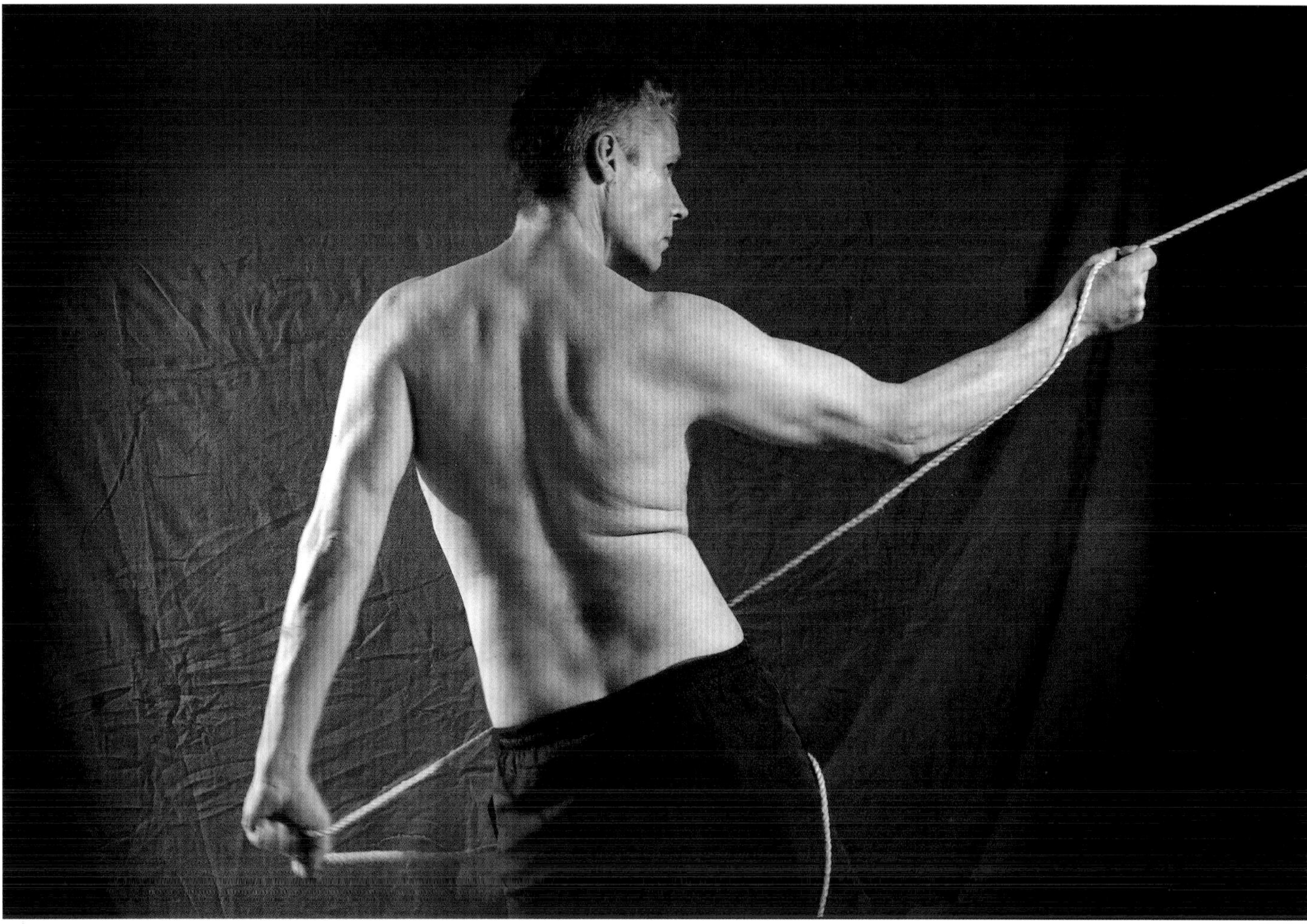

10 · The Beautiful Antagonist

I return to the drawing with renewed energy. If I may give myself one affirmation, it is my eternal optimism. If you lack optimism, then fake it until it becomes true inside. Tell yourself you are a magnificent artist as you draw, as there will be plenty of time during the break for critique. Of all the skills I've acquired, my optimism is my main strength; I credit my mother for this, as she displayed that trait in abundance.

I continue highlighting with erasers and detailing with pencils. Despite the shortness of the raised arm, I enjoy rendering the beautiful antagonistic nature of the triceps and biceps as they work in sync. The triceps are lengthening to allow the biceps to contract and shorten, and the opposite is happening on the straight arm.

The back-lit photo is my crutch now, and I cling to it for the much needed strength it provides. I work an oily sheen into the flesh by contrasting the darks and lights more. I add "gold" spots to the sarong with an eraser; this feels a touch feminine for a fisherman, but I like the spots too much to let them go. To counter this, I draw a rugged face. This is a more interesting face than the previous one, but it may not be an improvement as the head is now larger, making the arm appear shorter still.

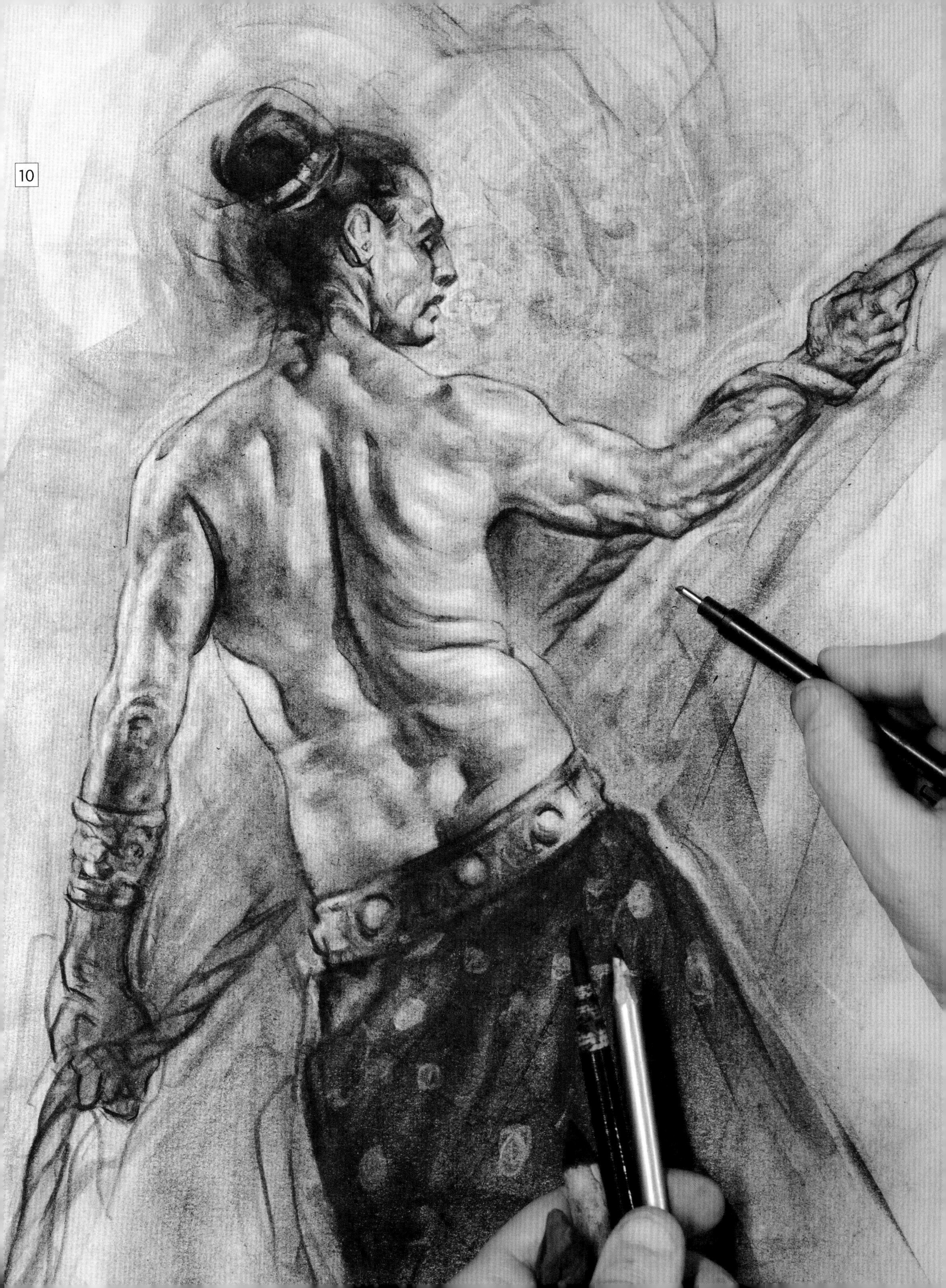

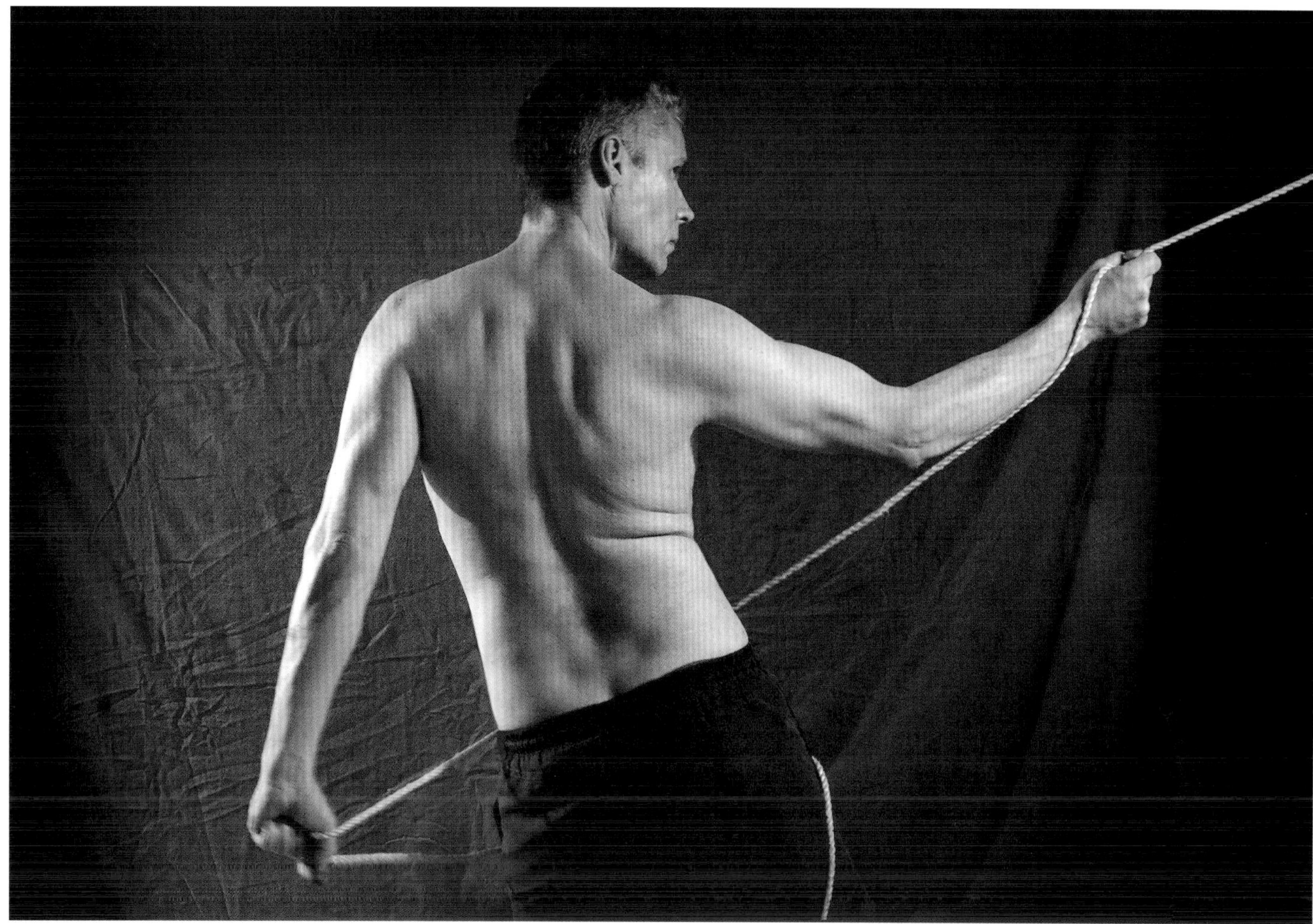

11 · An Old Dog

As I suspected, the continued rendering has killed a lot of the gestural energy of the earlier stages, and I counter it with further swirls of charcoal to express an abstract storm and windy rain. From this point onwards, I fight to regain my footing with a more scattered pattern of dots on the sarong and jangly gold to the head dressing.

The rendering and line work recover the drawing in some way, as all those hard-fought-for skills are on show. An old dog can put up one hell of a fight when it's cornered. To the average eye, this is now an adequate drawing, but it falls well below my original aim due to its proportional flaws. I continue past this point, to the result shown at the beginning of this workshop, to further flash more style around for my penance.

Earlier, when I referred to this as a "failed drawing", it was an attention-seeking call to arms, as there are no real failures in art, only learning experiences. If we don't experience "failure", then there is no moving forwards. Embrace the fear! Experimentation wins out when playing the long game of art, despite the pitfalls, and I'm all-in as far as the long game goes.

As with most longer studies, I'm left with a drawing more rendered than I would like, but for all its flaws, I've gained further knowledge of how muscles shapeshift and work together and have planted the knowledge into my subconscious art engine for future drawings.

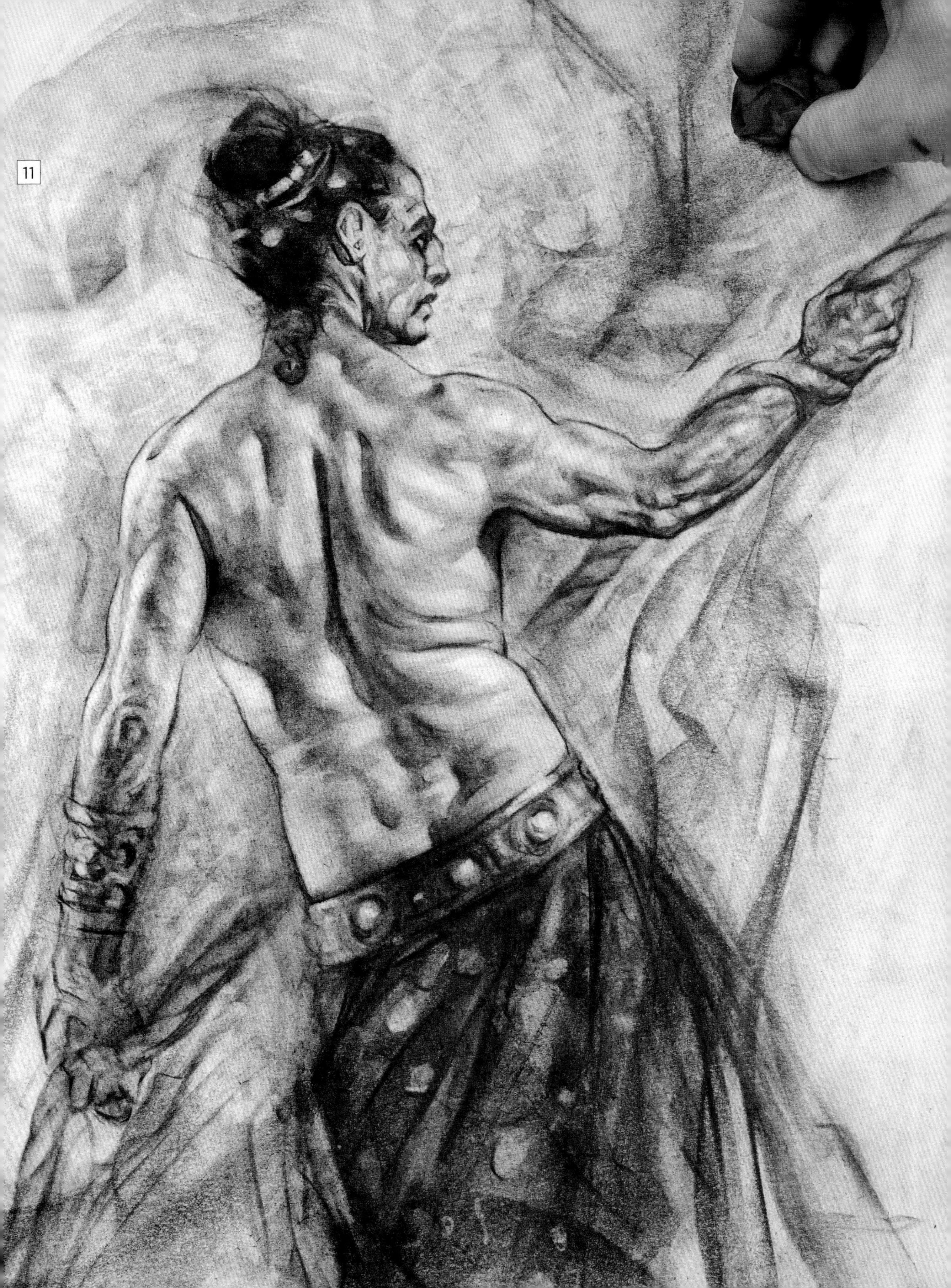

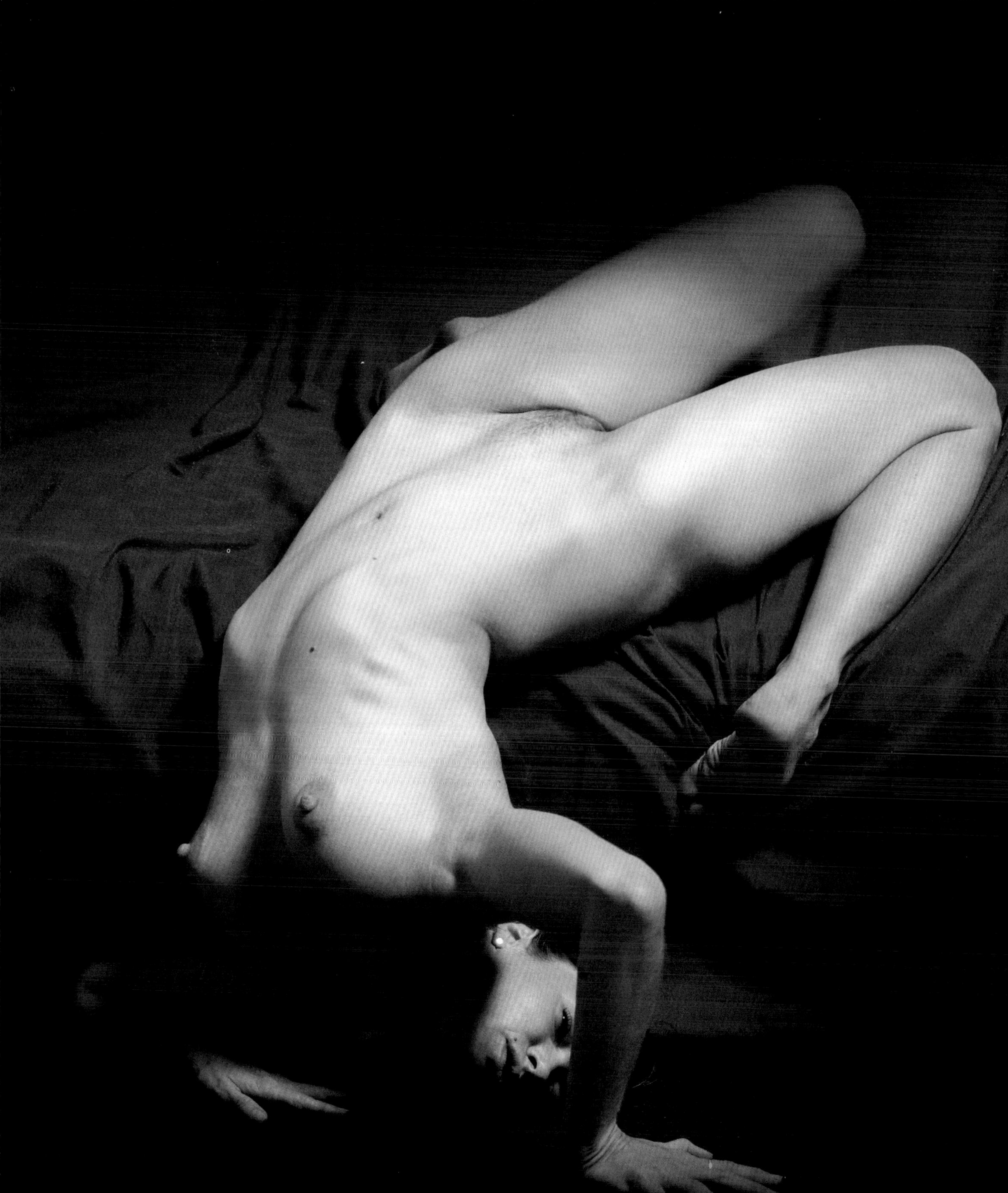

most essential and enduring in your life."

George Leonard (1923–2010)

THE PLATEAU

EVERY ONCE IN A WHILE, I meet up with two artist friends of mine, Richard Denham and Andrew Trimmer, to talk art. We are an art brotherhood in search of a name. On one occasion, they were both enthusing about a book by George Leonard called _Mastery: The Keys to Success and Long-Term Fulfillment_. That title would have had me swaying past the book in a store, as it sounds like a get-rich-quick kind of deal, but it turned out to be about discipline, particularly the discipline found in martial arts, and it touched on a buried weakness of mine: the will to surrender.

Surrendering to the discipline of practice was an echo from my past when I first surrendered to ego, which I will discuss further in this workshop. It became obvious that I had been working with these principles on a subconscious level for many years but, like a good psychiatrist, Mr Leonard made this clear to me in his book when he spoke of the "plateau".

What is a plateau, besides being a large area of high, flat land? In martial arts, it's the period of repetition needed to acquire a skilled move, one so fluid that it can be done instinctively, almost without thinking. In art, the plateau is often rushed as it's the period when we seem stuck in one place and are no longer learning anything new. With art, as in all skills, we need to practise repetition in order to master our medium – be it pencil, oils, or most of all, expressive mark-making. We need to surrender to the fact that this takes discipline and time.

Once we accept the discipline of practice, we experience an unexpected bonus: the joy of the plateau. The moment I learned to surrender and enjoy the learning experience, I realised what true art is – not the final destination but a lifetime of practising the process of art itself. By enjoying the practice of each new skill, I found myself always in the moment and never in pursuit of something else.

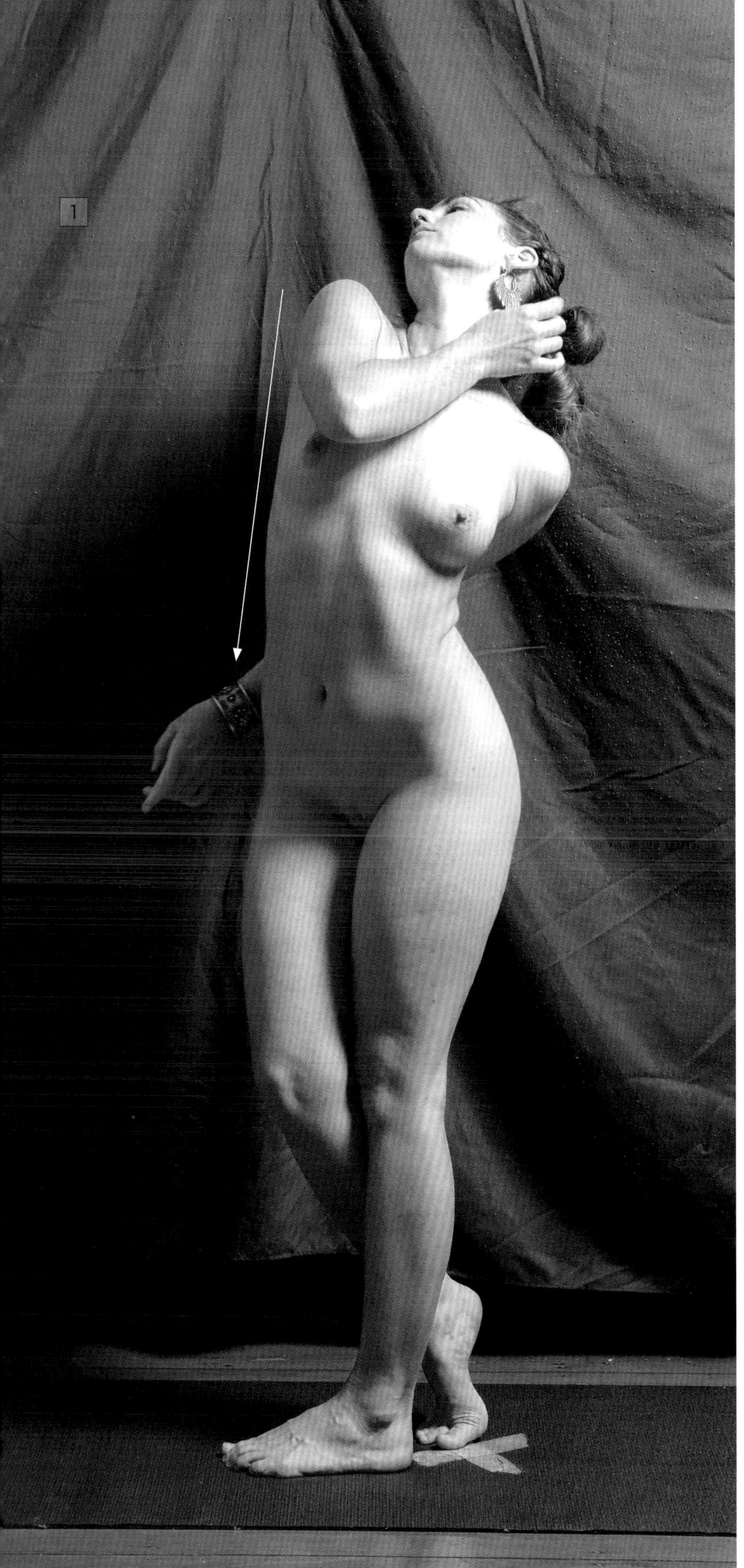

THE STORMBRINGER

Charcoal and pencil
on A2 newsprint

Today we will draw Katy while discussing the anatomy of style and the disciplines of art. As a young artist, I was driven by my love of art and my devotion to drawing. I believed that love and devotion were the only disciplines needed to scale each new wall and reach each new plateau, but one day, many years into my career, I realised that my taste in art had changed. I faced a colossal wall carved with the unforgiving words "Why are you unhappy?"

"I want to draw with more style and freedom," I replied. "What's stopping you?" the wall asked. "I'm a photo-realist. My work makes people gasp with admiration," I replied. "If I change now, I won't be as impressive."

"Then surrender your ego," the wall demanded. And in my silent surrender a giant wall toppled and I ascended to a new plateau.

I wrote down three words that would anchor me in future moments of doubt: Love, Devotion, and Surrender, and in doing so I changed everything.

Good fortune had gifted me the first two disciplines of love and devotion, yet the act of surrender proved difficult. In my quest for artistic freedom I was all over the place, painting and drawing, obsessed with high ambitions, leaving little time to practise each new skill. With this headless chicken approach my art seemed to get worse. I needed to slow down. I surrendered to the fact that true progression takes time, and honed my skills until I reached each new plateau. I learned once more that surrender could be a discipline. Art, I discovered, was not like anything else.

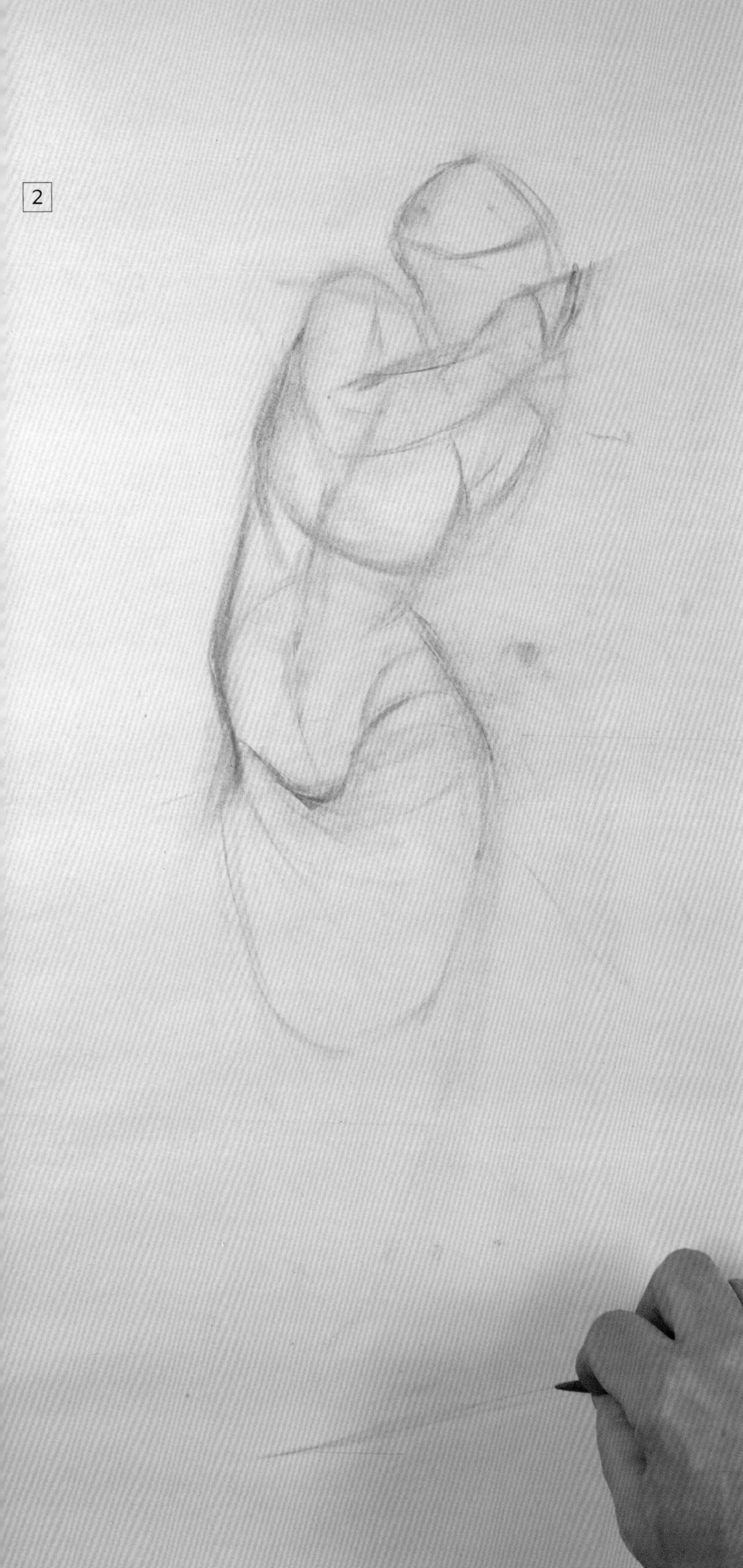

In the past when I art directed my models like mannequins, adjusting every finger and tilt to echo the sketch, I invariably ended up with stiff poses. I needed to surrender my ego once more and allow the model interpretive freedom. The fact that Katy's poses are so fluid is the result of her own artistic disciplines. The fact that I managed to harness this force of nature in a photo is the result of my discipline to surrender to Katy's interpretations.

1 · What's Wrong with this Photo?

Let's take a little time to praise the camera and its ability to capture a frozen moment of motion. If this pose were from life, Katy would start to flag and shift microscopically and would lose the energy found in the split second the photo was taken. Let's also study the problems with this photo. Firstly, Katy's left hand looks odd and it kills the rhythmic flow. Secondly, the stretch side of the body is almost a straight line. These are just the obvious problems, so I need to stay on high alert as I draw.

2 · Sweet Surrender

I start with the rhythmic flow of the figure, back and forth from one side to the other. I used to measure proportions with care, treating them with great reverence, but I ended up with dull drawings. Once I surrendered to rhythm more as my proportional guide, my drawings were no longer so "correct", but they were more interesting, gestural, and filled with life.

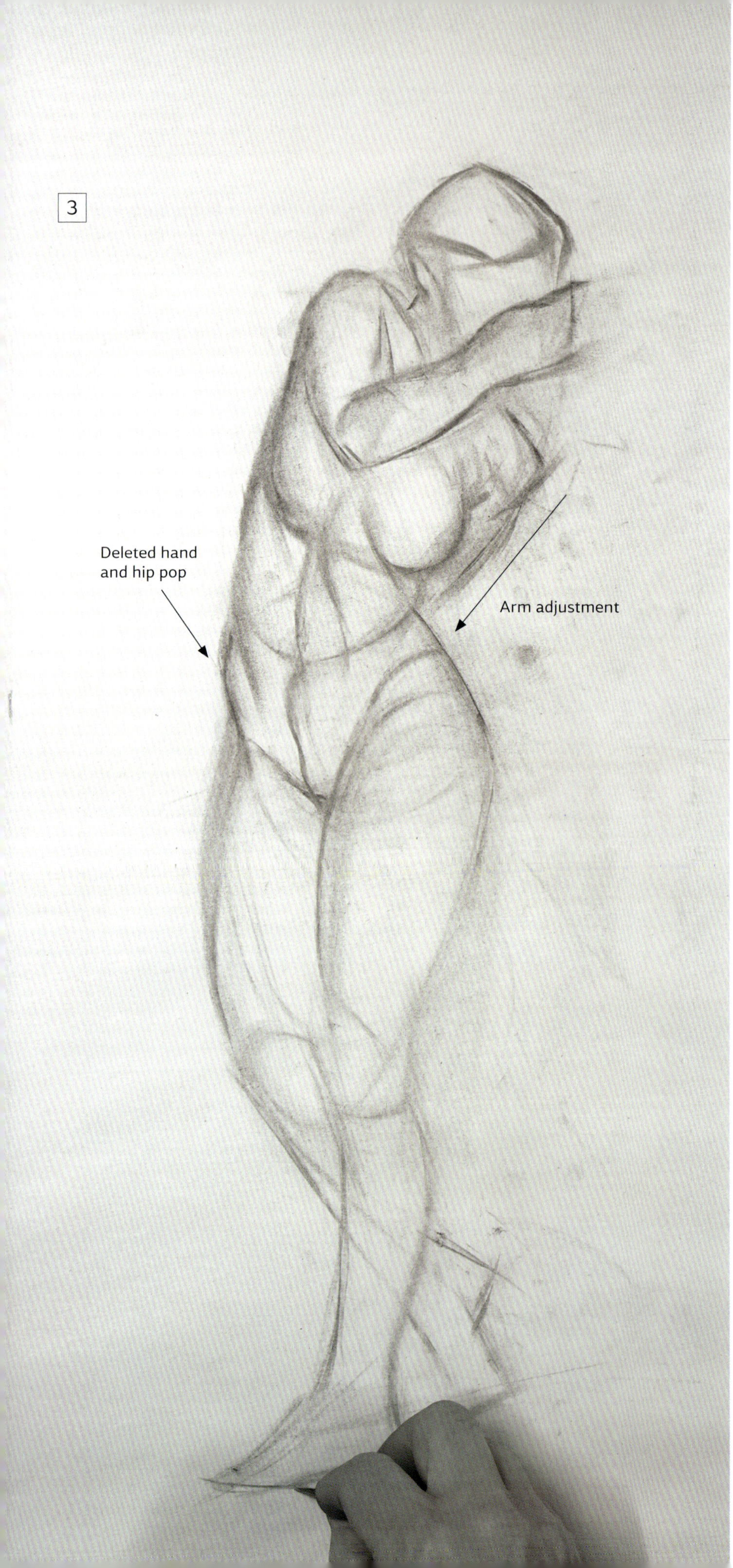

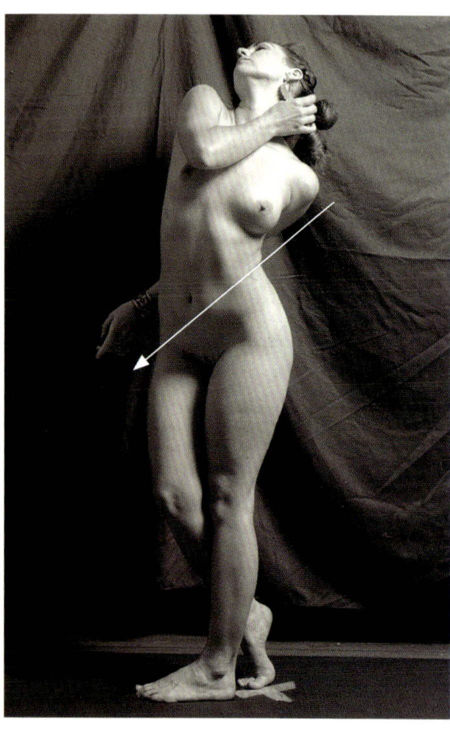

3 · The Lifeless Dummy

Here I've interpreted the photo reference towards the dynamic. The stretch side has more gesture due to the hip popping forwards more, with increased overlaps and undulations all the way down. I delete Katy's hand as it looks odd, like a lifeless dummy's hand. I've also dropped her left arm in order for the deleted hand to appear as if it's behind her back. Many hours of study committed to the love and devotion of craft have made possible this balance of gesture and structure.

4 · Play the Accordion

With the extra bend of the torso I make sure the pinch side is counterpoised with wider distances on the stretch side, like an accordion. Imagine a line through the nipples, rib pinch, and hip crests to see what I mean. At this stage I title the drawing *The Stormbringer*, which sets the mood to come.

The Accordion

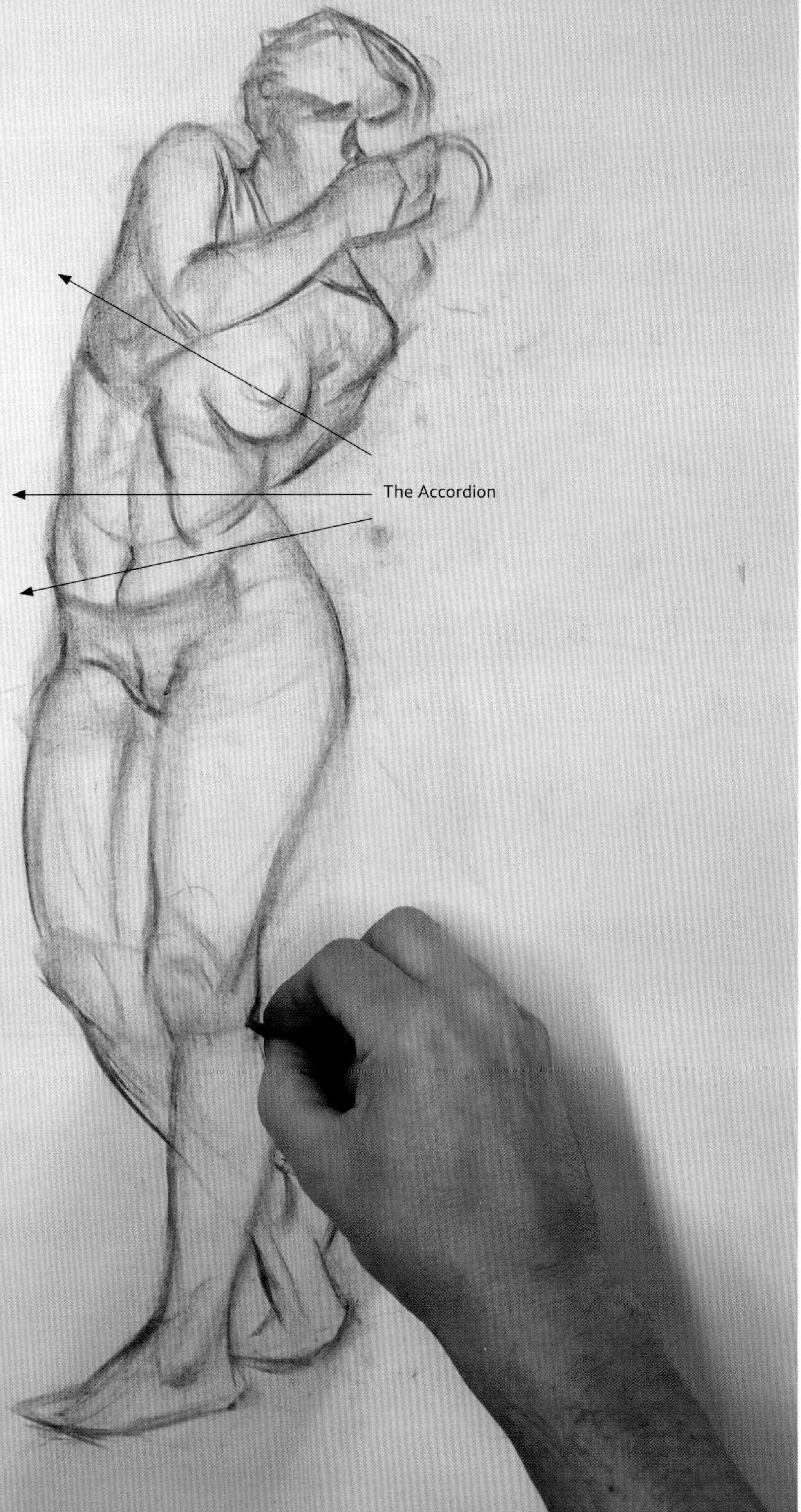

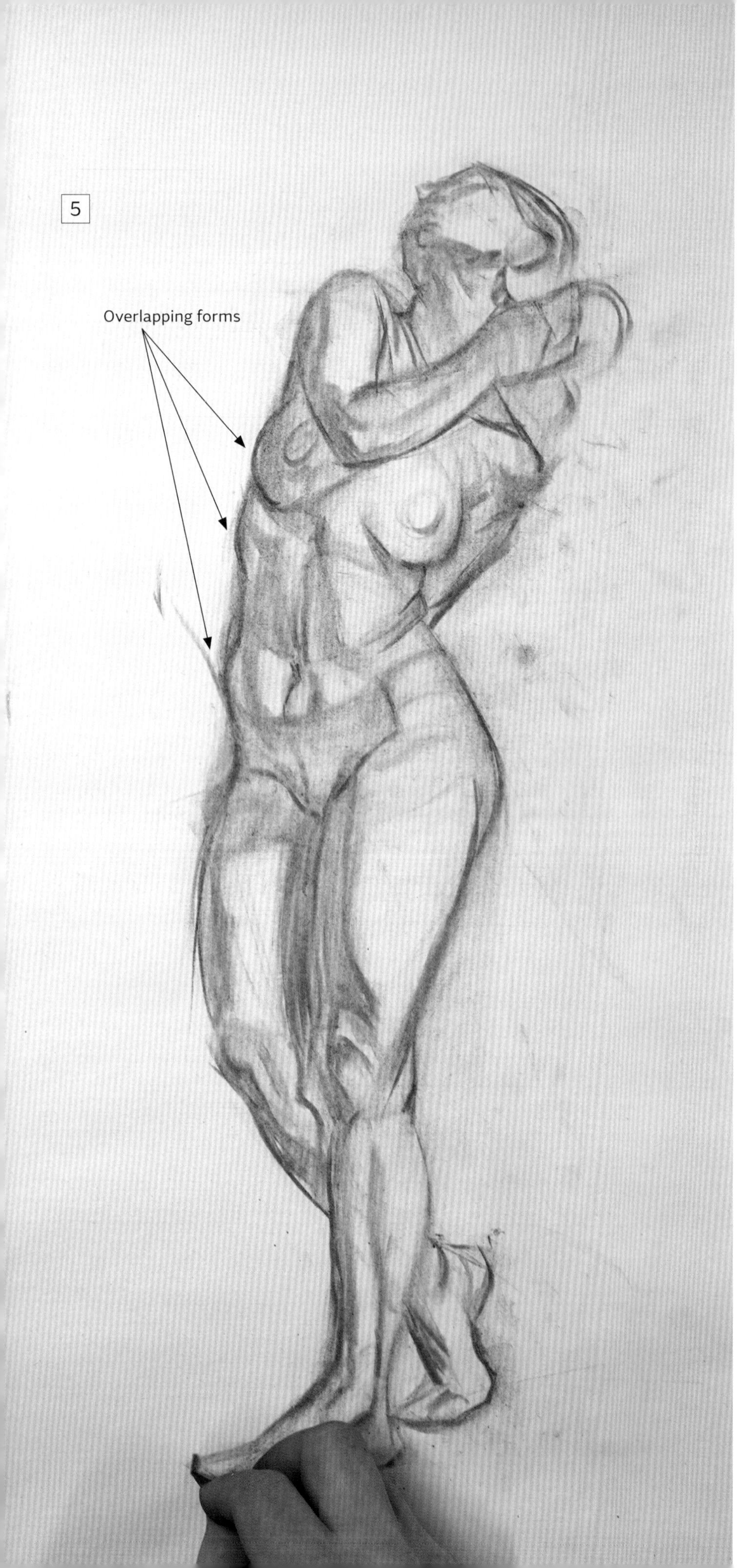

5

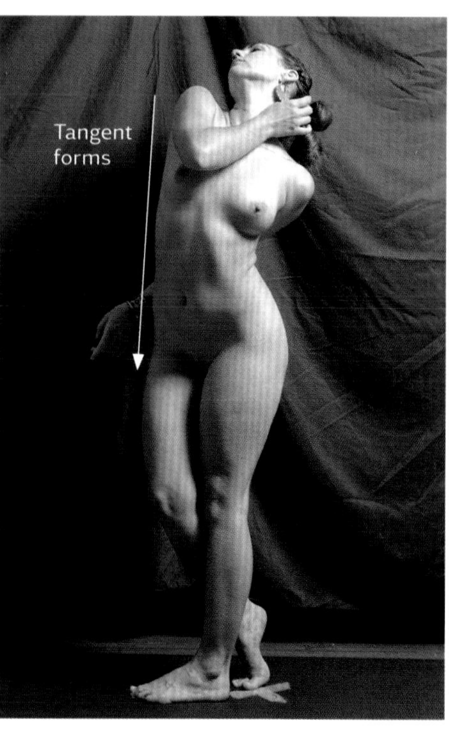

5 · The Lost Depth

I block in the core shadows. The stretch side of the photo reference was visually flat due to tangent lines (converging lines that destroy the illusion of depth). Study the flatness brought about by tangents in the photo, compared to the newly applied overlapping forms of the drawing. I have overlapped Katy's ribcage with her right breast and pushed the hip and the tenth rib forwards to regain the lost depth. If your photo reference lacks depth, see if you can create overlapping forms.

6 · Surrender to the Rhythm

Using a tissue I soften the forms. My figure is shorter in proportion but the natural rhythm gained is more important. If I were to go in now and make the legs longer, it would kill the organic rhythm, and the drawing would become horribly stiff. I feel that surrendering to the rhythm was the right choice, and I lay in gestural lines on top of the structures.

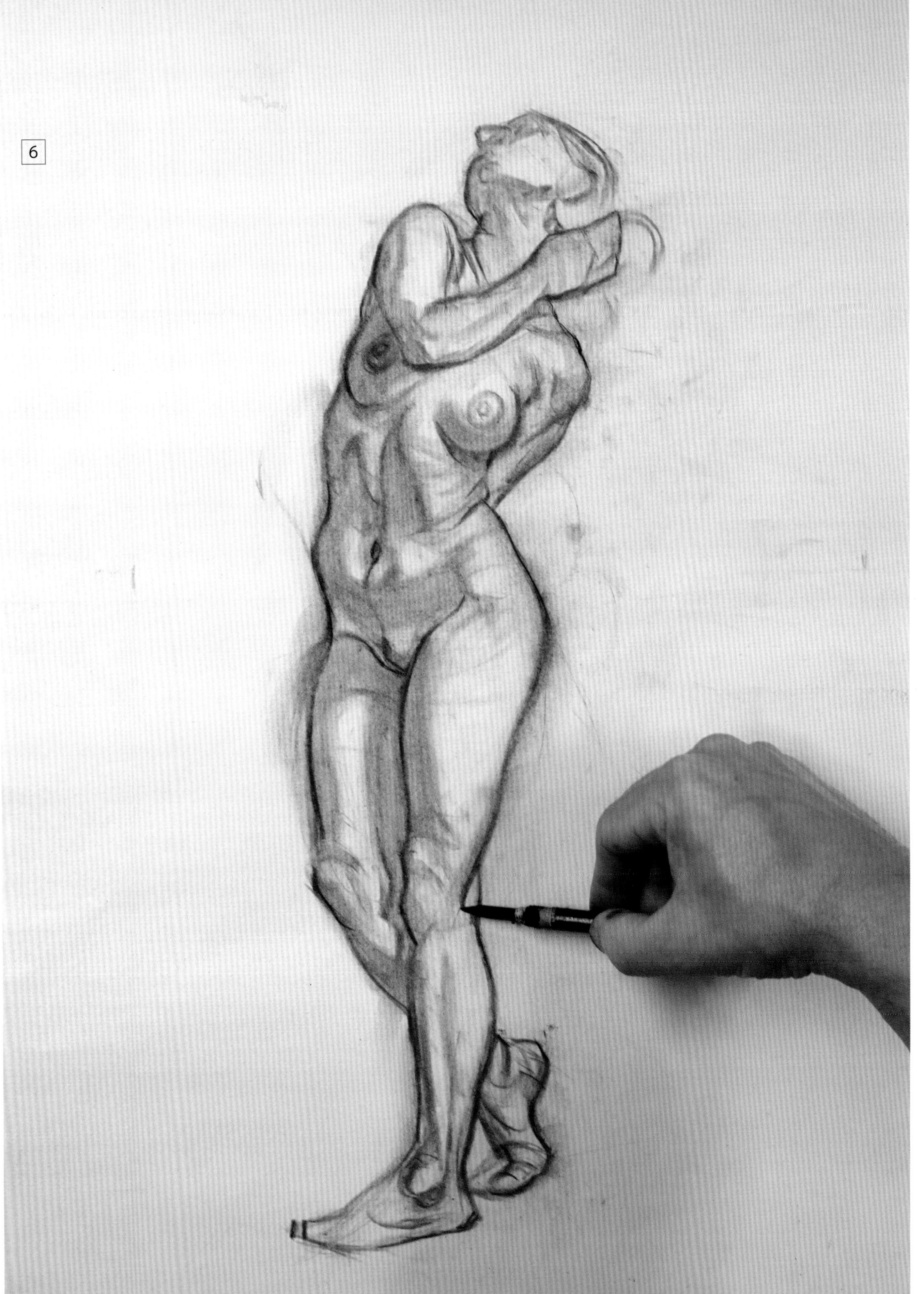

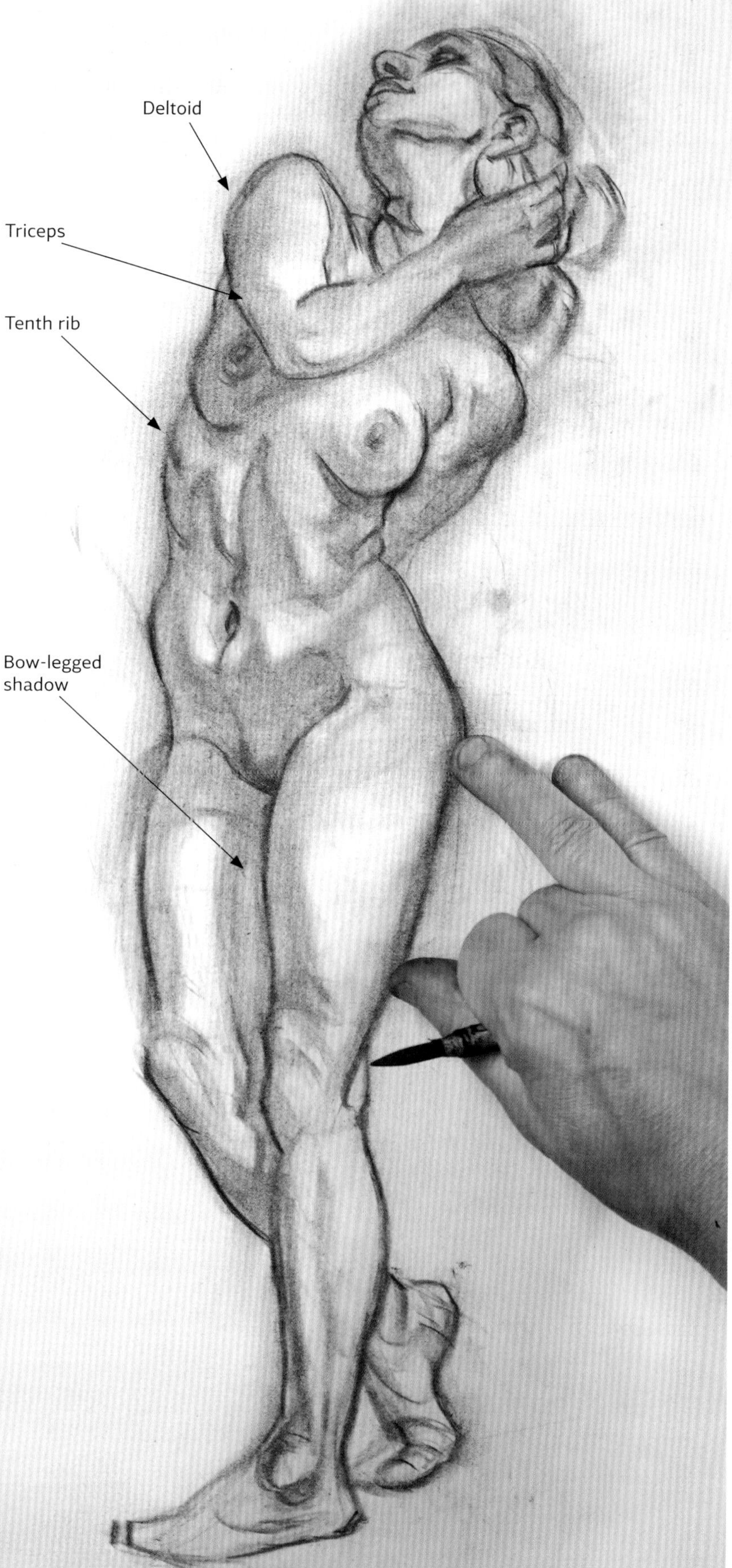

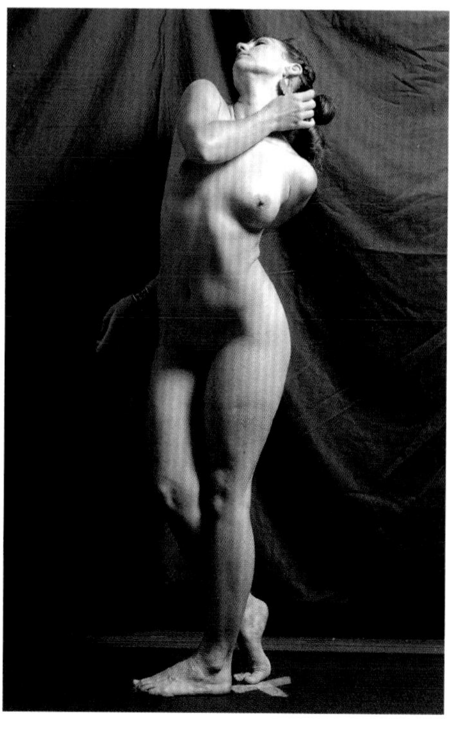

7 · Stay Focused

I bring out Katy's right shoulder and triceps and overlap the ribcage across the obliques to continue to find more illusion of depth with overlaps. As I smudge tone I'm aware that the head had grown bigger as I added details, and I make a note to myself to trim it down later. For now, I'm on a mission to find depth and don't want to be distracted with fixes that could kill my focus and rhythm. I also note that the cast shadow of Katy's left leg has created a bow-legged look to her right leg.

8 · If it Looks Wrong, it is Wrong!

I step back and assess the drawing. I decide the cast shadow of the arm should drop over the ribcage instead of across the breast. It now reads more clearly and dimensionally and has more gestural appeal. Remember my art law "If it looks wrong, it is wrong, even if it's right"? This conundrum is always guaranteed to raise student's eyebrows during my live workshops.

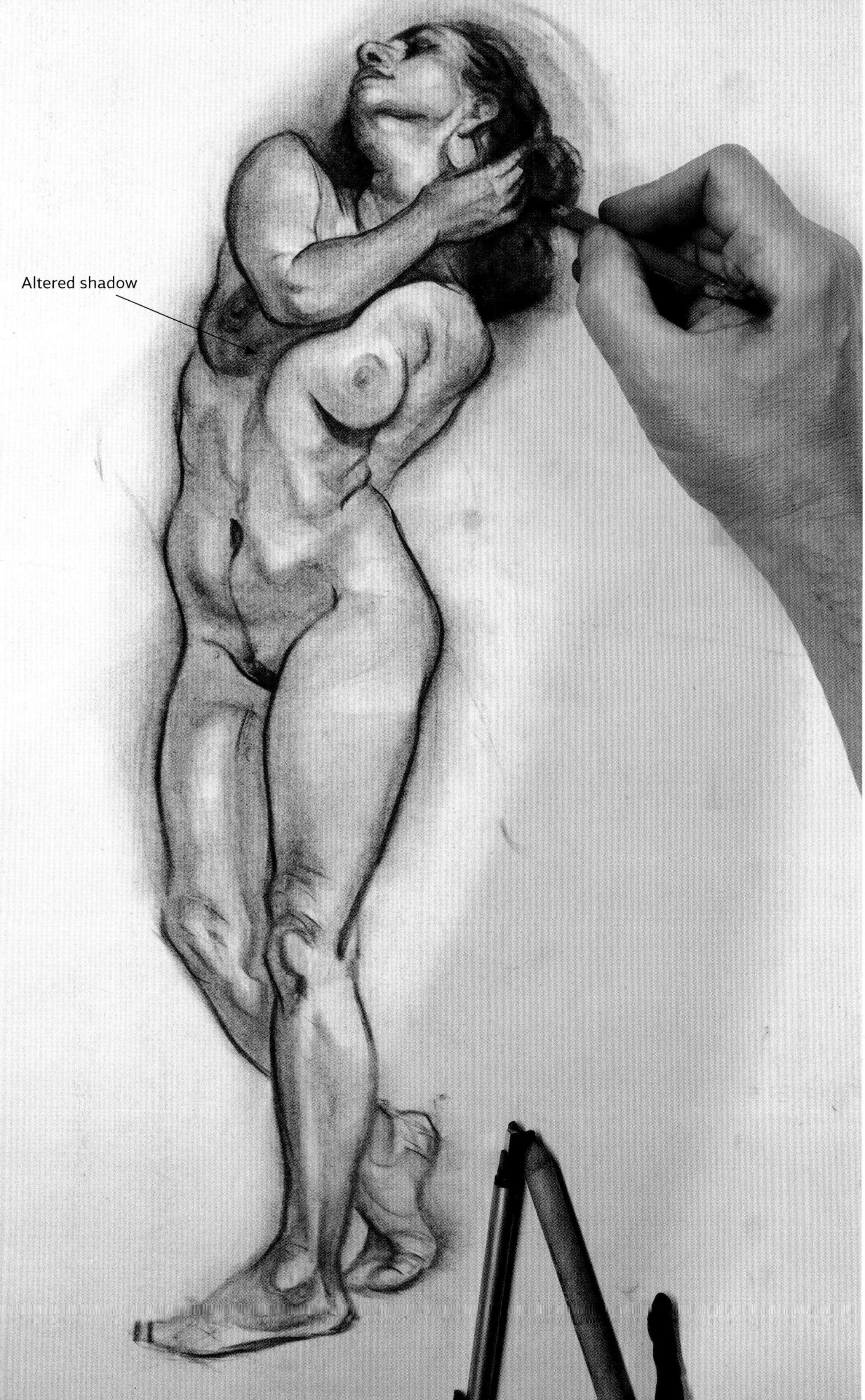

8

Sfumato mist

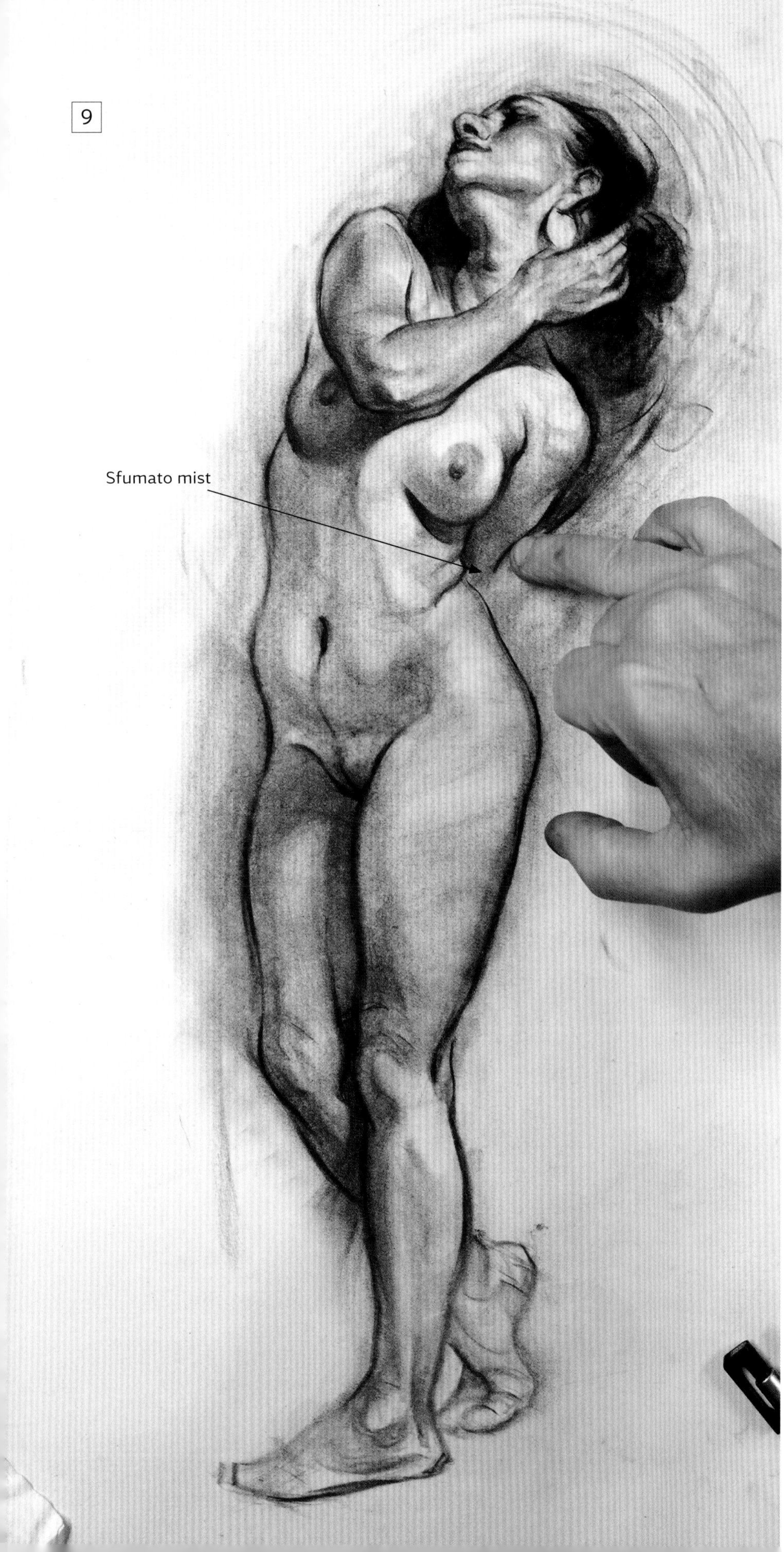

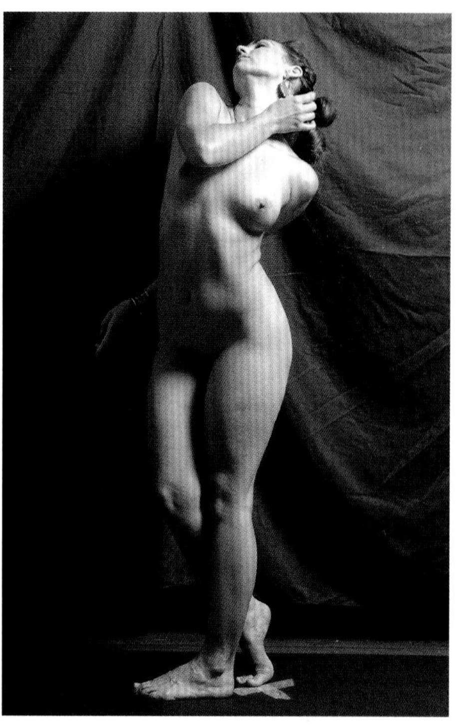

9 · Energy and Purpose

We have done a lot of work taming this photo, and it's paying off with fresh energy and rhythm. I work on the edges, softening core shadows and fading Katy's left arm into a sfumato mist. I slant her head, making it more dynamic and smaller. The head needs to be smaller still, and I think on it as I highlight the upper torso. Planning ahead as I work adds energy and purpose to my hand; this is different from multi-tasking, where we constantly interrupt the flow of one thing only to do another thing just as badly.

10 · A Metaphorical Storm

Alternating between my drawing tools, I reduce the head and fade the right leg into shadow to kill the bow-legged appearance. With this new shadow shape, I'm considering both story and style and plan to run a line of action through the body in the shape of a metaphorical storm. I'm always going forwards, always thinking ahead.

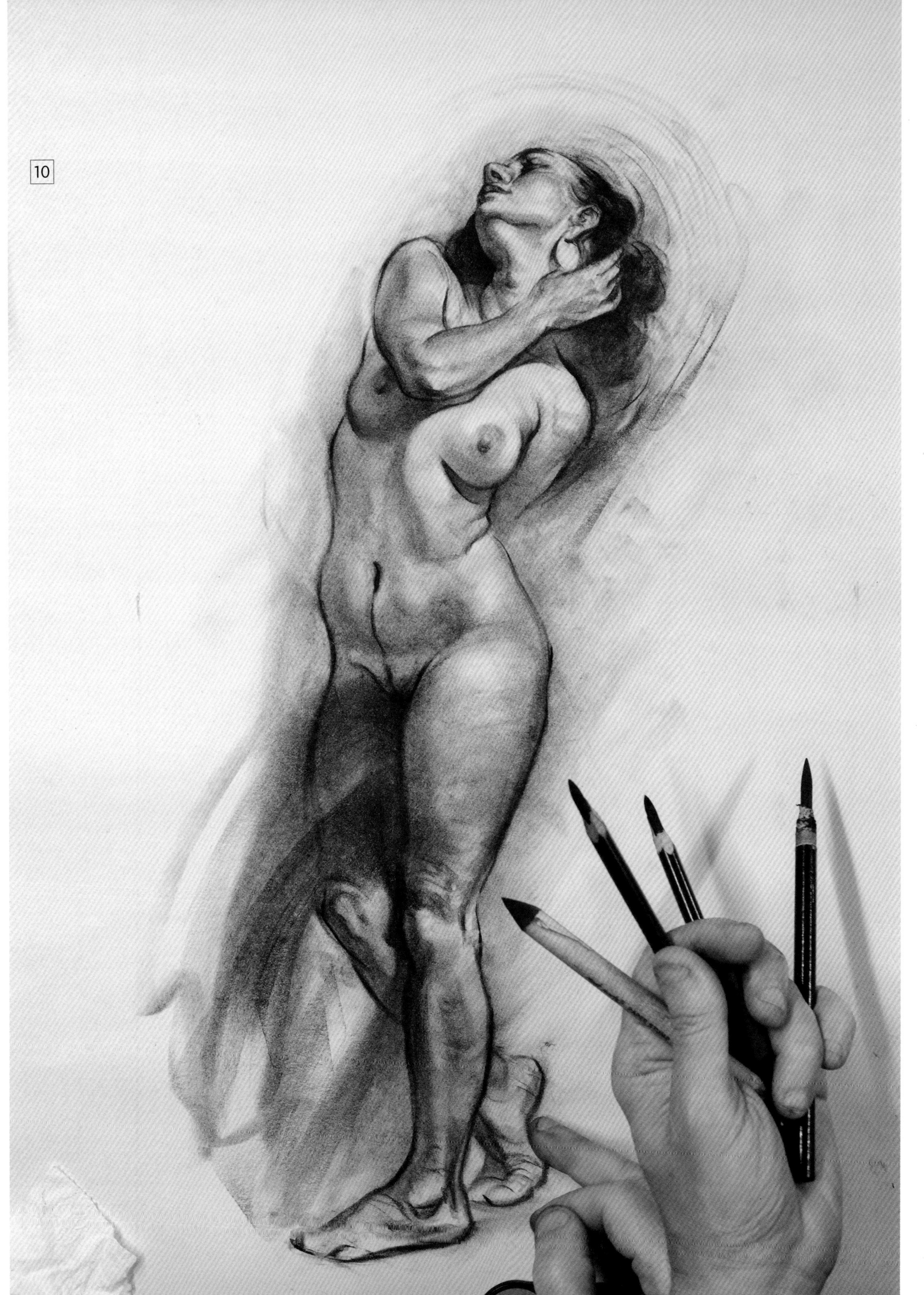

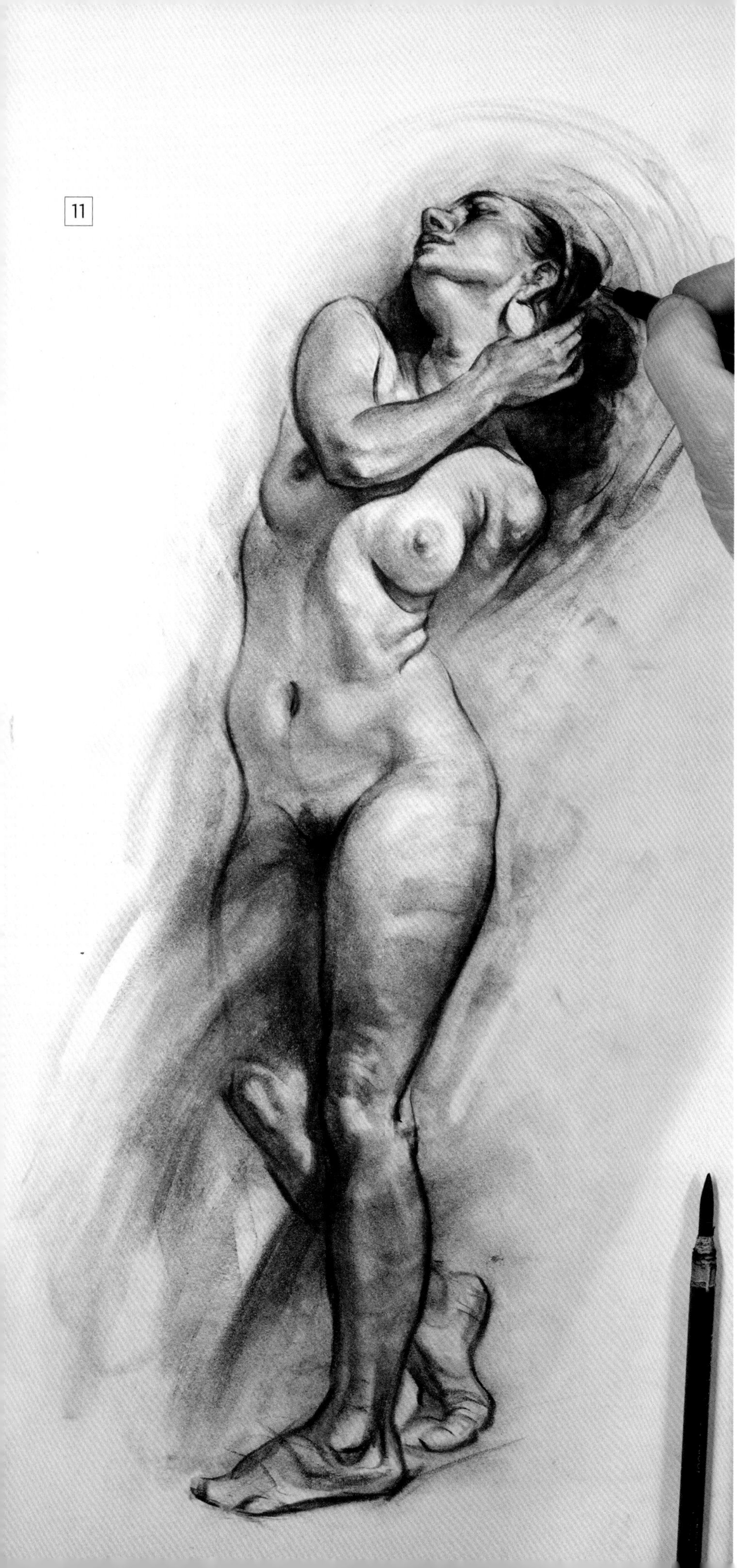

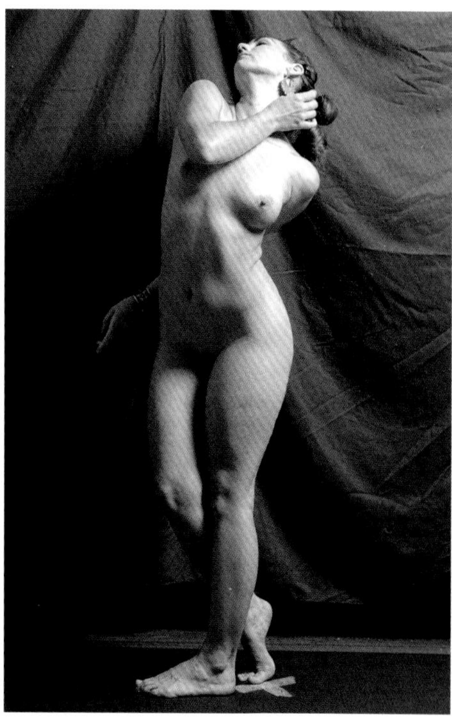

11 · An Insecure Decision

Katy's hand may seem big here next to her foreshortened forearm, but I find hands and feet look better bigger rather than smaller. If I were to make the hand smaller, it would feel like an insecure decision. When we look at the photo, in terms of photo distortion, it's actually the head that's too small. Here I add subliminal rhythm with gold headbands that echo the shape of the skull. The mono eraser is excellent for this.

12 · Engage the Storm

Now it's time for the metaphorical storm. Using a block of compressed charcoal, I engage the gestural hand with fluidity set at maximum, to bring out the raging tempest. Compressed charcoal is dark and may hinder confidence with its stark nature. To draw with bold confidence, try practising on some scrap newsprint before drawing on your art. Light strokes building to dark is the best approach.

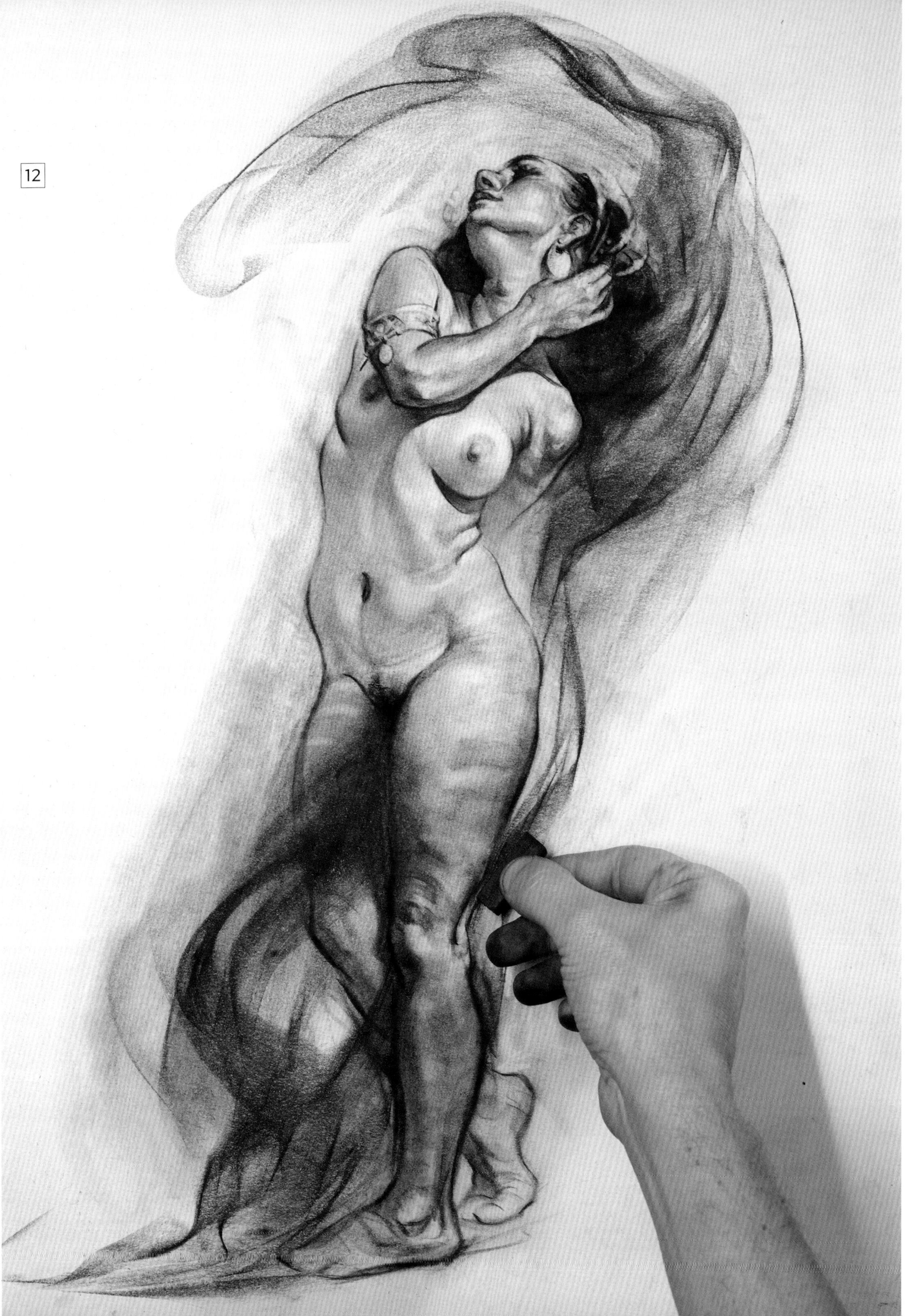

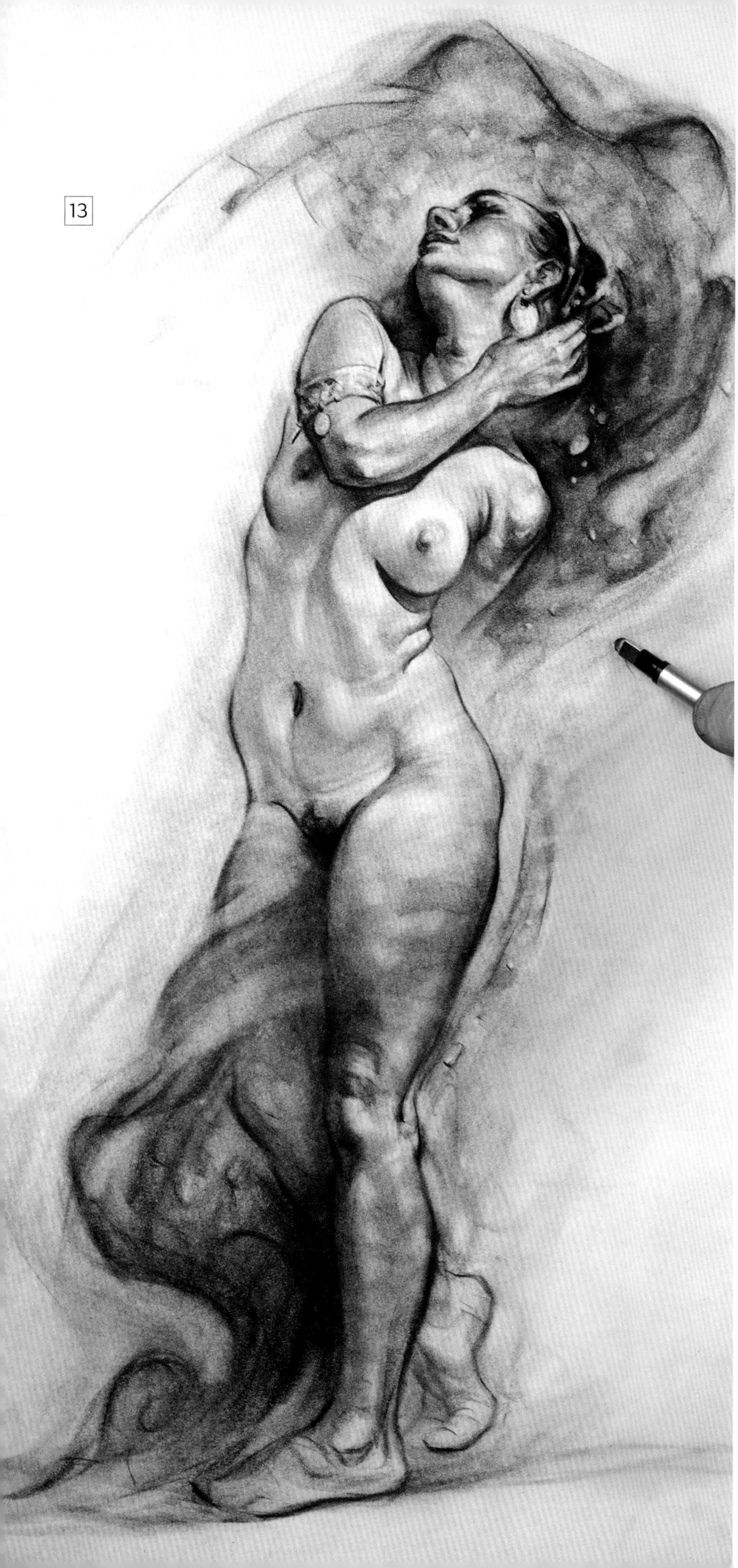

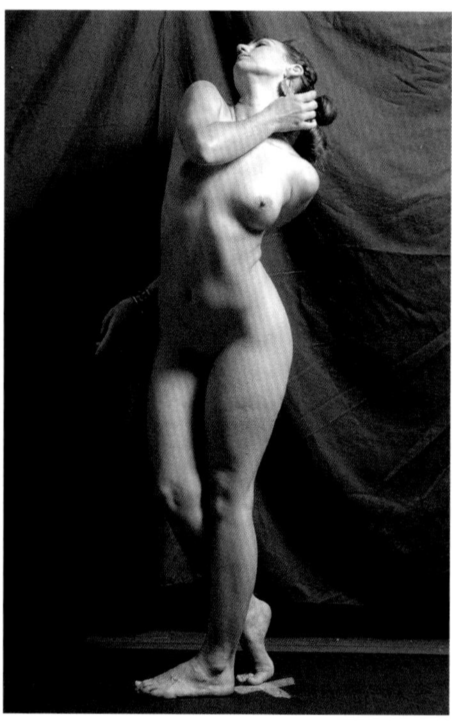

13 · It's a Kind of Magic

Reshaping the gestural lines to represent a storm has killed some gestural flow. There are trade-offs as we draw, but keeping our disciplines in place while also taking chances enables us to learn something new. The next time I use this rhythmic charcoal technique, I'll surrender more to the natural rhythm and not try to control it as much. This is a balancing act that watercolourists know all about. Sometimes we must let the medium do as it likes in order to find freshness and energy. It's also exciting when the art surprises the artist: it's a kind of magic.

14 · Love, Devotion, and Surrender

We are a world away from the photo now, and the micro changes to structure and gesture have created a style that's uniquely mine. And if you have drawn along, your drawing is uniquely yours. Embracing the disciplines of love, devotion, and surrender don't limit our art: they offer us freedom of expression.

14

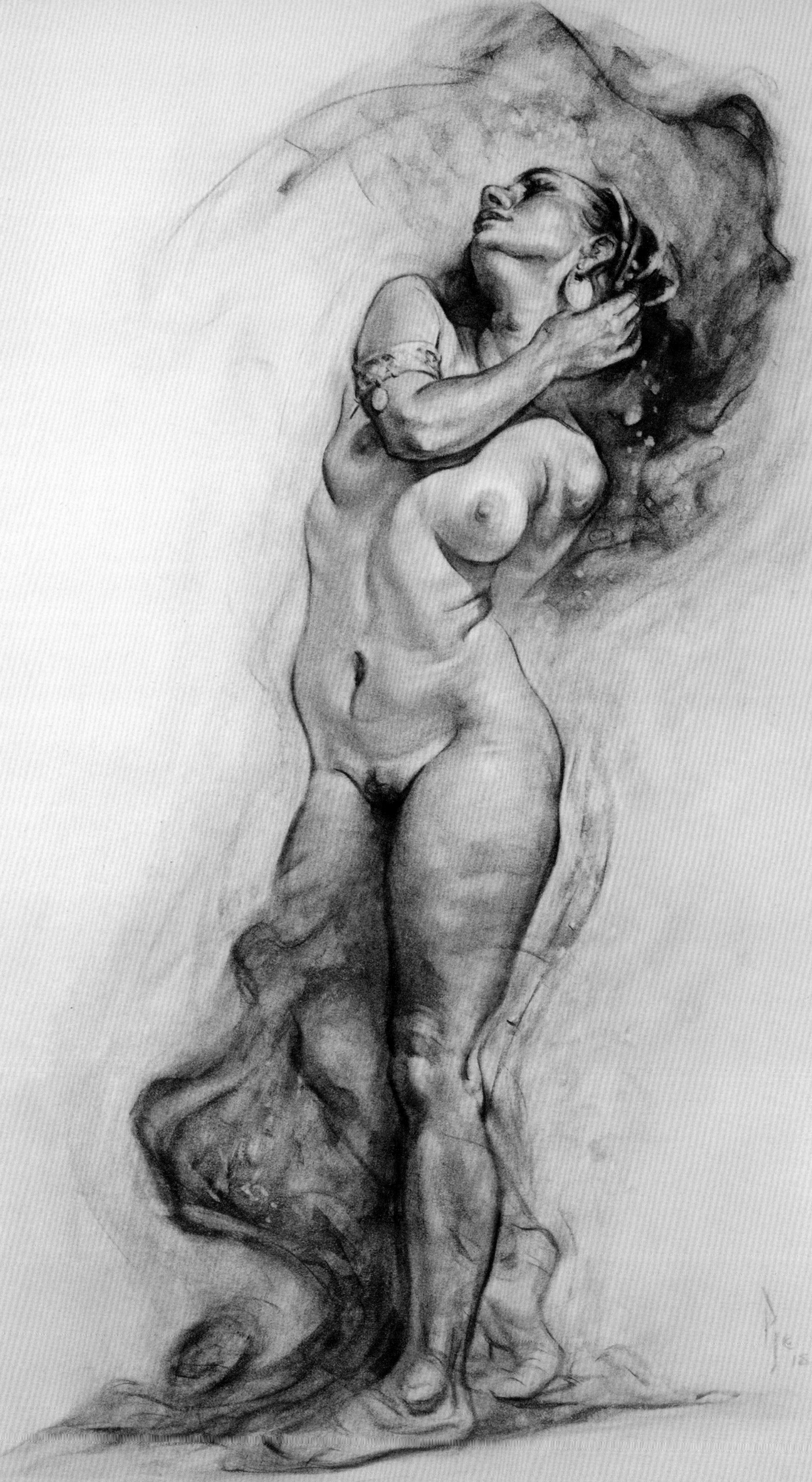

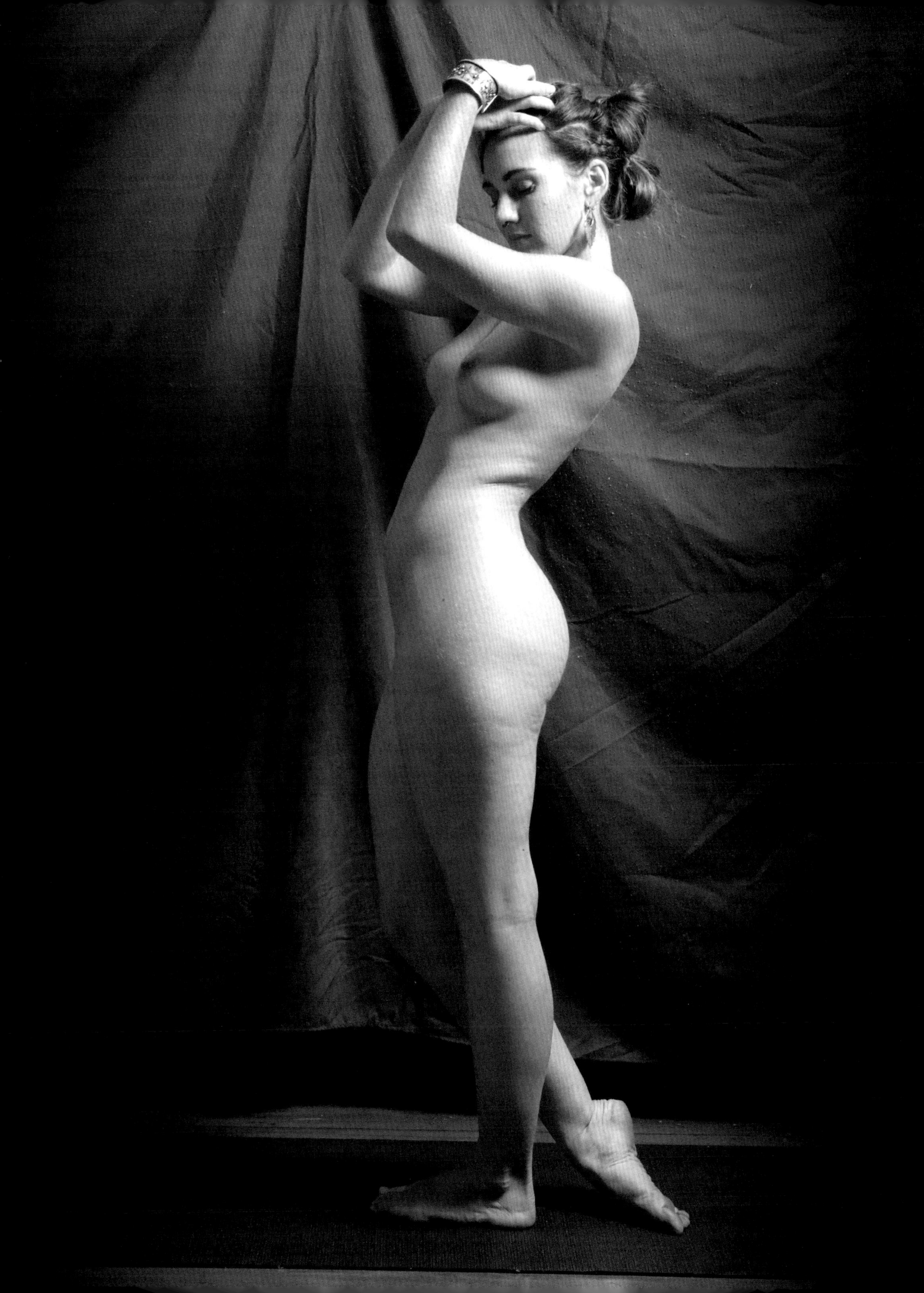

PART TWO

PRAISE FOR THE CAMERA

FOR MOST OF THIS BOOK, I've cast aspersions on the magic box that is the camera, with its primitive processing brain and wonky eye. As I look back at myself with some reproach, I feel a little cruel. For, after all, if we strip away the technological marvel of this creation, we are left with only a dim-witted servant. The problem is that the camera has become the master of many artists and has achieved a level of malignancy that is unparalleled in art history. The servant has become the master.

So, how do we regain control of an automation that is running amok, spreading lies about proportions and depth? We must first lose the fear of its control. In this final part of our exploration of working with photos, I will show how we can regain mastery and lead with our emotions and our artistic nature to the fore.

Opposite is a photo of the model and dancer Katy Woods. The camera has told mostly the truth here, due to the fact that Katy has stayed within its focal plane. None of her limbs are coming towards or away from us in a drastic manner; she stands within the 2D realm of up and down and side to side, and therefore retains her proportions almost as our human eyes see her. She has been shot with a 50mm prime lens from a distance, and then the surrounding background, the outer area of the lens containing the most distortion, was cropped out. That's as good as it gets through the eye of the camera. A student took a photo of me at a weekend workshop a while back with her iPhone, and it looked as if my head had been sucked into a vortex just off-screen. If you are on a budget, I recommend buying a good secondhand camera from a professional photographer who is upgrading.

Here, apart from the inevitable tonal banding "sudden value shifts", the flesh is blending without too much information missing, so all is tip-top. Let's now look at some less fortunate photos and, along the way, praise our poor one-eyed friend.

Left: Model Katy Woods

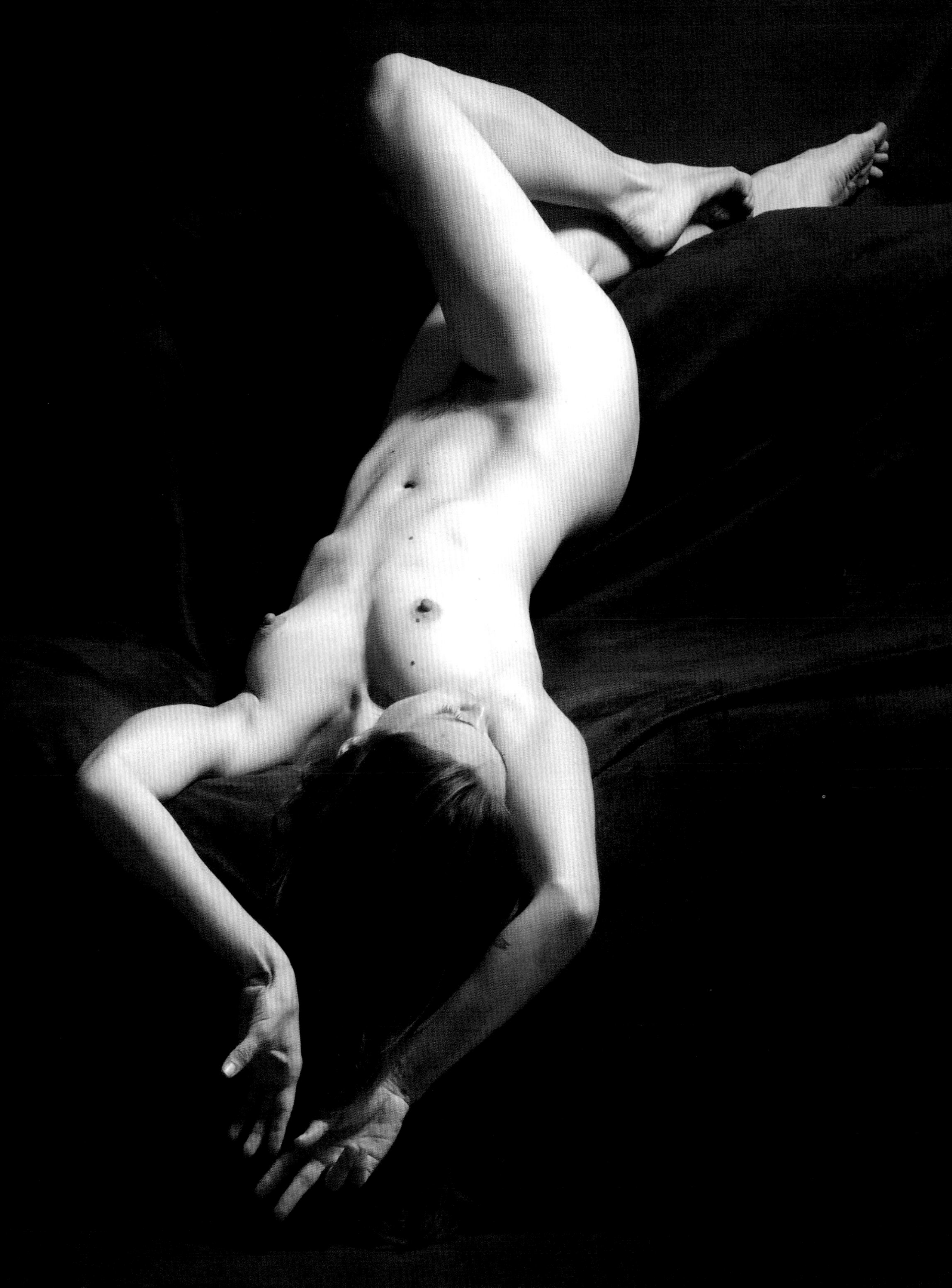

WORKSHOP EIGHT

LEARNING TO SEE

WE HAVE ALL at some point watched an artist at work and wondered how they make it look so easy, when it comes so hard to us. If we don't want to overthink this, we could say that it's down to "talent" and stroll off uninformed. I recently watched Rodger Dean paint a picture, and he spent two-thirds of the process looking and thinking before making a flawless mark. That flawless mark, of course, came from a lifetime of application, passion, and study. Once we understand that all artists work hard to achieve their vision, we have opened our minds to following that same path. The only problem then is that we can't read an artist's mind. When an artist gives a workshop, there are moments when they are quiet. Ironically, this is the artist most likely working with their deepest thoughts.

In this workshop, we will not draw the figure but instead analyse and understand what we are looking at. This is that quiet moment I have just talked about – the inner workings of the artist's mind. I often talk about my process of Analyse, Understand, and Draw: A.U.D. We can always see the drawing part of an artist's process, but here I will stop short of mark-making to show the other two-thirds of that process, which are the most important. For without understanding, we may as well try grabbing a handful of smoke.

As we are working with photos, there is more analysing to do with regards to distortion and depth, but most of what we will examine in this section contains the same thought processes I use when drawing from life.

Left: Model Alana Brekelmans

A Pearl of Wisdom

One of my favourite quotes is, "It is necessary to keep one's compass in one's eyes and not in the hand, for the hands execute, but the eye judges." This pearl of wisdom was uttered by none other than the great Michelangelo. But what did he mean?

Well, in academic art circles, there is a method known as "sight size", which is a bit of an oxymoron as it requires measuring with tools. For instance, artists might use a plumb line, which is a line with a weight at the end. When held up, the line will find a perfect straight, regardless of uneven ground. With a plumb line, we can relate how certain landmarks of the body line up. It's a marvellous method to begin with, and to continue with if it's your preference, but I prefer the Michelangelo method for one solid reason: gesture.

I've watched masters of academic art maintain gesture using the sight size method, but I've chosen the path of "learning to see" the lines of measurement as imaginary lines, as to me, it's simply more natural.

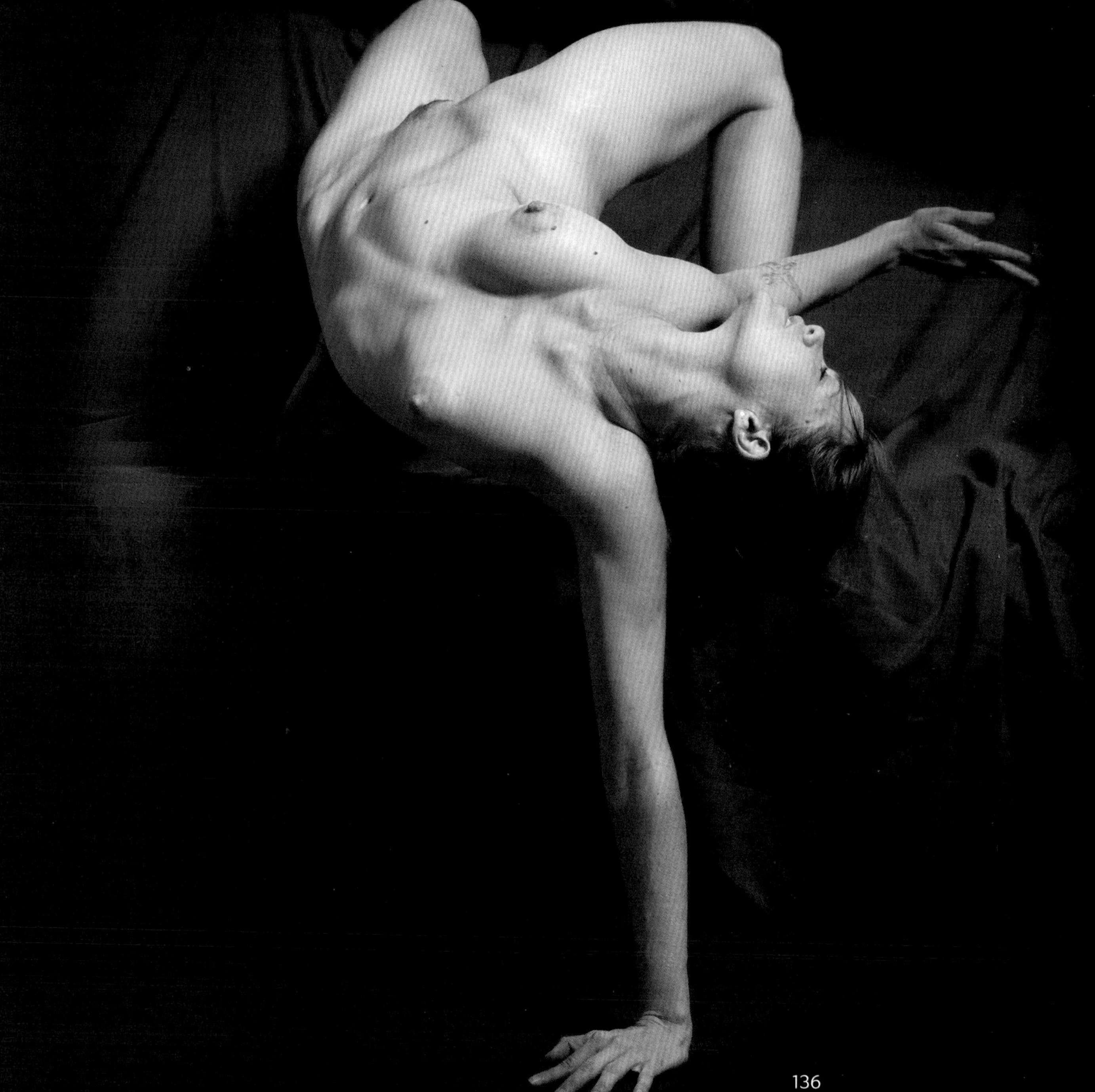

Learning to See

Let's look at the plumb line idea. Imagine I'm holding the weighted line with one eye closed. I hold the line high enough that it runs through the whole body. I then move the line across any pose, especially a difficult pose like this one, and search for relationships. I've found three examples: the nipple to the index finger, the bottom lip to the top of the ear, and the bottom of the chin to the insertion of the biceps femoris tendon. A useful exercise would be to try the plumb line method to begin with and then see if you can learn to see these relationships with imaginary straight lines. I've found using imagination much more enjoyable and no longer use the sight size method as it's not as necessary in my analytical approach to drawing the figure. Still, we can learn a lot from it, as we shall see.

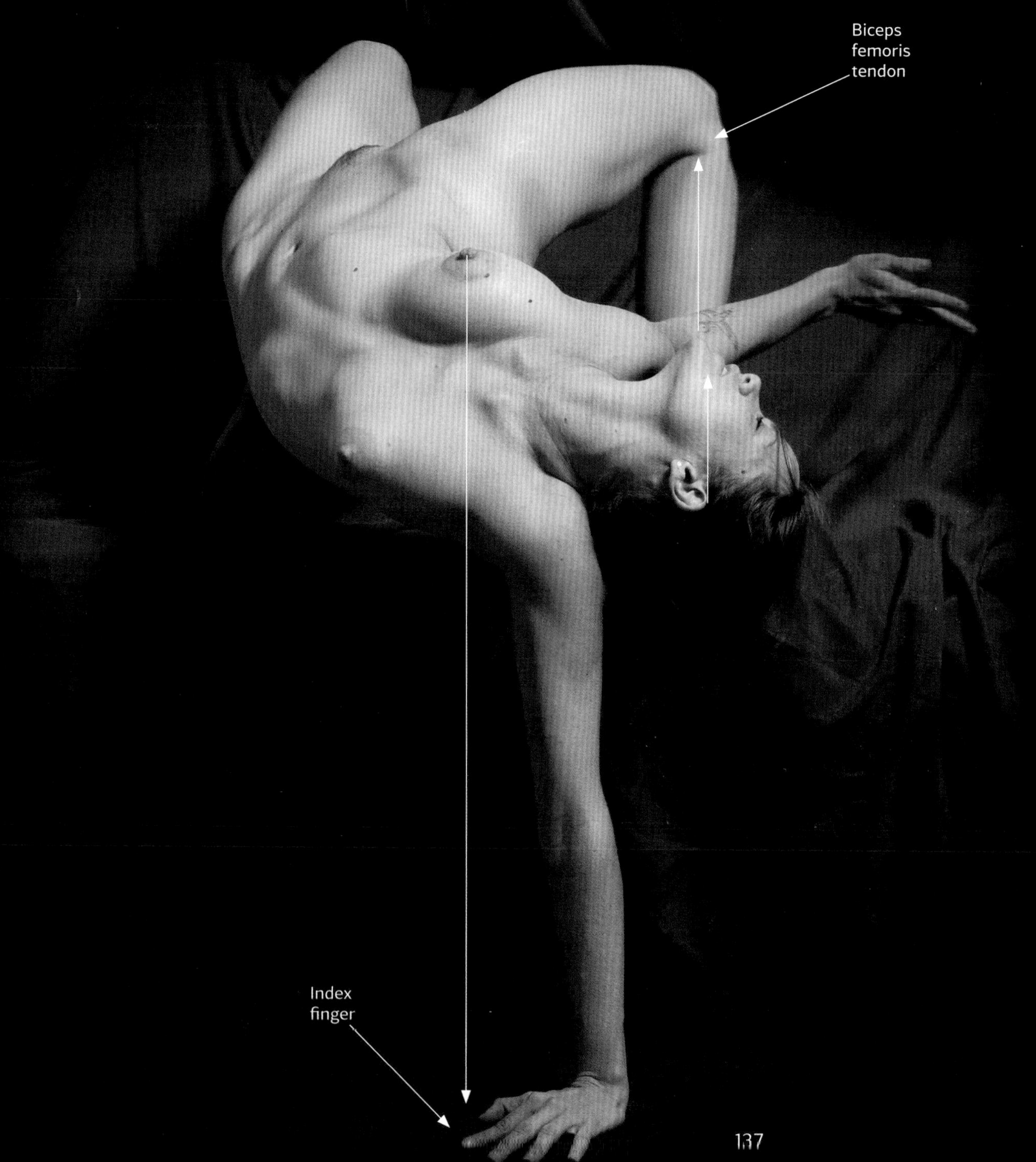

The Mind's Eye

A plumb line that finds up and down relationships is a great start, but it's a pretty narrow experience. What if we hold the line taut in both hands and turn it at angles? Now a whole world of relationships opens up. See here how the accordion rhythm of the body looks as we measure lines across its landmarks, such as the hip bone ridges, clavicle peaks, the nipples, and the ridge of the ribcage. I also note the ear position as it's a great indicator of how the head is tilted. As the figure is not standing straight, we observe that the landmarks have shifted to our advantage, giving us fluid asymmetry. Here I'm showing the inner workings of my mind's eye when analysing a figure before making a mark on paper, using the sight size method.

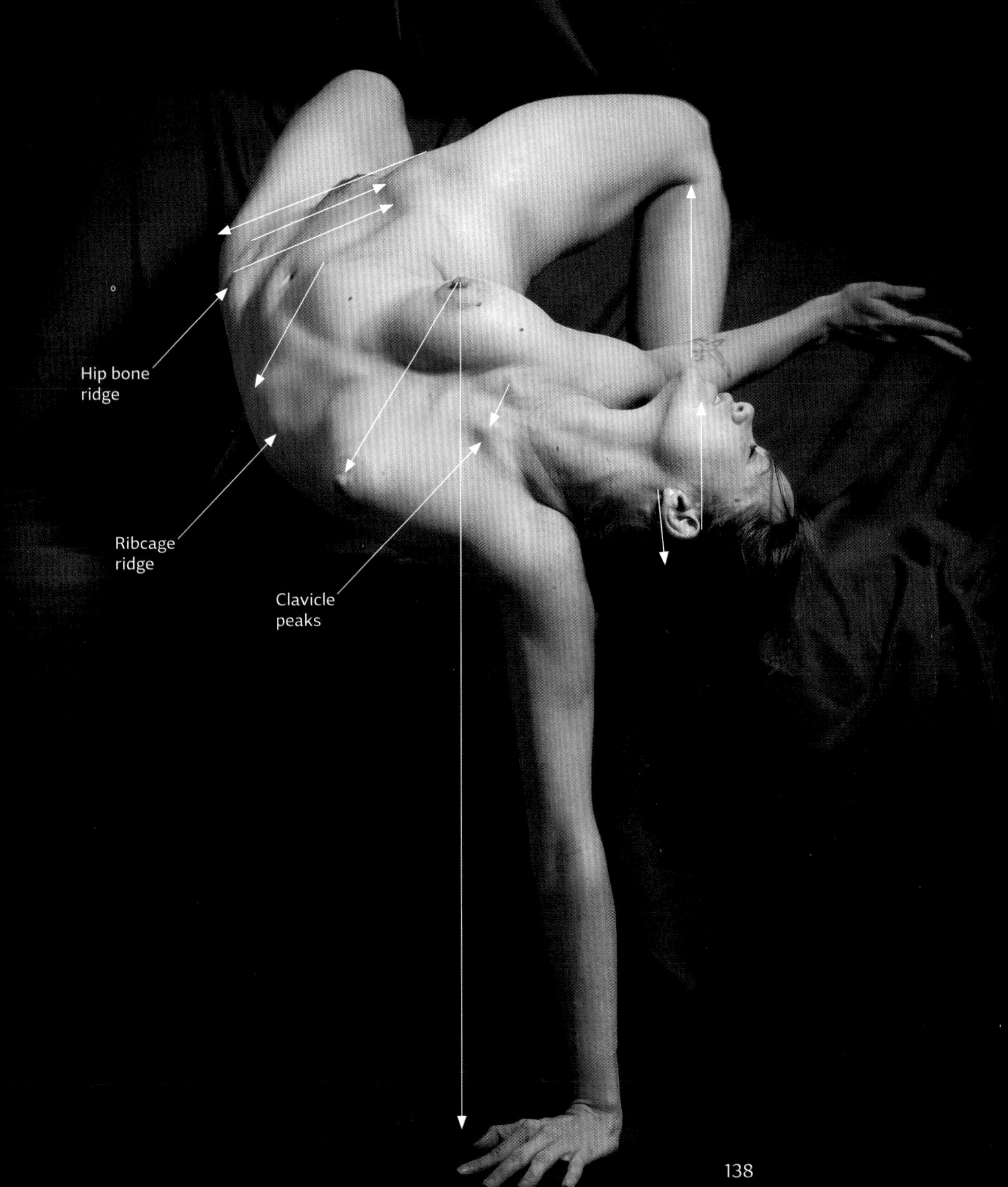

The Mermaid's Net

Another key process when analysing the relationships between landmarks of the body is to imagine a net cast over the figure; this is often referred to as an "envelope", but I prefer "net" as it's more evocative. Here we can almost imagine a mermaid struggling to get free. I run the net from one knee to the other and on to the outmost fingers, then up to the ribcage and hips. The space between the net and body is known as "negative space" and helps us see shapes that break down the figure into a more manageable set of steps rather than one muddled mass. Casting a net can also help us fit the figure onto the page; I will often draw a net if I need to do this. The net idea is recommended if you find your figure drawings often run off the page.

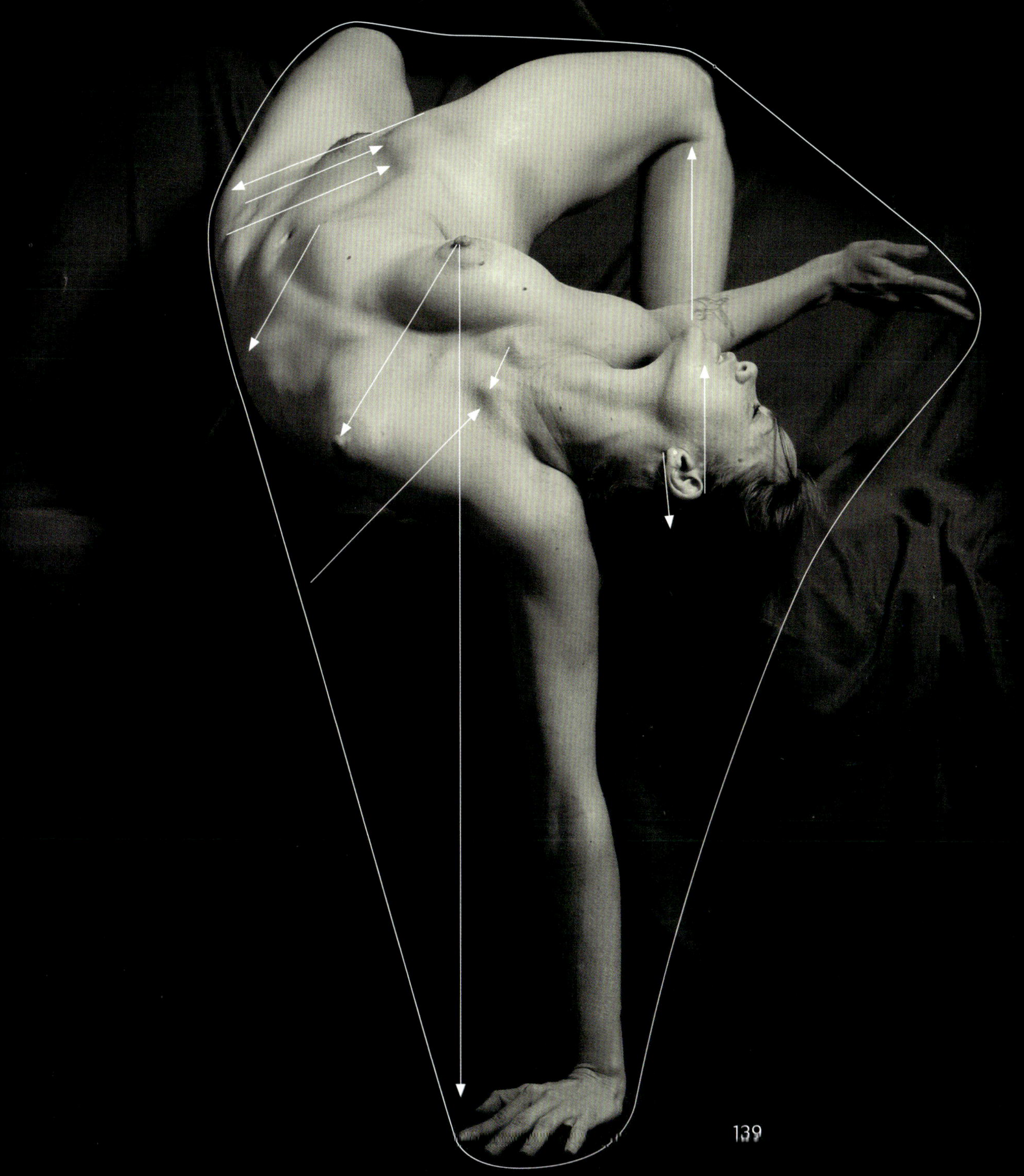

Mass Analysis

If you refer back to my drawings you will see that I don't begin a drawing with the lines shown in this section, apart from the occasional net, but they are constantly in my mind's eye when analysing relationships. With these imaginary markers I can draw gesturally without needing to use plumb lines or pencil measurements, which is the classic artist's method of closing one eye and using a thumb and pencil to measure. As we are working from a photo

I take extra note of overlaps to help with the illusion of depth. Note the overlaps of the breast, the gluteus maximus – which is also overlapping its own tendon – and the biceps femoris after the tendon. Here I also analyse smaller plumb lines, gauging the negative space between the chin and nose, then the nose and forehead. This I analyse as I draw big shapes to small shapes. You could think along the lines of big mass analysis to small mass analysis.

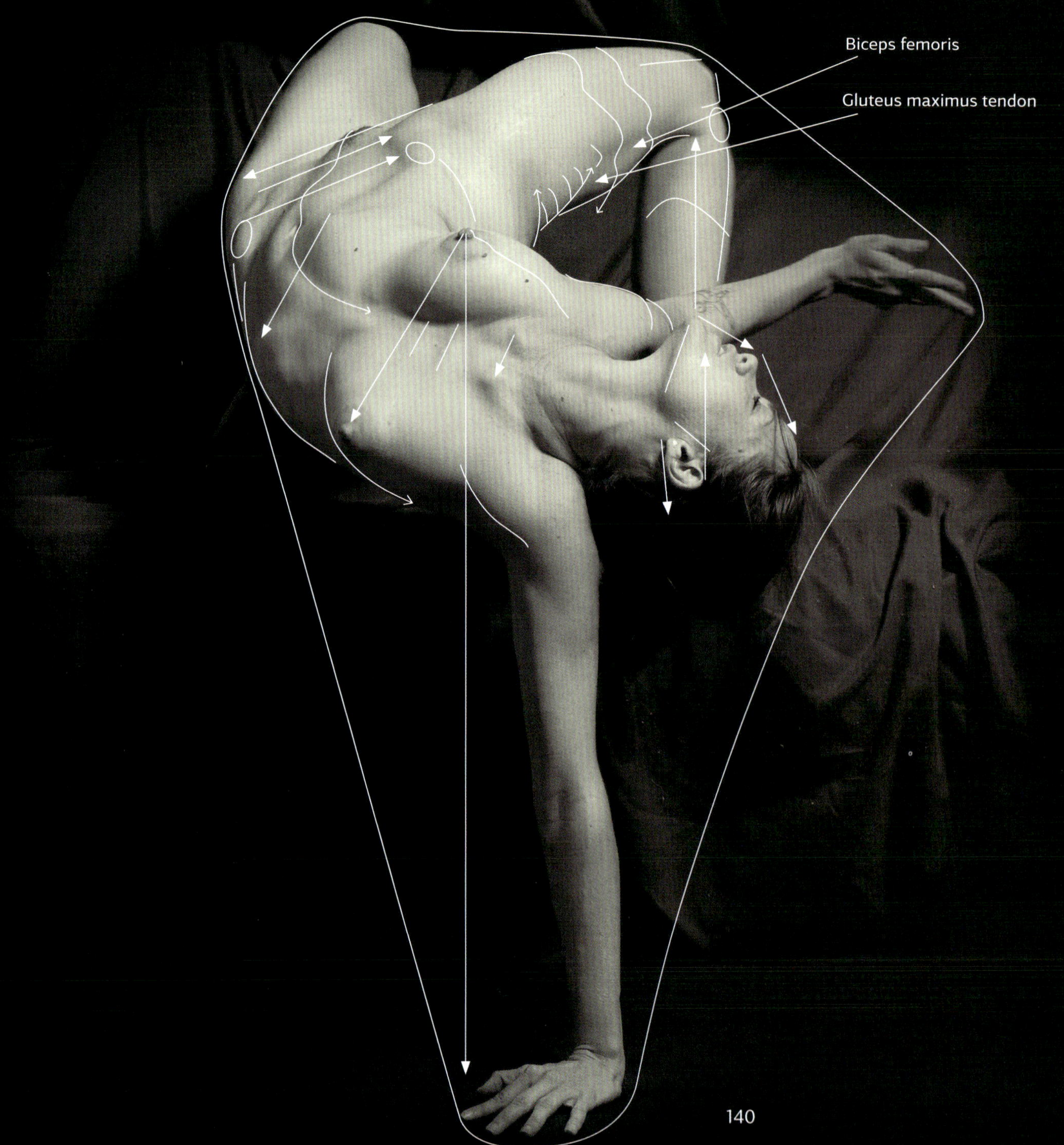

Analyse, Understand, and Draw

Another analytical process is to understand the figure in 3D space. Here, photos have one supreme advantage over life drawing in that we can draw on the "virtual model". If you have a program such as Photoshop, which I've used here, start by drawing contours on the body as if it has dimension. This helps us understand the anatomy as dimensional, rather than mindlessly copying a flat illusion of form onto a page. Note the interlocking shapes of the arm as a structural idea here, and the box nature of the hand. In this example, most thought processes are on show, plus the analyses of structural muscle shapes. Remember, not all of these thought processes are happening simultaneously, meaning I don't draw all this beforehand. I analyse everything broadly to begin with, then continue the analysis as I draw.

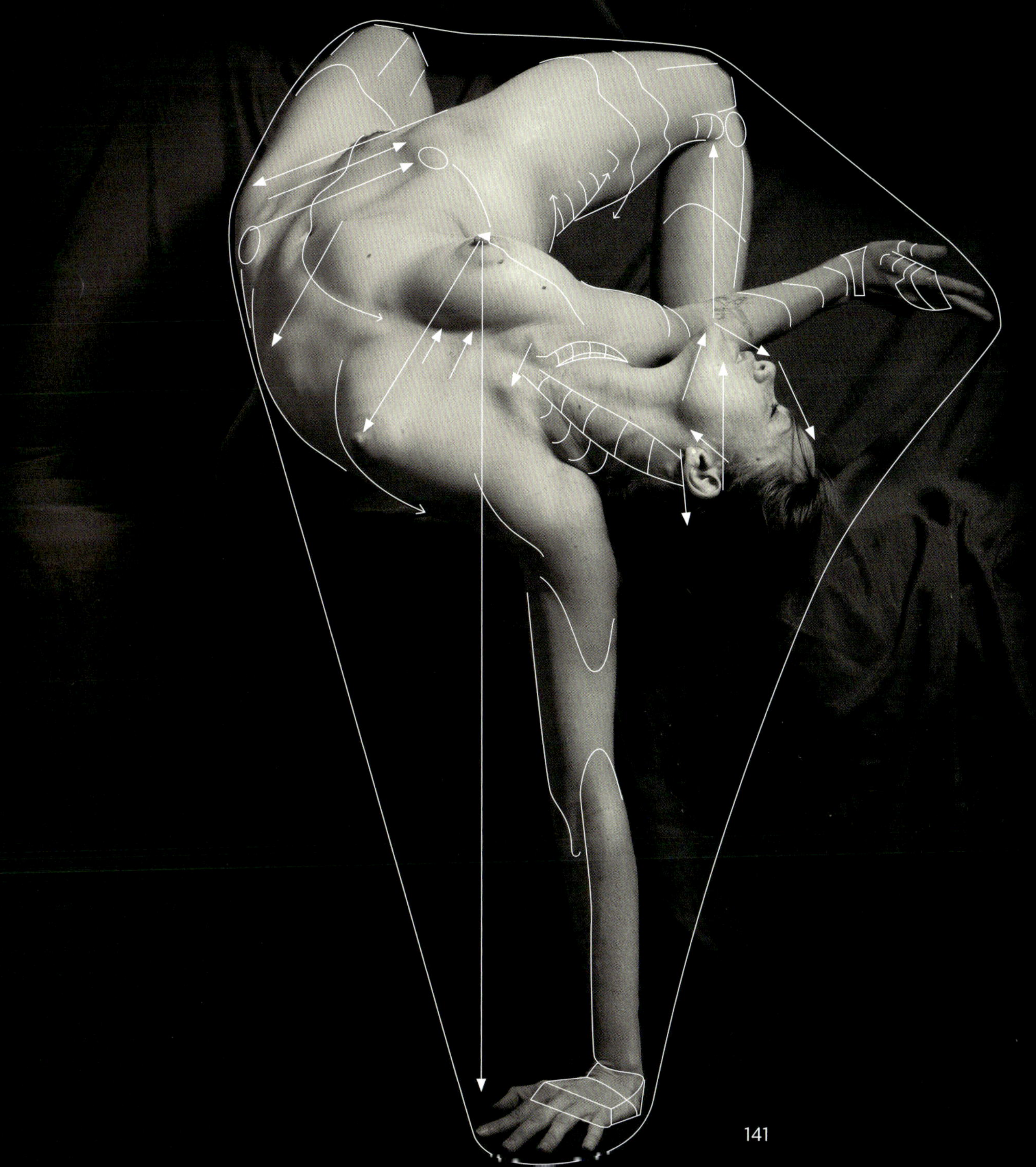

The Horizontal Zone

Let's look at a pose more perspectively warped by the camera's eye than our human eyes would see. This is more of a fly's-eye view, with Alana being relatively 100 feet long. Here the torso alone is longer than the legs, due to the extreme foreshortening of the lens. We get natural foreshortening through our vision, of course, but we need to learn the difference when analysing photos, otherwise our drawings will look like poor renditions of photos with all the flaws intact.

Finding the midpoint of the greater trochanter hip bone to the top of the head is a good way to get a notion of what a basic midway point would be on a standing figure. Once we see the extreme nature of the distortion we can reign it in a bit. This is when

hand measurements are "handy". The hand on the floor is in the 2D non-distorted horizontal zone. We can check it now as a basic length for other hand-long landmarks, such as the clavicles, the sternum, the sternum to the tenth rib, and the length of the top of the foot.

We could also use it for the chin to the hairline, but the camera has done an excellent job, and I see no unnatural foreshortening here. It feels like the natural foreshortening seen through human eyes. Using yardsticks such as hand lengths as a basic guide, we then use our feelings to avoid falling into the trap of shoehorning measurements. We need to learn to feel as well as to learn to see what is wrong.

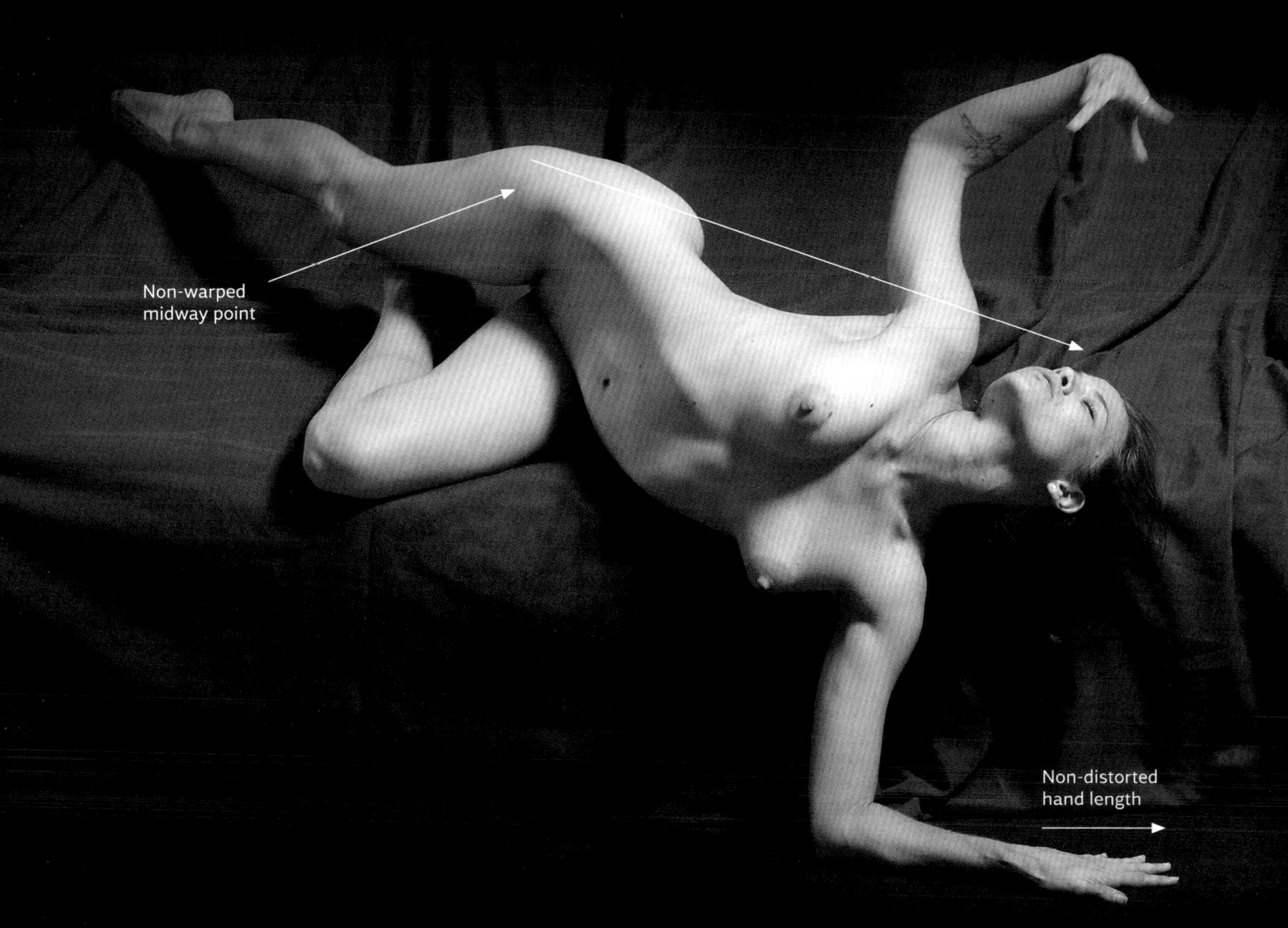

The Vertical Zone

We know that the camera struggles with the idea of the third dimension (depth), but modern cameras, especially 50mm fixed lenses, do very well with any objects on the straight vertical or horizontal plane, and this is why a 50mm lens is the photographer's first choice for portrait photography.

The focal depth from the nose to the cheek and the side plane of the face to the ear is not a big deal and will look perfectly normal, but once we have a leg or arm come forwards or go backwards in space the camera is literally out of its depth. For that reason, I always look for objects on the vertical and horizontal against which to judge the camera's eye. There are photo apps that fix camera distortion, but they usually distort something else in the process of doing so. I encourage artists to learn to see distortion; for one thing we won't always have our computer programs with us, and for another, we will have gained stronger "learning to see" skills.

Here, the most obvious objects on the basic vertical and horizontal planes are the upper portion of the arm leaning on the floor and the almost horizontal forearm and hand. These are the least distorted elements, from which we can judge everything else. The breasts are also within the same vertical depth (plane), even though they are slightly tilted. Learning to play the horizontal and vertical two-dimensional game simplifies our quest for proportions.

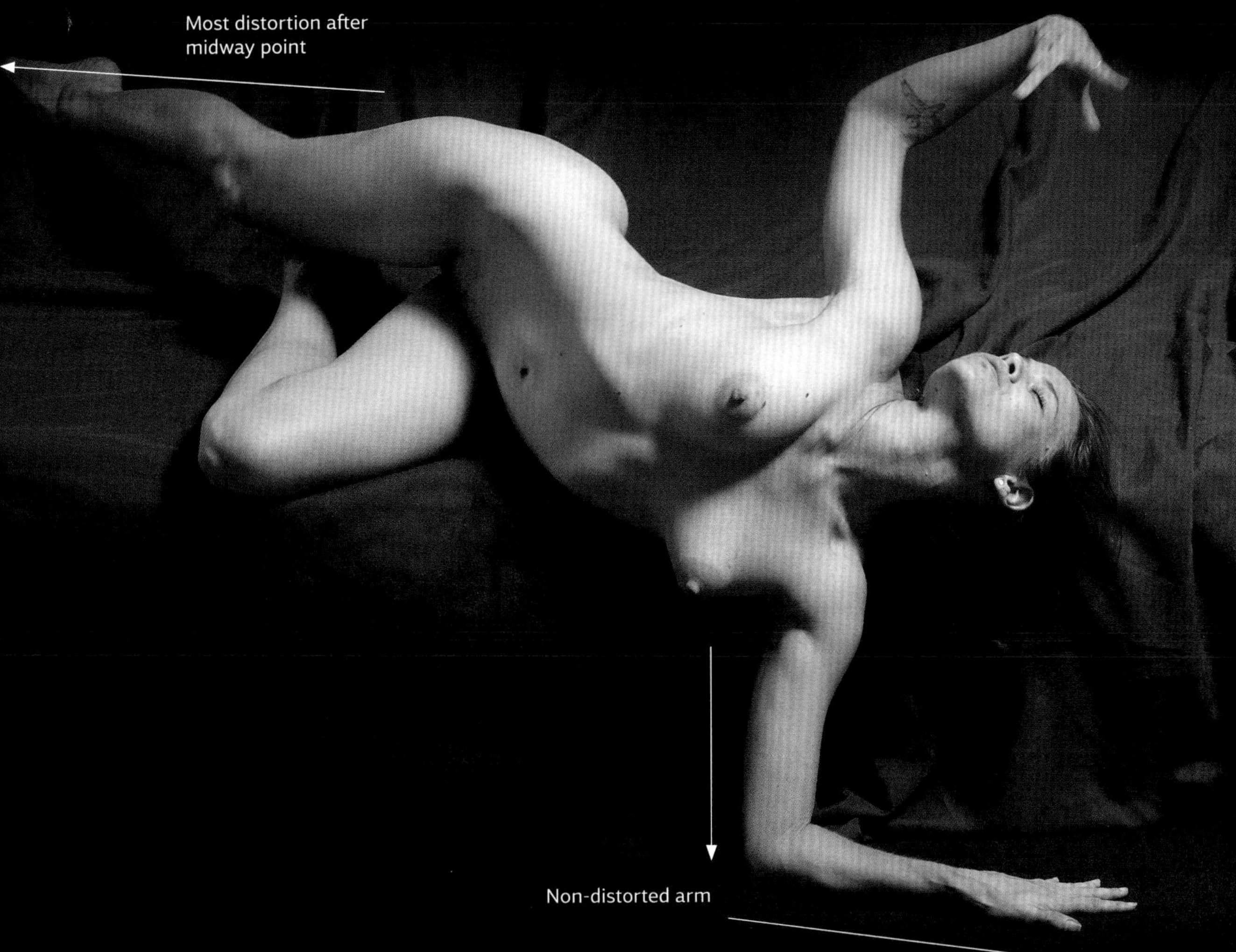

Our Friend James

When we work from photos we are gifted a frozen pose that is both a curse and a godsend. Gone are the slight movements of the model over time, and also the play of muscles changing due to fatigue. As the model gets tired they engage fresher muscles to take over from tired muscles, and in a standing pose the body often hunches forwards. This particular pose would be unsustainable after five minutes at best. For this kind of pose and also action poses the camera is an incredible asset to the artist. So here I'm praising the camera, as I should, as it's a miracle of technology – we just need to be wary of its shortcomings.

One shortcoming of the camera is in its flattening of form. There is hardly any definition in the torso here. The mid-tones merge together, as do the light tones and highlights. One trick is to bring the photo into Adobe Photoshop or a similar program and bring the levels together. In doing so we reveal hidden forms. The old book cover artists, such as James Avati, would create three separate exposures of the same photo to get a clearer idea of light and form and obtain lighting ideas to dramatise their work, taking information from each exposure. I do this for my paintings.

In the photo opposite I've dimmed the light using Photoshop levels to reveal more mid-tones. This has killed all the information in the shadows, but between both exposures we have the information we need to find anatomical detail. We must then avoid the trap of drawing everything in both exposures, otherwise we will end up with an over-detailed drawing; it's just a way to see forms that got lost in the exposure and then choose what we want to emphasise.

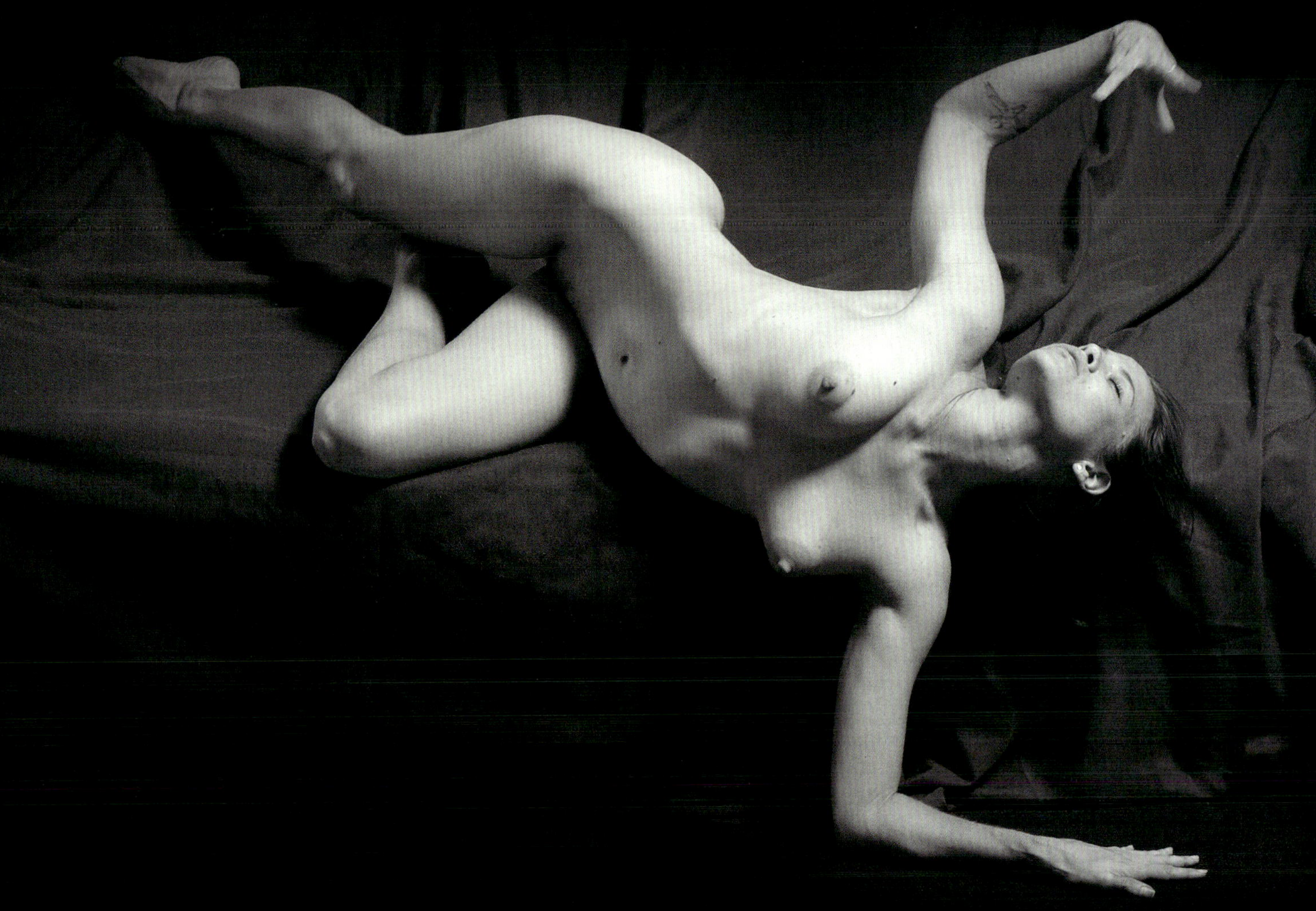

A Deeper Chiaroscuro

Here I've adjusted the levels to reveal more anatomy within the lighter areas. This creates a deeper chiaroscuro light. You can now use this more dramatic light to draw or paint like the Old Masters and let the details disappear into the shadows, or use it along with the original photos to simply see the anatomy that wasn't so obviously visible.

This is further praise for the camera. Although I could recreate this light using studio equipment, it would take much longer than the time spent pulling three sliders around in a computer program.

Note how we are almost box-shaped at the lateral side of our body and how it makes us aware of the gestural ledge leading down the leg, all the way from the corner of the ribcage. If we put our hands at the side of our ribcage, we may be surprised by how

flat that area is. We only feel the curve as we push over the tenth rib to the front. I consider the tenth rib to be the "corner" point of the torso. The term "core shadow" makes clear sense here as we can see the "corner" change from light into dark. The major landmarks, such as the iliac crest and the tenth rib, are clearer to see in this darkened photo due to their sharp, bony edges, but the main benefit is finding those muscles lost in overexposed light, such as the junction where the latissimus meet the ribcage.

Note how the gluteus comes from the side to disappear behind the obliques. This is why I sometimes call the gluteus the "behind and side" and also the "behind and under", as we see it from the front in certain poses that look through the legs. The gluteus maximus is the bulkiest muscle in the body.

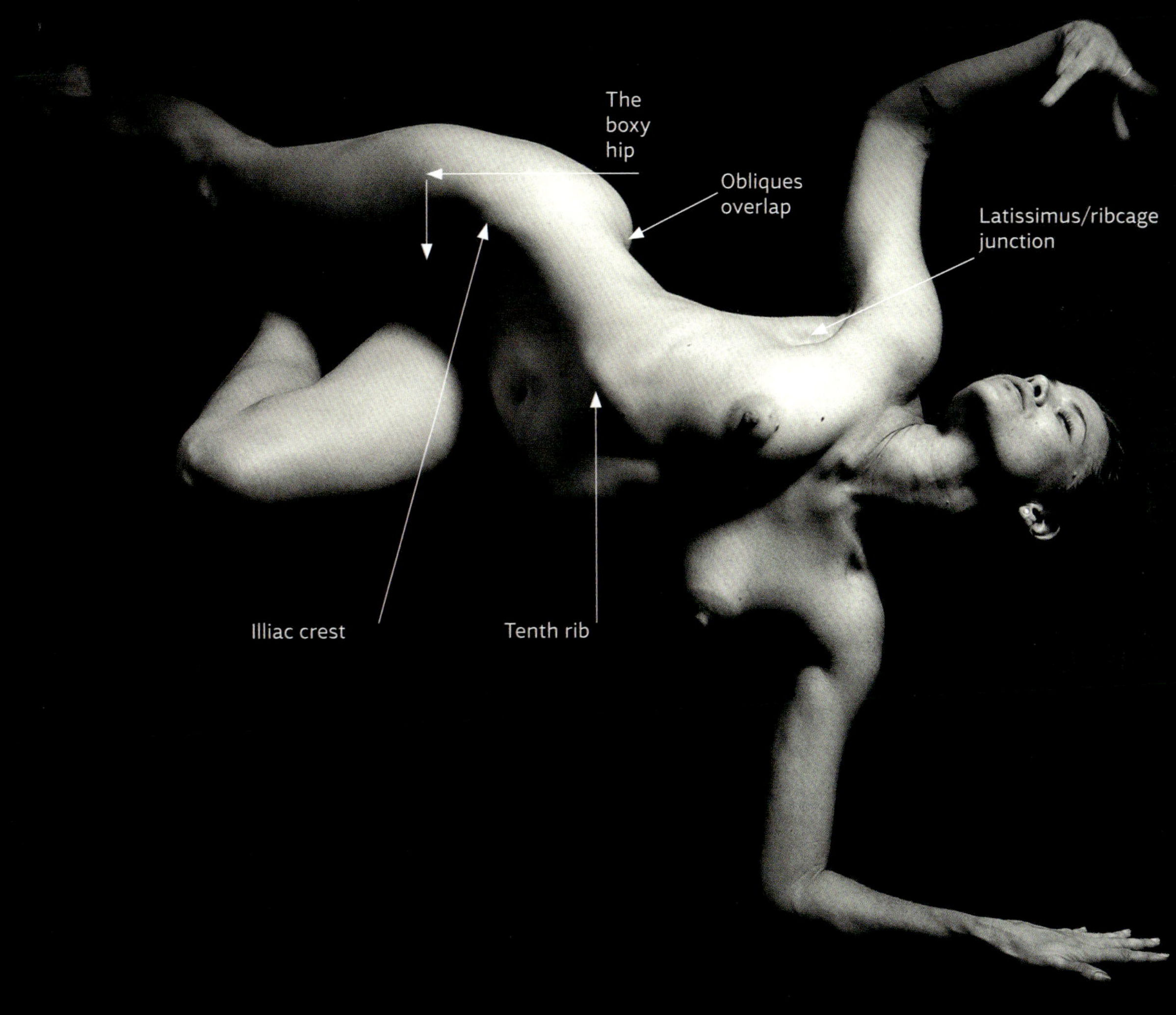

The Simple Contour Game

Let's play the simple contour game! When working with a nude model, we have the opportunity to see how the flesh turns. This gives us the chance to practice adorning the body with imaginary jewellery. And if we are working in the realm of fantasy art, we need to train our imagination.

Some artists set up a photoshoot and hire costumes and jewellery, and it's a whole heap of fun. I highly recommend getting together with friends to dress up and act. It was a great bonding experience when I was teaching my early fantasy workshops at a college in Brisbane, Australia. The students loved it, and more than 10 years later they often spoke of it as a college highlight, as it was for me too as a young, fledgling teacher. The only drawback to working with costumed models is that it can lead to a misunderstanding of form. Clothes hide form, and if we are always working with clothed models it's very easy to lose our sense of the figure, and before long we become lazy. Eventually, our anatomy skills deteriorate to the point where we need to have every piece of adornment worn and adjusted in the photoshoot to begin with.

By playing the simple contour game we will always be equipped to add any jewellery or adornments on the fly. By drawing contours and arrows on photos, we train our eyes to see direction and volume. I often see students add fantasy elements that come at us in the wrong dimension. Look how wrong the dark contour line on the raised arm below is. It's clearly the wrong shape along which to draw an imaginary bracelet. Try the simple contour game. It's quick, fun, and very important for fantasy artists.

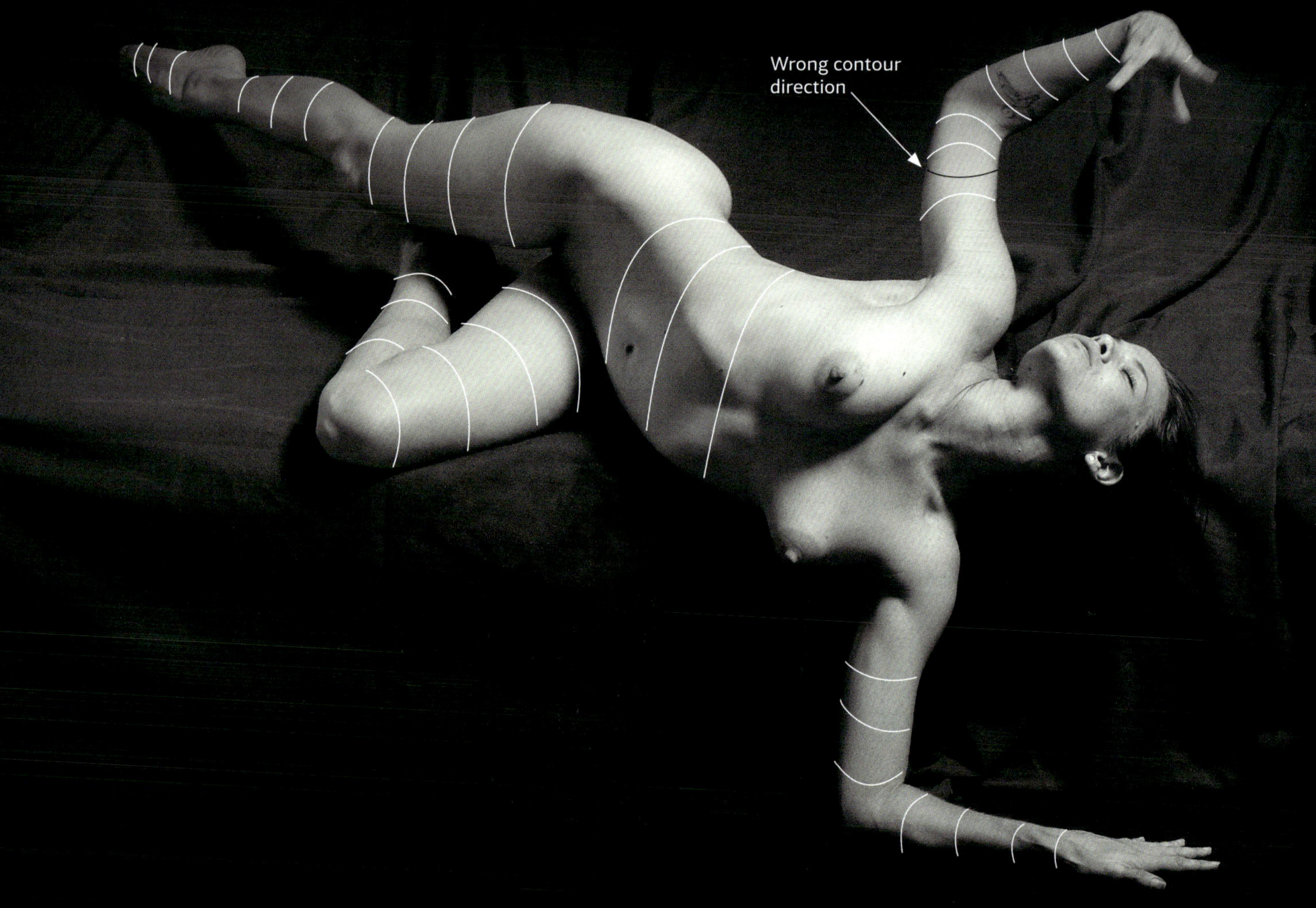

The Complex Contour Game

Anatomy is complex enough "the right way up" and in a pose like this, it can take the wind out of the sails of even the most seasoned artist. Again, this is when photography is the artist's friend. By drawing anatomy over the photo, we become better acquainted with the forms before committing to a drawing on paper. I do this kind of draw-over mostly for my online students during Q&A sessions to illustrate what's in my mind as I draw, and I find that it adds to my own internal art engine. In other words, we all benefit from this analysis, regardless of our experience levels.

By playing the contour game, we gain a deeper understanding of how the muscle and flesh shapes change as they contract or compress under weight or via gravity. Note the huge difference between the shape of each breast here. The upper breast is being pulled up by the raised pectoralis, which is attached to the upper arm, which in turn compresses the breast into a new shape against the hard ribcage. The lower breast, by contrast, is pulled down by gravity, with very little pressure against the ribcage.

Note also the bulge of the adductor magnus of the upper leg under the pull of gravity, compared to the flatter adductors of the lower leg flattened by compression. See the box-like nature of the bent knee compared to the cone-like nature of the extended knee. Study the separation of muscles and plane changes, then try it yourself. It is very rewarding.

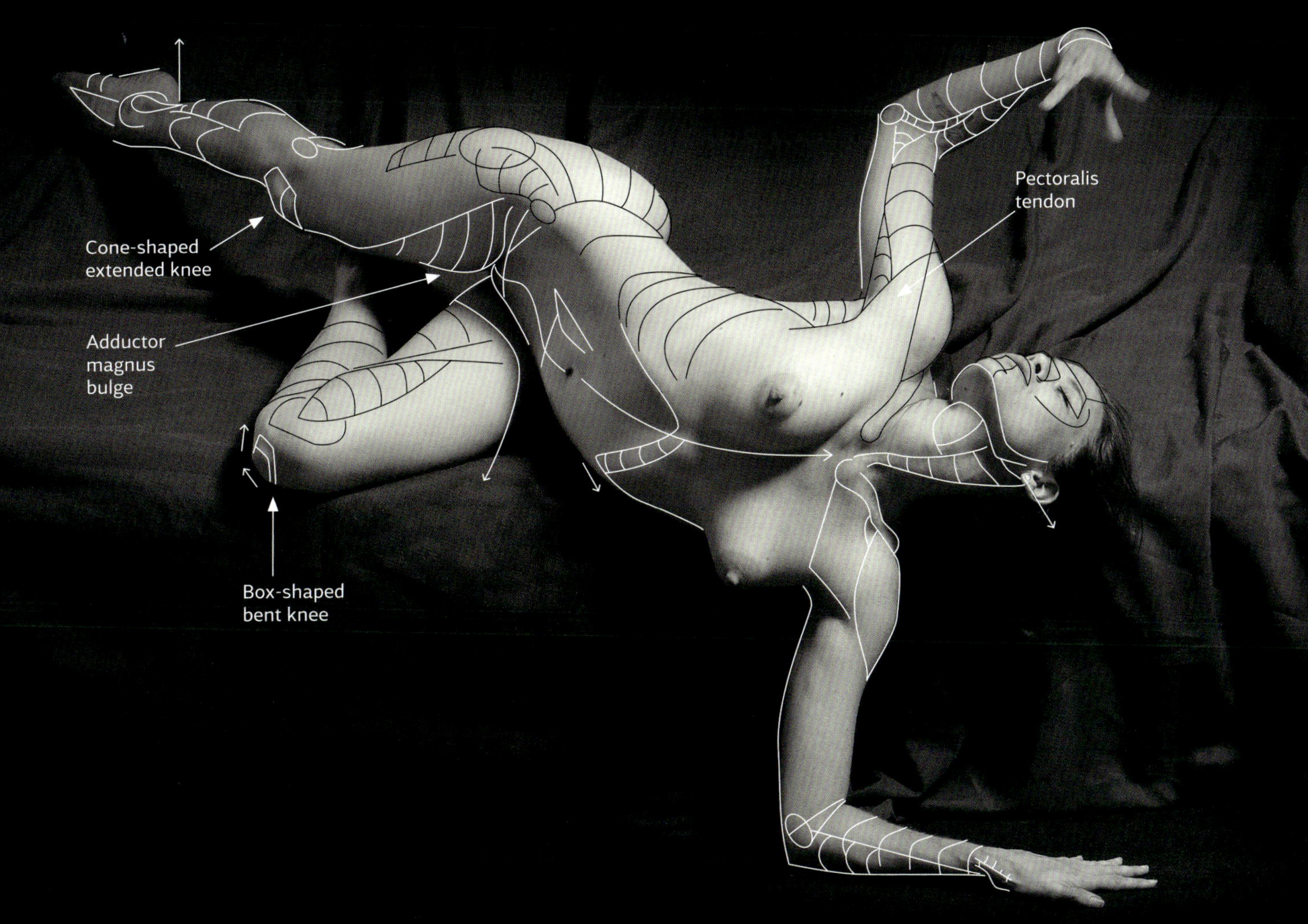

Vertical Stripes

Although this is a foreshortened pose, it's not so much the torso that is distorted; it is the furthest thigh that is more foreshortened than our eyes would see, which is only noticeable because of the lower leg seeming wider on the vertical, less distorted, 2D plane. So why does the torso seem so long? Apart from some natural foreshortening, there are a few reasons. First off, the obliques are being stretched, and also the ribcage is being elongated. There are intercostal muscles between the ribs that allow the ribcage to expand. In this pose, they are allowing the ribcage to become slightly longer. With arms raised we see a tube-like torso that optically appears longer, just as vertical stripes appear longer than horizontal stripes.

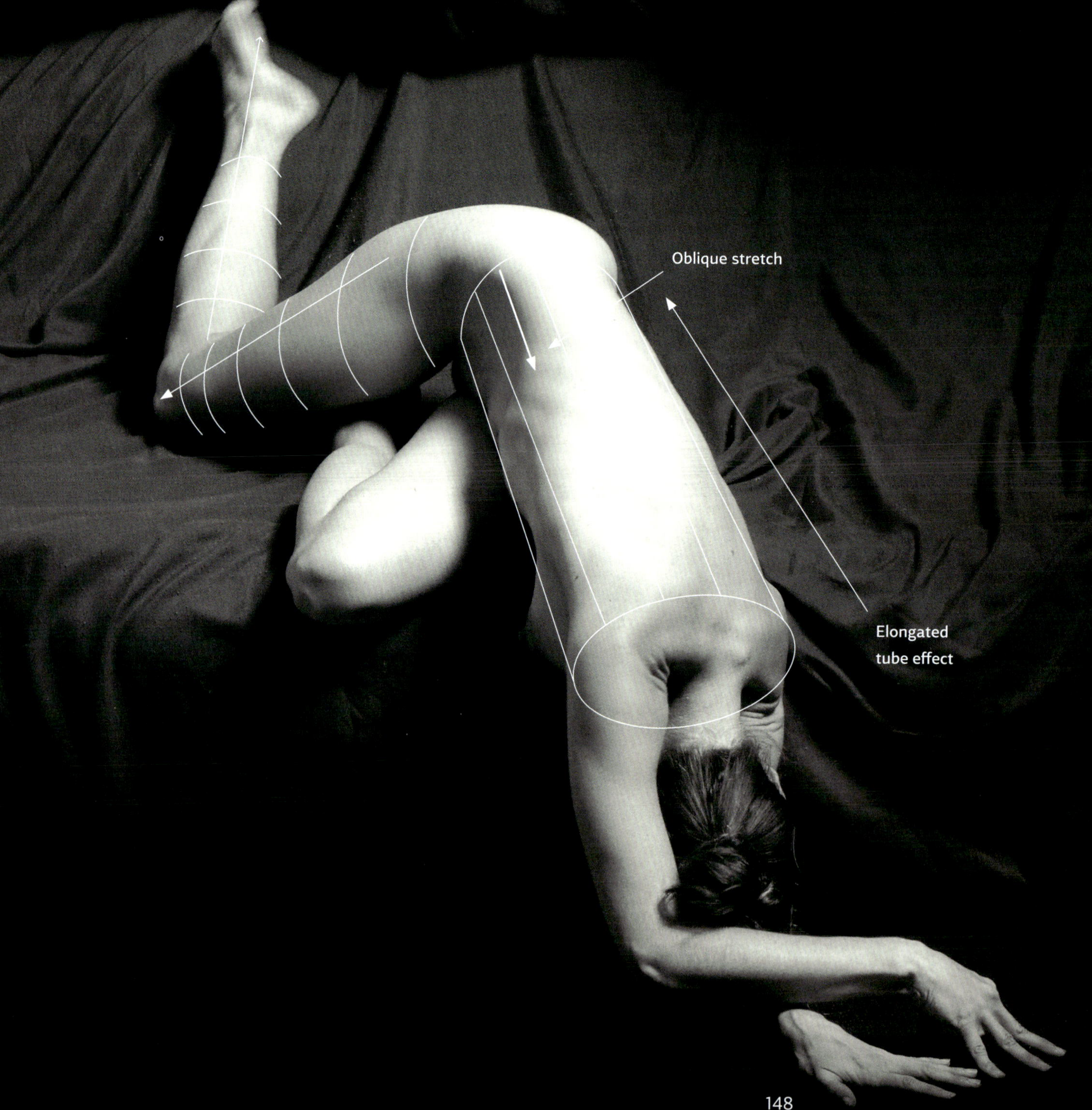

The Egon Schiele Effect

Now you may think that I regard photo distortion as the enemy, and I do when photos are traced without any understanding, making us incumbent slaves fearful of stepping out of line. But here's the rub: I actually admire artists who play with proportions, such as Egon Schiele and Jenny Saville. What makes their work so exciting is they know anatomy well enough to make personal distortions that are not reliant on camera distortion. How can we tell the difference? Well, let's take the ribcage as an example. If it retains its egg-shaped nature, we can make it a longer egg, whereas the camera might distort it into a skewed egg.

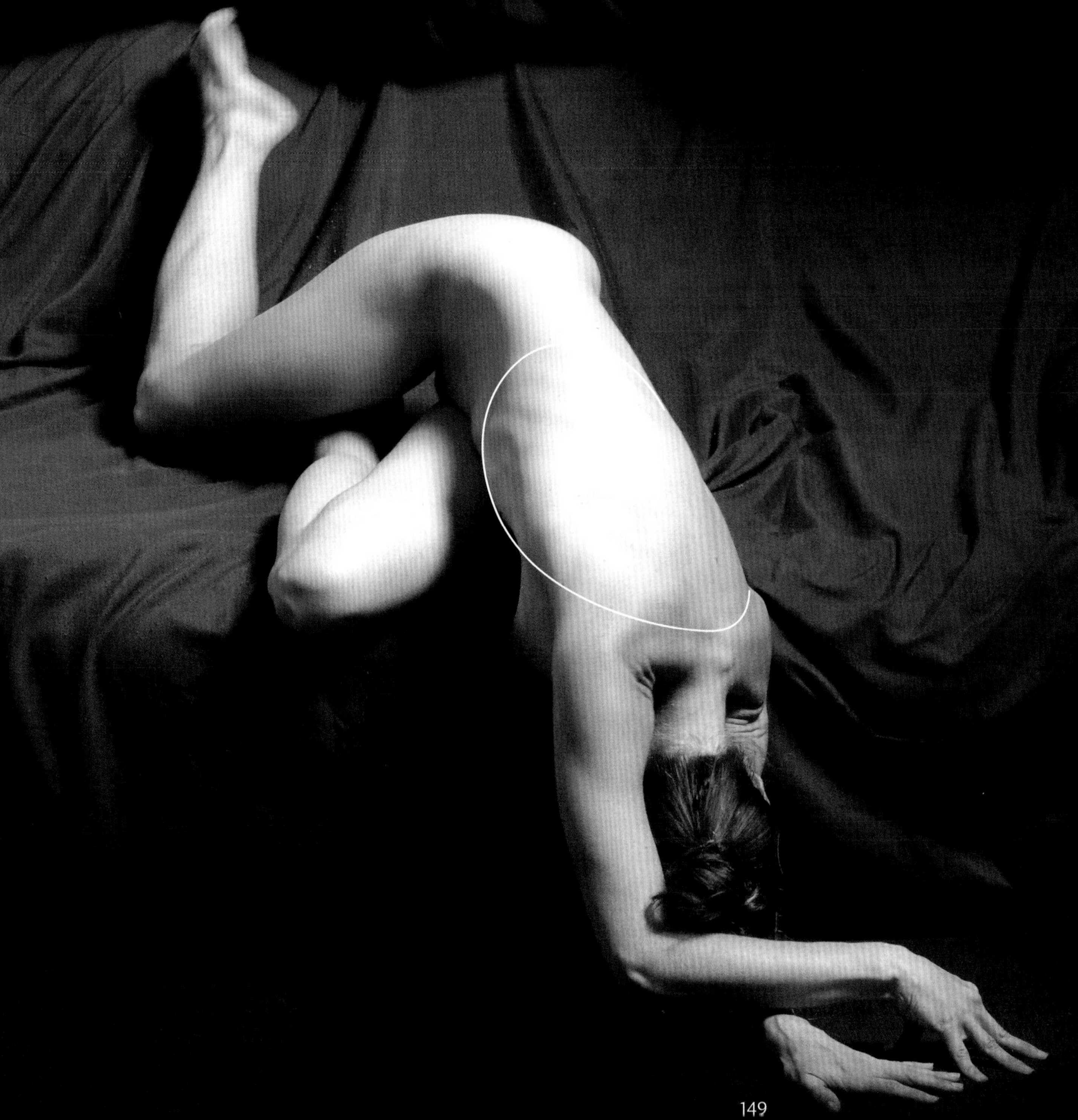

Becoming the Master

When we understand the weaknesses of the camera's lens, we can become the master rather than the slave. By seeking the body's landmarks, we can draw on top of the photo to find a simple structure. Landmarks are usually bones. The tenth rib almost always makes itself known, as does the seventh vertebra (the top of the ribcage). Therefore we can trace an egg shape to see if it's distorted by the camera. Here it looks pretty good. From this point, we can play the shapes game. The knees always box-off, especially in a lateral side view, with some top showing, as in both legs here. Note the pinch of the acromion process bone when the arms are raised. We can wrap the hot-air balloon shape of the deltoid around the pinch.

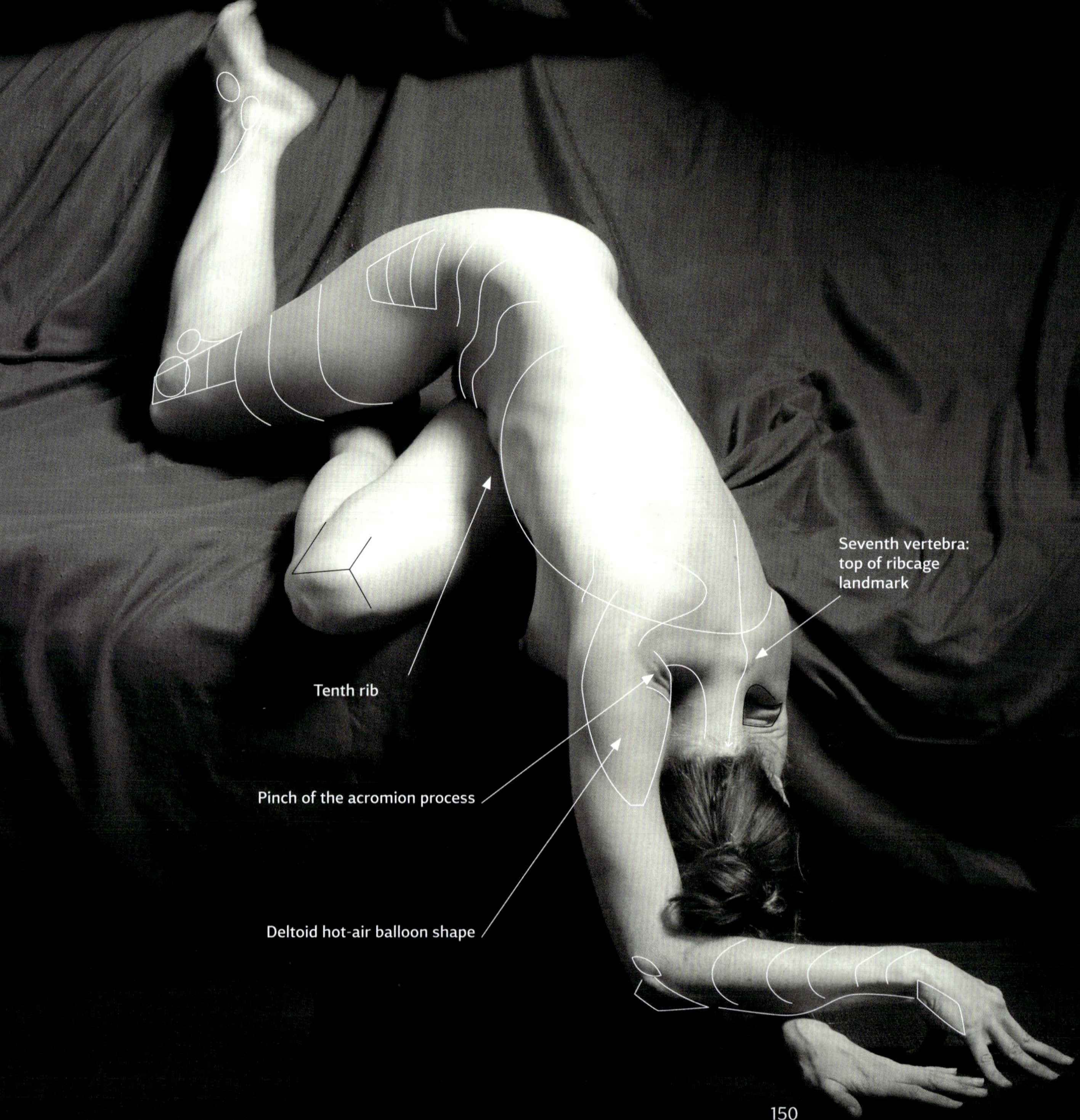

A Fluid Figure

What the great masters of art were most interested in wasn't so much getting the proportions "correct" but making the relationships of forms harmonious. In the art deco period, it was all about geometric shapes complementing one other. With most figurative artists, it's the opposite. We want our figure to look fluid, not stiff. When we have found our structural shapes, we can link them with gesture, adjusting the flow to our own will. Here I'm exploring muscles and also shadows that I will almost certainly make more gestural in my drawing. Note how I'm chasing rhythms down the body, especially in the arm and hand.

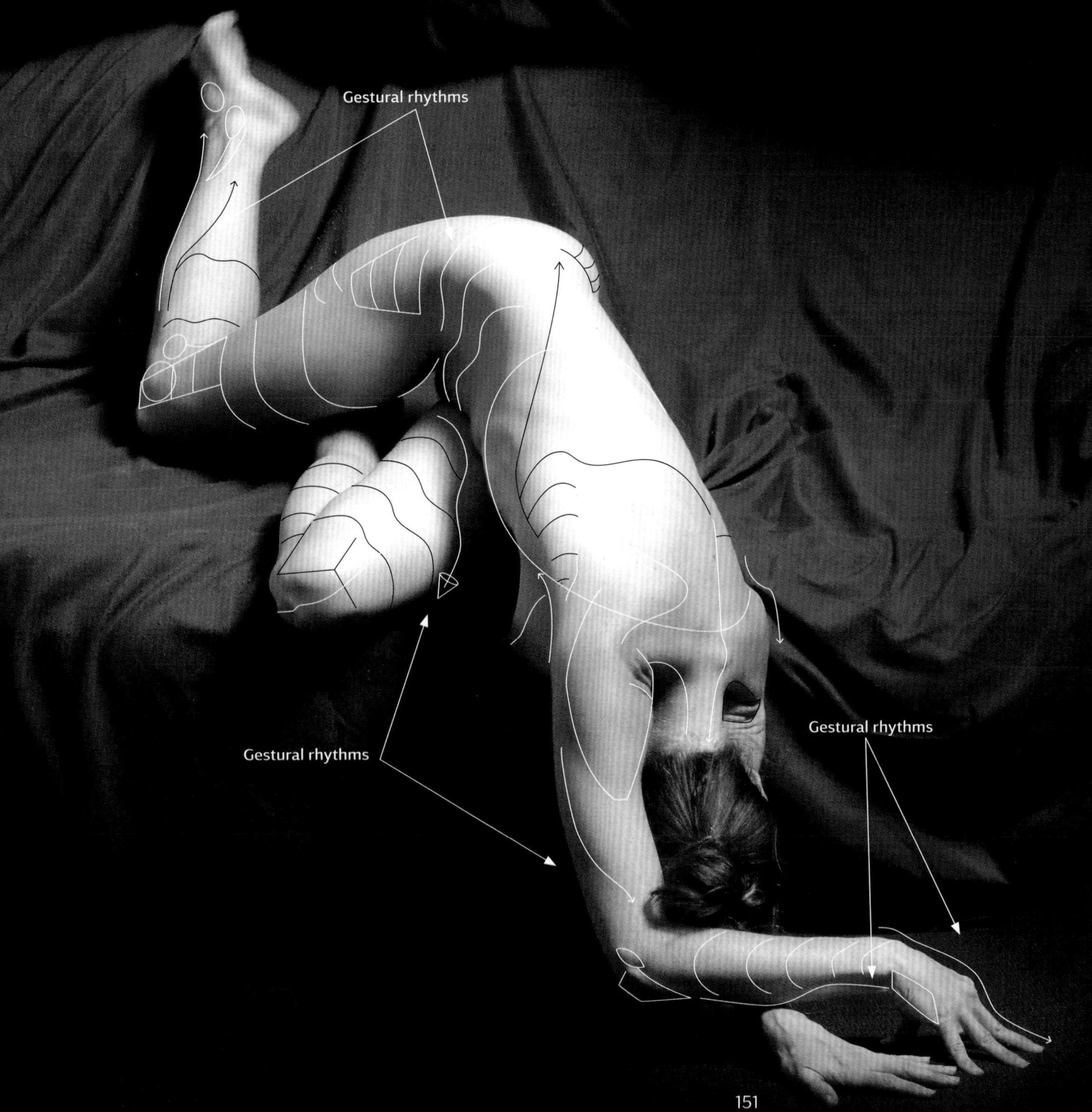

Finding Freedom

With all the anatomy and structural analysis done, we can start thinking of style. Remember, I'm doing all this analysis internally. With photos and computers, we can draw on top of the photos, as I've done here, but it's best to train our eyes to see this on the live model. If we use every aid we need, eventually we will no longer need to draw over a photo first. We can then consider ourselves free from slavery and draw with our eyes as the master decision-maker. As we don't have a standing figure here, we can learn to see the halfway point to make the figure easier to proportion. In a standing figure pose, halfway would be roughly the hip bone area; in this pose, with the arms raised, it's around the lower part of the scapula.

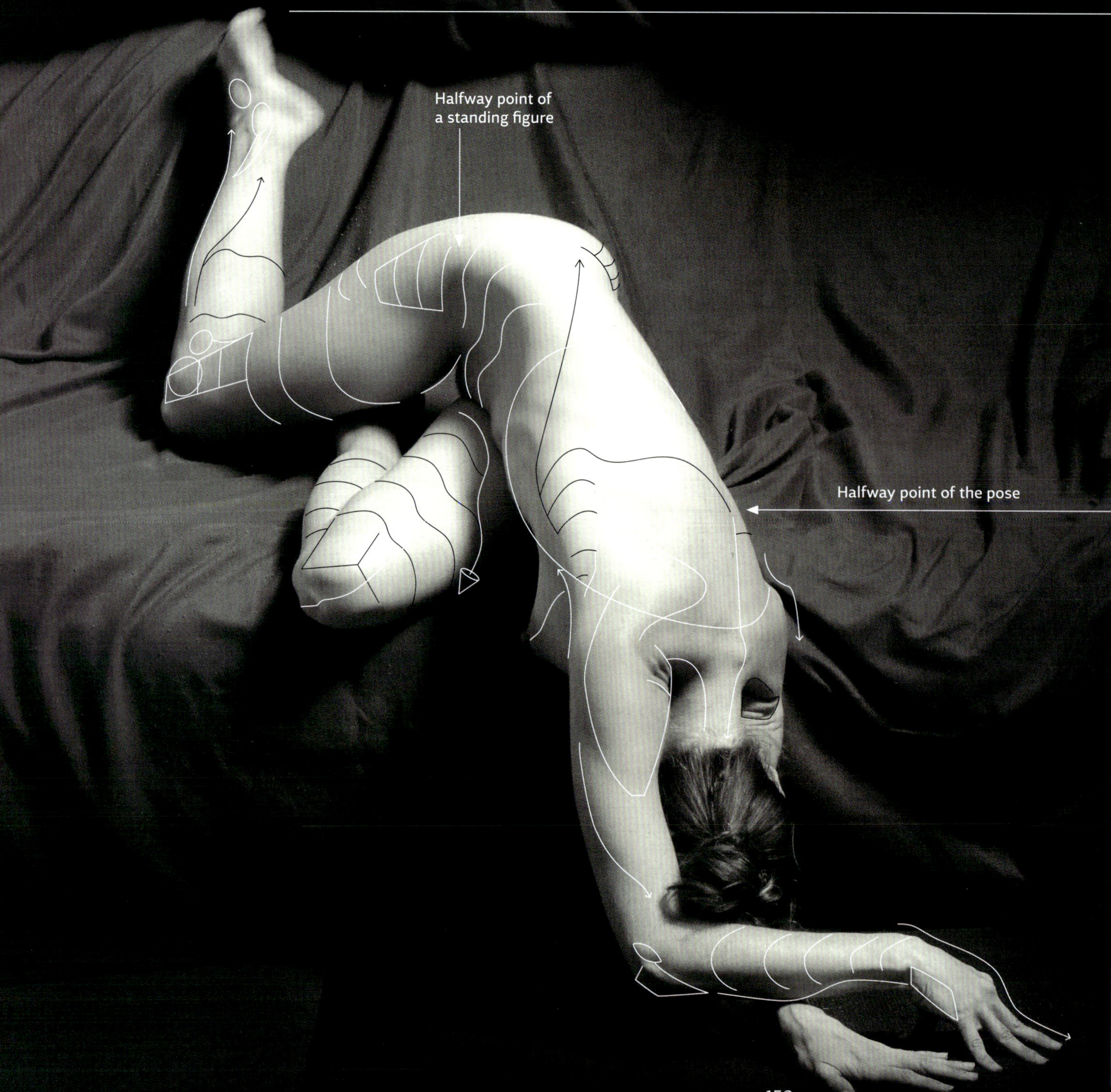

The Shooting Arrows Game

When considering 3D depth, it's fun to imagine thick-headed arrows shooting into space. Play with the idea, using arrows to show the directions of the head, limbs, and torso. As the arrows head away, make the underside of them wider or narrower, based on how deep or shallow you think the structures are being foreshortened. Note how the arrowhead showing the direction of the forearm has very little curve, indicating that it's heading towards us only slightly and therefore has basically no foreshortening to it, whereas we can see underneath the arrowhead indicating the thigh going away from us and the top of the arrowhead of the thigh coming towards us. Playing this game trains our eyes to see 3D space in a 2D photo.

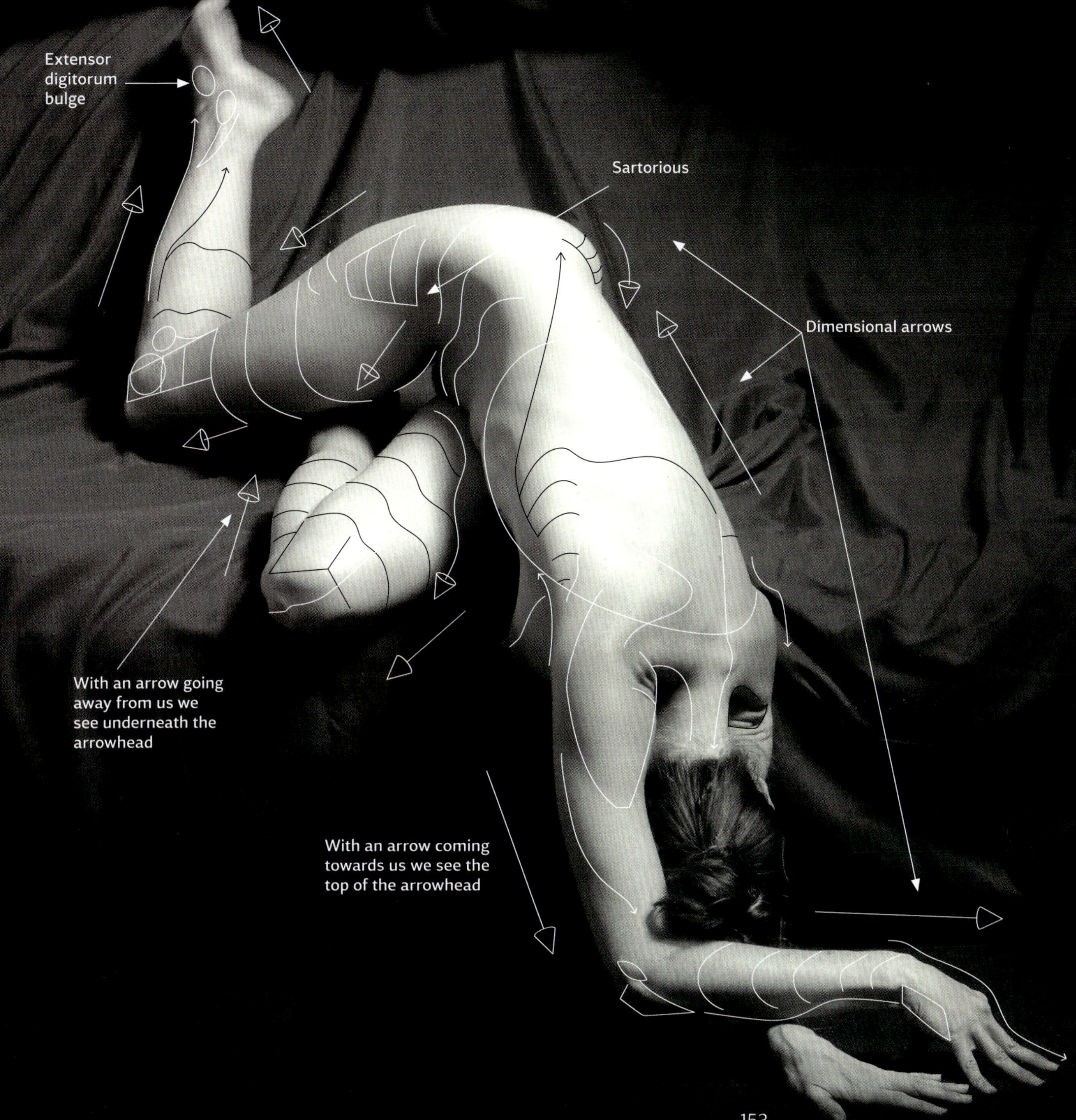

Finding Gold

Let's look at an artistic pose seen from an unusual viewpoint. Here I've flipped the photo to create a supernatural pose. This is an example of photography giving us the power to experiment with poses beyond the abilities of any life model. We can easily imagine a vampire defying the laws of gravity to peer in a high window, for instance. I usually present Alana with thumbnail sketches, then let her continue the idea using her inner emotions; in other words, to become the vampire! My artworks are an art collaboration and would be severely diluted with an inferior model. When you find a great model, treasure them like gold.

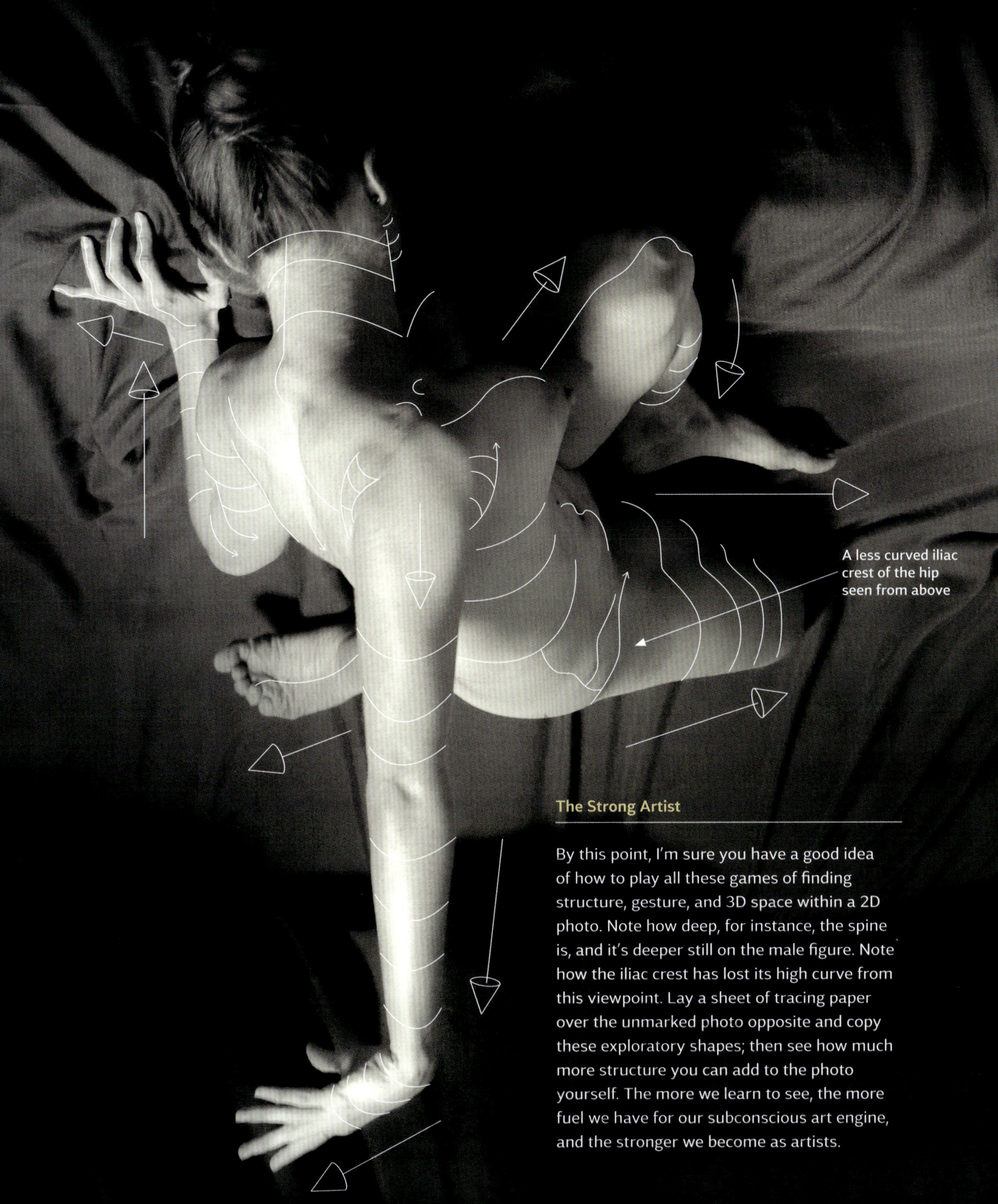

The Strong Artist

By this point, I'm sure you have a good idea
of how to play all these games of finding
structure, gesture, and 3D space within a 2D
photo. Note how deep, for instance, the spine
is, and it's deeper still on the male figure. Note
how the iliac crest has lost its high curve from
this viewpoint. Lay a sheet of tracing paper
over the unmarked photo opposite and copy
these exploratory shapes; then see how much
more structure you can add to the photo
yourself. The more we learn to see, the more
fuel we have for our subconscious art engine,
and the stronger we become as artists.

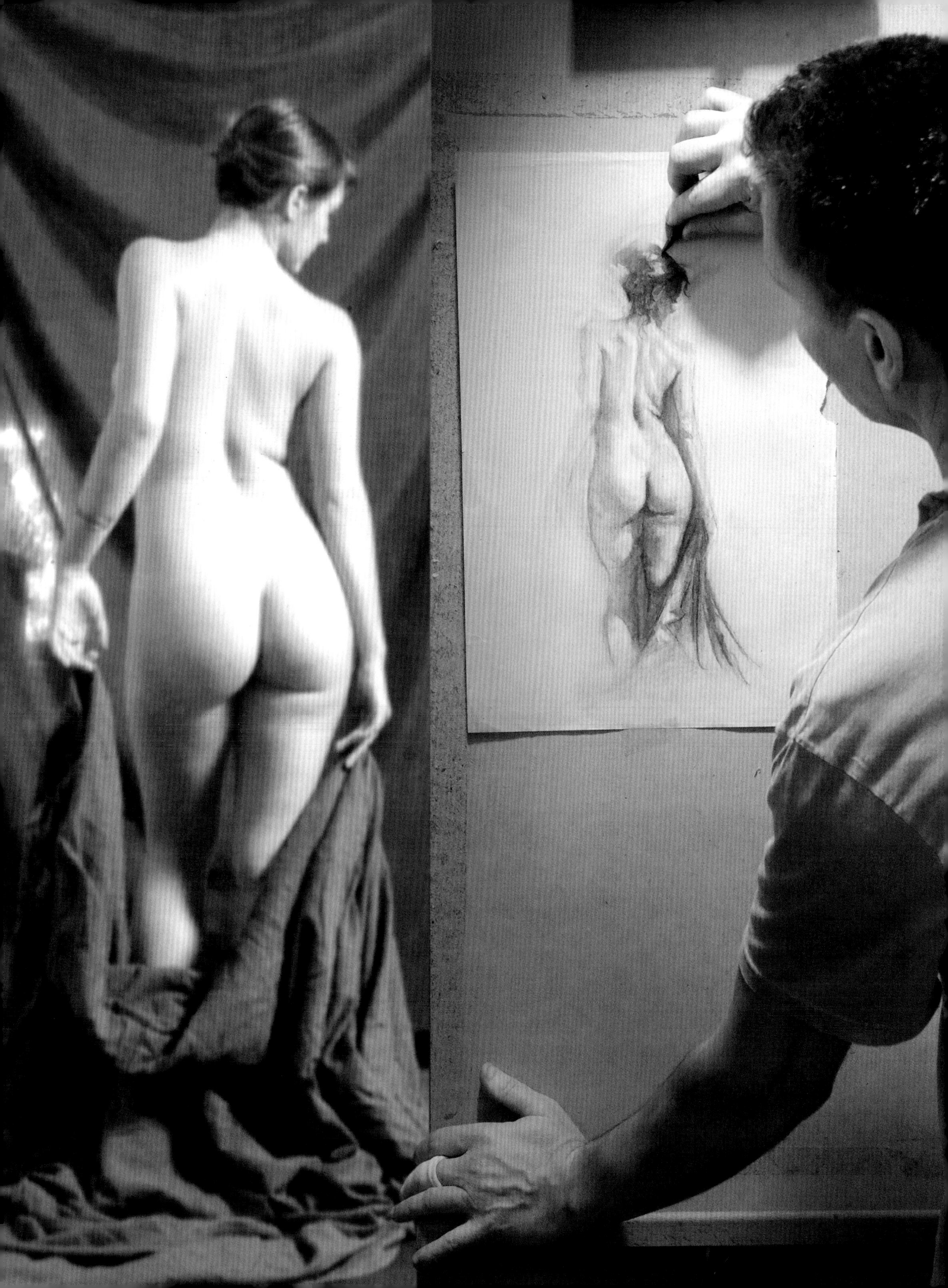

"The creative process is a process of surrender, not control."

Julia Cameron (1948–)

AFTERWORD

IN PURSUIT OF ART

DRAWING THE NUDE FIGURE creates a timeless image, carved from our ancestors' endurance and evolution over hundreds of thousands of years and unblemished or dated by the clothes of fashion. What better a subject to rejoice in than the extraordinary specimens we have become. We are a body landscape, sometimes embellished with exotic markings, tattoos, or jewellery, or posed simply unadorned in all our original splendour. By interpreting the human figure with line and tone, we scratch our individual marks on paper and canvas to leave eternal memories of our common humanity and our connection to one another.

I believe that art is the ultimate expression of who we are. In this joyful act of creation, we leave a lasting impression of our brief time and place in the world, as did the artists before us and the artists to come. For me, drawing and painting the figure has been the most challenging and fulfilling of all artistic pursuits, and through my art and teachings I hope I have inspired you to find the same bounty.

And so it comes time to say farewell and close the curtain on another series of workshops. I trust these adventures in art have been as enjoyable for you as they have been for me. For my art companions who are reading these words after taking online or live workshops with me, I thank you once again for joining me here in spirit and for being part of the ever-growing community of artists exploring the spiritual and emotional appreciation of the human figure.

Until next time, I wish you all the best of luck with your artistic adventures.

Patrick J. Jones
Brisbane, Australia

Left: Patrick collaborating with model Katy Woods for a series of drawings

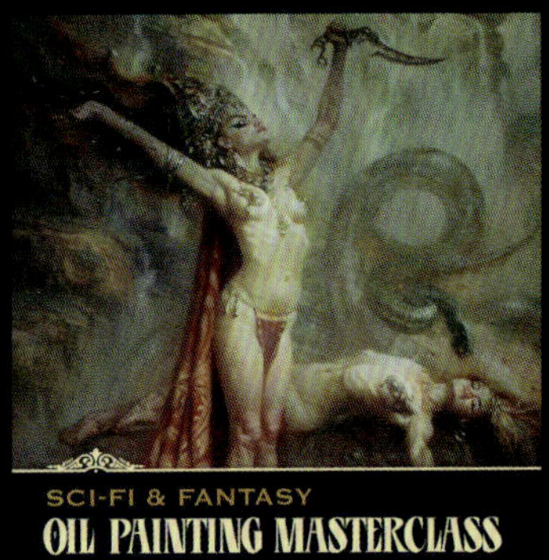

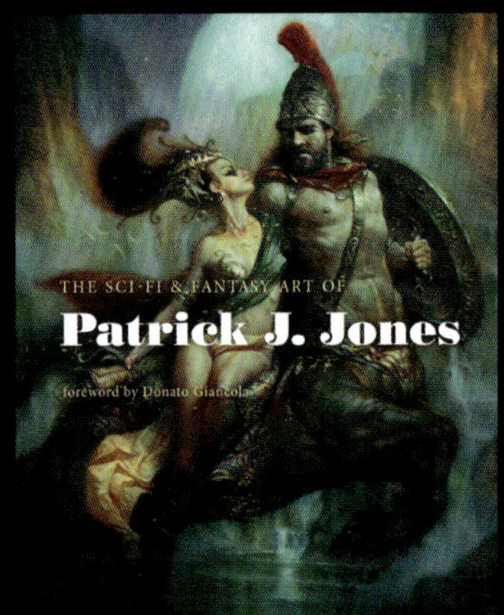

Other available titles by Patrick J. Jones
Sci-fi & Fantasy Oil Painting Masterclass
– foreword by Jeff Mircola
The Sci-fi & Fantasy Art of Patrick J. Jones
– foreword by Donato Giancola

www.koreropress.com
@koreropress

To continue with Patrick's teachings, take a virtual seat
in his studio as he draws and paints. Movie tutorials are
available for download from his online school, along with
upcoming news of live and online classes.

www.pjartworks.com
@patrickjjonesillustrator

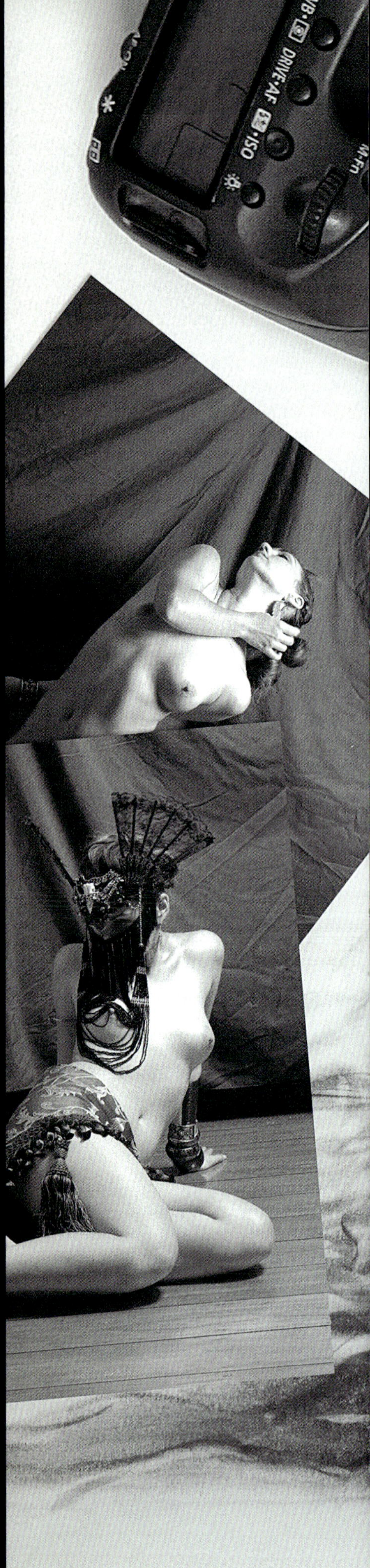

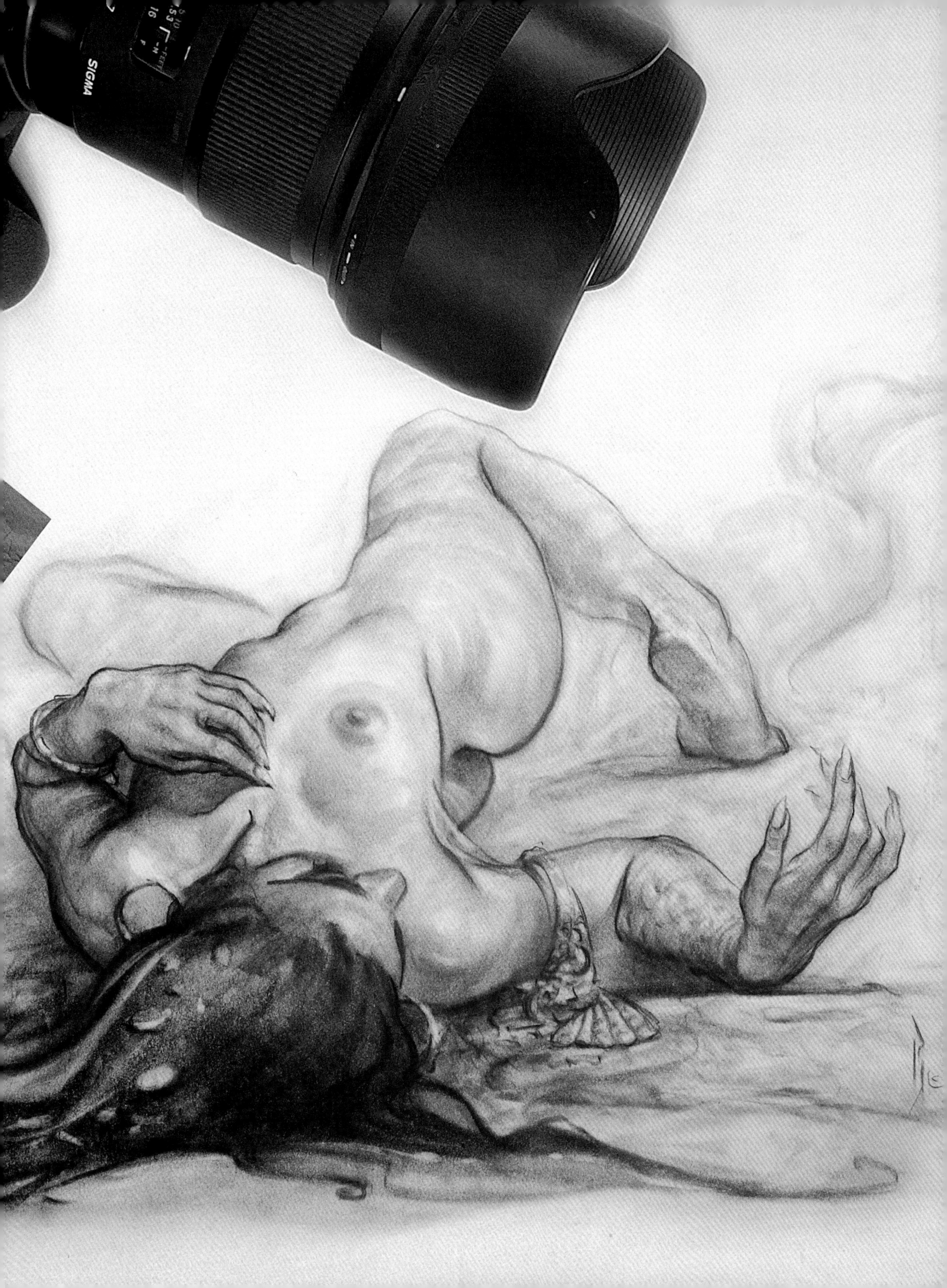

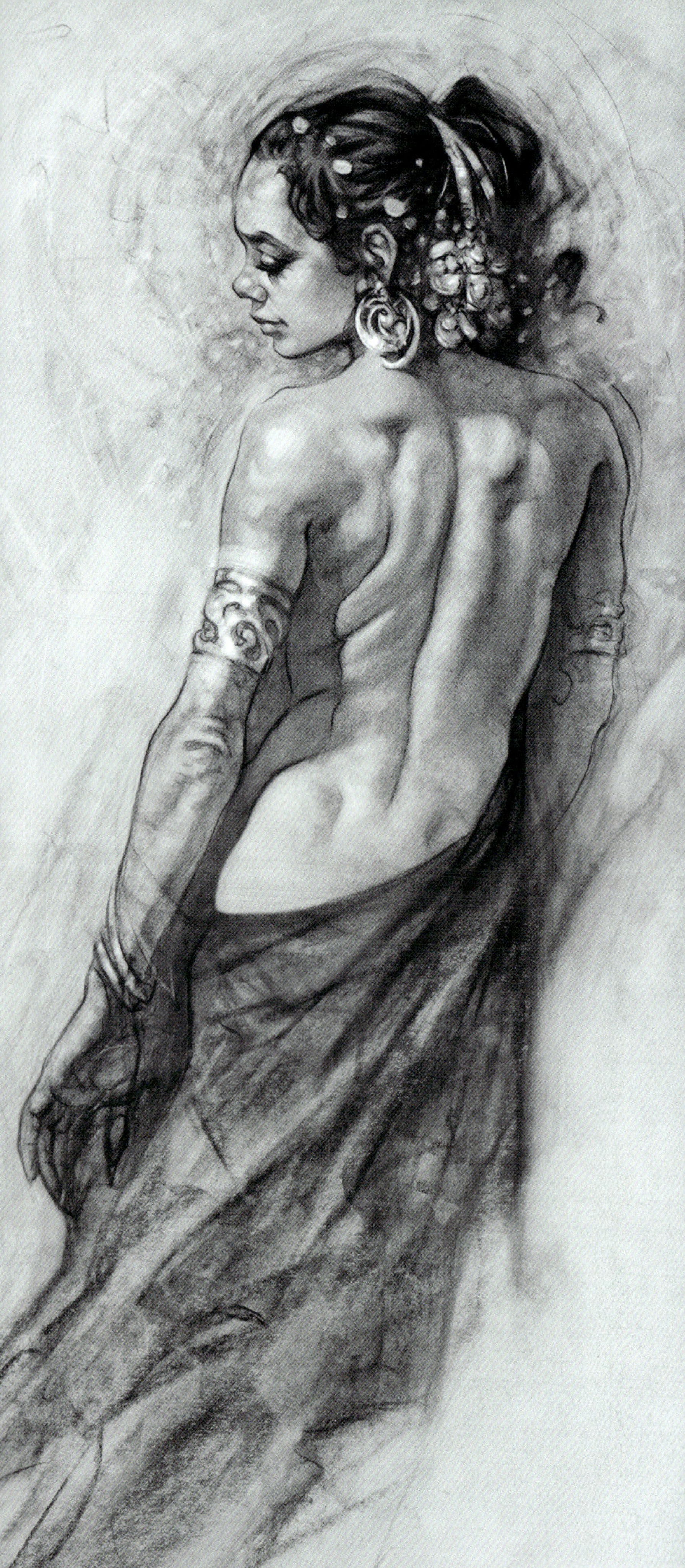

Thanks...

To Steve Huston, for writing the wonderful foreword to this book.

To my artistic model collaborators Alana Brekelmans and Katy Woods, for lending their incredible artistic voices expressed here in my drawings. This book would be a lesser achievement without you.

To Claire Howlett, for commissioning the original workshops for *ImagineFX* magazine, and the ImagineFX team for their support of my art over the years, especially Clifford Hope, Beren Neil, and Daniel Vincent.

To Mercedes Harford and the Leeton Model Agency, for welcoming me and introducing me to the artists and models of my adopted home of Brisbane, Australia.

To my publisher, Yak El Droubie, for his humour and friendship, and for bringing these books into the world.

For my eternal childhood friends of Belfast, who are far away but forever in my mind.

For my parents, Patrick and Sally, for being my inspiration.

For my kids, Dean and Daryl, for making me prouder every day.

For my beautiful wife, Cathy, my eternal sunshine.